Love and Marriage in the Age of Chaucer

By the Same Author

The Devil, Demonology, and Witchcraft, 1968; 2d ed., 1974. British edition, *Towards the Death of Satan*.

Divine Providence in the England of Shakespeare's Histories, 1970.

Love and Marriage in the Age of Chaucer

HENRY ANSGAR KELLY

CORNELL UNIVERSITY PRESS

ITHACA AND LONDON

First published 1975 by Cornell University Press.
Published in the United Kingdom by Cornell University Press Ltd., 2-4 Brook Street, London W1Y 1AA.

International Standard Book Number 0-8014-0881-4
Library of Congress Catalog Card Number 74-10414

Printed in the United States of America by York Composition Co.

For Dominic Tancred Kelly

Acknowledgments

Most of the research for and writing of this book was done in 1972, in Rome, while I was on leave of absence and on sabbatical from the Department of English of the University of California at Los Angeles; my work was assisted by a fellowship from the John Simon Guggenheim Memorial Foundation. By invitation of John Leyerle, I announced some of my findings in the paper "Courtly Love, Clandestine Marriage, and Virtuous Sex," in a symposium on marriage in the Middle Ages at the open session of the Committee on Centers and Regional Associations of the Mediaeval Academy of America, in Los Angeles, April 15, 1972. A more specialized version of this paper appeared as "Clandestine Marriage and Chaucer's *Troilus*" in *Viator* 4 (1973) 435–457, published by the University of California Press; I draw upon it by permission of the Regents of the University of California.

I would like to thank Professor Leyerle for his advice and encouragement and to acknowledge here the valuable assistance of Martin Bertram and Father Leonard Boyle, who aided me in the canonical aspects of this book, and of G. Karl Galinsky, who made helpful suggestions for the chapters on Ovid. I wish to express my appreciation to the Vatican Library and the American Academy in Rome for providing facilities for researching and writing the book. The manuscript was read for Cornell University Press by Winthrop Wetherbee and Jerome Taylor, and I am most grateful to them for their sympathetic and constructive criticism. Finally, I wish to thank Jeanne Louise Carrière for her assistance in preparing the manuscript for publication.

HENRY ANSGAR KELLY

University of California, Los Angeles

Contents

Contents

Abbreviations

Acton   John Acton (Iohannes de Athon), *In constitutiones legitimas Angliae glossemata*, published with the *Provinciale* of Lyndwood (*q.v.*)

Andreae   John (Iohannes) Andreae, *In primum-sextum Decretalium librum novella commentaria*, Venice 1581, repr. Turin 1963.

Andrew the Chaplain   Andreas Capellanus, *Ars honeste amandi*, tr. John Jay Parry, *The Art of Courtly Love*, Columbia University Press, New York 1941. Copyright 1941 by Columbia University Press.

Benoit   Benoit de Saint-Maure, *Le roman de Troie*, ed. Léopold Constans, 6 vols., SATF, Paris 1904–1912.

Boccaccio   *Filocolo, Filostrato,* and *Teseida* in *Tutte le opere* 1–2, general editor Vittore Branca, I classici Mondadori, Milan 1967 and 1964. Vols. 1, 2 © 1967, 1964 Arnoldo Mondadori Editore. *Decameron,* ed. Vittore Branca, ed. 2, Florence 1965. © 1965 Casa Editrice Felice Le Monnier.

Burgh   John Burgh (Iohannes de Burgo), *Pupilla oculi*, Paris 1527.

CFMA   Les classiques français du moyen âge.

Chaucer   *The Works of Geoffrey Chaucer*, ed. F. N. Robinson, ed. 2, Houghton Mifflin, Boston 1957. © 1957, 1961 F. N. Robinson.

DDC   *Dictionnaire de droit canonique*, ed. R. Naz, Paris 1935–1965.

Donaldson   E. Talbot Donaldson, *Speaking of Chaucer*, London 1970.

EETSes   Early English Text Society, extra series.

Gist   Margaret Adlum Gist, *Love and War in the Middle-English Romances*, Philadelphia 1947.

Gower   John Gower, *The Complete Works*, ed. G. C. Macaulay, 4 vols., Oxford 1901. The two volumes constituting *The English Works* were printed for EETSes 81–82, 1900–1901, repr. 1969.

Gratian, *Decree*   *Concordia discordantium canonum*, ed. Emil Friedberg, *Corpus iuris canonici* 1, Leipzig 1879, repr. Graz 1959. For the Ordinary Gloss, one must go to earlier editions.

Guido of Le Colonne   Guido de Columnis, *Historia destructionis Troiae*, ed. Nathaniel Edward Griffin, Mediaeval Academy of America Publications 26, Cambridge, Mass., 1936, repr. New York 1970.

Lawlor   John Lawlor, ed., *Patterns of Love and Courtesy*, London 1966.

Lewis   C. S. Lewis, *The Allegory of Love*, London 1936, repr. 1969.

Lyndwood   William Lyndwood, *Provinciale*, Oxford 1679; repr. Farnborough, Hants., 1968.

Machaut   Guillaume de Machaut, *Oeuvres*, ed. Ernest Hoepffner, 3 vols., SATF, Paris 1908–1921.

Newman   F. X. Newman, ed., *The Meaning of Courtly Love*, Albany, N.Y., 1968.

Ordinary Gloss to the Bible   *Biblia sacra*, Venice 1588.

Ordinary Glosses to Canon Law   See under Gratian and X.

Ovid   Publius Ovidius Naso, *Opera*, Loeb Classical Library.

PG, PL   J. P. Migne, ed., *Patrologia graeca* and *Patrologia latina*.

Rochester Register   *Registrum Hamonis Hethe diocesis Roffensis, A.D. 1319–1352*, ed. Charles Johnson, Canterbury and York Society, Oxford 1948.

Roman   Guillaume de Lorris and Jean de Meun, *Le roman de la Rose*, ed. Félix Lecoy, CFMA 92, 95, 98, Paris 1965–1970. © 1965, 1966, 1970 Éditions Champion.

Sarum Manual   *Manuale ad usum percelebris ecclesie sarisburiensis*, ed. A. Jeffries Collins, Henry Bradshaw Society 91, London 1960.

SATF   Société des anciens textes français.

Sheehan   Michael M. Sheehan, "The Formation and Stability of

Marriage in Fourteenth-Century England: Evidence of an Ely Register," *Mediaeval Studies* 33 (1971) 228–263.

Van de Voort   Donnell Van de Voort, *Love and Marriage in the English Medieval Romance*, Nashville 1938.

X   *Decretales Gregorii IX*, ed. Emil Friedberg, *Corpus iuris canonici* 2, Leipzig 1881, repr. Graz 1959. For the Gloss, see earlier editions.

Love and Marriage in the Age of Chaucer

Introduction

Multa renascentur quae iam cecidere, cadentque
Quae nunc sunt in honore.

(Much that has fallen shall be born again, and what is now
held in honor shall fall.)

—Horace, *Ars poetica* 70–71

C. S. Lewis used these lines as an epigraph for his *Allegory of Love*, first published in 1936, which contains his classic statement of the code of courtly love. Though Horace was speaking of word usage, Lewis applies his prophecy to literary tastes and conventions. Nowadays his own book shows that it applies equally well to modern critical theories, for the concept of courtly love that he accepted as an operative code in the upper-class life and literature of the Middle Ages has been found defective.

Lewis has been singled out for criticism not because courtly love was his invention—it was already a widespread delusion before his time—but because he wrote on it so well. I love C. S. Lewis and all his works, including *The Allegory of Love*, but I believe that sometimes, like all men, he was misguided. John Lawlor, speaking for all of Lewis's friends who contributed to a volume of essays in his honor, published after his death, assures us that it would have afforded him the liveliest satisfaction that they should on occasion qualify or oppose his contentions. I have written the following pages in this spirit of affectionate debate, and I share Lawlor's regret that we cannot now look to Lewis "to challenge, to re-order, and where necessary to confute, what we have written."[1]

1. John Lawlor, *Patterns of Love and Courtesy* (London 1966) Preface.

Lewis takes the theory of courtly love for granted: "Every one has heard of courtly love, and every one knows that it appears quite suddenly at the end of the eleventh century in Languedoc." The characteristics of this highly specialized love "may be enumerated as Humility, Courtesy, Adultery, and the Religion of Love."[2] The inclusion of the characteristic of adultery is the most peculiar and entrancing aspect of the theory, and the one most open to attack; and it is the one that interests me most in this study, for it postulates the incompatibility of love and marriage.

This doctrine is truly astonishing, and, of course, as "almost every one" now knows, patently unhistorical. That is to say, though there were certain individual cases both in literature and in life in which love and marriage were incompatible, or thought to be incompatible, there was never a seriously or generally held opinion that love was impossible within marriage. In Part I of this study I examine some of the more frequently alleged proof-texts for the law of incompatibility and discuss the theoretical bases set forth by its modern proponents, in order to see how and where they have gone astray.

The most astounding thing about the theory of courtly love is that it ever achieved currency among scholars. One reason for its success, no doubt, was the insidiousness of its growth. It began as a small tumor in an essay by Gaston Paris in 1883, and then by rapid multiplication and metastasis increased its range and its claims. According to Paris, courtly love first made its appearance in French literature in *Le chevalier de la charrette*, or *Lancelot*, of Chrétien de Troyes, though he can find contributing elements earlier, both in real life and in literature—especially that of the troubadours. Later manifestations appeared in the great prose romances of the Round Table, and it reached its apogee in the prose *Lancelot* of some forty or fifty years later.[3] By Lewis's time, most scholars agreed with him that courtly love started at the end of the eleventh century, and held that it could be traced at least to the end of the fourteenth, thus spanning three centuries or more.

2. C. S. Lewis, *The Allegory of Love* (London 1936, repr. 1969) 2.
3. Gaston Paris, "Lancelot du Lac 2: *Le conte de la charrette*," *Romania* 12 (1883) 459–534, esp. 519–532.

A short account of the way in which courtly love was eventually overtaken by doubts and disbelief will provide a background for this book. The credit for the first frontal attack on the code must go, it seems, to Donnell Van de Voort. Just two years after the appearance of *The Allegory of Love*, he published a thesis at Vanderbilt University in which his specific intention is "to demonstrate that those parts of the code of courtly love relating to a system of idealized immorality have no place in the English prose or metrical romances," but that, on the contrary, in this body of writings "the sacredness of marriage and the desirability of morality in love are consistently emphasized."[4] In working out his demonstration, however, he goes outside English literature to draw the same conclusions for French romances, including the prose *Lancelot*. His attack against courtly love lacks finality chiefly because of his failure to come to grips with the *Lancelot* of Chrétien de Troyes and the *Ars honeste amandi* of Andrew the Chaplain. He admits to being stymied only by Chaucer's *Troilus and Criseyde*, "the one work examined in this study whose hero and heroine may be conceded to act in accordance with the principles of courtly love" (132) as defined by Lewis.

But in spite of the fact that Van de Voort's work was directed by a distinguished medievalist, Walter Clyde Curry, its message was lost.[5] Even when it was noticed and read, its full import and importance were not realized. Margaret Adlum Gist cites it in a thesis written under the direction of another well-known medievalist, Albert C. Baugh, and published in 1947. A belated reading of Van de Voort brings home to her only the conclusion, which she adds in her preface, that "the attitude of the Engish authors toward sex and marriage was not noticeably influenced by the French concept of courtly love."[6] She finds, also belatedly, a similar conclusion in the 1933 Leipzig University thesis of Kurt Lippmann, who maintains that "the English poets, with the ex-

4. Donnell Van de Voort, *Love and Marriage in the English Medieval Romance* (Privately printed: Nashville 1938) Preface.
5. The book was listed in the 1944 bibliography of the Modern Language Association and in the bibliography compiled by F. X. Newman, *The Meaning of Courtly Love* (Albany, N.Y., 1968).
6. Margaret Adlum Gist, *Love and War in the Middle-English Romances* (Philadelphia 1947) vii; cf. 8 n. 17.

ception of Chaucer and Gower, had slight interest in and little understanding of the French concept of courtly love" and that "they fitted the concepts of courtly love wherever possible to a marital rather than an extramarital pattern."[7] Moreover, even Gower, though he understood the system, did not approve of it. Lippmann cites the earlier judgment of William George Dodd that the English poet frankly condemned the adulterous love "which was inherent in the courtly system."[8] A similar assertion of English preference for marriage was made by Constance West in 1938, writing about Anglo-Norman romances; Gervase Mathew in 1947 and John Lawlor in 1956 developed her contention to include romances written in English.[9] Lippmann also refers to Eugène Vinaver's assessment of Thomas Malory; according to Vinaver, writing in 1929, Malory had a stronger matrimonial orientation than did his sources, in which romantic love was "treated with the characteristic freedom of courtly romance."[10]

It is, in fact, such a take-it-or-leave-it attitude that is to be found in many French (and English) romances rather than Van de Voort's "conventional morality" or Lewis's compulsive adultery. In 1940, Sidney Painter saw that the works of Marie de France reflect an attitude of this sort combined with a liking for marriage: "Marie preferred to have her lovers find their solace in marriage, but if love and matrimonial obligation were in conflict, love always won."[11] He fails to notice, however, that the same

7. Gist 8; see Kurt Lippmann, *Das ritterliche Persönlichkeitsideal in der mittelenglischen Literatur des 13. und 14. Jahrhunderts* (Meerane in Sachsen 1933) 56–72. Lippmann is expanding upon the insight of Levin L. Schücking, *Die englische Literatur im Mittelalter*, Handbuch der Literaturwissenschaft 4, ed. Oskar Walzel (Wildpark-Potsdam 1927) 66.

8. William George Dodd, *Courtly Love in Chaucer and Gower*, Harvard Studies in English 1 (Boston 1913, repr. Gloucester 1959) 89.

9. C. B. West, *Courtoisie in Anglo-Norman Literature* (Oxford 1938) esp. 167–169; Gervase Mathew, "Marriage and *Amour courtois* in Late Fourteenth-Century England," *Essays Presented to Charles Williams* (London 1947) 128–135; John Lawlor, "The Pattern of Consolation in *The Book of the Duchess*," *Speculum* 31 (1956) 626–648. Sarah F. Barrow, *The Medieval Society Romances* (New York 1924) 33, saw such a preference even in the French romances.

10. Eugène Vinaver, *Malory* (Oxford 1929, repr. 1970) 46. Cf. Barrow 34.

11. Sidney Painter, *French Chivalry: Chivalric Ideas and Practices in Medieval France* (Baltimore 1940, repr. 1961) 131. J. S. P. Tatlock, "The

combination appeared in the rest of French romance as well. This is a point that was made later by Justina Ruiz de Conde, in a Radcliffe thesis written in 1945 and published in 1948. She finds in Spanish literature a virtually absolute preference for marriage, but in France only a relative preference: in case of conflict in French romances, the priority goes to love rather than to marriage. Furthermore, when the love ends in marriage, the story normally ends at the same time, so that married love itself is usually not described—the fortunate couple simply lives happily ever after.[12]

As we shall see later, Ruiz de Conde also understood and correctly applied the principles of clandestine marriage, which I take up in Part III below; but, as with Van de Voort, her message was not received, at least by students of French and English literature.

Beginning in 1951, the theory of courtly love came under attack, and the attack has continued to this day, from another direction. D. W. Robertson, Jr., believes that works presumably illustrative of such a code, like the *Ars honeste amandi* or Chrétien's romances, are nothing but ironic and humorous broadsides against "idolatrous passion," which is how Robertson defines carnal love.[13] He sees nothing new or extraordinary about the rule that

---

People in Chaucer's *Troilus*," *Publications of the Modern Language Association* 56 (1941) 85–104, esp. 85–89, points out that many medieval romances end in marriage, and objects to the indiscriminate application of the term "courtly love" to medieval romantic love. According to Tatlock, romantic love first appeared *in literature* only in the eleventh or twelfth century, but he believes that it must have occurred now and then in real life centuries before. (I take up the question of earlier literary manifestations of romantic love below.)

12. Justina Ruiz de Conde, *El amor y el matrimonio secreto en los libros de caballerías* (Madrid 1948) 122, 153–155. I wish to thank Michael Gerli for bringing this work to my attention. Cf. Christopher Brooke, "Gregorian Reform in Action: Clerical Marriage in England, 1050–1200," *Cambridge Historical Journal* 12 (1956) 1–21, reprinted in his *Medieval Church and Society* (London 1971) 69–99, esp. 98: "In every age and every stratum of courtly literature there are hints that the union of love and marriage is both possible and desirable; it is surprising in how many romances it is a married couple who live happily ever after." Brooke believes that girls of the twelfth and thirteenth centuries as a matter of course took for their motto the words of Matthew of Vendôme's heroine, "Respuo moechari, volo nubere"—"I repudiate adultery, I wish to marry" (96, 99).

13. D. W. Robertson, Jr., "The Doctrine of Charity in Medieval Literary

love so defined was incompatible with marriage; it was simply orthodox Christian doctrine. Such irrational passion could, he admits, exist within marriage, but even then it would be incompatible with the Christian ideal and doctrine on marriage. Robertson recognizes no sympathetic treatment in the Middle Ages of love that is both sensuous and idealistic (what I call serious or romantic love); and he believes that no orthodox Christian could admit the good or sinlessness of sexual delight even within marriage. Virtuous, or "courteous," love of man for woman could have no sensual element in it.[14]

Robertson's more extreme views cannot bear very much reality, as we shall see in the course of this study. But his assessment of the *Ars honeste amandi* has proved a valuable stimulus to dismantling the theory of courtly love on a less eccentric basis. He seems to be right in denying that Andrew the Chaplain was swayed by foreign influences—"by scurrilous Albigensian doctrines, by Arabic or Andalusian cults of sensuality, if such indeed existed, or by obscene neo-Platonic heresies."[15] He is no doubt also right in viewing Andrew's work as a satire, though he is too rigid in his interpretation of it as a piece of sardonic moralism. R. E. Kaske seems much closer to the truth when he suggests that it is "an intellectually controlled, witty, and often satiric analysis of sexual love itself, with the emphasis falling elsewhere than on its moral aspects—such as, perhaps, on the comedy created by the differing attitudes of men and women, further complicated by differences of social rank."[16]

Gardens: A Topical Approach through Symbolism and Allegory," *Speculum* 26 (1951) 24–49, esp. 36–39; "Some Medieval Literary Terminology, with Special Reference to Chrétien de Troyes," *Studies in Philology* 48 (1951) 669–692, esp. 691; more recently, "The Concept of Courtly Love as an Impediment to the Understanding of Medieval Texts," in Newman 1–18, esp. 3.

14. Robertson, *A Preface to Chaucer* (Princeton 1963) 428–432, 454–457, 463–464, 471.

15. Robertson, "The Subject of the *De amore* of Andreas Capellanus," *Modern Philology* 50 (1952–1953) 145–161, esp. 161.

16. R. E. Kaske, "Chaucer and Medieval Allegory," a review of Robertson's *Preface to Chaucer*, *English Literary History* 30 (1963) 175–192, esp. 191–192. Douglas Kelly, "Courtly Love in Perspective: The Hierarchy of Love in Andreas Capellanus," *Traditio* 24 (1968) 119–147, in rejecting Robertson's ironic humor finds no humor at all in Andrew's treatise; he

   In 1965, E. Talbot Donaldson, in "The Myth of Courtly Love," adopts such a modified Robertsonian view of Andrew: "He was producing a *jeu d'esprit* by rewriting Ovid's *Art of Love* and *Remedies of Love* for his own time."[17] This judgment, in fact, corresponds to the assessment of Andrew made a generation earlier by Constance West: "Though the *De amore* is regularly taken as the work of all others in which the theory of courtly love is set forth, its tone, especially in the third part, which is a *Remedia amoris*, is often more in keeping with the cynicism of Ovid than with the seriousness of courtly love."[18] Donaldson goes on to draw more or less the same conclusion that Van de Voort arrived at in the same year West was writing. "I do not believe," says Donaldson, "that the proposition, which is insisted upon by Andreas [Andrew the Chaplain], that love can exist only extra-maritally, was ever much practiced—that it ever had much counterpart in reality. It does not even seem to have had much effect on the subsequent literature of supposedly courtly love."

   Donaldson's essay, especially since its more accessible reprinting in 1970, has been widely accepted as delivering the *coup de grâce* to courtly love. But Francis Utley, in reviewing this and other recent studies, is reluctant to let Donaldson demolish the code completely, although he seems to give a qualified affirmative to his title question, "Must We Abandon the Concept of Courtly Love?" He readily admits that it is more sensible to speak of "medieval love" than "courtly love," and he stresses the great

---

appeals unconvincingly to a "gradualistic" viewpoint to maintain that Andrew approved of "courtly love" on one level (the worldly), while recognizing that it was disapproved of by God and the teachings of the Church on another level (the eternal). A better perspective is provided by John C. Moore, "Love in Twelfth-Century France: A Failure in Synthesis," in the same volume of *Traditio* (429–443): "One takes that writer [Andrew] seriously at one's peril" (437); "It seems to me that the entire work can be considered as a piece of sophisticated humor, produced for the same audience who enjoyed the goliardic poetry, and aimed at the two extremes, the one which said all good comes from love and the other which said no good comes from love" (n. 47).
   17. E. T. Donaldson, "The Myth of Courtly Love," *Ventures: Magazine of the Yale Graduate School 5* (1965), reprinted in his *Speaking of Chaucer* (London 1970) 154–163, esp. 160.
   18. West, *Courtoisie* 4.

variety of love in the Middle Ages. In speaking of Lewis's four
characteristics of the courtly code, he acknowledges that adultery
has been "overplayed," but defends the other three, and emphasizes that others besides Andrew the Chaplain codified an Art of
Love in the Middle Ages. He fails, however, to deal with the
modern belief that these notions were a novelty in the eleventh
century, except for alluding to the findings of Peter Dronke.[19]
Dronke asserts that the supposedly new aspects of medieval romantic love are universal in time and place.[20] But I attempt to
show in Part II that these so-called courtly characteristics were
directly inspired in large measure by the romantic tales of Ovid.
(It should not be necessary to demonstrate that Ovid's more
frivolous *Ars amatoria* was the inspiration of the medieval Arts of
Love that Utley speaks of.)

In the book as a whole I am chiefly concerned with the works
of Geoffrey Chaucer and John Gower and their sources, with
special emphasis on Chaucer's *Legend of Good Women* and
Troilus and Criseyde and Gower's *Confessio amantis*. In order to
come to a better understanding of love and marriage in these
works I consider it necessary to examine the technicalities of
medieval views on sexuality and love within marriage, numerous
aspects of which are not generally known to literary critics. The
whole area of canon law in particular is an unexplored land for
many scholars, and I hope that the chapters on clandestine marriage and matrimonial sin will serve as an introduction to some of
its mysteries. Closely related to canon law is the subject of confessional casuistry, that is, the analysis of cases of conscience for
use in the sacrament of penance. Other religious viewpoints on

19. Francis L. Utley, "Must We Abandon the Concept of Courtly Love?"
Medievalia et humanistica 2.3 (1972) 299–324.
20. Peter Dronke, *Medieval Latin and the Rise of European Love-Lyric,*
2 vols. (Oxford 1965) 1.2. Dronke does stress that the concepts of Christian
mysticism gave a peculiar tone to medieval love. I myself tend to think that
it was romantic love that gave a peculiar tone to Christian mysticism,
though clearly the influence was reciprocal. In Chap. 12 below, "The
Mystical Code of Married Love," I attempt to show how we can distill
evidence of virtuous romantic love even from some of the most ascetic of
mystical writers.

marriage, some of them quite similar to those found in these analyses, but others radically different, appear in the writings of the theologians, philosophers, and scriptural exegetes, and especially in the nuptial liturgy and in works dealing with mysticism and the spiritual life.

Besides Ovid, Chaucer's most important literary source as a romanticist was Boccaccio, and I give a great deal of attention to his works. Perhaps I should say here that, when discussing the first-person narratives of these and other authors, I have found it cumbersome and not very helpful to distinguish between the author and an assumed persona, and do not propose to resort to the practice as a general rule. It is to be presupposed, of course, that an author will strike various fictional attitudes when he includes himself as a character or active narrator in his works. I make an exception in the case of Gower's *Confessio amantis*, for he insists on the distinction between himself and his self-characterization as a lover.

When citing texts in foreign languages, I have usually attempted to give at least the sense of each passage, if not an exact translation. For Ovid, I have generally used the translations of the Loeb Classical Library; for other authors, unless otherwise indicated, the translations are my own. In the interests of clarity, I have normalized the spelling of all medieval Latin citations, even those taken from inedited manuscripts. For the sake of convenience, I normally refer to the latest or most readily available editions of ancient and medieval authors; but for the vast majority of passages cited, the questions of textual variants or emendations are unimportant, and other editions would serve as well.

There is no agreement among modern scholars on the form to be used for the personal names of medieval authors. I follow the policy of Anglicizing them whenever hallowed tradition does not forbid it. Thus, I have not changed "Jean de Meun" to "John of Meun," but I use "John Acton" rather than the Latin form "Iohannes de Athon," though I often give an alternate form of an author's name in the first full-reference footnote. Sometimes I translate Latin epithets or appellations: "Laurence of Spain" rather than "Laurence Hispanus (or "Laurentius Hispanus")"; but sometimes, following the model of "John Duns Scotus," I let it stand: "Peter Comestor" rather than "Peter the Eater"; "John Andreae" rather than "John of Andrew" (or "John son of Andrew" or "Iohannes Andreae" or "John d'Andrea" or "Giovanni d'Andrea").

PART I

Hymenaeus Amorque: The Compatibility of Love and Marriage

Protinus Andromedan et tanti praemia facti
Indotata rapit. Taedas Hymenaeus Amorque
Praecutiunt; largis satiantur odoribus ignes;
Sertaque dependent tectis; et ubique lyraeque
Tibiaque et cantus, animi felicia laeti
Argumenta, sonant.

(Forthwith the hero claims Andromeda as the prize of his
great deed, seeking no further dowry. Hymen and Love
shake the marriage torch; the fires are fed full with incense
rich and fragrant; garlands deck the dwellings; and everywhere lyre and flute and songs resound, blessed proofs of in-
ward joy.)

—Ovid, *Metamorphoses* 4.757–762

Ful is the place of soun of minstralsye,
Of songes amorous of maryage.

—Chaucer, *The Legend of Hypermnestra* 2615–2616

Chapter 1

Guinevere, Marie of Champagne, and Heloise Reviewed

Lancelot and the *Ars honeste amandi*

In the interests of exorcizing once and for all the categorical imperative of adultery from our concept of medieval romance, it will be instructive to compare the reasons given by Gaston Paris and C. S. Lewis for the alleged enmity between love and marriage. For Paris, the first characteristic of courtly love is that it is illicit and furtive: it involves the kind of behavior that one could not imagine of a man toward his wife, such as the lover's constant fear of losing his mistress, of not being worthy of her, of displeasing her. None of this, he says, can be reconciled with a husband's calm and public possession of his lady.[1]

It was possible, however, and quite common, for marriage as well as love to be both illicit and furtive, rather than calm and public, as we shall see in the chapters on clandestine marriage. Furthermore, Paris does not allow for the possibility that these qualities could characterize the period of courtship, before the lady definitively gave herself to her lover, as a bride or a mistress.

The adultery that C. S. Lewis requires of love includes fornication, as well as adultery in the strict sense: "The poet normally addresses another man's wife" (2–3); but sometimes the lady in question is unmarried, and so is the man. The reasons he gives for the general dissociation of love and marriage are: (1) arranged

1. Paris, "Lancelot du Lac 2: *Le conte de la charrette*," *Romania* 12 (1883) 518: "Il est illégitime, furtif. On ne conçoit pas de rapports pareils entre mari et femme; la crainte perpétuelle de l'amant de perdre sa maîtresse, de ne plus être digne d'elle, de lui déplaire en quoi que ce soit, ne peut se concilier avec la possession calme et publique."

[31]

marriages did not take love into consideration; and (2) the preva-
lent view of theologians and other churchmen was that passionate
love, even within marriage, was more or less wicked (13–18).
Neither of these, however, would be sufficient to account for the
principle allegedly held by the medieval poets and their contemporaries that love was *impossible* within marriage. First of all,
not all marriages were arranged; furthermore, what was to prevent
love from developing once the marriage was arranged? Donnell
Van de Voort even argues that arrangements of this sort often
worked out for the best emotionally as well as socially, especially
since the daughter frequently had a say in the matter. "Riches
have always married riches, and power, power; such matches are
no doubt calculated to produce the happiest results," and the romances usually bear this out.[2] As for Lewis's second point, we
shall find universal agreement among churchmen that marriage
excused passion of at least some, if not all, of its sinfulness. Even
if this were not so, however, one could not argue that love would
be impossible for a married couple, but only that love would be
indifferent to marriage—that on the moral level whether or not
the lovers were married (or to be married) would not be an issue.

Later on, when analyzing the *Ars honeste amandi* of Andrew
the Chaplain, Lewis better justifies his stipulation of adultery:
"The love which is to be the source of all that is beautiful in life
and manners must be the reward freely given by the lady, and
only our superiors can reward. But a wife is not a superior" (36).
This view, which is at least speciously plausible, would perhaps
have merit if it could be shown to have a widespread incidence
in literature. In fact, it does not: one rarely, if ever, reads of marriageable lovers in serious romances refusing to marry because the
the woman will lose her dominant role over the man; if the sub-

2. Van de Voort 11–12. See also John F. Benton, "Clio and Venus: An
Historical View of Medieval Love," in Newman 19–42, esp. 21: "The influence of family alliances, property rights, desire for legitimate offspring,
social status, and the prospect of companionship all worked to make marriage attractive to the participants." And "the ideal of marriage, if not
always the reality, was that there should be love between the spouses." On
happily arranged matches of interest in medieval England, see John Lawlor,
"The Pattern of Consolation in *The Book of the Duchess*," *Speculum* 31
(1956) 626–648.

ject arises, the lady is normally allowed to keep her sovereignty, at least to some extent; or else both the man and the woman cede the mastery to the other, and a state of equality or mutuality results.[3]

Lewis professes to derive the notion of female sovereignty as the reason for the necessity of adultery from Andrew's *Ars*, in the alleged letter of the Countess Marie of Champagne. But he is mistaken: that is not the basis of her opposition to marriage. She treats the man and the woman equally: "Lovers give each other everything freely, under no compulsion of necessity, but married people are in duty bound to give in to each other's desires and deny themselves to each other in nothing."[4]

Her reasoning is no doubt based directly on Ovid:

> Non legis iussu lectum venistis in unum:
> Fungitur in vobis munere legis amor.

That is, "Not by the law's command have you come into one bed; for you love performs the work of law."[5] There is no sign in Andrew's *Ars* of the doctrine of the superiority of the woman over the man.[6]

3. Taking Chaucer as an example, we can cite *Troilus and Criseyde* 3.169–175 and *The Franklin's Tale* 728–798 (see below, Chap. 2); cf. also Jason's proposal to Medea in Benoit's *Roman de Troie*, and that of Aeneas to Dido in Machaut (below, Chap. 8). The Wife of Bath, whether she knows it or not, provides an example of mutuality, in her account of her marriage to her fifth husband, and also in the marriage of the knight to the Loathly Lady (*Wife of Bath's Prologue* 817–825; *Wife of Bath's Tale* 1230–1256, esp. 1255–1256: "And she obeyed hym in every thing / That myghte doon hym plesance or likyng"). All citations of Chaucer are from *The Works of Geoffrey Chaucer*, ed. F. N. Robinson, ed. 2 (Boston 1957).

4. Andreas Capellanus, *The Art of Courtly Love* 1.6.7, tr. John Jay Parry (New York 1941, repr. 1969) 106–107. For the Latin text, see *Andreae Capellani regii Francorum De amore libri tres*, ed. E. Trojel (Copenhagen 1892).

5. Ovid, *Ars amatoria* 2.157–158, ed. and tr. J. H. Mozley, Loeb Classical Library (London 1929, repr. 1962).

6. The seventh rule of the King of Love in *Ars* 1.6 dialogue 5 (81), which reads: "Being obedient in all things to the commands of ladies, thou shalt ever strive to ally thyself to the service of Love," refers not to the lover's subordination to his beloved, but to his courtesy and service to all ladies; cf. rule 11: "Thou shalt be in all things polite and courteous." The lady's sovereignty over her lover is a doctrine ascribed not to Marie Countess of Champagne, but to Marie Viscountess of Ventadour, by the

The dictum of the Countess Marie does serve to show, however, that at least some basis for the modern courtly-love rule of the incompatibility between love and marriage can be found in medieval literature. Other examples of such a doctrine are often alleged, and it will be useful to examine some of the better-known ones.

Let us look first at Chrétien's *Lancelot*. At the end of the work, just before Chrétien breaks off without finishing the story, we are told of a great tournament arranged by a "parlement" of the ladies of the court. Their object is to find suitable husbands for themselves, and when the disguised Lancelot performs so splendidly, they all wish to marry him. When he disappears from the scene, they refuse to marry anyone else, since they cannot have him whom they desire.[7] There is then, no animus against marriage as such in this poem, and the *Lancelot* cannot be said to differ from Chrétien's other works in this respect. Perhaps then we should conclude that the reason why marriage is never considered between Lancelot and Guinevere is that she is already married, rather than that Lancelot deliberately chose her as a mistress because she was married.

Perhaps too we can even generalize from this episode after the fashion of Gaston Paris and replace his theory with another, which we might call the Code of Courtly Courtship: "When one falls in love, one seeks to marry one's beloved, if at all convenient; if not convenient, then one gets along as best one can." This formula, of course, is simply a restatement of the pattern discerned by Justina Ruiz de Conde: preference for marriage, but

---

Provençal poet Gui d'Ussel in a debate written early in the next century (before 1219); she is made to contest the opinion, supposedly held by the poet himself, that lady and lover should eventually be equal. Gui has another debate, this time with his cousin Elias, over the advisability of marrying one's lady. Gui opposes marriage, because it would be wrong for a man either to court his lady after marriage or to treat her rudely and brutally. Elias responds that he would like nothing better than to marry his lady: a husband has his joy without torment, but a mere lover has it mixed with pain. See Maurice Valency, *In Praise of Love* (New York 1958, repr. 1961) 66, 149–150. For the texts, see Jean Audiau and René Lavaud, *Nouvelle anthologie des troubadours* (Paris 1928) 195–201.

7. *Le chevalier de la charrete* 5361–6056, ed. Mario Roques, CFMA 86 (Paris 1958, repr. 1970).

priority to love.[8] The attitude is nicely summed up by the King of Hungary's daughter in the late medieval romance *The Squire of Low Degree*.[9] She tells the squire of her hope

> That my father so fayne may be,
> That he wyll wede me unto thee,
>
> . . . . .
>
> That we might our dayes endure
> In parfyte love that is so pure.
> And if we may not so come to,
> Other wyse then must we do.   [259–267]

Whether the love is marriage-oriented or not, however (I am still generalizing from *Lancelot*), the common "doctrines"—moral, religious, or intellectual—which would cast the lovers in an unfavorable light are frequently held in abeyance. Thus, in the episode of the tournament, there is no sign of antifeminism or of the familiar complaint about the evils of marriage or sexual pleasure. Nor in the treatment of the affair between Lancelot and Guinevere is there any suggestion on the author's part that they are culpable, on grounds of adultery, treason, or perjury. Such charges occur only when Kay is falsely accused of lying with the queen. Lancelot formulates this principle of abeyance himself:

> Car, sanz faille, molt en amande
> Qui fet ce qu'Amors li comande,
> Et tot est pardonable chose.[10]

8. Above, Introd.
9. Ed. W. H. French and C. B. Hale, *Middle English Metrical Romances* (New York 1930) 721–755.
10. *Chevalier* 4393–4395: "For unquestionably he is much better off who does all that Love commands, and whatever he does is pardonable." I do not agree, obviously, with those who interpret the poem as condemning the love of Lancelot by way of irony. See Francis L. Utley, "Must We Abandon the Concept of Courtly Love?" *Medievalia et humanistica* 2.3 (1972) 320, on the overly facile use of irony as a solution to difficulties of interpretation. I do not mean, of course, to deny the comic aspects of the poem. As pointed out by Fanni Bogdanow, "The Love Theme in the *Chevalier de la charrette*," *Modern Language Review* 67 (1972) 50–61, "Chrétien delights in making gentle fun at the expense of his hero. . . . But while not idealizing Lancelot, Chrétien is careful not to vilify him" (54). Bogdanow appeals to Eugène Vinaver's concept of Chrétien as "ideologically uncommitted" to explain that he "is not desirous of idealizing either marriage or extramarital love" (50). See, for example, Vinaver's *The Rise of Romance* (New York 1971) 32.

Gaston Paris cites the *Ars honeste amandi* in support of his reading of *Lancelot* because of the connection of both works with the Countess Marie of Champagne, who gave Chrétien the *matière* and *san* of the story and who appears as a judge on matters of love in Andrew's book. But in recent times Marie has been exonerated from the charges of having encouraged the kind of love that Andrew describes, and Andrew's connection with her court has been seriously questioned.[11] He does not in fact claim to be her chaplain. He is Andrew the Lover, Chaplain of the Royal Court, which no doubt refers to the court of the King of Love.[12]

C. S. Lewis attributes courtly love in part to "Ovid misunderstood" (7–8). We shall see that it is he who misunderstood Ovid, not the authors of the Middle Ages. In particular, Andrew the Chaplain was perfectly aware of the Ovidian character of his *Ars honeste amandi*.[13] With much more justice we could say that courtly love was created in the nineteenth and twentieth centuries

11. See John F. Benton, "The Court of Champagne as a Literary Center," *Speculum* 36 (1961) 551–591. Andrew dates the letter from Marie of Champagne 1 May 1174, but his book was probably composed in 1186 or in the decade following, therefore after the *Lancelot* (generally dated ca. 1177–1181). Perhaps the prominence that Chrétien gave to Marie in the *Lancelot* inspired Andrew to concoct his letter from her.

12. Andrew 1.6.7 (104); cf. pp. 80 and 107 for some of the many references to the King of Love.

13. It should be noted, however, that Ovid's *Remedia amoris* is not a total rejection of love, like Andrew's *Reprobatio;* rather it is designed to help one recover from being jilted by one's beloved, or to escape from an unsuitable love affair. One can agree, of course, that the *Remedia* served as a model for a more thoroughgoing repudiation of love than Ovid envisaged. But by no stretch of my imagination, at least, can I regard the *Remedia* itself as a treatise "supplying techniques by means of which one might extricate oneself" from the snare of "idolatrous passion," as it has been described by D. W. Robertson, Jr., "The Concept of Courtly Love," *Newman* 3. It is true, of course, that not only the *Remedia* but also the *Ars amatoria* was *sometimes interpreted* in the Middle Ages to be serving an entirely moral purpose. See Robertson, *A Preface to Chaucer* (Princeton 1963) 356, citing Fausto Ghisalberti, "Medieval Biographies of Ovid," *Journal of the Warburg and Courtauld Institutes* 9 (1946) 10–59. But I tend to agree with Edwin A. Quain, "The Medieval *Accessus ad auctores*," *Traditio* 3 (1945) 215–264, 225: "It is impossible to suppose that the medieval writer really believed that Ovid, for instance, had a high moral purpose in writing the *Ars amatoria*."

by "Andrew misunderstood," because his precepts on love were taken seriously.

In the sample dialogues that Andrew gives to aid men in winning over women, there is no word of the place of marriage in the scheme of love until the fifth exchange, in which a set of rules of the King of Love is set forth. The fourth rule specifies: "Thou shalt not choose for thy love anyone whom a natural sense of shame forbids thee to marry."[14] Marriageability therefore is a criterion of suitability. In the seventh dialogue, however, the woman objects that she is already married and loves her husband. The man denies that marital affection can ever be true love, for love is "an inordinate desire to receive passionately a furtive and hidden embrace" (100). This explanation corresponds to Paris's, but nothing more is made of it. In fact, it is contradicted later on (2.2:153): "Love increases, too, if it happens to last after it has been made public."

The man and woman of the seventh dialogue agree to abide by decision of the Countess Marie, who judges against married love, but for different reasons. One of them we have already seen when discussing the countess's letter: the marriage agreement binds the partners to satisfy each other's desires, and therefore does away with the freedom necessary to love. She adds that one's honor cannot be increased by receiving what one has a right to. This reasoning too is contradicted later in the *Ars* (2.6:167): "All lovers are bound, when practicing love's solaces, to be mutually obedient to each other's desires."[15]

A further reason given by the countess to explain the incompatibility of love and marriage is based on two precepts of Love: (1) "No woman, even if she is married, can be crowned with the reward of the King of Love unless she is seen to be enlisted in the service of Love himself outside the bonds of wedlock." (2) "No one can be in love with two men."[16] No justification is given for

14. Andrew 1.6.5 (81), referred to again in 1.8 (143), and repeated in 2.8 rule 11 (185).
15. This contradiction was pointed out by Robertson, *Preface to Chaucer* 444.
16. Andrew 1.6.7 (107). The second rule is no. 3 in the list given in 2.8 (184). The first rule appears neither here nor in the list in 1.6.5 (81–82).

the out-of-wedlock rule; it is simply an arbitrary fiat. The countess's final reason depends on yet another rule of Love, "He who is not jealous cannot love," and true jealousy is held to be impossible for man and wife.[17]

It is frequently assumed that, according to Andrew, true love must be adulterous in the strict sense or, even more specifically, that the *lady* must be married. But there is nothing in the foregoing to suggest this. The only rule of the King of Love on the subject runs thus: "Marriage is no real excuse for not loving" (2.8.1). In the eighth dialogue, examples are given of unmarried virgins who have loved truly, and we also learn that true lovers are accustomed to marry (121), and are therefore free to marry.[18] They do not marry each other, of course, for that is fatal to love (2.14:156). At one point in the eighth dialogue, however, the man and woman seem to assume that love is possible between man and wife. When the woman mentions her grief as an impediment to love, the man says that only grief for a dead *lover* can impede love, according to Love's precept, which stipulates a two-year period of mourning (114–115). After further discussion, in which the man cites the Countess Marie as his authority for holding it impossible to love his own wife, the woman admits that it is her husband she is grieving for. He responds: "According to the rule of the law you may after the years of grief for your husband have elapsed lay aside all sadness and join the soldiery of lovers" (116–117).[19]

In the Latin it reads: "Nulla etiam coniugata regis poterit amoris praemio coronari, nisi extra coniugii foedera ipsius amoris militiae cernatur adiuncta."

17. The rule given here is the second in the list of 2.8 (184).

18. The good character of the maidens here named—Blanchefleur, Isolde, and Anfelis—is open to question, especially that of the latter two.

19. Cf. 2.8 rule 7 (185). There was no legal period of mourning in force in the Middle Ages. According to Roman civil law, a widow had to mourn for one year and could not remarry within that time, but this restriction was specifically revoked by Popes Alexander III and Innocent III; their edicts are collected in the *Decretals of Gregory IX* 4.21.4 (*Super illa*, here ascribed to Urban III) and 5 (*Cum secundum*), ed. Emil Friedberg, *Corpus iuris canonici* (Leipzig 1879–1881, repr. Graz 1959) 2.731–732. Both popes refer to 1 Corinthians 7.39, as does the man in Andrew's dialogue (118): "The Apostle clearly permits a woman to marry again immediately after the death of her husband," though he says it does not apply if there might

This, in summary, is the varied doctrine of Andrew the Chaplain on the incompatibility of love and marriage. Striking as it is, there is little or no reference to it or use of it in the literature of succeeding generations, not only in England, where (as far as we know) Andrew was not heard of, but also in France, Italy, and Spain, where his work was known.

We must conclude that the opposition between love and marriage was very much a minority view, and hardly a serious one, contrary to what the theorists of courtly love have assumed. A corollary of the courtly-love theory was that in cases where the matrimonial status of the characters was in doubt, adultery was to be assumed. Our new code, on the contrary, demands that we follow the principle enunciated in the revised *Code of Canon Law:* In all doubtful cases the presumption of the law is on the side of marriage, and the burden of proof rests on those who impugn it.[20]

The *Roman de la Rose*

We may apply this canon of presumption to Guillaume de Lorris's *Roman de la Rose*. There is no reason to suppose that the Rose is a married lady; it is rather more likely that she is an unmarried virgin. The same is true even for Jean de Meun's Rose, for Jean has Guillaume say that he was the first man to go that route.[21] Similarly, there is no reason to suppose that Guillaume's love for the Rose is not to end in marriage. At least we hear of no theoretical opposition to marriage from Lorris or any of his characters.

The same is not true of Meun's section, however. In particular, the Lover's Friend has harsh things to say against marriage—or more accurately, against the generality of men (that is, the male of

---

be confusion of descent (i.e., if she is pregnant or possibly pregnant by her first husband).

20. *Codex iuris canonici* 1014 (Rome 1917) 291: "Matrimonium gaudet favore iuris; quare in dubio standum est pro valore matrimonii, donec contrarium probetur."

21. *Le roman de la Rose* 21627, ed. Félix Lecoy, CFMA 92, 95, 98 (Paris 1965–1970): "Car g'i passai touz li prumiers." Cf. below, Chap. 5, in the section "John's Status as a Lover." The best treatment of the themes of love and marriage in the *Roman* is to be found in Alan M. F. Gunn, *The Mirror of Love: A Reinterpretation of "The Romance of the Rose"* (Lubbock, Texas, 1952).

the species) who enter into marriage. His general principle is that love must be mutual, for love and mastery do not mix:

> Onques amor et seigneurie
> Ne s'entrefierent compaignie
> Ne ne demorerent ensemble:
> Cil qui mestroie les dessemble.   [8421–8424]

Specifically, he says, true love cannot last when the husband domineers over his wife and treats her like his property:

> Bone amour n'i peut durer,
> Tant s'entrefont maus andurer,
> Quant cil veut la mestrise avoir
> Du cors sa fame et de l'avoir.   [8433–8436]

In so saying, he admits that love is possible for married people, as long as both husband and wife are willing to abide by the law of the matrimonial contract, according to which neither husband nor wife is to dominate; they are to be equals and companions.

> [Sa fame] ne redoit pas estre dame,
> Mes sa pareille et sa compaigne,
> Si con la loi les acompaigne,
> Et il redoit ses compainz estre
> Sanz soi fere seigneur ne mestre.   [9396–9400]

No husband will be loved by his wife if he wants to be her lord. Love dies in such a case, for love must be free in order to survive:

> Ja de sa fame n'iert amez
> Qui "sires" veust estre clamez;
> Car il convient amors morir
> Quant amant veulent seignorir.
> Amor ne peut durer ne vivre,
> S'el n'est en queur franc et delivre.   [9407–9412]

According to this view, then, marriage should result in the freedom necessary to love, if only the partners would obey its laws. This concept of marriage is just the opposite of that set forth in the letter of the Countess of Champagne in Andrew's *Ars honeste amandi*, and might seem to be very optimistic for its time. Most churchmen, of course, stressed the wife's equality with the husband to some extent—particularly in the symbolism of Eve's formation from Adam's side, whereby God showed that a wife was to be neither mistress nor servant but companion.[22] Realistically speaking, however, the woman was considered equal mainly in the matter of sexual intercourse, the right to the carnal *debitum*. In most other matters, she was to be subordinate and obedient to her husband.[23]

If Amis has a favorable view of marriage in theory, in practice he is pessimistic: Lovers who marry may find that in spite of themselves their love is no longer able to endure; for the man beforehand acted as servant and she was mistress, but now he acts as lord and master over his onetime lady:

> Por ce revoit l'en ensement,
> De touz ceus qui prumierement
> Par amors amer s'entreseulent,
> Quant puis espouser s'entreveulent,
> Envis peut entr'eus avenir
> Que ja s'i puisse amors tenir;
> Car cil, quant par amors amoit,
> Serjant a cele se clamoit
> Qui sa mestresse soloit estre;
> Or se claime seigneur et mestre
> Seur li, que sa dame ot clamee
> Quant ele iert par amors amee.   [9413–9424]

The reasoning contained in these lines may strike us as similar to that which C. S. Lewis professed to find in Andrew the Chaplain. No doubt it was this passage in the *Roman* that led him, at least in part, to that erroneous judgment. Such an interpretation of the *Roman*, however, would be almost as erroneous. The Friend does not hold that love is impossible within marriage; it is merely difficult—especially in cases where love was not mutual beforehand but was dominated by the desires of the lady.

In this section the Friend reserves his harshness almost exclusively for men who destroy love within marriage by becoming tyrannical over their wives. The long tirade of the Jealous Hus-

22. See, for example, Peter Lombard, *Sentences* 2.18.3 (PL 192.688), and John Gower, *Mirour de l'omme* 17521–17532.

23. See Gratian, *Decretum* 2.33.5.12–13 (the canons *Est ordo* and *Haec imago* of Augustine) and 18–19 (the canons *Adam per Evam* and *Mulier debet* of Ambrose), Friedberg 1.1254–1255. Cf. René Metz, "Recherches sur la condition de la femme selon Gratien," *Studia gratiana* 12: Collectanea Stephan Kuttner 2 (1967) 377–396.

band is offered as an example of such misbehavior. In the course
of his polemics, he attacks marriage as an institution, and approves
of Heloise's opposition to it. She objects, first, that the conditions
of marriage are too difficult, even though the woman be wise—for
she well knows the nature of woman:

> Trop sunt dures
> Condicions de mariage,
> Conbien que la fame soit sage;
> Car les livres avoit veüz
> Et estudiez et seüz,
> Et les meurs feminins savoit,
> Car tretouz en soi les avoit.   [8740–8746]

Heloise makes no more of this typically antifeminist utterance,
though the Jealous Husband does, as we shall see. Her next argument is that she wants Abelard to love her but to claim no right
over her other than what she freely gives, with no lordship or
mastery:

> Et requeroit que il l'amast,
> Mes que nul droit n'i reclamast,
> Fors que de grace et de franchise,
> Sanz seigneurie et sanz mestrise.   [8747–8750]

Her desire to love freely might seem to hearken back to the
Countess of Champagne's letter in Andrew the Chaplain; but the
countess, like Ovid, was speaking of the *mutual* constraint that
follows upon the marriage contract, while Heloise seems clearly
to be referring to the kind of male domination that Amis later
discusses and that the Jealous Husband himself is guilty of.[24] Furthermore, we do not get the idea that love is impossible within
marriage, but only that it is less preferable to unmarried love.
This is especially true in their circumstances, for she adds that, if
they do not get married, they will be able to pursue their studies
without being tied down; and another advantage would be that
their joys would be greater on the occasions when they met to-

---

24. In the original letter, however, the spirit does seem to be that of
Ovid and Andrew: Heloise preferred to be mistress rather than wife so that
only her own charms would tie him to her, not the force of any nuptial
bond ("ut me ei sola gratia conservaret, non vis aliqua vinculi nuptialis
constringeret"). *Historia calamitatum*, ed. J. Monfrin (Paris 1959) 78.

gether (8751–8758). This latter sentiment, "Absence makes the heart grow fonder," was perhaps inspired by Ovid's advice in the *Ars amatoria*, although it is a counsel that can apply to the married as well as to the unmarried, as is shown by Ovid's three examples, all of them of married couples.[25]

However, concludes the Jealous Husband, Heloise's arguments were in vain. Abelard loved her so much that he married her, and thus it turned out badly:

> Mes il, si conme escrit nous a,
> Qui tant l'amoit, puis l'espousa
> Contre son amonestement,
> Si l'en meschaï malement.   [8759–8762]

Here we have a clear example of love that led to marriage. Marriage brought great disaster upon Abelard and Heloise, but it did not destroy their love; if anything, it increased their devotion to one another. (I am not now referring to the truth of the matter in real life: the authenticity of their letters is suspect,[26] and the romantic quality of their love as manifested in the letters is quite problematical;[27] rather, I am continuing to rely solely on the account of the Vilains Jalous in the *Roman*, for this version would have had the most immediate effect on poets in the age of Chaucer.) Even after she became abbess of the Paraclete, she continued to write, without shame, to her lover (*amis*). If, in her arguments against marriage, she declared that she wanted love without lordship or mastery, nevertheless she loved him so much that she called him father and lord: "Tant amoit / Que pere et seigneur le clamoit" (8777–8780). She proved that she meant it by marrying him against her better judgment. She told him, as abbess, long

25. *Ars amatoria* 2.345–356. The couples are Phyllis and Demophoon, Penelope and Ulysses, and Laodamia and Protesilaus. Ovid perhaps would not have considered Phyllis married, but no doubt the medieval reader would have. See below, Chap. 8.

26. John F. Benton, "Fraud, Fiction, and Borrowing in the Correspondence and Abelard and Heloise," *Actes du Colloque international Pierre Abélard–Pierre le Vénérable* (Paris 1974). See also Benton and Fiorella Ercoli Prosperetti, "The Style of the *Historia calamitatum*: A Preliminary Test of the Authenticity of the Correspondence Attributed to Abelard and Heloise," *Viator* 6 (1975).

27. R. W. Southern, "The Letters of Abelard and Heloise," in *Medieval Humanism* (New York 1970) 86–104.

after they had come to grief: "If the Emperor of Rome should wish to take me as his wife and make me mistress of the world, I would prefer, with God as my witness, to be called your whore than to be crowned empress."[28]

The Jealous Husband draws three conclusions from this episode. First, there was probably never another woman like Heloise, and it was probably her learning that enabled her to keep her female nature in check. Second, Abelard should have followed her advice. And, third, marriage is an evil bond: "Mariages est maus liens" (8795–8803). That is, he resumes where he had left off and continues to berate his wife; in condemning her behavior he concludes that all women are basically whorish and intractable:

> Toutes estes, serez, et fustes,
> De fet ou de volenté pustes;
> Car, qui que puist le fet estaindre
> Volenté ne peut nus contraindre.
> Tel avantage ont toutes fames
> Qu'eus sunt de leur volentez dames.   [9125–9130]

As I pointed out before, Amis disapproves of the Jealous Husband's whole manner of discourse. But it does not necessarily follow that he disapproves of everything that the Husband has said. Just as Amis was pessimistic about the ability of most men to refrain from acting the jealous or domineering husband, he is also harsh at times toward women. Furthermore, we cannot automatically conclude even that the Jealous Husband means everything he says, or that the Friend takes all of his own sentiments literally.

Exemplary Hits and Misses

We must remember, first of all, that the medieval tendency to use exempla to illustrate morals can be very misleading, because of the practice of telling whole stories rather than simply alluding to

28. "Se li empereres de Rome,
    Souz cui doivent estre tuit home,
    Me daignet volair prendre a fame,
    Et fere moi du monde dame,
    Si vodroie je mieuz," fet ele,
    "Et Dieu a tesmoigne en apele,
    Estre ta putain apelee,
    Que empereriz coronee."   [8787–8794]

the appropriate aspects of the stories. We all know that compari-
sons limp, and that the longer the analogies are the more halting
they are likely to be. In medieval literature, however, the situation
often reaches paraplegic proportions. Writers frequently include
a wealth of detail that is antithetical to the moral at issue, or to
other morals that the author wishes to enforce. Dozens of examples of this effect can be seen in John Gower's *Confessio amantis*,[29] and Chaucer's *Clerk's Tale* is a particularly flagrant instance.
Chaucer follows Petrarch in having the Clerk deny the moral of
the story to be that wives should be humbly obedient like Griselda, for such submission would be both undesirable and intoler-
able. Rather, Griselda's patience under her husband's afflictions
should teach us all to be patient under the trials sent by God
(1142–1162). This is almost like saying that Griselda was ill-
advised to bear with Walter, who was perverse and unjust
(though God knows what would have happened to her had she
rebelled); but since she did bear with him, she can provide us with
an example of constancy, *mutatis mutandis*. The *mutanda*, however, are so numerous and distracting that it might hardly seem
worth the effort to make the changes.

Chaucer increases the difficulty by accentuating Walter's in-
justice and inhumanity, thereby making him still more removed
from God's loving providence, and by making Griselda herself
seem perverse in obeying him (when, for example, she delivers
her children to him to be murdered). To makes matters worse, in
the stanza that comes after Petrarch's moral, the Clerk goes on,
without warning, to speak as if the moral of the story really were
the one that he (and Petrarch) had just rejected, namely, that
wives should obey their husbands:

> It were ful hard to fynde now-a-dayes
> In al a toun Grisildis thre or two;
> For if that they were put to swiche assayes,
> The gold of hem hath now so badde alayes
> With bras, that thogh the coyne be fair at ye,
> It wolde rather breste a-two than plye.   [1164–1169]

As a matter of fact, of course, the Clerk's implied moral is just as
easily derivable from the story as Petrarch's. Once again, Gri-

29. See below, Chap. 5, in the section "Marriage Neglected."

selda's patience provides the point of contact between moral and exemplum, and the other elements are *mutanda;* this time we would have to transform Walter to a just husband rather than to a just God.

In the same way, the point of applicability of the Jealous Husband's moral ("Marriage is bad") to his exemplum is Heloise's conviction that marriage was bad for her and Abelard. But in the course of telling her story he brings out a number of features that serve to undermine his sardonic view of women and their relations with men: Heloise is a stirring example of wisdom, fortitude, constancy, and of a love so strong that it could endure even the rigors of marriage. Like Petrarch, the Husband is a bit uncomfortable with the story, and he tries to explain Heloise away as totally untypical. But the over-all impact of his exemplum remains "counterproductive." Whether Amis or Jean de Meun was aware of the resulting irony, we do not know; but there it is.

Satirical Hyperbole

Apart from the pitfalls of exemplary inappropriateness, we must guard against the hyperbole characteristic of satirical and hortatory modes of discourse.[30] In these contexts, vices and the incidence of vices are often exaggerated beyond measure in the heat of the moment, without qualifications or exceptions. Thus, immediately after giving an example of a jealous husband's abusive treatment of his wife, Amis characterizes "woman" as shameless, stubborn, ignorant, deceitful, and vicious,[31] and then proceeds to expound the ideal of mutual love within marriage, which assumes that both men and women are capable of the reason and modera-

---

30. For instances of hyperbole in the context of spiritual exhortation and counsel, see below, Chap. 5, in the sections on "John's Status as a Lover" and "An End of All His Work," and Chap. 12, "Spiritual Counsel for Troilus."

31. Fame ne prise honor ne honte
     Quant riens en la teste li monte,
     Qu'il est veritez sanz doutance
     Qu'en fame n'a point de sciance.
     Vers quan qu'el het et quan qu'el aime,
     Valerius neïs la claime
     Hardie et artificieuse
     Et trop a nuire estudieuse. [9383–9390]

tion that such love demands. Later he says that he, like Solomon, has looked for a good woman and never found one. He (or Jean) forgets momentarily that he is addressing the Lover and says that if "you" in your search should find such a woman, hold her fast (9887–9898). After further attacks on woman in general, he suddenly addresses the Lover again: "Thus it is with your Rose, the most precious thing you could possess."[32] He simply takes for granted that she is not to be included in the universal condemnation of woman, or acts as if the antifeminist lines had never been spoken.

The Antigamy of Misogyny

A final caution must be raised about the nature of antifeminism in particular. When a character is antifeminist, or when an author is an antifeminist mood, he is usually opposed to marriage, not because it interferes with love or makes love impossible, but because love itself, in the romantic and ennobling sense, is impossible, given the fundamental and irremediable peversity of women. Women can only pretend a genuine love in order to entrap men into marriage, which from their point of view is simply a means of exploiting their husbands and indulging their vices all the more. The movement of thought, then, is from being antiwoman to being antilove, and finally, *per consequens*, antimarriage.

This is the basic and constant attitude of the Jealous Husband, and we must not be thrown off by the seemingly profeminist trimmings of the Heloise exemplum. It is not the constant attitude of the Friend, but when he indulges in it he does so wholeheartedly. Sometimes antifeminist sentiments are placed in the mouths of women, like Chaucer's Wife of Bath, or her model La Vielle in the *Roman de la Rose*. Such women embody and preach the sort of deceitful and self-serving love that the Jealous Husband spoke of, and their views of marriage usually correspond to it.

---

32. Ausinc, compainz, de vostre rose,
    Qui tant est precieuse chose
    Que n'en prendriez nul avoir
    Se vos la poïez avoir,
    Quant vos en serez en sesine. [9957–9961]

According to La Vielle, for instance, Nature made women free; that is to say, they are promiscuous by nature. Marriage was instituted by wise men to check the quarreling that such promiscuity gave rise to, but marriage by no means changed woman's roving character (13845–14008). She goes on to say that men are the same; the law of marriage is too strict in confining one man to one woman. No man would refuse to love her when she was in her prime, whether he were vowed to marriage or religion, if only he knew her thoughts and the nature of all women in general. Or rather, no one would refuse to do so except perhaps a madman who, afflicted with love like a head cold, were to remain loyal to his beloved:

> Se ne fust aucuns forsenez
> Qui fust d'amors anchifrenez
> Et leaument s'amie amast.   [14109–14111]

When antifeminism remains unyielding and contemptuous, it obviously has nothing to do with the love and marriage that constitute the subjects of this study. But occasionally satire does yield to sentiment, and fabliau to romance. Thus, even the Wife of Bath, if we can believe her, achieved mutuality and fidelity in her fifth marriage, and so did the protagonists of her tale in their marriage.[33] And, of course, a similar shifting of modes is to be had in Jean de Meun's contribution to the *Roman de la Rose* as a whole.

33. See n. 3 above.

Chapter 2

Criseida and Criseyde

The Romantic Boccaccio on Love and Marriage

Sometimes antifeminism or "antiamorism" makes only a small appearance in a work given over principally to romantic love. Boccaccio's *Filocolo* provides a good example: it is mainly the story of the love of Florio and Biancifiore, a love that is noble and ennobling, passionate and faithful, furtive yet matrimonial, approved of by the gods and by God. In the interlude at Naples, in which there is a series of judgments concerning love like those in Andrew the Chaplain's *Ars honeste amandi*, Fiammetta as judge shows that her usual view of love and marriage corresponds to that practiced by Florio. For instance, in answer to a dilemma proposed by Menedon, which was to serve as the basis for Chaucer's *Franklin's Tale*, she explains that the wife's oath to make love to another man was null and void because of her marriage vows, by which she had become one body with her husband and sworn to remain content with him alone.[1] The love that the other man has for her is condemned as mere lustful desire ("libidinoso disio").[2] But a bit later, in delivering another judgment, she can

1. "La donna, con ciò sia cosa ch'ella sia membro del marito, o più tosto un corpo con lui, non potea fare quel saramento sanza volontà del marito, e se 'l fece, fu nullo, però che al primo saramento licitamente fatto subsequente puote derogare, e massimamente quelli che per non dovuta cagione non debitamente si fanno; e ne' matrimoniali congiungimenti è usanza di giurare d'essere sempre contento l'uomo della donna, e la donna dell'uomo, né di mai l'uno l'altro per altra cambiare." *Filocolo* 4.34.2, ed. Antonio Enzo Quaglio, *Tutte le opere* 1, I classici Mondadori, ed. Vittore Branca (Milan 1967) 408.
2. *Ibid.* 4.34.4. Even though Boccaccio was by his own admission an indifferent student of canon law, he would naturally realize that the wife could not commit herself to another man even with her husband's permission, so

rule out the possibility of virtuous love between man and woman.[3]

Similarly, Criseida's betrayal of Troiolo in the *Filostrato* provokes an antifeminist outburst. Young women are fickle and vain:

> Giovane donna e mobile e vogliosa
> È, negli amanti molti; e sua bellezza
> Estima più ch'allo specchio; e, pomposa,
> Ha vanagloria di sua giovinezza,

and so on. In spite of this general denunciation, however, Boccaccio does not mean to deny that individual women, even young ones like the fourteen-year-old Biancifiore, can be mature and faithful in love; for he goes on to speak of perfect women with stable desires:

> Perfetta donna ha più fermo disire
> D'essere amata, e d'amar si diletta.[4]

Fiammetta in the *Filocolo* is like Perry Mason in that she must win every case; and it does not really matter that her arguments are sometimes not up to the standard of "what has always and everywhere been true," or that they are inconsistent with her own views expressed elsewhere. The same is true of Boccaccio himself: he will support love and/or marriage when it suits the story; otherwise not. On this score, then, there is little difference whether one accepts the traditional view, as I do, of dating the *Filostrato* after the *Filocolo*, or adopts the reverse dating.[5] The

---

that, realistically, the knight was stupid and criminal to permit it. But Boccaccio, like Chaucer after him, had to ignore this consideration in order to make the story work.

3. *Ibid.* 4.44.4–9; cf. 4.46.18: "Questo amore è reo, e se egli è reo, è da fuggire." Contrast this with 2.9.8, where Boccaccio says that Providence arranged it so that the love of Florio and Biancifiore would be kept honorable through marriage (the original passage is quoted below, Chap. 9).

4. *Filostrato* 8.30–32, ed. Vittore Branca, *Tutte le opere* 2 (Milan 1964) 224–225.

5. Branca's reasons for dating the *Filostrato* before the *Filocolo* are not convincing (see his edition, 3–4). The *Filocolo* seems the more juvenile work, especially in plot construction (see below, Chap. 12). The fact that the *Filostrato* makes no mention of Fiammetta need only mean that Boccaccio had not yet hit on the idea of continuing his allusions to her in his later works. The fact that the *Filocolo* makes no reference to Troiolo and Criseida among its many allusions to ancient lovers, on the other hand, suggests that Boccaccio had not yet given them his attention. The Mondadori *Opere* was obviously planned on the assumption that the *Filocolo* preceded

fact that extramarital love is defended in the *Filostrato* does not indicate either a tightening up or relaxing of Boccaccio's own morals, as far as we can judge from his later practice. He simply follows the needs of the plot in each instance.

But if we can deliver no opinion about Boccaccio himself, we can make judgments about his characters and plots. Before we consider the particulars of the antimatrimonial *Filostrato*, then, it may be enlightening to look at a large sampling of his love stories to ascertain their prevailing tendencies. The *Decameron* with its hundred tales will prove ideal for such an examination. In Chapter 1 we formulated a hypothesis, virtually a priori, that serious lovers as a general rule favor marriage. Let us see if it holds true of the *Decameron*.

Thirty of the tales have no direct bearing on the theme of love between man and woman. Of the remaining seventy, thirty-four may be characterized as fabliaux, in which love is treated lightly, with emphasis usually placed upon the trickery involved in getting the lovers together. The remaining thirty-six, on the other hand, treat the subject more seriously. I realize that such divisions cannot be sharply drawn in every instance, particularly since Boccaccio rarely achieves true seriousness of tone even for the most tragic of his *novelle*, as Erich Auerbach has pointed out.[6] Still, a rough division should prove serviceable enough for a general discussion.

All of the stories that I classify as love-fabliaux center around extramarital affairs. Only three of them are matters of simple fornication, however, and in one of them the desired act is frustrated.[7] There are, in addition, five stories of grave fornication, that is, involving priests or nuns.[8] The remaining twenty-six deal

---

the *Filostrato;* and though Quaglio accepts Branca's dating (see Branca's "Profilo biografico," also in vol. 1, pp. 40–43), his introduction still presupposes the *Filocolo*'s precedence: "Le malinconiche meditazioni di Florio anticipano il languido sospirare di Troiolo" (47, 51).

6. Erich Auerbach, *Mimesis*, Doubleday Anchor ed. (New York 1957) 202–203. Vittore Branca, *Boccaccio medievale* (repr. Florence 1964) 28 n. 25, is "stupefied" by Auerbach's judgment but does not really refute it.

7. *Decameron* 2.2 and 8.10; frustrated in 2.5. Simple fornication occurs alongside adultery in 9.6. I use the second edition of Branca's *Decameron* (Florence 1965).

8. *Decameron* 1.4, 3.1, 3.10, 8.4, 9.2.

with adultery; in all but one it is the husband who is cuckolded, and in the lone exception the delinquent husband is caught by his wife before the act.[9]

As for the more serious love stories, Fiammetta's admonition against coveting other men's wives, "La maritata in niun modo è da disiderare" (4.52.1), seems to be in operation most of the time. Or, at least, if a man does desire a married woman, often enough she refuses him because of the love—or at least the loyalty—she bears toward her husband.[10] There is, in fact, only one clear instance of the sort of love envisaged in Andrew's *Ars honeste amandi* between a man and a married woman.[11] There are a few examples of such love between a man and a widow or a single girl.[12] There are no examples of a preference for adultery; but, of course, the same is true of Andrew's protagonists, who argue simply for extramarital love (that is, they are indifferent to whether it is fornication or adultery). There is only one example in the *Decameron* of a refusal of lovers to marry when marriage is seemingly considered; and even then no theoretical or philosophical reason is given. We are only told that the widow Elena did not wish to marry again because she was in love with a youth of her own choice and enjoyed herself with him in complete free-

9. *Decameron* 3.2–6, 8; 4.2, 10; 5.10; 6.7; 7.1–10; 8.1–2, 8; 9.6, 10. The would-be adulterer is in 9.5. Priest-adulterers appear in five of the stories: 3.8, 4.2, 7.3, 8.2, 9.10. No story in the *Decameron*, whether serious or frivolous, deals with incest, except for the metaphorical incest of spiritual kinship ridiculed in 7.10. There is no example of grave fornication or grave adultery in the serious love stories.

10. So in 1.5, 4.8, 5.9, 10.4, 10.5; cf. 2.9. In 2.8, the Count of Antwerp refuses a "Potiphar's-wife" offer. In 10.7, a girl falls hopelessly in love with the married King of France, but adultery is desired on neither side. In 10.4 and 10.5, when the would-be adulterers get their opportunity, they refuse it out of honor; cf. 10.6 (lust repressed). Love and/or loyalty in marriage is also exemplified in 10.9 and 10.10.

11. *Decameron* 3.7: the lover disguised as a friar maintains to his mistress that she has moral obligations to her lover. Cf. 4.9, which is too tragic (the husband makes his wife eat her lover's heart, and she kills herself); 2.7 is not serious enough (a woman is the mistress or wife successively of eleven different men). In 2.10, the husband is an old man, and his wife openly lives with another man.

12. *Decameron* 1.10 (widow); 4.5 and 4.7 (single girls). In 9.1 a widow successfully rejects the advances of two would-be lovers.

dom.[13] Perhaps we are to understand that marriage with such a youth would not have been allowed by her guardians, or would not have been considered proper.[14] Ironically this is virtually the only story in the *Decameron* in which one of the lovers tires of the other: Elena's young man falls in love with another woman. Such defections are almost unheard of among lovers who marry.[15]

There are numerous instances of lovers who desire to marry and actually do marry as a matter of course.[16] Sometimes lovers are seemingly indifferent to marriage, but not opposed to it.[17] When they are able to marry, they do so, four times out of five.[18]

13. *Decameron* 8.7.4: "La quale, rimasa del suo marito vedova, mai più rimaritar non si volle, essendosi ella d'un govinetto bello e leggiadro a sua scelta innamorata; e da ogni altra sollicitudine sviluppata . . . spesse volte con lui con maraviglioso diletto si dava buon tempo."

14. See below, Chap. 7. Cf. *Decameron* 5.9 and 10.9 for examples of family pressure brought on widows to remarry.

15. A possible exception occurs in 4.3, though the marriage of the three pairs of lovers after their elopement is problematical: we are only told that the men lived like barons with their *donne* (sentence 19). One of them, Restagnone, who had once loved Ninetta very much, found his love for her decreasing now that he possessed her without hindrance: "Potendola egli senza alcun sospetto ad ogni suo piacere avere, gl' incominciò a rincrescere e per conseguente a mancar verso lei l'amore" (20).

16. *Decameron* 2.3, 2.8, 3.9, 4.6, 5.1, 5.2, 5.3, 5.5, 5.8, 10.8, and, apparently, 4.3 (see previous note). Cf. 4.8: the boy's parents prevent marriage; and in 4.1 the girl's father refuses to let her remarry. In 2.10, a married woman marries her lover after her husband's death. In 5.9, a married woman who rejected a lover's advances accepts him and marries him after her husband dies.

17. *Decameron* 5.4, 5.6, 5.7. In 4.4, the lovers are killed before we can see what they would have done. In 2.6, when the girl's father proposes marriage, Giannotto replies that he always wished it and would have asked for it long ago if he thought it would have been granted.

18. I do not include 2.7 in my computations: two of Alatiel's eleven men marry her, namely Osbech and the King of Garbo; the Duke of Athens cannot marry her because he has a wife; Antioco cannot marry her because she is already married to Osbech; the two Genoese cannot very well marry her, since they possess her at the same time; Marato and Constantine simply enjoy her without further ado; Pericone desires to marry her if she is not married, or have her as mistress if she is (she is in fact not married, but he never gets around to marrying her); the Prince of the Morea loves her so much that he treats her as a wife rather than as a mistress; and the merchant who poses as her husband eventually succumbs to the temptation of having intercourse with her.

Obviously not all of the lovers who marry have the same motivation. Some of them seem to have no religious or moral objections to fornication or adultery.[19] Sometimes such objections exist on one side only.[20] But in one case the lovers would rather die than enter into an affair without marriage; and in another, the girl is prepared to reject her beloved if he is not willing to marry her.[21] Some of these differences in motivation and character are due to the demands of the plot, but others are not. In the story of Andreuola and Gabriotto, for instance, the lovers meet many times together, to the great delight of them both. Perhaps we are to assume that they have sexual intercourse before they marry each other, or perhaps not. Their marriage is a secret matter between themselves alone, seemingly because Gabriotto is of a lower estate than she. Their reason for marrying is to ensure that nothing but death can end their delightful love.[22] However, the story immediately preceding ("The Pot of Basil") and the one immediately following ("The Leaf of Sage") describe lovers in almost identical circumstances and with similarly tragic endings, but in neither case is marriage mentioned.

In conclusion, we can say that there is an almost overwhelming statistical preference for marriage among the serious lovers of the *Decameron;* but the preference is an entirely personal and circumstantial matter and is in no way subject to reliable prediction. The "canon of presumption" in Boccaccio's case must cede to one of vague probability.

19. See the tales mentioned in nn. 15 and 17 above. In 2.10.37–38 the lady justifies her adultery: if living with her lover, Paganino, is a mortal sin, so is living with her impotent old husband Ricciardo. She feels that she is Paganino's wife, whereas with Ricciardo she seemed to be his whore. During Ricciardo's lifetime Paganino treats her honorably as his wife (16); and when Ricciardo dies, Paganino, knowing her love for him, marries her: "conoscendo l'amore che la donna gli portava, per sua legittima moglie la sposò" (43).

20. See above, n. 10. The tragic events of 4.8 offer a particularly good example.

21. *Decameron* 2.8 (Giannetta and Giachetto) and 2.3 respectively.

22. *Decameron* 4.6.9: "In un bel giardino del padre di lei e più volte a diletto dell'una parte e della altra fu menato; e acciò che niuna cagione mai, se non morte, potesse questo lor dilettevole amor separare, marito e moglie segretamente divennero."

The *Filostrato*

When we examine the *Filostrato*, therefore, we must do so with
an open mind, and not presuppose that Boccaccio or his characters are committed beforehand to any doctrine for or against
marriage. This much can be said, however: the nature of the plot
is such that even though Troiolo and Criseida are marriageable,
they cannot get married, at least publicly, because their marriage
would interfere with the course of the foregone conclusion;
Criseida would not be delivered to the Greek camp if she were
known to be Troiolo's wife. The same reason forbids her to have
any other husband.[23] Boccaccio therefore, without further ado,
has his characters engage in an illicit affair, a matter of "simple
fornication."

All three of the principal characters clearly realize that the love
affair will be dishonorable: Troiolo enunciates the principle that
love is above the law; it leads even to incest (2.19–20)–though,
as we saw, it did not go to such extremes even in the *Decameron*.
Pandaro demonstrates to Criseida that adultery, at least, and even
cuckoldry would be acceptable to him, when he says that he
would give Troiolo his own wife if he had one (2.52).

Pandaro admits that the sort of love that he and Troiolo have
in mind would not be proper for a worthy lady:

> Né creder, Troiol, ch'io no veggia bene
> Non convenirsi a donna valorosa
> Sì fatti amori. [2.25]

But he believes that all women experience amorous passions of
this sort and are held back only by a fear of shame. Criseida, being
a widow, desires; if she denies it, she is not to be believed (2.27).[24]

---

23. This latter point was made by N. E. Griffin in his introduction to *The
Filostrato of Giovanni Boccaccio* (Philadelphia 1929) 84–87; but he was concerned with the rules given in Andrew's *Ars honeste amandi*, which, he
believed, demanded an adulterous affair.

24. When he says, "La mia cugina è vedova e disia," he no doubt means
that because she is a widow she desires sexual pleasure more strongly than
would a virgin. Such at least is Fiammetta's doctrine in *Filocolo* 4.54.8: "Le
pulcelle a tale effetto per diletto non corrono le prime volte, però che egli è
loro più noia che piacere; avvegna che a quella cosa che diletta, quante più
fiate si vede o ode o sente, più piace, e più è sollicito ciascuno a seguirla."

Troiolo fears that she will keep up her pretence of virtue when Pandaro informs her of his love:

> E se nel cor l'avesse, per mostrarti
> D'essere onesta, non vorrà 'scoltarti.   [2.30]

His apprehension is partially realized. Criseida knows immediately that there is to be no question of marriage, but rather that her yet unnamed admirer wishes to enjoy the pleasures proper only to a husband without becoming her husband:

> Chi dee aver di me piacer intero
> Se già non divenisse mio marito?   [2.45]

She puts Pandaro off by saying that ever since her husband died she has removed herself from love: she mourns him and ever shall (2.49).

Criseida's sentiments on this point are sincere; she loved her husband till he died and still cherishes the love she bore him. This must be kept in mind during the soliloquy that follows. In spite of her temporary misogamy, she has no fundamental philosophical objection to married love.

When she is alone, Criseida proceeds to talk herself into the affair: she is young, beautiful, childless; though "honesty" forbids such love, she will be prudent and hide it; to do as others do is no sin; later will be too late; besides, it would be delightful (2.69–72). Then she adds, "Now is no time for a husband" ("Ed ora non è tempo da marito," 2.73). That is, she might as well accept Troiolo as a lover since she has no plans or inclination to be married to someone else. She is, in fact, still officially mourning her husband, since she wears black.[25]

But even if marriage were proper for her at this time, she continues, she finds a number of reasons for rejecting it. First of all, to keep one's freedom is always wiser than to lose it:

> E se pur fosse, la sua libertate
> Servare è troppo più savio partito.

Second, the love to be found in a nonmarital alliance always brings intense pleasure:

25. Cf. above, Chap. 1, n. 19.

> L'amor che vien de si fatta amistate
> E sempre tra gli amici assai gradito.

Third, husbands always get tired of their wives, no matter how beautiful they are, and soon seek new pleasures:

> Ma, sia quanto vuol grande la biltate
> Che a' mariti tosto non rincresca,
> Vaghi d'avere ogni di cosa fresca.   [2.73]

Finally, stolen water is better than free wine, and the stealth and furtiveness of unmarried love are sweeter than a husband's embraces:

> L'acqua furtiva assai più dolce cosa
> È che il vin con abbondanza avuto;
> Così d'amor la gioia che sia nascosa
> Trapassa assai del sempre mai tenuto
> Marito in braccio.   [2.74]

On leaving her to her own thoughts, Pandaro had told her to consider the affair as a religious duty: "Fatti con Dio e fa il tuo dovere" (2.67). Now, accordingly, she concludes this part of her meditations by affirming her belief that God has sent this love and that it should be enjoyed:

> Adunque vigorosa
> Ricevi il dolce amore, il qual venuto
> T'è fermamente mandandolo Iddio,
> E soddisfa al suo caldo disio.   [2.74]

It is typical of Boccaccio's application of the "principle of abeyance" that even though an act is freely admitted to be dishonorable in the eyes of men, it is not portrayed as an offense against God (Criseida's facile rationalization, "Come gli altri far non è peccato," hardly counts).[26]

---

26. Even when Boccaccio says in the *Filocolo* that God prevented Bianci-fiore from becoming Florio's mistress, he characterizes the avoided fault not as a sin but as a dishonor to her noble line (see n. 3 above). Sometimes, of course, his characters do speak in terms of theological sin; cf. above, n. 19. Fiammetta says that to desire or take another man's wife "è commettere contra le divine leggi, e eziandio contra le naturali e positive; alle quali offendere è un commuovere sopra di sé la divina ira, e per consequente grave giudicio" (*Filocolo* 4.52.1–2).

Then, however, Criseida has second thoughts about her decision: unmarried love has its drawbacks too. It is full of grief and brings on jealousy worse than shameful death. Besides, Troiolo is of higher rank than she and will desert her; or if their love is long-lasting, it will become known and ruin her reputation. We leave her in a state of indecision; she spends a long time, we are told, wavering back and forth, not knowing whether to accept or reject the love that has been offered to her (2.75–78).

In summary, let me repeat that Boccaccio was not in the habit of drawing on a tradition that held love and marriage to be incompatible. If he was influenced by Andrew the Chaplain in setting up his "questions of love" in the *Filocolo* and *Filostrato*, he does not seem to have been influenced by Andrew's antimatrimonial doctrine, even in Criseida's monologue. Her remark on the attractions of furtiveness is perhaps an exception, but it could just as easily have been inspired by Ovid's "Utque viro furtiva venus, sic grata puellae."[27] It could even have been prompted by Boccaccio's study of canon law. John Andreae of Bologna (d. 1348), the great lay commentator on the *Decretals of Gregory IX*, said: "Saepe etenim clandestine contrahuntur, testante Solomone, Prover. 9: 'Aquae furtivae dulciores sunt, et panis absconditus suavior.'" That is, "People often marry clandestinely, for, as Solomon says in Proverbs 9, 'Stolen waters are sweeter, and hidden bread is more pleasant.'"[28]

Andreae's dictum also shows that secrecy is not always contrasted with marriage. Similarly, openly avowed love need not be matrimonial. The love that Ovid celebrates in the *Ars amatoria*

27. Ovid, *Ars amatoria* 1.275 ("And as stolen love is pleasant to a man, so is it also to a woman"); cf. 1.33. Ovid gives reasons for preferring specifically adulterous love in *Amores* 2.19: the more carefully Corinna's husband guards her, the more his own desire is increased; 3.4: the *amor mariti* makes the wife more desirable to another—she becomes an *adultera cara*.

28. Iohannes Andreae on X 4.3: *De clandestina desponsatione, In primumsextum Decretalium librum novella commentaria* (Venice 1581) 4.21v, citing Prov. 9.17. Andreae began his commentary around 1311 and completed it by 1338, though portions of it were made available during the intervening years. See Stephen Kuttner, "Joannes Andreae and His *Novella* on the *Decretals of Gregory IX*," *The Jurist* 24 (1964) 393–408; Kuttner's article is a reprint with additional notes of the introduction to the Turin 1963 reprint of the *Novella*.

and *Amores*, whether secret or open, is always illicit. At the beginning of the *Filostrato*, Criseida does, it is true, contrast secret love with married love and thereby talks herself into an illicit affair with Troiolo. Later on, however, when she returns to the argument for secrecy in opposing Triolo's suggestion of flight (4.152–153), there is no indication that she thinks of the flight as resulting in marriage. As Robert apRoberts says, marriage *or any other state* which destroys the condition of secrecy, stealth, and restricted access does not possess the peculiar and distinctive quality of love as it is envisaged in the *Filostrato*.[29] Or, at any rate, this is how Criseida regards the matter.

The Morality of Chaucer's Lovers

Like Boccaccio, Chaucer enjoyed describing the woes of cuckolded husbands and the exploits of their wives in the fabliaux of *The Canterbury Tales*. But his preference for marriage in his serious romances was not just general, as with Boccaccio, but absolute. He strove to portray his lovers as sympathetically as possible and therefore normally made them as moral as possible. In *The Legend of Good Women*, for example, he passes over the crimes of a Medea and a Philomela in silence, and omits the *Aeneid*'s account of Dido's insane fury.

Chaucer does not omit Dido's suicide, but he attaches no blame to it, following a long tradition of exempting lovers' self-slaughter (actual or attemped) from the normal rules of morality; in fact, we could almost elevate the tradition into a Theory of Courtly Suicide. Writers in this tradition do not simply accept pagan views of suicide in pagan settings, as Shakespeare does in *Julius Caesar* and *Antony and Cleopatra* (while in the Christian settings of *Hamlet* and *Othello* he makes it clear that the Almighty has set a canon against self-slaughter). For even in Christian love stories like *Romeo and Juliet*, suicidal characters are often treated with approval from a divine as well as a human point of view, with no condemnation of their actions nor allusion to the doctrine that self-slayers are destined for hell. Thus Boccaccio frequently

29. Robert P. apRoberts, "Love in the *Filostrato*," *Chaucer Review* 7 (1972–1973) 1–26, esp. 7.

describes attempts or deeds of suicide by lovers, even completely moral lovers like Florio (see *Filocolo* 2.21), without alluding to Christian doctrine; though he as well as Chaucer can make use of this doctrine in other contexts, when it does not jeopardize the sympathetic standing of the central lovers of the story.[30]

Chaucer is especially careful in matters of sexual morality. He never portrays his romantic lovers as knowingly committing fornication or adultery. As D. S. Brewer puts it, "Chaucer nowhere celebrates illicit love"; there is always, in his serious love stories, "an explicit connection between love and marriage."[31] We shall see this assertion confirmed in detail later.

We saw that in the case of Boccaccio, the presumptive favor enjoyed by marriage could give rise to no more than probable conclusions; but in the case of Chaucer we should be able to arrive at practically certain knowledge, especially since he was not acquainted with the *Ars honeste amandi*, the only work in which we have found a principle of the complete incompatibility of love and marriage. Thus, for example, when a question is raised of the nature of the relationship between the Man in Black and the Lady White in *The Book of the Duchess*, we would have

---

30. Thus in *Decameron* 4.6.24, Andreuola is dissuaded from killing herself after her clandestine husband has died; she would thereby go to hell, while her husband is no doubt in heaven: "Figliuola mia, non dir di volerti uccidere, per ciò che, se tu l'ai qui perduto, uccidendoti anche nell'altro mondo il perderesti, per ciò che tu n'andresti in inferno, là dove io son certa che la sua anima non è andata, per ciò che buon giovane fu." In 5.8.21, Nastagio has a vision of a lover who killed himself and went to hell: "Come disperato m'uccisi, e sono alle pene etternali dannato."

In his dream in *The Book of the Duchess*, Chaucer tells the knight that if "ye for sorwe mordred yourselve, / Ye sholde de dampned in this cas" with as much justice as Medea was for killing her children, and Phyllis and Dido for killing themselves. Of Dido: "Which a fool she was!" (lines 724–734). In contrast, suicide in the *Legend* is treated sympathetically, and even St. Augustine is called upon to approve of Lucretia:

The grete Austyn hath gret compassioun
Of this Lucresse, that starf at Rome toun. [1690–1691]

Gower, in the *Confessio amantis*, considers suicide a fault of rashness, not of despair, and gives as an example the story of Pyramus and Thisbe (3.1323ff.).

31. D. S. Brewer, "Love and Marriage in Chaucer's Poetry," *Modern Language Review* 49 (1954) 461–464.

to conclude to its moral probity even if we did not have an as-
surance of it in these lines:

> My lady yaf me al hooly
> The noble yifte of hir mercy,
> Savynge hir worship, by al weyes,
> Dredles, I mene noon other weyes.   [1269–1272]

The same benefit of the doubt must be given to *Troilus and
Criseyde,* which even Brewer sees as constituting something of an
exception to Chaucer's general practice; but it is an exception dictated by the exigencies of the plot. For Chaucer, as for Boccaccio,
the working out of the story forbade Troilus to claim Criseyde as
his wife. Boccaccio solved the problem by making their love illicit.
Brewer believes that Chaucer dealt with it in much the way that
we have seen Chrétien handle the story of *Lancelot* (I am not
saying, of course, that Chaucer knew the *Lancelot*); that is to
say, he deliberately obscured the fact of the love's illicitness by
treating it as licit.

I shall maintain later that, far from holding the normal canons
of morality in abeyance from their love, Chaucer actually made
it licit by maneuvering the lovers into a clandestine marriage.
Brewer was no doubt unaware that such a union was recognized as
valid by the medieval Church; furthermore, he believed that
Chaucer was relying on the alleged courtly-love prohibition
against marriage. But in spite of these blind spots, his analysis
remains basically correct. That is, he is right in thinking that
Chaucer set himself the task of "castigating" the unchaste love
depicted in his Italian source.

The transformation presented Chaucer with a number of problems. For example, Boccaccio's lovers had to keep their love secret
because it was dishonorable; in Chaucer's version, the love is
honorable but it must be kept secret lest people think it dishonorable.[32] It is not an entirely irrational situation; Boccaccio himself
would create a similar set of circumstances later, in the *Decameron.*[33] But Chaucer's treatment sometimes results in the im-

32. For Chaucer's express justification of the need for secrecy, see below,
Chap. 9.
33. *Decameron* 4.6.23: Andreuola and Gabriotto marry clandestinely, and

pression that Troilus, or Criseyde or Pandarus, shares the opinion
that there would be something dishonorable about their love if it
were made known. For instance, when Pandarus says to Troilus,

> Wel thow woost, the name as yet of here
> Among the peeple, as who seyth, halwed is;
> For that man is unbore, I dar wel swere,
> That evere wiste that she dide amys, [3.267–270]

the implication seems to be that now she is doing something amiss;
and that indeed is precisely the meaning of the lines Chaucer is
translating from Boccaccio:

> Tu sai ch' egli è la fama di costei
> Santa nel vulgo, né si disse mai
> Da nullo altro che tutto ben di lei. [3.8]

The false impression in this case, I believe, is due to Chaucer's
imperfect modification of his source.

I realize that this conclusion might seem an easy way out to
most critics, who would generally be reluctant to admit a lack of
full authorial control in Chaucer's masterpiece. One could, of
course, appeal to his well-established gifts of irony and humor and
find a positive motive in his failure to adapt Boccaccio at this
point. Pandarus's suggestiveness here would be in keeping with
the vague air of prurience that we notice in him elsewhere as he
busies himself about his niece's affair, and it would confirm the
obvious truth that Pandarus's canons of morality are not as rigorous as those of Troilus. I admit the possibility of such a reading
but still find it rather more likely that Chaucer has simply slipped.
If we are willing to admit such an explanation here and elsewhere,
his negligence might strike us as downright carelessness at times;
but we must remember that medieval storytellers were not so
concerned about consistency as we tend to be nowadays.[34]

To take another example, the almost contradictory qualities that
appear in Criseyde have been taken as evidence of great subtlety

after Gabriotto's death Andreuola determines to act in such a way as to
preserve her honor and keep their secret love hidden: "Vorre' io che noi
prendessimo modo convenevole a servare il mio onore e il segreto amor tra
noi stato." Her fault, as she saw it, consisted in taking a husband without
her father's knowledge: "Umilmente perdono vi domando del fallo mio,
cioè d'avere senza vostra saputa chi più me piacque marito preso" (38).

34. See the section "Exemplary Hits and Misses," above, Chap. 1.

on Chaucer's part, whereas they may be, often enough, simply a result of his failure now and then to refine the words and actions given her by Boccaccio. Similarly, relics of Troiolo's immoral intentions could be cited as proof that Chaucer disapproved of Troilus's love—as when he offers one of his sisters to Pandarus as a reward, or even Helen, his brother's wife, or "any of the frape" (3.409–413). But instead of seeing it as a manifestation of his moral turpitude, we should regard it, if not as a rare attempt to give Troilus a sense of humor[35] or as an example of Troilus's almost culpable naïveté, simply as a "jaunty passage" resulting from "a careless adjustment of old and new."[36] As for the ruses that Troilus resorts to in order to win Criseyde, which have confirmed his viciousness in the minds of some readers,[37] they should rather be overlooked, along with his suicidal tendencies, as part of the approved behavior of medieval lovers.[38]

Criseyde's Stand on Marriage

With these considerations in mind, let us see how Chaucer dealt specifically with the passage in the *Filostrato* in which Criseida gave her objections against marriage. As in the *Filostrato*, so in the *Troilus*, there is no evidence of a general doctrine of the incompatibility of love and marriage. Rather the contrary. When Pandarus speaks of those who have loved "paramours," he says:

> Day by day thow maist thiselven se
> That from his love or ellis from his wif
> A man mot twinnen of necessite,
> Ye, though he love hire as his owene lif.[39]   [5.337–340]

35. So Neil D. Isaacs, "Further Testimony in the Matter of *Troilus*," *Studies in the Literary Imagination* 4.2 (Oct. 1971) 11–27, esp. 16. Another attractive explanation is that of Donald R. Howard. *The Three Temptations: Medieval Man in Search of the World* (Princeton 1966) 137 n. 86: "It is an avowal of good intentions and loyalty, not of depravity—an exaggerated protestation of friendship which . . . carries the implication that the friend would forbear to ask so much."

36. Elizabeth Salter, "*Troilus and Criseyde*: A Reconsideration," in Lawlor 99–100.

37. For example, D. W. Robertson, Jr., "The Concept of Courtly Love as an Impediment to the Understanding of Medieval Texts," in Newman 14.

38. I discuss this point further below, Chap. 5, in the section "Trouthe and the Matrimonial Bond."

39. The importance of this passage was pointed out by John Lawlor,

When Criseyde tells Diomede much later that her heart belonged entirely to her dead husband (5.974–978), she is not being completely sincere, since she is denying her relationship with Troilus, but she is not expressing an outlandish sentiment, and Diomede does not deny the possibility of such marital love.

Boccaccio's Criseida, we recall, spoke against the idea of her marrying someone else, as an excuse to have an affair with Troilus out of wedlock. Chaucer's Criseyde, on the contrary, speaks against marriage (to Troilus or anyone else) as a reason for not accepting Troilus's love, no matter how faithful he professes to be. That this must be her meaning is certain if we do not wish to accuse Chaucer once again of negligent adaptation; but this reading is not altogether clear at first sight, and her monologue therefore demands a close analysis.

In the *Filostrato*, Criseida first argued in favor of taking Troilus as a lover, then against it; and though Boccaccio says that she continued to waver back and forth, he gives no further arguments for either decision. Chaucer on the other hand prefaces his account of her soliloquy by saying that "now was hire herte warm, now was it cold," and he gives more than one wave of her fluctuation. Like her Italian counterpart, Criseyde starts out warm: even though she refrained from loving him, she tells herself, it would be a good thing for both of them simply to keep up their acquaintance; it certainly would not do to offend him, for that would put her in danger. Drunkenness is wrong, but not moderate drinking, and the same is true of love; since Troilus has honorable intentions ("he meneth in good wyse"), there is nothing wrong in his feelings for her. He is a upright man—he would not boast of her, nor would she give him the opportunity. What if people perceive that he loves her? No harm in that; men often love

---

"The Pattern of Consolation in *The Book of the Duchess*," *Speculum* 31 (1956) 628–629, whose criticism of the alleged courtly-love ban against marriage unfortunately stopped short of Continental literature. This same passage, of course, refutes the thesis of Ernst Käsmann, " 'I Wolde Excuse Hire Yit for Routhe': Chaucers Einstellung zu Criseyde," *Chaucer und seine Zeit*, Symposium for Walter F. Schirmer, ed. Arno Esch (Tübingen 1968) 97–122, esp. 115–119, that "love paramours" is always illicit. "Paramours" is also used for virtuous love by the *Purity*-poet and Lydgate (below, Chap. 11 n. 23).

women without their consent. As long as a lady could keep her
honor, Troilus would be the worthiest man in all Troy to be her
love; and he loves Criseyde. He is hurt, and she can heal him. It
is no wonder that he loves her, of course, for she is admittedly
one of the loveliest women in all the city (2.698–749).

Then comes the crucial stanza:

> I am myn owene womman, wel at ese,
> I thank it God, as after myn estat,
> Right yong, and stonde unteyd in lusty leese,
> Withouten jalousie or swich debat.
> Shal noon housbonde seyn to me, "Chek mat!"
> For either they ben ful of jalousie,
> Or maisterfull, or loven novelrie.   [750–756]

In the first four lines she continues giving reasons for warming to
Troilus: She is her own mistress, in comfortable circumstances,
and unfettered—like a mare that is not kept tied but allowed to
roam at its leisure in a pleasant pasture—for there is no one to be
jealous of her. Then she suddenly turns cold at the idea of tying
herself down to anyone (including Troilus). She is free and wants
to keep it that way. No husband is going to checkmate her. For
husbands are either always jealous, or domineering, or unfaithful
woman-chasers.

The first line of the next stanza shows not only that her mental
climate is now unsettled ("What shal I doon?"), but also that the
burden of her thoughts immediately preceding has been *against*
loving Troilus, not for it: "To what fyn lyve I thus?" That is,
what is the purpose of her living a free and unfettered life? In
the next line, "Shal I nat love, in cas if that me lest?" she has
warmed again to her subject, and gives more reasons for accepting
Troilus. She is no nun ("I am naught religious"); that is, if she
had entered a religious order and taken a vow of chastity, such
love would be wrong; but since she did not, she would be perfectly justified in going ahead with it, as long as she kept it honorable both in deed and in the public estimation:

> And though that I myn herte sette at reste
> Upon this knyght, that is the worthieste,
> And kepe alwey myn honour and my name,
> By alle right it may do me no shame.   [760–763]

But then a "cloudy thought" comes upon her horizon and turns her cold again: since she has no ties, why enslave herself to love—

> Allas, syn I am free,
> Sholde I now love, and put in jupartie
> My sikernesse, and thrallen libertee?   [771–773]

It turns out that this objection is similar to the one she had earlier against marrying: the joys of love are full of fears, and lead to constraint and pain and lamentation. When love's sorrows come, the wretched women can do nothing but weep; they are slandered, and the men are always unfaithful (776–805).

Then her mind clears and warm weather returns, as she says, "He which that nothing undertaketh, / Nothyng n'acheveth." But immediately another thought makes her tremble, and thus she continues to waver, "now hoot, now cold" (806–811).

We see, then, that just as Pandarus could speak of a man's "love paramours" for his beloved or his wife, so too Criseyde could suspect all men of being untrue to their women, whether married to them or not. Husbands "loven novelrie" (756) and

> men ben so untrewe
> That right anon as cessed is hire lest,
> So cesseth love, and forth to love a newe.   [786–788]

As for Criseyde's two other objections to husbands, namely that "they ben ful of jalousie, / Or maisterfull," she deals with Troilus's supposed jealousy at greath length before she gives herself up to him completely (3.799–1054). On the question of his mastery over her, she had already made herself clear:

> "But natheles, this warne I yow," quod she,
> "A kynges sone although ye be, ywys,
> Ye shall namore han sovereignete
> Of me in love, than right in that cas is;
> N'y nyl forbere, if that ye don amys,
> To wratthe yow; and whil that ye me serve,
> Chericen yow right after ye disserve."   [3.169–175]

This is almost the same undertaking that Arveragus makes to Dorigen before he marries her:

> Of his free wyl he swoor hire as a knyght
> That nevere in al his lyf he, day ne nyght,

> Ne sholde upon hym take no maistrie
> Agayn hir wyl, ne kithe hire jalousie,
> Bot hire obeye, and folwe hir wyl in al,
> As any lovere to his lady shal,
> Save that the name of soveraynetee,
> That wolde he have for shame of his degree.
> [*Franklin's Tale* 745–752]

For her part, Dorigen is determined "to take hym for hir hous-bonde and hir lord, / Of swich lordshipe as men han over hir wyves" (742–743). But Arveragus assumes no more sovereignty "than right in that cas is," to use Criseyde's qualification.

That true love should lead to mutuality in marriage was not a new doctrine, something that Chaucer would have discovered for himself only when writing *The Canterbury Tales*. It was a commonly held view—we have seen Jean de Meun's use of it in the *Roman de la Rose;* and it is espoused with great vigor by Thomas Usk in his *Testament of Love*, a work written a year or so after the *Troilus*, which draws upon the *Troilus* and Chaucer's translation of Boethius. Love, the female personification modeled on Boethius's Philosophy, says that when her servants marry in her presence, "two that wern firste in a litel maner discordaunt, hygher that oon and lower that other, ben mad evenliche in gree to stonde."[40]

We may conclude that Criseyde's objections to loving Troilus are only temporary and that when she overcomes her arguments against accepting him as her lover she also disposes of her reasons against having him as her husband.

---

40. Thomas Usk, *The Testament of Love* 1.9, ed. W. W. Skeat, *Chaucerian and Other Pieces*, supplement to *The Complete Works of Geoffrey Chaucer* (Oxford 1897) 40–41.

PART II

The Age of Ovid

What seyth also the epistel of Ovyde
Of trewe wyves and of here labour?
>   —Chaucer, *The Legend of Good Women* G 305–306

Chapter 3

Ovid's Endorsement
of Married Love

The Serious Lovers of Antiquity

Another thesis in Lewis's *Allegory of Love* which should be
marked for a fall concerns the treatment of love by classical authors. Lewis maintains that "in ancient literature love seldom rises
above the levels of merry sensuality or domestic comfort, except
to be treated as a tragic madness" (4). Dido is one of his examples of the last-named category, of lovers who go mad and are
plunged into crime and disgrace. We have already spoken of
Chaucer's more romantic treatment of Dido. This view of her is
not his own invention, however, but rather Ovid's, in the epistle
he gives her in the *Heroides:*

> But who wol al this letter have in mynde,
> Rede Ovyde, and in hym he shal it fynde.
> [*Legend of Good Women* 1366–1367]

Even in *The House of Fame*, where Chaucer is explicitly sum-
marizing "Virgile in *Eneydos*," Dido's character is based more on
"the Epistle of Ovyde, / What that she wrot or that she dyde"
(378–380). Lewis, however, thinks of Ovid as providing only
examples of the first category of classical love, that of "merry
sensuality." For his second category, Lewis may be right in reading Homer as simply acknowledging "the comfort and utility of
a good wife" and Odysseus's love for Penelope as the same sort
of attachment that he has to "the rest of his home and possessions." But Chaucer did not know Homer; he modeled his portrait
of Penelope instead on Ovid's characterization of her in the *Heroides*, where she loves with a greater fidelity and tenderness than

many a heroine of medieval romance. For example, Boccaccio's Madonna Adalieta, when her crusader husband Torello is given up for dead, finally succumbs to the entreaties and threats of her relatives and agrees to remarry.[1] Ovid's Penelope, on the contrary, resists her father's insistent demands that she take another husband: "Let him chide on—yours I am, yours must I be called. Penelope, the wife of Ulysses, ever shall I be." And eventually it is her father who relents, overcome by her faithfulness and her virtuous entreaties.[2]

Lewis, of course, has in mind only the domestic Roman comedy of Ovid's *Ars amatoria*, *Remedia amoris*, and *Amores*, and not his serious treatment of the lovers of Greek legend in the *Heroides* and *Metamorphoses*. He rightly says that Ovid presents rules of how to win and keep one's beloved in the *Ars amatoria* with only mock seriousness. He is also right when he says that in the Middle Ages "the very same conduct which Ovid ironically recommends could be recommended seriously by the courtly tradition" (7). For instance, if, as the editors of Boccaccio's *Filocolo* assume, the *Ars amatoria* is "il santo libro d'Ovidio" studied by Florio and Biancifiore to learn how to enkindle the holy fires of Venus (1.45.6), the two young students clearly take its instructions with the utmost seriousness. But the examples they give of love affairs are invariably taken from Ovid's serious treatments of love; they refer, for instance, to Ariadne, Theseus, and Phaedra, and to Phyllis and Demophoon (2.17.7, 11). Ovid himself, in fact, alludes

---

1. *Decameron* 10.9.96. It is not quite fair to judge her love as less than Penelope's, of course, since she had what was taken to be certain knowledge of her husband's death; furthermore, her remarriage was demanded by the story line.
2. Ovid, *Heroides* 1.81–86, ed. and tr. Grant Showerman, Loeb Classical Library (London 1914, repr. 1963):

> Me pater Icarius viduo discedere lecto
> > Cogit et immensas increpat usque moras.
> Increpet usque licet—tua sum, tua dicar oportet.
> > Penelope coniunx semper Ulixis ero.
> Ille tamen pietate mea precibusque pudicis
> > Frangitur, et vires temperat ipse suas.

The most recent edition of the *Heroides* is that of Heinrich Dörrie (Berlin 1971). For a good discussion of the love themes, see W. S. Anderson, "The *Heroides*," in *Ovid*, ed. J. W. Binns (London 1973) 49–83.

to the same or similar lovers in his light amatory verse,[3] which
simply shows that at least some of his principles by their very nature can be applied to weightier contexts as well.

But Lewis is dead wrong, I believe, when he says or implies that
the romancers of the Middle Ages in general failed to appreciate
the humor and irony of Ovid's Roman comedies. When Chaucer,
for instance, says of the Wife of Bath:

> Of remedies of love she knew per chaunce,
> For she koude of that art the olde daunce,
> [*General Prologue* 475–476]

who can doubt that he has mastered all the nuances of Ovid's old
dance himself and that he is making a new joke by equating the
remedies against love with the rules for obtaining love?[4] Boccaccio, too, had obviously been a diligent and accurate student of the
classical *artifex amoris*. As for twelfth-century French writers,
Lewis himself says of the author of the *Concilium in Monte Ro-
marici*: "The French poet has taken over this conception [of a
mock religion in Ovid's *Art of Love*] with a full understanding of
its flippancy, and proceeded to elaborate the joke in terms of the
only religion he knows—medieval Christianity" (20). It was
Lewis's great mistake that he did not see that Andrew the Chaplain prepared his *Ars honeste amandi* in precisely the same spirit.

It is, therefore, very much an understatement that "Chaucer
knew Ovid and may well have seen the similarity between Ovidian and courtly *amor* better than he saw the difference."[5] What, in

3. E.g., *Ars amatoria* 1.527–564 (Ariadne and Theseus, and Bacchus) and
2.353–372 (Phyllis and Demophoon, Penelope and Ulysses, Laodamia and
Protesilaus, Helen and Paris).
4. For the true import of the remedies of love, see above, Chap. 1 n. 13.
Ovid specifies travel as a remedy against love (*Remedia* 214ff.); the Wife
of Bath goes on pilgrimage to remedy (that is, satisfy) her need for love.
Chaucer uses the term in its original sense in *The Book of the Duchess*
567–568 ("May noght make my sorwes slyde, / Noght al the remedyes of
Ovyde"), as pointed out by Richard L. Hoffman, "The Wife of Bath as a
Student of Ovid," *Notes and Queries* 2.11 (1964) 287–288.
5. Donald R. Howard, *The Three Temptations* (Princeton 1966) 115. This
admission effectively negates Howard's thesis that Chaucer deliberately
anachronized the "courtly love of the French school" by placing it in
ancient Troy.

fact, is the difference between medieval and Ovidian love, once we clear away the obfuscations of the theory of courtly love? Or, for a moment, to consider Lewis's Four Marks of Courtly Love, do we not find, in the *Heroides*, Humility, Courtesy, Adultery, and the Religion of Love"? Paris, himself married, pays his suit to Helen, another man's wife, and is answered in much the same way as Andrew the Chaplain's *nobilis* in the fifth dialogue.[6] Hercules, while married to Deianira, courts Queen Omphale, like Lancelot courting Queen Guinevere, and humbles himself before her as her slave, performing at her whim deeds that would have shamed a warrior in ordinary circumstances.[7] Who could be more courteous —that is, noble—than Prince Protesilaus, or the Trojan warriors that his doting wife Laodamia speaks of: each one fights cautiously, bearing with him his mistress's recent commands?[8] Protesilaus is Laodamia's god; Hero is Leander's goddess as well as mistress; Venus has given Helen to Paris.[9] It may not be possible to find the perfect courtly lover in Ovid; but, after all, even in the Middle Ages only Lancelot really fills the bill.

All such examples would be a mere evasion of the real question of what constitutes the novelty of medieval love, were they not useful in demonstrating that the answer to the question is not as

6. *Heroides* 5, 16, and 17.
7. *Heroides* 9.53–118. This, of course, is only Deianira's limited view of Hercules's true predicament. See G. Karl Galinsky, *The Herakles Theme* (Oxford 1972). Ovid's ninth epistle is cited as a precedent for the medieval "service of love" by Tom Peete Cross and William A. Nitze, *Lancelot and Guinevere: A Study on the Origins of Courtly Love* (Chicago 1930) 91. Joseph Coppin, *Amour et mariage dans la littérature française du nord au moyen âge* (Paris 1961) 7, cites a still more familiar and more ancient precedent for such love-service, namely, Genesis 29.20: "So Jacob served seven years for Rachel, and they seemed but a few days, because of the greatness of his love." Coppin remarks, "Si l'amour a été 'inventé,' l'invention rémonte loin." For a partial survey of the rich tradition of romantic love in Greek and Roman authors before Ovid's time, see Elizabeth Hazelton Haight, *Romance in the Latin Elegiac Poets* (New York 1932) 3–124.
8. *Heroides* 13.145–156.
9. *Heroides* 13.159; 18.66, 95; 16.35. For lists of lovers' characteristics that occur both in the light and serious amatory verse of Ovid, see Foster E. Guyer, "The Influence of Ovid on Chrestien de Troyes," *Romanic Review* 12 (1921) 97–134, 216–247, esp. 120–122, and Thomas A. Kirby, *Chaucer's Troilus: A Study in Courtly Love*, Louisiana State University Studies 39 (Baton Rouge 1940) 8–14.

easy as has often been thought. Medieval romance is basically Ovidian; it is Ovid medievalized. What then are the medieval elements? Naturally, the doctrines and customs of paganism's "tremendous rival" and successor are everywhere reflected, as are new secular institutions like knighthood and feudalism. And, of course, different stories have different circumstances, and even the same story changes with each retelling. But apart from this, perhaps some general distinctions could be hazarded immediately. Women, for example, are more often romantic than men in Ovid, whereas in medieval tales there are more languishing males and more cruel and demanding mistresses. The latter characters, however, could easily have been borrowed from Ovid's light verse. As I have indicated already, we can agree that later authors treated his mock-serious themes seriously without concluding that they misunderstood him. Another possible generalization (which may admit of the same explanation) is that it was easier to die of lovesickness in the Middle Ages than in Ovid's time.

But instead of trying to multiply such statistical statements of divergence, let us examine Ovid's serious love poetry closely to see precisely what kind of romantic experiences poets like Chaucer and Gower could have drawn upon.

The Solitary *Heroides*

When we look at the first fifteen epistles of the *Heroides*, we can immediately perceive an important reason for the romantic imbalance in favor of women noted above. The only work that Ovid dedicated almost exclusively to the graver sentiments of love was designed to consist solely or largely of epistles from Women in Love. And since they are Women in Love in Distress, a high percentage of the men to whom the letters are sent are bound to be unworthy of their love. But his later series of three double epistles, in which the man writes first and the woman replies, not only partially redresses the balance but also shows that there was a precedent in his own practice for the creation of romantic heroes.

Of the solitary heroines, only Penelope is destined to be reunited with her lover. She is happily married; but perhaps that is only because, unlike Deianira, she does not have certain information to confirm her fear that her husband is "captive to a stranger love."[10] The stories as a whole demonstrate the truth and compatibility, in the pagan world, of two principles which came to be impossible of reconciliation in Christian times: (1) Lovers invariably marry;[11] (2) Marriage is no excuse for not loving. The reason, of course, for their compatibility in pre-Christian times is that one could easily get a divorce or simply abandon one's previous spouse and remarry. Jason, for instance, left his first wife Hypsipyle and moved on to Medea.[12] We shall see that the same sort of thing happened with great frequency in Chaucer's time, but it was not done openly, for second marriages were regarded as bigamous and invalid.[13]

From another perspective, it could almost be said that Ovid's case histories in the *Heroides* demonstrate that love and marriage are incompatible, or generally so. The reason is that the men nearly always "loven novelrie," whether or not they are married to their fancies of the moment.[14]

Protesilaus, however, is an exception, for he remains faithful, so far as we are told.[15] Lynceus, of course, had to leave Hypermnestra, since her father was out to kill him. Hypermnestra refused to assassinate him, lest she violate the sacred symbols of their wedding service, but she seems to place greater stress on kinship loyalty than on marital love: she regards him perhaps even more as a brother (he is her first cousin) than as a husband.[16]

Canace's lover, Macareus, is her literal brother; but far from abandoning her, when he finds out that she is pregnant and about

10. *Heroides* 1.76. In the Middle Ages, Ulysses was thought to have played an active role in his captivation. See below, Chap. 5.
11. The only exception is the captive Trojan widow, Briseis, the original of Criseida, whom Achilles does not marry or promise to marry, though she considers him her husband (*vir*) as well as master and brother (*Heroides* 3.52). We are not told if Sappho and Phaon married.
12. *Heroides* 6 and 12.
13. See below, Chap. 6 and Chap. 7.
14. See *Heroides* 2 (Demophoon abandons Phyllis), 5 (Paris abandons Oenone), 6 (Jason abandons Hypsipyle), 7 (Aeneas abandons Dido), 9 (Hercules abandons Deianira), 10 (Theseus abandons Ariadne), 12 (Jason abandons Medea). See Chap. 8 below for the marital status of Phyllis, Hypsipyle, Dido, Ariadne, and Medea.
15. *Heroides* 13.
16. *Heroides* 14.9–10, 123–130.

to give birth, he promises to marry her. Her father, Aeolus, god of the winds, sentences both mother and infant to death when he discovers her shame, without realizing, apparently, that his son Macareus was her partner.[17] Whether such a brother-sister marriage as Macareus proposed was thought possible for the children of the gods, as it was for the gods themselves (for instance, Juno and Jupiter), we are not told. Ovid makes no reference to an incest law here, as he does when Phaedra unsuccessfully attempts to seduce her stepson Hippolytus. She uses the precedent of brother-sister marriage (presumably among the gods) to justify her proposal.[18] But Phaedra, of course, is not suggesting marriage, especially since her own husband, Hippolytus's father, is still very much in evidence. He (Theseus) had first married, or promised to marry, Phaedra's sister Ariadne, and then abandoned her for Phaedra. Phaedra alludes to this history but does not seem to include it among the unnatural or incestuous unions she names, as would the Christians of the Middle Ages.[19]

Orestes is another lover who cannot be accused of abandoning his beloved. His cousin Hermione was first married to him, but then her father married her to Pyrrhus, from whom she has withheld her consent. Hermione calls on Orestes to demand his rights by force, as Menelaus (her father) did when he was deprived of Helen (her mother). Orestes will rescue her if a *cura pia* moves

17. *Heroides* 11.
18. *Heroides* 4.134: "Fas omne facit fratre marita soror." In the *Metamorphoses* (9.454–665), the story of Byblis, who loves her brother, is told as a lesson that girls should love only what is lawful ("ut ament concessa puellae"). She too cites the example of the gods' marriages, though she admits that they have their own laws ("sunt superis sua iura," 500). She mentions that more than one son of Aeolus lay with his daughters: "At non Aeolidae thalamos timuere sororum" (507), but there is no indication that the sisters' *thalami* are meant as bridal beds; nor does Byblis ever suggest that she can get married to Caunus.
19. *Heroides* 4.53–66. According to medieval law, even a promise to marry in the future followed by intercourse would constitute marriage (see below, Chap. 7). And marriage or intercourse with close inlaws was considered as incestuous as with close blood relatives, according to the standard interpretation of Leviticus 18 and 20. Cf. the objections that Henry VIII was to raise against the validity of his marriage to his sister-in-law Catherine of Aragon. See my article "Canonical Implications of Richard III's Plans to Marry His Niece," *Traditio* 23 (1967) 269–311.

him (8.15). This is really the only reference Hermione makes to his feelings. Her love for him is clearly passionate, but we have no way of judging his attitude toward her.

Hector is held up by Oenone as a perfect and faithful husband, a *certus maritus*. Her own husband, Paris, who has turned out to be Hector's brother, is just the opposite. She upbraids him for his failure to follow this ideal; he has become a pursuer of women like himself, women who abandon their *legitimi viri*, and she warns that Helen, unfaithful in the past, may be unfaithful to him (5.77–78, 99–108).

Dido too complains that Aeneas has betrayed the ideal of mutual fidelity—he had given her hope that he would be her *vir mansurus;* but then he too (so she says) had abandoned his first wife. She regrets now that she has been unfaithful to the *pudor* that she owes to the memory of her first husband, Sychaeus (7.84, 97–108). Similarly, Deianira, who fears that Hercules will now marry Iole, reminds him that she, his first wife, is the only woman he has ever loved without sin: "Me quoque cum multis, sed me sine crimine amasti" (9.137). Theseus's vow of marriage (or, more likely, betrothal) to Ariadne was false—his *fides data* an empty word and he a *vir periurus* (10.76, 116). Jason is similar: he is Medea's *vir infidus* (12.210) as well as Hypsipyle's *maritus lentus* (6.17).

Almost all of the unfortunate ladies of the *Heroides* are still waiting and hoping for the return of their men. This is true even of Dido, who like Briseis brings herself to admit that if she cannot be wife, she will be content with something less (7.167, cf. 3.69). But Dido's patience is fast running out, and as she ends her letter, she prepares to kill herself, as does Phyllis. Deianira too resolves to kill herself, when she gets word of how Hercules has died through her doing. She blames her madness for what has happened: "Quo me furor egit amantem?" (9.145). But obviously she was not mad in Lewis's sense. She meant no harm—she did not know that Nessus's shirt was poisoned. She was simply trying to use every device possible to win back the love of the man that she had married. Admittedly, their union had been inadvisable, because she was his social inferior: "As the ill-mated steer yoked miserably at the plough, so fares the wife who is less than her mighty lord." It is no *honor* but rather an *onus* to marry thus, and she warns womankind rhetorically, "Would you be wedded happily, wed your equal" (9.29–32).[20]

Of Lewis's examples of criminal or shameful madness, only Medea fits the description, in Ovid's characterizations. Dido certainly does not, as I have already said; and Phaedra, though she will like Medea bring about the death of the man who spurns her, is presented as too calculating in her lust to be declared insane. Medea, however, is possessed by a god ("deus qui nunc mea pectora versat") impelling her to revenge (12.211).

Canace too was possessed, but by the God of Love; and whereas Medea burned with no ordinary fires ("nec notis ignibus arsi") when she first loved Jason (12.33),[21] Canace's flame was more moderate ("incalui . . . corde tepente"). It had the result of producing in her alone, of all these epistolary heroines, the symptoms of lovesickness: she grew pale and thin, could scarcely eat or sleep, and continually moaned, though in no physical pain (11.25–30). That she was in no danger of death from her malady was perhaps owing only to the fact that Macareus "remedied" it (in the Wife of Bath's sense of the word). However, her symptoms almost do double duty for her pregnancy, which would have been fatal were she not revived by Macareus's promise of marriage. In the end, only her father's discovery of the child forces death on her, by her own hand.

It is the sorrow rather than the disease of love that almost causes Laodamia to die when her beloved husband parts from her to go to the Trojan War. When she is finally and with great

---

20. Oenone has something of the same complaint: when she first knew Paris, he was, for all he or she knew, no more than a slave; but now that he is revealed to be a Trojan prince, she fears that he despises her as a rustic (5.11–12, 87–88).

21. In contrast to Medea's "ruin" at first sight ("et vidi et perii," 33), Sappho thinks she may, like the Wife of Bath, have been born inclined to love easily, though she admits that she may also have acquired her soft character because of the interests that she devoted herself to, especially her art (15.79–84). Ovid's authorship of Sappho's letter has been doubted (it does not appear in the earliest manuscripts), but the letter is now generally thought to be his. Ovid's friend Sabinus, in fact, wrote an answer from Phaon to such a letter of Sappho's by Ovid, as Ovid himself tells us (*Amores* 2.18.34).

difficulty revived from her deathlike faint, her pain returns, and her agitation is shown by the rapid movement of the verses, which have as many short syllables as are possible in a distich:

> Ut rediit animus, pariter rediere dolores.
> Pectora legitimus casta momordit amor. [13.29–30]

Just how passionate *legitimus amor* can be even in *casta pectora* is shown by her fantasy of Protesilaus's return to her: "When shall I clasp you, safe returned, in my eager arms, and lose myself in languishing delight? When will it be mine to have you again close joined to me on the same couch, telling me your glorious deeds in the field? And while you are telling them, though it delight to hear, you will snatch many kisses nonetheless, and will give me many back."[22]

Just as Oenone had envied Andromache her faithful Trojan husband, so too Laodamia envies the new bride at Troy who can arm her husband herself every time he goes into battle, and while she gives him his weapons, can receive his kisses:

> Ipsa suis manibus forti nova nupta marito
> Inponet galeam dardanaque arma dabit;
> Arma dabit, dumque armo dabit, simul oscula sumet.
> [13.139–141]

As we have already seen, such a warrior will bear himself more carefully while fighting and return safe and sound to the bosom of his mistress. For though she is married to him, she is still his *domina* and can command him:

> Ille, ferens dominae mandata recentia secum,
> Pugnabit caute, respicietque domum. [145–146]

The Double Epistles

It is probable that the double epistles came later than the fifteen single letters: that is, during the composition of the *Meta-*

22. Quando ego, te reducem cupidis amplexa lacertis,
  Languida laetitia solvar ab ipsa mea?
  Quando erit, ut lecto mecum bene iunctus in uno
  Militiae referas splendida facta tuae?
  Quae mihi dum referes, quamvis audire iuvabit,
  Multa tamen capies oscula, multa dabis. [13.115–120]

morphoses.[23] They certainly represent a great advance in the psychology of love. The naturalness with which Ovid portrays the workings of his lovers' minds makes much of the earlier series look very artificial indeed. One reason for this improvement is that we now hear both sides of the story; and another contributing factor is the stage at which the story is begun. Now it is not old and usually betrayed love which is recollected in sorrow, but new and reciprocal love. Instead of the bitter lees, we have living wine, where "passion is either awakening or at its height."[24]

The lightest tone is to be found in the first of the three exchanges, that between Paris and Helen. The tragedy of the Trojan War is hinted at, but only ironically, through Paris's relentlessly optimistic judgment of omens and probabilities (16.41–50, 341–378). He has learned the *ars amatoria* perfectly and exercises it skilfully on Helen. I need not give particular details of his lines of approach except to say that his intentions are always honorable—after a fashion; for he has not only adultery but marriage in mind. Helen is, he says, of all the women in the world, best suited to be his wife. Oenone is next best (he does not really say that he is actually married to her), but he can now think of no one but Helen (97–106). She need not fear "disparagement" (in the medieval sense) in marrying him, for his family is as noble as they come (173–174). (Oenone, we remember, condescended to marry him even though she thought him a mere slave.)[25]

Menelaus, Helen's husband, has served as the unconscious means of bringing Paris to her, by receiving him as his guest—which was done "not without the counsel and approval of the gods." Paris professes to regard Menelaus as something of a clown ("rusticus iste"), and he bursts with anger and envy ("rumpor et invideo") when he sees him fondling his wife. He manages only with difficulty to prevent an overt explosion as he struggles to conceal his madness ("luctor celare furorem") (129–130, 221–224, 237).

23. See E. J. Kenney, "Liebe als juristisches Problem: Über Ovids *Heroides* 20 und 21," *Philologus* 111 (1967) 212–232, esp. 213. A new dating of the early *Heroides* is promised in Howard Jacobson, *Ovid's Heroides* (Princeton 1974).

24. L. P. Wilkinson, *Ovid Recalled* (Cambridge 1955) 107; also in the revised and abridged edition, *Ovid Surveyed* (Cambridge 1962) 43.

25. See above, n. 20.

Once again, then, we have a sub-Ludovician love-madness in a fairly serious context. Paris is certainly infatuated, but he is only playing at being mad. The only shameful crime he commits is the theft of his host's wife, and he tries to convince Helen that it is no crime at all. She is not to worry over a violation of *venus marita*, for her beauty necessitates it. Jupiter and Venus do this sort of thing, and she is Jupiter's heiress (she is the daughter of Leda and the "swan"). She can scarcely be chaste, therefore. Yet at the same time he assumes that she can be faithful to him, and her exhorts her to practice chastity later, when she is his wife. They will commit sins now, perhaps, but their marriage will set everything straight: "Nunc ea peccemus quae corriget hora iugalis." After all, when Menelaus departed, he did tell her to look after Paris's needs (285–306).

Helen begins her reply by professing to be shocked at Paris's impudence and treachery. She has always been careful of her honor (*pudor*), and has never been unfaithful. No *adulter* has ever had her. And yet, she is not angry—for who becomes inflamed against a lover?—as long as the love that Paris offers is sincere ("non simulatur amor") (17.1–36).

If she were willing to receive his attentions, she would do so not because of his gifts to her but for his own sake. She admits that he is the sort of man she could readily love, but she exhorts him to be virtuous, like her. If only he had come before she was married! She would be made of iron if she did not love such a man, and she freely confesses that she is not made of iron. But she immediately backs off from this virtual admission of love by saying that she resists loving someone who could hardly become her own: "Amare repugno / Illum quem fieri vix puto posse meum" (65–138). She is thinking, of course, of the permanent (or at least relatively stable) possession that comes from marriage.

She is not practiced, she says, in furtive love—or, literally, the theft of love ("veneris furtum")—but she proves an adept improviser. She tells him to "play on," but stealthily ("lude, sed occulte"), and begins to plan their affair (141–153). She is fearful, though, and holds back. She wishes she could proceed honorably (that is, become his wife in an honorable way). If only he had taken her off by force, she could have been "compelled" to be

happy ("sic certe felix esse coacta forem"). She calls up examples
of women abandoned by their husbands, namely, Hypsipyle and
Ariadne, and she knows that Paris too has abandoned Oenone
after loving her for many years. If she goes with him now, people
would condemn her; he will be jealous later on, fearing her infidelity to him, and call her an adulteress; and she is worried about
the prophecy that Paris has so glibly dismissed (175–240).[26] She
finally leaves matters unresolved but says that they can communi-
cate through her maids.

The next set of letters, between Leander and Hero, provides
a great contrast to those of Paris and Helen. The lovers are tragic,
for the omens of Leander's death, which both of them have seen
(18.193–204, 19.195–204), are destined to be fulfilled immediately.
Furthermore, they are innocent of any violation of wedlock.
True, they too must keep their love secret because they fear the
opposition of Leander's parents; the reason seems to be that Hero,
a Thracian maiden, would be considered unworthy of a husband
from Abydos (18.13–14, 19.99–100). They would no doubt marry
if they could: Hero wishes that the sense of shame, or honor
(*pudor*), that forces them to love secretly would disappear, or
that their love would no longer be afraid of what men would say
of it (19.171–172). These lovers are not so innocent, of course,
that they do not give full rein to their passion. When Hero receives Leander dripping wet from his swim, they warm their
breasts together in close embrace and do much else that she is too
modest to write about (18.101–104, 19.60–64).

Leander, as we saw, worships Hero as both his *domina* and his
dea;[27] but she, being a realist, knows that she is his inferior not
only socially but physically, though the fire of their love is equal:
"Urimur igne pari, sed sum tibi viribus inpar" (19.5). She thinks
that this inequality of body must reflect a similar weakness of
character and mind:

> Fortius ingenium suspicor esse viris;
>   Ut corpus, teneris ita mens infirma puellis.   [6–7]

26. No doubt Ovid is suggesting that Helen and Paris together plotted his
famous public "rape" in order to save her honor.
27. "Quam sequor ipsa dea est" and "Dominae placuisse laboro" (18.66,
95).

The result of her infirmity is that she does not bear easily the delays and obstacles to their love: "Non patienter amo!" (4).

What makes her all the more impatient is that she, like all women, has nothing else to do but think of love ("superest praeter amare nihil," 16), whereas men can distract themselves in hunting, tending to the fields, spending their time in the market-place or sporting arena, or passing the later hours of the day in drinking wine (9–14). Since, then, she does nothing but love Leander, who is her only pleasure, she loves him more than he could ever love her:

> Quod superest facio; teque, O mea sola voluptas,
>   Plus quoque quam reddi quod mihi possit amo.   [17–18]

Perhaps we are meant to take this as evidence that, in Ovid's view, not only are there more passionate women than there are passionate men, but also that women are more passionate than men, since one's occupations affect one's character ("abeunt studia in mores").[28]

Among his accounts of his own fairly lightweight passions, Ovid includes an *alba*, in which he rebukes the dawn for coming on so fast while he is in the arms of his *domina*.[29] Leander recalls that he and Hero uttered similar complaints when he had to leave her after his first swim to her tower (18.111–114).[30] Such outbursts are not techniques of the art of love such as Paris might use on Helen, but heartfelt manifestations of love, whether that love be "comic" or tragic.

The story in the final exchange of letters somewhat resembles that of Paris and Helen. Acontius has fallen in love with Cydippe and attempts to take the place of her husband. In this case, however, she has not yet married her intended spouse, and Acontius does not seek to insinuate himself beforehand as her lover, but wishes to be her lawful husband from the outset; their marriage can be brought about without committing any sin:

28. These are Sappho's words, *Heroides* 15.83 (see n. 21 above).
29. *Amores* 1.13. This poem contains the line used by Marlowe's **Dr.** Faustus to tragic effect: "Lente currite, noctis equi!"
30. John Gower draws on this passage in *Vox clamantis* 1.4.

> Coniugium pactamque fidem, non crimina posco;
>   Debitus ut coniunx, non ut adulter amo.   [20.7–8]

Unlike Paris, Acontius fell in love with Cydippe at first sight, without having heard about her or knowing who she was. Like Troiolo after him, he simply saw a girl in a temple and was stricken by her.[31] He moved quickly, by writing a betrothal vow on an apple and throwing it before Cydippe. When she picked it up and read it, she inadvertently bound herself to him. In his letter to her, Acontius blames Amor for his fraud: it was his advice that made Acontius cunning in the law ("iuris vafer"), and it was he who dictated the words of the vow. Acontius prays that the god may enable him to bind her to him with yet more knots (21–40).[32]

Acontius even compares himself to Paris—not to the smooth seducer of Ovid's epistle, but to the traditional Paris who seized Helen by force. He admires a man who was virile and used force to become a *vir* (husband), and he threatens to do the same to Cydippe if his *artes* are of no avail (47–50).[33] He seeks to bind her to him, but only because he is himself bound to her by love and shall always remain so. She may punish him as if he were her slave, and command him like a mistress ("dominae more"), if only he can plead his cause in person (75–90).[34]

The time for Cydippe to marry has come, but she is often ill in bed. Acontius attributes her malaise to Diana, in whose sanctuary she made her vow; the goddess, he says, must be trying to keep her from violating it. He is in agony when he thinks that her fiancé may be in her room with her, ministering to her sickness, caressing and kissing her as he does so. He is an adulterer in so doing, for she is pledged to be Acontius's wife. True, her first

31. We get the impression from Boccaccio that Troiolo has never seen Criseida before, yet there is no explanation of how he knows who she is, which he does. It is the same with Chaucer's hero.

32. Cf. Kenney, "Liebe" 213.

33. On Paris as rapist, see n. 26 above, and below, Chap. 4, in the section "The Unsung Heroines."

34. Lines 91–92, in which he complains that he is arraigned *in absentia* and loses his case because he has no one to plead it, are used by Gower, *Vox clamantis* 1.1385–1386.

engagement was not to him, but it was arranged by her father,
whereas Cydippe herself swore this one. Mere men were the father's witnesses, but Diana was hers. Her father will be only
mendax if his undertaking is broken, but she will be *periura*
(107–162).

Cydippe's marriage to Acontius would be a love match, he tells
the fiancé, whereas the latter in his arranged betrothal does not
yet love her, but only may come to do so: "Idque ego iam, quod
tu forsan amabis, amo" (168). The assumption by C. S. Lewis and
others that all marriages in the Middle Ages were matches of interest and had nothing to do with love has been refuted by historical evidence.[35] But it could also have been opposed by Ovid's
common sense: the interest that motivates men is not infrequently
love; and, conceding Lewis's point that interests change, we can
agree with Acontius that it is possible for them to change for the
better—a man may come to love even his prearranged bride, as in
the case of Cydippe's fiancé.

As Acontius sees it, his own credentials as a prospective husband
are complete. He has a good name and wealth; but even though he
could offer nothing else, he loves her: "Amplius utque nihil, me
tibi iungit Amor" (223–226). She should have sought such a husband even if she were not sworn to one; and since she is sworn,
she should take him even if he were not such:

> Appeteres talem vel non iurata maritum;
> Iuratae vel non talis habendus erat.   [227–228]

He has been wounded by Love's arrows, she by Diana's; but
Cydippe can heal them both (229–234).

Cydippe's letter, like Helen's, begins as a rebuke which gradually gives way almost unconsciously to an admission of love. She
asks him why he did not woo her instead of resorting to trickery.
Her betrothal to him is invalid—she did not really take an oath,
since it is not the mouth but the mind that swears: "Quae iurat,
mens est." But she is afraid that he is right in saying that Diana
holds her bound, which she finds most unfair (21.1–14). Each
time the marriage sacraments are prepared, her limbs grow weak

35. Lewis 13; see above, Chap. 1.

and useless. Three times Hymenaeus has fled from her room, having found there only tears and the fear of death (129–168).

If Acontius is not lying about his love for her, let him pray for her, at least so that she may not die and thus deprive him of his hope. He is not to fear that her husband-to-be takes liberties with her. True, he sits by her bed as often as he can, but he remembers that it is the bed of a virgin. He seems to sense that something is wrong, too, and that she is offended with him, and he silently groans and sighs. Having recounted this in her letter, Cydippe is embarrassed to think that she has thereby confessed her feelings for Acontius (183–204).

Cydippe has also revealed that Acontius has sold his rival short: he obviously loves her already in spite of the parental negotiations that brought them together. It is obvious too that Cydippe does not suffer simply from a "fever of unknown origin"; the symptoms are those of Love's darts, not Diana's. She admits as much a bit later when she plays on Acontius's name, which means "javelin" in Greek (209–212). She finally confesses that she has told her mother about the oath she was deceived into making. The rest is up to Acontius. She has nothing more to say—except that she longs to be united to him: "Cupio me iam coniungere tecum" (241–247). Like Acontius, she now desires to enter a *coniugium* with him, to possess him *ut coniunx.*

In summary, the double epistles can hardly fail to strike us as very "medieval." It is no wonder that one of Andrew the Chaplain's dialecticians draws upon the sophistries of Ovid's Paris.[36] And though Chaucer and Gower do not retell the love stories of this series of Ovidian letters, there can be little doubt that they were influenced by their sentiments, whether directly or indirectly.[37] L. P. Wilkinson is more emphatic in speaking of Chau-

36. *Ars honeste amandi* 1.6.8 (116), referring to *Heroides* 16.74ff.
37. Chaucer claims to have written of "the dreynte Leandre for his Erro" in his *Saints' Legend of Cupid* (*Man of Law's Tale* 61–69); if he did so, however, the account has not survived in the twelve manuscripts of *The Legend of Good Women* that have come down to us, though "Herro" does make an appearance in the *Legend's* prologue (F 263). The same is true of "the teeris of Eleyne" (*Man of Law's Tale* 70) and "Eleyne" (*Legend* F 254); but Helen, of course, sheds no martyr's tears in Ovid's version of

cer: "The yielding of Criseyde, more subtle and lifelike than any treatment in medieval poetry of such a theme, was undoubtedly influenced by the yielding of Helen to Paris in Epistle XVII."[38]

The *Metamorphoses:* Romance and Antiromance

Another work by Ovid that purports to deal seriously with love is the *Metamorphoses*. But much of it concerns the unnatural endings caused by perverse or promiscuous lust. On the celestial level we are led through Jupiter's seemingly insatiable desires for earthly women and exposed to the almost totally unrelieved nastiness of his wife Juno. Theirs is a marriage completely devoid of love; his indifference to her is matched by her jealousy and desire for revenge. Their union seems to confirm Ovid's general characterization of conjugal society in his *Ars amatoria:* "Keep far away, quarrels and bitter-tongued affrays! With soft words must love be fostered. With quarrels let wives pursue husbands and husbands wives, and deem that they are ever at issue with each other; this befits wives: the dowry of a wife is quarrelling."[39]

There is virtually no sign in Juno of the beneficent patroness of marriage, except when she makes a perfunctory appearance with Venus and Hymenaeus at the wedding of Iphis and Ianthe.[40] It is said that the Furies rather than Juno were at the wedding of Tereus and Procne (6.428–432), but it would have suited Juno's fierce character to have joined them. Even in the story of Ceyx and Alcyone, Juno responds to the latter's prayers not because she pities her, but simply because she is annoyed: she can no longer stand to be prayed to on behalf of a dead man, and she wishes to

---

her story. In the *Metamorphoses* she does weep, but only at the loss of her beauty in old age (15.232–233). For the Helen Chaucer must have had in mind, see below, Chap. 4 in the section "The Unsung Heroines." Gower draws on the double epistles in *Vox clamantis* 1.4 (*Heroides* 18.112; see n. 30 above), 1.1385–1386 (20.91–92; above, n. 34), 1.1612 (19.52), 3.1952 (17.190), 5.211 (16.231), 6.69–70 (19.13), 6.750, 752 (17.130, 234). See *The Major Latin Works of John Gower*, tr. Eric W. Stockton (Seattle 1962).

38. *Ovid Surveyed* 192.

39. *Ars amatoria* 2.151–155, ed. and tr. J. H. Mozley, Loeb Classical Library (London 1929, repr. 1962).

40. *Metamorphoses* 9.796, ed. and tr. Frank Justus Miller, Loeb Classical Library (London 1916, repr. 1966–1968).

drive Alcyone's mourning hands from her altar. She is not concerned at all about offering consolation to the widow in her grief; Morpheus is simply to tell Alcyone of Ceyx's fate (11.583–588).[41]

The love affairs of the gods are not, of course, always sordid or extramarital. When Cupid in revenge for an insult pierces Apollo with his golden arrow, causing him to love Daphne, daughter of the river god Peneus, his love for her is indistinguishable from his desire to marry her: "Phoebus amat, visaeque cupit conubia Daphnes." Marriage is just as inseparable from love in Daphne's mind. Because she was pierced by Cupid's leaden arrow, she hates them both—she flees from the very name of lover (amans) and has no regard for Hymen, love, or marriage: "Nec quid Hymen, quid amor, quid sint conubia curat"; and she hates wedding torches as if they were something criminal (1.474–490).

The ending of the story can hardly be described as happy. Though Apollo is the inventor of medicine, he suffers from a wound his arts cannot heal. But Daphne escapes his pursuit by having her father change her into a laurel. Apollo, however, does not seem as disconcerted by this transformation as might be expected; he simply declares, "Since thou canst not be my bride, thou shalt at least be my tree"; and both he and the girl-tree seem strangely satisfied with this arrangement.

Sometimes the loves of the gods end more conventionally (in human terms). After Ariadne is abandoned by Theseus, Bacchus brings her "embraces and aid," which, we must infer, are inclusive of love and marriage. The oppressive thrust of the poem toward metamorphosis is happily fulfilled this time by an accidental rather than a substantial change: Ariadne's crown and not she herself is transformed into a constellation (8.176–181). Similarly, when Pluto seizes Proserpina and takes her off to the underworld to be his queen, only her habitat is changed. But the incidence of human-to-subhuman mutations in her story is fearfully high (5.385–571).

There are very few such happy endings in the *Metamorphoses*. Even in the story of Proserpina, one can hardly say that there is

41. For the miseries that Juno actively provokes, see 1.601ff., 722ff.; 2.466ff.; 3.256ff.; 4.420ff.; 7.523ff.; 9.176ff., 284ff.; 14.781ff.

mutual love. Her marriage to Pluto becomes a matter of negotia-
tion between relatives. Jupiter, her father and Pluto's brother,
thinks that Pluto will do very nicely as the girl's husband and
desires her mother Ceres to consent to the match. Proserpina's
consent is not sought, nor is it forthcoming, until Jupiter hits upon
his celebrated compromise of allowing her to spend half of the
year in the upper world. Then Proserpina is happy, but only, it
seems, because she can be with her mother again. Whether she
ever came to love her husband we are not precisely told, though
she does not deny it when Orpheus says as much to her (10.29).

Another arranged marriage in which the girl has no noticeable
voice is that of Perseus (son of Jupiter and Danaë) and Andromeda; but in this case the prospective husband approaches the
girl's parents rather than seizing her, after he has been struck by
her beauty. The parents agree to the marriage if he can save her
from the sea monster that threatens her. He does so, and only
then does he "seize" her. Since we are told that Hymenaeus and
Love wield the torches at their wedding, we may assume that the
love that Love inspires or celebrates is mutual and that the music
and songs are "happy arguments of the joyful spirit" of Andromeda as well as of Perseus, even though we are not told of
her explicit consent (4.670–672).[42] Perseus continues his "knightly"
deeds on her behalf even after marriage. When her uncle and
former fiancé Phineus breaks in upon their celebration and tries to
take her by force, Perseus immobilizes him and his allies by letting them gaze on the head of Medusa. This is the only kind of
metamorphosis in their story, and the fortunate couple are allowed to depart from Ovid's pages untransformed and happy
(5.1–249).

On the purely or nearly human level, we encounter a model
human love very early in the piece. Deucalion, the Noah figure,
loves his wife Pyrrha passionately and would follow her into the
sea if necessary (1.350–362). Luckily it is not necessary, and since
they are the product of a subhuman-to-human metamorphosis,
they have paid their debt to Ovid's theme, and so can be left in

42. For the text describing the wedding celebration, see the epigraph for
Part I, above.

peace. The same is true in the story of Pygmalion and his statue. Pygmalion starts off as an antifeminist, who, disgusted with the vices that Nature has given in such abundance to the female mind, lives unmarried, "sine coniuge caelebs." But he falls in love with the woman his art has created and desires the gods to enable him to marry her. Venus complies, gives her life, and witnesses the marriage that she has made ("coniugio quod fecit adest dea") (10.243–295).

Another beneficent and nondegrading metamorphosis brings the love of Iphis for Ianthe to the happy wedding at which, as we saw, the gods of love and marriage participated. Iphis, a girl, has been reared as a boy to protect her from her father's command to have his child killed if it is female (his reason: girls are burdensome and weak). At the age of thirteen she is engaged to another girl, Ianthe. She loves her desperately, though with heavy conscience: for Nature, mightier than all the gods, forbids such homosexual affection. The goddess Isis takes pity on her and provides the perfect remedy by changing her sex (9.669–797).

Hymenaeus leaves the wedding of Iphis and Ianthe to attend another, that of Orpheus and Euridyce. Theirs too is basically a story of fervent married love, but their tale turns tragic at Euridyce's death. Orpheus follows her to Hades because (as he tells Pluto and Proserpina) he has been conquered by the god Amor, by whom they too were joined together. But his love for her also makes him violate the condition that he not look back at her as she returns to the upper world with him (10.1–57). What spoils the tale as a story of romance, however, is the moral metamorphosis that Orpheus then imposes upon himself: he becomes a homosexual. He sets himself to sing of boys loved by (male) gods and of girls punished for unnatural lust (78–154). The only girl he sings of who fits in this latter category is Myrrha, who commits incest with her father, thereby polluting the compact (*foedus*) of mighty Nature (352–353). But Orpheus, unlike Iphis, apparently does not recognize homosexuality as unnatural and punishable; and, though he is torn apart by Bacchantes in punishment for scorning women, his death does not function as a punishment but rather as a reward. The Bacchantes instead are punished metamorphotically by Bacchus, whereas Orpheus escapes metamorphosis and rejoins Euridyce in the nether world (11.1–84). But though he has emerged from his pederastic cocoon, the episode takes the edge off the romance between him and his wife.

Pygmalion's adventure is one of the stories told by Orpheus in the course of his song; but though Myrrha is Pygmalion's great-granddaughter, there is no hint that his love is condemned as unnatural. Like Iphis, he went through the proper "channels," and the irregularity of his affections was remedied by celestial intervention. Much, in fact, of Orpheus's song deviates from his announced subjects of divine-human pederasty and illicit female lust. The story of Adonis, Myrrha's son by her father, is an example, as is the story of Atalanta that Venus tells Adonis: Atalanta has been warned that a husband will be the death of her; but because she is very beautiful, many men love her and (naturally) want to marry her. But of all those who agree to her test (racing with her) and its death penalty for failure, she is moved only by Hippomenes; if she had been destined to marry, he is the only one with whom she would wish to share her bed. Hippomenes wins the race by Venus's connivance; but when he forgets to thank her, Venus arranges to have him and Atalanta transmuted into lions. The point of the story for Adonis is not that he should avoid vengeful goddesses like Venus, but rather that she should avoid vicious beasts like lions (10.503–739). Thus, once again, Ovid has robbed his story of its tragedy and even of its pathos by the inappropriateness of its conclusion.

Ringing the Changes on Faithful Love

The most human and touching of the love stories of the *Metamorphoses* are those of Pyramus and Thisbe, Cephalus and Procris, and Ceyx and Alcyone.[43] The first is the story of young and tragic love, like that of Leander and Hero. The lovers are not separated by the sea, however, but by a single wall shared by their two houses. As times goes on, their love grows; they would willingly come together under the law of marriage, but their parents

43. The story of Philemon and Baucis deserves mention as a portrait of enduring marital affection. Their request to the gods they served that they might die at the same time is granted, after a fashion: they both become trees together and lose consciousness (8.631–719).

forbid it; what the parents cannot prevent is the ardor they feel
for each other, in equal measure, in their captive souls:

> Tempore crevit amor; taedae quoque iure coissent,
> Sed vetuere patres; quod non potuere vetare,
> Ex aequo captis ardebant mentibus ambo.   [4.60–62]

Though they cannot be united by the *ius taedae*, their faithful
love joins them together in their hour of death: "quos certus
amor, quos hora novissima iunxit" (156). They are allowed to die
decently, without the indignity of some animal, vegetable, or
mineral half-life; only their blood is metamorphosed, giving its
color to the mulberry's fruit, which serves as a lasting memorial
of their devotion.

The tale of Pyramus and Thisbe is one of the world's great
love stories; and if Shakespeare could bring himself to burlesque
it in *A Midsummer Night's Dream*, it was only after he had used
its plot of divided family and double suicide to tragic effect in
Romeo and Juliet.[44]

A somewhat similar story of star-crossed but unmetamorphosed
lovers is that of Cephalus and Procris. This time there is no
parental opposition: rather the contrary, for Procris's father sanc-
tioned the marriage, and Cephalus not only seemed happy but was
so in fact: "Pater hanc mihi iunxit Erechtheus, / Hanc mihi iunxit
amor; felix dicebar eramque" (7.697–698). But scarcely a month
after their wedding, Cephalus was snatched away by the goddess
Aurora. He refused her adulterous advances, however, for he
loved only Procris; she was always in his heart and on his lips; he
kept talking of the sacraments of their marriage and the fresh embraces of their bridal chamber, first covenants of his now deserted
bed:

> Ego Procrin amabam;
> Pectore Procris erat, Procris mihi semper in ore.

---

44. Ovid's comparison of the bleeding Pyramus to a broken lead pipe
(4.122–124) has been taken as evidence of parody in his account. The simile
is certainly ludicrous and inappropriate, and if Ovid recognized it as such
he is guilty of bad taste in the first degree. I, for one, however, would prefer
to dismiss him on the lighter charge of inadvertent bad taste. It is worthy of
note that the purpose of the simile is to "justify" the metamorphosis, and
Ovid's metamorphoses are often in dubious taste.

> Sacra tori coitusque novos thalamosque recentes
> Primaque deserti referebam foedera lecti. [707–710]

Another goddess might have performed some spiteful metamorphosis on Cephalus.[45] But Aurora was more subtle in her
revenge, and Ovid more subtle in his retelling of the story. She
made Cephalus jealous of Procris and simply metamorphosed his
appearance (*inmutat figuram*) so that he could spy on her (722).
Cephalus tempted Procris's fidelity and unjustly found fault with
her. She left him in indignation, but after three years he suc-
ceeded in obtaining her forgiveness. They lived sweet years together in harmony (752); he was happy in his wife and she in
her husband, and mutual cares and love bound them together:

> Coniuge eram felix, felix erat illa marito;
> Mutua cura duos et amor socialis habebat. [799–800]

But then Procris by a fatal misunderstanding became jealous of
Cephalus: she had heard him address the breeze, "aura," and she
believed him to be in love with some nymph. She went to spy on
him, and he, thinking her a wild beast, killed her with the javelin
she had given him. But before she expired, he set her jealous fears
to rest, and she seemed to die content (808–862). Cephalus, however, lived on: it is he who tells the story, amid sighs and tears for
his remembered happiness.

Much of the central books of the *Metamorphoses* is taken up
with impious deeds provoked by unnatural or excessive love: first,
there is Tereus's rape and mutilation of Philomela, and her revenge (6.424–674), and then Medea's exploits (7.1–424); after the
"normal" but unfortunate love of Cephalus and Procris comes the
story of Scylla's sacrifice of her father to her passion for Minos,
with allusions to Pasiphaë and the Minotaur (8.1–158); then
comes Byblis's love for her brother Caunus (9.447–665),[46] and
Myrrha's incest with her father.

---

45. Circe, for instance, changed Picus to a woodpecker when he insisted
on not violating his marriage covenant by an extramarital love: "Nec
venere externa socialia foedera laedam" (14.380). On the various transforma-
tions discernible in Cephalus and Procris, see William S. Anderson, "Mul-
tiple Changes in the *Metamorphoses*," *Transactions of the American Philological Association* 94 (1963) 1–27, esp. 10–14. I am grateful to Margo
Kipps for drawing my attention to this article.
46. See n. 18 above.

Finally, though some glimpses of sanity have been caught along the way, there is a sustained treatment of devoted marital love in the story of Ceyx and Alcyone, which corresponds in many ways to the history of Laodamia and Protesilaus. Ceyx is Alcyone's *carus coniunx* and she is his *amans* (11.440, 450). When we are first introduced to Ceyx, he names peace and marriage as his main interests: "Pacis mihi cura tenendae / Coniugiique fuit (297–298). The two concerns are interrelated, as we can see from Alcyone's successful efforts to prevent Ceyx from attacking a wolf that an enemy has sent (383–388). Unfortunately, however, she is not able to dissuade him from going to consult an oracle. Like Laodamia, Alcyone watches her husband's departing ship until she can see it no more.[47] Then she throws herself upon her marriage bed, thereby renewing her tears; for she is reminded that part of her is gone (461–473). And Ceyx, in the midst of the storm that overwhelms his ship, can think of nothing but his wife, and he keeps calling her name until he drowns (544–569).[48]

We have seen how even Juno is constrained to do an act of kindness to Alcyone, grudging though it is. Morpheus takes on the shape of Ceyx and appears to Alcyone in her sleep. He speaks no words of comfort, but simply describes his death and tells her to lament for him. She does so, bitterly, and when she goes to the seashore the next morning to relive his departure, she sees his corpse. Ceyx's last wish had been that the waves would bear his body to Alcyone and that she would bury him. Instead, however, she attempts to join him in death by leaping into the sea. But before she can touch the waters, she is transformed into a bird, a halcyon, and, through the pity of the gods, so is Ceyx. Their love is thereby able to endure, and their matrimonial bond is preserved even in their winged state: "Tunc quoque mansit amor, nec coniugale solutum / Foedus in alitibus." They mate and become

47. *Heroides* 13.15–22.
48. This is another passage that some modern critics have found deliberately humorous and satirical, and they cite Dryden's rather ludicrous translation of the lines in his *Fables* as confirmation of this reading. But it may well be that Dryden considered the passage infected by those "boyisms" of untimely wit that he deplored rather than admired in Ovid. See Wilkinson, *Ovid Surveyed* 193.

parents, and serve as an example in praise of love that lasts to the end: "Ad finem servatos laudat amores" (650–750).

Thus, by means of the metamorphosis, the pathetic story of Ceyx and his wife has a happy ending of sorts, or rather a bittersweet one; for though we are told that their love went on unchanged after their transformation, we can hardly be expected to believe it or to accept the change as fully appropriate. Yet there is no question that such endings were often accepted at face value by Ovid's medieval imitators—for instance, by Guillaume de Machaut in his *Dit de la fontaine amoureuse* and John Gower in the *Confessio amantis* when they retell the story of Ceyx.[49] The same is true even of *Ovide moralisé*, in the final analysis (11.4148–4155),[50] after some preliminary allegorizing of the birds to contrary effects (4133–4147). But when Chaucer tells the same story in *The Book of the Duchess*, he has Alcyone simply die of sorrow three days later and omits the metamorphosis entirely. "It would have marred his tale," had he included it; "Chaucer has better taste than Ovid, and far more concern for morality."[51]

These judgments of L. P. Wilkinson on the "distastefulness" of metamorphosis and on the relatively low quality of Ovid's moral concern have been challenged, in effect, by Brooks Otis in his efforts to see Ovid as an epic poet. He finds the metamorphosis of Ceyx and Alcyone "the mystic moment when the powers of nature achieve a perfect harmony, when humanity finds itself at one with nature in a kind of cosmic sympathy."[52] He is right to associate this feeling with Wordsworth; but such a sentiment distracts from the kind of moral that Chaucer and Gower, and, according to Otis, Ovid himself, wished to draw.

Even less convincing is Otis's justification of the metamorphosis as the only possible means of mitigating tragic actions. Without

49. *Confessio amantis* 4.2927–3123. For Machaut, see the beginning of Chap. 4, below.

50. *Ovide moralisé*, ed. C. de Boer et al., 5 vols., Verhandelingen der Koninklijke Akademie van Wetenschappen te Amsterdam 15, 21 30.3, 37, 43 (1915–1938) 4.219.

51. Wilkinson, *Ovid Surveyed* 194. For *The Book of the Duchess*, see the beginning of Chap. 4, below.

52. Brooks Otis, *Ovid as an Epic Poet*, ed. 2 (Cambridge 1970) 255.

the metamorphosis, he says, "death would be the only result of the steadfast devotion of Ceyx to Alcyone and Alcyone to Ceyx. It is, therefore, the metamorphosis that saves the day and validates Ovid's positive estimate of mutual or conjugal love" (272). Yet he praises the story of Pyramus and Thisbe as bearing the same theme (277), without feeling the need for some kind of reduced animal life for the principals. Ovid's approbation is clear enough without distributing such poetic justice. Furthermore, Ovid had other, more satisfying alternatives for the conversion of tragedy into melodrama: Ceyx could have had his life restored, as almost happened to Euridyce, or he could have been decently reunited to Alcyone in their human forms in the next world, as eventually did happen to Euridyce and Orpheus.

"The West's First Champion of Conjugal Love"

In summary, it may be said that in the *Metamorphoses*, as in the *Heroides*, love can easily be insincere or go wrong, whether in marriage or out of it; it happens thus more often than not, in fact, and it is usually the man who is at fault and the woman who is victimized. But when the love is mutual and serious, it can serve as the basis for the greatest possible human happiness. Such love is exclusive and faithful and always aims toward marriage; adultery and infidelity are never praised or condoned on the human level—which is the only level that really counts.

In 1938, two years after C. S. Lewis first published *The Allegory of Love*, Brooks Otis declared that Ovid is really two love poets: on the one hand, he is "the urbane and witty amatory elegist"; and, on the other, he is "the sympathetic connoisseur of the master passion as it met him in the field of legend and myth."[53] A generation later, Otis elaborated more fully on this second Ovid, "the West's first champion of true, normal, even conjugal love." In this phase of Ovid's writing, "the pathological, isolating *eros* is assessed and deliberately contrasted with the normal, human love of two mutually responsive personalities. It is actually conjugal love—the love of husband and wife—that con-

53. Otis, "Ovid and the Augustans," *Transactions and Proceedings of the American Philological Association* 69 (1938) 188–229, esp. 229.

stitutes the ethical apex of Ovid's amatory scale. And it is just here
that Ovid is most original: nobody in classical or Hellenistic or
previous Roman literature really anticipated him."[54]

Lewis, then, was partially right in his judgment of the classical
writers and their failure to treat romantic love seriously. There
was, however, a major exception, the later (or "middle") Ovid.
Anyone familiar with the stories and sources of Chaucer and
Gower should have focused on this exception immediately and
realized its overwhelming importance in defining the nature of
love in the Middle Ages.[55] This is not to say, of course, that Ovid
would have been regarded in the Middle Ages precisely as we see
him today, or that everyone would have assessed him in the same
way.[56] But even some of those who were determined to rescue

54. Otis, *Ovid as an Epic Poet* 266, 277. He is speaking principally of the
Metamorphoses, in contrast even to the *Heroides*. But as the preceding
analysis has shown, many of the epistles contain the same sort of understanding and comparison of unwholesome and wholesome love as the *Metamorphoses*, without the disadvantage of being marred by the metamorphoses.
A case could be made for considering Catullus, Tibullus, and Propertius as
occasional champions of conjugal love as well as habitual romanticists. See
Georg Luck, "The Woman's Role in Latin Love Poetry," in *Perspectives
of Roman Poetry*, ed. G. Karl Galinsky (Austin, Tex., 1973). But these poets
exercised little perceptible influence on the Middle Ages. Ovid's title as a
champion of true, normal, and conjugal love has been disputed on the
grounds that noble as well as ignoble love in the *Metamorphoses* leads to
pain and disaster (Robert Coleman, *Classical Review*, n.s. 17[1967] 49). But
the same is true of the works of Shakespeare and of many others who have
written tragically of romantic love. Furthermore, we have seen many examples of love in the *Metamorphoses* that is not tragic but rather ends happily.
Even in the tragic stories, love is not always the cause of disaster; more
often the tragedy results from the ill will of one of the gods.
55. Cf. W. P. Ker, who wrote before the universal acceptance of *amour
courtois:* "They found in Ovid the form, at least, of devotion, and again the
Art of Love was not their only book. There were other writings of Ovid
and works of other poets from whom the Middle Ages learned their lesson
of chivalrous service. . . . What made by far the strongest impression on
the Middle Ages was . . . the poetry of the loyalty of the heroines, the
fourth book of the *Aeneid*, the *Heroides* of Ovid, and certain parts of the
Metamorphoses. If anything literary can be said to have taken effect upon
the temper of the Middle Ages, so as to produce the manners and sentiments of chivalry, this is the literature to which the largest share of the
influence must be ascribed" (*Epic and Romance* [London 1897] 395–396).
56. See Salvatore Battaglia, "La tradizione di Ovidio nel Medioevo," *La
coscienza letteraria del Medioevo* (Naples 1965) 23–50; and cf. above, Chap.
1 n. 13.

Ovid as an approved *auctor* could perceive different intentions in his various works on love. For instance, the twelfth-century *Accessus ad auctores* in use in the monasteries of Benediktbeuern and Tegernsee described Ovid as writing the *Ars amatoria* to instruct youths on how to acquire mistresses and treat them well once acquired, and to teach girls the same thing. Some youths, however, too much given over to pleasure, sought virgins as well, and even went after matrons and their own kinswomen; and virgins submitted themselves to married men as well as to the unmarried. Whence it was that Ovid came to be hated by his friends and others. He later repented and sought to win back those whom he had offended by writing the *Remedia amoris* as medicine against illicit love.[57] He wrote the *Heroides*, on the other hand, with the intention of commending legitimate marriage or love. He describes illicit and foolish love not for its own sake but for the purpose of commending legitimate love and reprehending the other. He is in fact the teacher of good morals in these epistles, and the extirpator of evil.[58]

We may easily suppose that an author like Chaucer would have a more sophisticated view of Ovid than this—that he would not, for instance, consider that Ovid's main intention in the *Remedia*

57. *Accessus ad auctores*, ed. R. B. C. Huygens, rev. ed. (Leiden 1970) 34: "Ovidius iste amandi librum composuit, ubi iuvenes amicas acquirere, acquisitas benigne tractare docuit, et puellas id idem instruxerat. Quidam autem iuvenes, voluptati nimium oboedientes, non solum virgines verum et ipsas matronas et consanguineas minime vitabant, virgines coniugatis sicut non uxoratis se pariter subiungebant. Unde Ovidius ab amicis et ab aliis in maximo odio habebatur; postea poenitens, quos offenderat sibi reconciliari desiderans, vidensque hoc non melius posse fieri quam si dato amori medicinam adinveniret, hunc librum scribere aggressus est, in quo pariter iuvenibus et puellis irretitis (consulit) qualiter contra illicitum amorem se armare debeant."

58. *Ibid.* 30: "Intentio sua est legitimum connubium vel amorem commendere, secundum hoc triplici modo tractat de ipso amore, scilicet de legitimo, de illicito, et [de] stulto: de legitimo per Penelopen, de illicito per Canacen, de stulto per Phylliden. Sed has duas partes, scilicet stulti et illiciti, non causa ipsarum, verum gratia illius tertii commendandi interserit, et sic commendando legitimum, stultum et illicitum reprehendit. Ethicae subiacet, quia bonorum morum est instructor, malorum vero exstirpator. Finalis causa talis est, ut visa utilitate quae ex legitimo procedit et infortuniis quae ex stulto et illicito solent prosequi, hunc utrumque fugiamus et soli casto adhaereamus."

amoris was to combat illicit love. A great Ovidian of the present century has said, "Ovid, the whole Ovid, never was better understood than in the Ages of Faith, and no one ever so lived him through as Geoffrey Chaucer."[59] Our perception of both Ovid and Chaucer has changed in the fifty years since these words were written, but I venture to say that they hold today with even greater force than they did originally.

59. Edward Kennard Rand, *Ovid and His Influence* (Boston 1925) 149.

Chapter 4

Chaucer and the
Martyrology of Love

Ovid as Mother Lode

The preceding chapters have shown that there was no principle
of incompatibility between serious love and marriage in Chaucer's
own writings or in any of his Latin, Italian, or remoter French
sources and precedents; rather, there was a positive impetus in
most lovers toward marriage. The same is true of Chaucer's more
recent French models. Though by no means all of the loves they
described were conjugal or licit, there was no pressing need in
principle not to marry, and no reason why marriage must interfere with or put a stop to love, if love or the seeds of love were
there to begin with.

The most important continental influence upon the young
Chaucer was Guillaume de Machaut, canon, poet, and musician.
Chaucer's first major work, *The Book of the Duchess,* a memorial
to Blanche, first wife of John of Gaunt, is filled with echoes or
imitations of Machaut's poetry. He was following Machaut's example when he introduced Ovid's story of Ceyx and Alcyone,
and he found in Machaut the same high regard for their conjugal
love as he found in Ovid: "Car, sans mentir, / Elle l'amoit plus
que rien d'amour fin."[1] It was this highest and noblest of love,
amour fin, here ascribed to Alcyone, that critics of the last century metamorphosed into *amour courtois* and excluded from wedlock.

Chaucer did not rely, of course, entirely on Machaut for his

1. Guillaume de Machaut, *La fonteinne amoureuse* 550–551 (*Oeuvres*
3.162).

account of Ceyx and Alcyone, but went directly to Ovid. Chaucer's relation to Ovid was in many ways like Ovid's relation to his predecessors. "When he wanted a Euripidean or Hellenistic *libido* he had no lack of models to draw upon; when he wanted truly mutual or conjugal love, he had to invent it or at least wrest it from very refractory material."[2] For example, Ovid purifies the Ceyx-Alcyone story by eliminating the idea that they were punished for an act of impiety. While he drops many of the traditional metamorphoses from his other tales, however, he retains it in this story, although it serves another purpose here than in earlier accounts. In his sources it functioned either as the punishment itself or as a "consolation prize" after the punishment.[3] Chaucer improved on Ovid by eliminating the metamorphosis of the lovers altogether, thereby making the tale like Ovid's own story of Pyramus and Thisbe, which Chaucer used later in *The Legend of Good Women*.[4]

Apart from Chaucer's dislike for making men into monkeys, as it were, he was faced with the superabundance of vicious love that Ovid allowed to enter his works without overt ethical transformation. Thus, when Chaucer was searching for good women to place in his legendary, he decided to include Philomela and Medea along with ladies of more estimable dossiers. But though he toyed with the idea of telling all—

> The crueltee of the, Queene Medea,
> Thy litel children hangynge by the hals
> For thy Jason, that was of love so fals[5]—

in the actual tale that he composed for Medea he makes no reference to any of the crimes she committed either on behalf of Jason

2. Brooks Otis, *Ovid as an Epic Poet*, ed. 2 (Cambridge 1970) 268.
3. *Ibid.* 232–233.
4. Chaucer omits even the memorial metamorphosis of the mulberry tree in his *Legend of Thisbe*. He uses the metamorphosis of Ariadne's crown in her legend to give the impression that she died of grief, whereas in fact she married again in the lifetime of her "husband" (see above, Chap. 3); and though he speaks of Alcestis as having been turned into a daisy (F 512), he makes it clear later that the flower is just symbolic of her—"in remembraunce of hire and in honour" (530)—while she herself leads a glorified life in paradise (564).
5. Introduction to *The Man of Law's Tale* 72–74.

or in revenge against him.[6] And though Philomela's sister Procne is said to be speechless "for sorwe and ek for rage" at Tereus's atrocities, Chaucer gives no hint of their counteratrocities but simply leaves them to dwell in their sorrow.[7] He also thought of including the story of Canace.[8] But evidently he came to the conclusion that her vice of incest was too closely connected to her love to be expunged:

> But certeinly no word ne writeth he
> Of thilke wikke ensample of Canacee,
> That loved her owene brother synfully.
> Of swiche cursed stories I sey fy![9]

Chaucer was obviously inspired by the example of the *Heroides* when he set about to gather together stories of women who had been faithful in love and suffered for it. Of the ten tales he actually composed, six of them deal with Ovid's epistolary heroines, namely, Dido, Hypsipyle, Medea, Ariadne, Phyllis, and Hypermnestra. In the prologue to the *Legend*, he mentions four more (Penelope, Hero, Laodamia, and Canace), not counting Helen.[10] And in the list of the introduction to *The Man of Law's Tale* an additional three appear: Deianira, Hermione, and Briseis. Phaedra's absence is understandable, but Oenone's is not.[11] Sappho's letter was probably unknown to him. Cydippe's sufferings were nothing more than a short prelude to anticipated bliss, and her fidelity to Acontius was never tested.

Chaucer draws on the *Metamorphoses* for the legends of Thisbe and Philomela, as we have seen (he also uses the *Metamorphoses* and other sources to fill out some of the other tales). For the legend of Lucretia he goes to Ovid's *Fasti*. The only non-Ovidian tale, therefore, is the first, the legend of Cleopatra. Of the fourteen

---

6. However, Hypsipyle, Jason's first wife, does pray that Jason will abandon Medea "and that she moste bothe hire chyldren spylle / And alle tho that sufferede hym his wille" (*Legend* 1571–1575).

7. *Legend* 2374, 2382.

8. *Legend* F 265, G 219. In F 554–561, Canace is by inference included among the "goode wommen alle, / And trewe of love."

9. Introduction to *The Man of Law's Tale* 77–80.

10. For Helen, see above, Chap. 3 n. 37.

11. Oenone does appear in a list of Ovidian *heroides* in *The House of Fame* 379–426.

other women that Chaucer named as subjects of his *Legend*, besides Ovid's heroines, two are from Greek mythology or history (Alcestis and Polyxena), two are Roman (Marcia and Lavinia), one is biblical (Esther), and one medieval (Isolde).[12]

A Work of Reparation

The immediate impulse for the compilation of his legendary, Chaucer assures us, came to him in a dream, in which such a work was commanded by the God of Love at the suggestion of Queen Alcestis as an act of penance and of reparation for his having translated the *Roman de la Rose* and told the story of Criseyde. At the end of the *Troilus*, Chaucer indicated that he had something of the sort already in mind:

> And gladlier I wol write, yif yow leste,
> Penelopees trouthe and good Alceste.   [5.1777–1778]

In so saying, he was forestalling a charge of antifeminism. Just before these lines, he pointed out that he did not invent Criseyde's guilt (1772–1776); and he continued his half-serious defense by saying that the story was meant as a cautionary tale not only for men but especially for women against false men:

> N'y sey nat this al oonly for thise men,
> But moost for wommen that bitraised be
> Thorough false folk (God yeve hem sorwe, amen!)
> That with hire grete wit and subtilte
> Bytraise yow! And this commeveth me
> To speke, and in effect yow alle I preye,
> Beth war of men, and herkneth what I seye.   [1779–1785]

This is not quite the same thing as saying that more men are false than women, but it allows his female audience to interpret it thus. Similarly, his warning against men in general suggests that all men

---

12. We have, then, twenty-four names in all. In his *Retractions*, Chaucer refers to *The Book of the Twenty-Five Ladies* among his "translations and enditings of worldly vanities." In the ballade of the *Legend*, nineteen ladies are named, including Alcestis (F 249–269, 283, 554–555). For a recent full-length study of Chaucer's poem, see Robert Worth Frank, Jr., *Chaucer and The Legend of Good Women* (Cambridge, Mass., 1972). Though he recognizes that the existence of courtly love has been challenged (6 n. 3), he continues to accept its concepts.

are false, or likely to be. (Another implication, which the ladies are not meant to pick up, is that women are more likely to be deceived by men than men by women, because men are more intelligent than women.)

Thus, if Chaucer were to expand upon these sentiments later, he would not be writing a palinode to the *Troilus,* since he would be retracting nothing but simply clarifying what he has already said. He tries to maintain the same posture in the prologue to the *Legend,* but without much success as far as his two interlocutors are concerned. The God of Love's charges against him are twofold: his *Romance of the Rose* is antilove, and *Troilus and Criseyde* is antiwoman. Specifically, by means of the *Romance,* which is a heresy against the law of Love, Chaucer induces wise people to abstain from Love's service. In the expanded prologue, the charge is elaborated further: Chaucer reveals his belief that anyone who loves *paramours,* "too hard and hot," is nothing but a fool. But the reason he believes this, says the god, is that he has entered his dotage and lost the spirit of youth (F 329–331, G 255–263). Second, in telling of Criseyde, he has made men have less trust in women (F 332–333). The alternate version of this charge is that, in showing how Criseyde forsook Troilus, he has revealed that women have done amiss (G 264–266). The implication, of course, is that a dishonor to one is a dishonor to all; just as Friar John in *The Summoner's Tale* is inclined to think that the indignity done him constituted a blasphemy against his holy convent as well (2182–2183); and, according to the Parson, women who sin with priests injure the whole Church.[13]

The God of Love demands to know why Chaucer does not write of good women, who outnumber the bad a hundred to one and certainly far outshine men (G 267–277, 301–304). Love does not, therefore, deny that the occasional wicked woman exists but believes that such should be passed over in silence; Chaucer's fault lay in throwing away the wheat and saving the chaff: "I seye, what eyleth the to wryte / The draf of storyes, and forgete the corn?" (G 311–312). And:

---

13. *Parson's Tale* 901; the reason, however, is that they thereby deprive the Church of the priests' prayers and worship.

> Let be the chaf, and writ wel of the corn.
> Why noldest thow han writen of Alceste,
> And laten Criseide ben aslepe and reste?   [G 529–531]

Love demands an answer from Chaucer but goes on to condemn him without waiting to hear it. Alcestis blames Love for
this, but she is really no more interested in Chaucer's answer than
he; rather she is concerned only to mitigate the intended punishment by suggesting a lighter penance. At first she says that perhaps Chaucer did not even write the *Rose* or the *Criseyde;* but by
the end of her plea it is clear that she takes his authorship for
granted and also assumes without further discussion that the contents of the works are slanderous, whether through ignorance,
ineptness, or malice (F 335–441).

Chaucer, however, does attempt a response. True lovers, he
says, should not take offense against him for showing disapproval
of false lovers; and whatever the intent of the original authors
who wrote about the Rose and Criseyde, his own was above reproach:

> To forthren trouthe in love and yt cheryce,
> And to been war fro falsnesse and fro vice
> By swich ensample—this was my menynge.   [F 472–474]

Therefore he explicily pleads "not guilty" to the antilove charge
and implicitly dismisses the antiwoman accusation as irrelevant:
for falseness is to be avoided, whether in men or in women. But
Alcestis tells him curtly that neither she nor Love is interested in
hearing his opinion of what is right or wrong in the matter.

> Lat be thyn arguynge,
> For Love ne wol nat countrepleted be
> In ryght ne wrong; and lerne that at me!   [F 475–477]

When Alcestis first proposes Chaucer's penance, she suggests
that he be required to write of women, whether virgins or wives,
who were true in loving all their life (F 438–439). She later repeats this instruction, with the further specification that he is to
condemn the male lovers who betray the women; but at the same
he is to speak well of love:

> Thow shalt, while that thou lyvest, yer by yere,
> The moste partye of thy tyme spende

In makyng of a glorious legende
Of goode wymmen, maydenes and wyves,
That weren trewe in lovyng al hire lyves;
And telle of false men that hem bytraien,
That al hir lyf ne do nat but assayen
How many women they may doon a shame;
For in youre world that is now holde a game.
And thogh the lyke nat a lovere bee,
Speke wel of love; this penance yive I thee.   [F 481–491]

This would almost be the same program that Chaucer claimed to
have had in writing *The Romance of the Rose* and *Troilus and
Criseyde*, were it not for Alcestis's profeminine and antimasculine
bias. The accent is still on woman's fidelity, as it was in the statement at the end of he *Troilus;* but now a new stress is given to
fidelity betrayed. In the *Troilus,* he envisaged telling of Alcestis
and Penelope, whose fidelity resulted in a happy reunion with
their husbands. Now, however, room must be made for a more
tragic kind of story; there are to be martyrs as well as "confessors" in this legendary.[14] In the end, the ten women whose tales
are actually told are all martyrs or quasi martyrs. Not even Alcestis is included: she was only a temporary martyr, for she was
restored to life (see F 513–516).

It is clear, though, that Chaucer originally intended to tell tales
principally of women like Alcestis. When he first sees her, without knowing who she is, he composes a ballade in her honor. In
it he says she surpasses the attributes of two men (namely, the
golden hair of Absalom and the friendly manner of Jonathan) and
those of eighteen women: the meekness of Esther; the wifeliness
of Penelope and Marcia; the beauty of Isolde, Helen, and Lavinia;
the fidelity and fame of Lucretia, Polyxena, Cleopatra, and
Thisbe; and the fidelity of Hero, Dido, Laodamia, Phyllis, Canace,
Hypsipyle, Hypermnestra, and Ariadne:

> Hyd, Absolon, thy gilte tresses clere;
> Ester, ley thou thy meknesse al adown;

14. Technically, only men were termed confessors in the Church's liturgy.
If a woman saint was neither a virgin nor a martyr, she was simply designated as *nec virgo nec martyr,* unless she could be termed a penitent, a
widow, or a queen.

> Hyd, Jonathas, al thy frendly manere;
> Penalopee and Marcia Catoun,
> Make of youre wifhod no comparysoun;
> Hyde ye youre beautes, Ysoude and Eleyne:
> My lady cometh, that al this may disteyne.
>   Thy faire body, lat yt nat appere,
> Lavyne; and thou, Lucresse of Rome toun,
> And Polixene, that boghten love so dere,
> And Cleopatre, with al thy passyoun,
> Hyde ye your trouthe of love and your renoun;
> And thou, Tisbe, that hast for love swich peyne:
> My lady cometh, that al this may disteyne.
>   Herro, Dido, Laudomia, alle yfere,
> And Phillis, hangyng for thy Demophoun,
> And Canace, espied by thy chere,
> Ysiphile, betrayed with Jasoun,
> Maketh of your trouthe neythir boost ne soun;
> Nor Ypermystre or Adriane, ye tweyne:
> My lady cometh, that al this may dysteyne.   [F 249–269]

Of the twelve ladies praised for their "trouthe," Chaucer implies that most or all of them suffered in maintaining it; but the primary accent is on faithfulness, not suffering. All nineteen ladies, including Alcestis, are later said to have been true in love (how true this is will be discussed later), and all are to be included in Chaucer's legend (F 283, 554–561).

The God of Love describes Alcestis as being so charitable and true that he has found no one else like her (F 442–446); she is the model and guide

> To any woman that wol lover bee,
> For she taught al the craft of fyn lovynge,
> And namely of wyfhod the lyvynge,
> And all the boundes that she oghte kepe.   [F 543–546]

Once again, then, the emphasis is on fidelity, especially marital fidelity, and not on martyrdom.

In the expanded version of the Prologue, the God of Love describes the sort of good and true women whose stories are contained in Chaucer's sixty books. To the two classes of clean maidens and true wives he adds a third, steadfast widows, described by "Jerome agayns Jovynyan." They were so true to their love that they preferred to suffer and die rather than to take a new love or be false;

> For alle keped they here maydenhede,
> Or elles wedlok, or here widewehede.   [G 294–295]

It would seem that Love is now talking about a different sort of club than is indicated by the ballade. For example, without serious adjustment, Helen and Isolde would certainly be excluded for having broken wedlock, as would Ariadne for her remarriage to Bacchus. Dido was not a steadfast widow; and Hero lost her maidenhood before she was able to become a wife, as did Phyllis. It is quite clear that these and most of the others were not acting primarily from the motive that Love gives them, namely, "verray vertu and clennesse," or that they "were so sore adrad of alle shame" that they preserved their reputation even at the price of their lives (G 297–301).

The Two Standards: Jerome and Ovid

The problem, of course, is that Chaucer has assembled his good women together under two completely different and sometimes contradictory criteria, one upheld by St. Jerome and the other by Ovid. The Hieronymian canon of conduct consists in the avoidance of "dishonorable" sex at all costs. The Ovidian requirement "of trewe wives and of here labour" (G 306) is to suffer greatly for love. The first involves fidelity to the abstract ideal of chastity; the second, fidelity to one's beloved. The two notably coincide when a wife's virtue is forced (Lucretia) or solicited (Penelope), or when a widow refuses to remarry (Marcia), or when a maiden preserves her virginity from attack out of love for her intended husband. No example of this last category occurs in the ballade; but Hermione, listed in *The Man of Law's Tale*, comes close to it.

The presence of "Marcia Catoun" in the ballade shows that Chaucer had Jerome's criterion in mind at the beginning as well as at the end of his project. But in the finished tales it is Ovid's standard that won out, at least ostensibly. Only Philomela suffers for chastity alone and not because of love for a man. Lucretia, as Ovid presents her in the *Fasti*, comes nearer to Jerome's ideal than to that of the *Heroides*, but Chaucer brings her closer to the latter by making her as concerned for her husband's name as for her own (1844–1846).

On the other side, however, many of Ovid's martyrs for love are brought closer to the Hieronymian norm. Hypermnestra, of course, is above reproach as she is. It is true that she does not suffer in defending her chastity, but she suffers for saving her husband's life. Thisbe is a combination of virgin and widow. She is not married to Pyramus, but she wishes to be; and when he dies, she kills herself. In so doing she resembles Porcia, whom Jerome praises because she was a virgin when Brutus married her, and she was unable to live without him. He contrasts her with Marcia, the wife of Cato Uticensis: she was not a virgin when she married Cato, and she could live without him; in fact, after bearing Cato's children, she agreed to do the same for another man, Hortensius, and went to live with him; after his death, she returned to Cato.[15] Just before this, Jerome praised Cato's *daughter* Marcia for refusing to remarry when her husband died (she, of course is the Marcia that Chaucer refers to in his ballade).

Cleopatra, the only non-Ovidian heroine in the *Legend*, has been adjusted to fit the Porcian model of virtuous widowhood. While Antony is roundly condemned for leaving his first wife, no mention is made of Cleopatra's previous alliances. Chaucer makes much of the fact that Antony and Cleopatra actually got married, a circumstance he would have found in Vincent of Beauvais's *Speculum historiale*, which the God of Love recommends to him as a source (G 307).[16] He treats the union as a true marriage, tacitly accepting the pagan ethic on the question. After Antony lost his honor, he despaired, went mad, and killed himself. Cleopatra thereupon killed herself out of love for him, to fulfill the marriage covenant she had made with him:

15. Jerome, *Adversus Iovinianum* 1.46 (PL 23.288): "Brutus Porciam virginem duxit uxorem; Marciam Cato non virginem; sed Marcia inter Hortensium Catonemque discurrit, et sine Catone vivere Marcia potuit; Porcia sine Bruto non potuit."

16. Vincent, *Speculum historiale* 6.53 (Douai 1624, repr. Graz 1965) 190, says simply: "Porro cum esset lascivus Antonius correptus amore Cleopatrae Aegypti reginae, repudiata Augusti sorore, ipsam sibi Cleopatram matrimonio copulavit."

> Now, love, to whom my sorweful herte obeyde
> So ferforthly that from that blisful houre
> That I yow swor to ben al frely youre—
> I mene yow, Antonius, my knyght—
> That nevere wakynge, in the day or nyght,
> Ye nere out of myn hertes remembraunce,
> For wel or wo, for carole or for daunce;
> And in myself this covenaunt made I tho,
> That ryght swich as ye felten, wel or wo,
> As fer forth as it in my power lay,
> Unreprovable unto my wyfhod ay,
> The same woulde I fele, lyf or deth—
> And thilke covenant, whil me lasteth breth,
> I wol fulfille; and that shal ben wel sene,
> Was nevere unto hir love a trewer quene.   [681–695]

The liturgical marriage contract in use in Chaucer's day obligated the wife to obey and serve her husband whether he is sound or sick, and to adhere to him while the life of both of them should last,[17] or, in the vernacular: "to have and to hold from this day forward, for better, for worse, for richer, for poorer, in sickness and in heal, to be bonner [meek] and buxom [obedient] in bed and at board, till death us depart."[18] Cleopatra went farther in her agreement: she would experience all that Antony did, for better or for worse, in life or in death.

Antony is not praised at the end of Cleopatra's legend. Although he "set all the world at no value" for her love (599–602), he did not die for it, as she did for his; and Chaucer expresses his skepticism at being able to find a man like her:

> Now, or I fynde a man thus trewe and stable,
> And wol for love his deth so frely take,
> I preye God let oure hedes nevere ake!   [703–705]

17. *Manuale ad usum percelebris ecclesie sarisburiensis* (Sarum Manual), ed. A. Jeffries Collins, Henry Bradshaw Society 91 (London 1960) 47: "Vis habere hunc virum in sponsum et ei oboedire et servire et eum diligere, honorare, et custodire sanum et infirmum sicut sponsa debet sponsum, et omnes alios propter eum dimittere et illi soli adhaerere quamdiu vita utriusque vestrum duraverit?" The bride answers, "Volo." This edition of the Manual is based on that of Rouen 1543 but is collated with fourteenth-century manuscripts.
18. *Ibid.* 48.

He is forced to qualify this judgment somewhat in the very next legend, where Pyramus kills himself for love of Thisbe:

> Of trewe men I fynde but fewe mo
> In alle my bokes, save this Piramus,
> And therfore have I spoken on hym thus.[19]   [917–919]

In none of the remaining tales is there to be found a man worth his salt, with the pale exception of Collatinus, Lucretia's husband. Even Lynceus, the husband Hypermnestra saved, is to be blamed for not taking her with him when he escaped from her father (2716–2722).[20] Of the other men, we have alluded to the two rapists, Tarquin and Tereus, in discussing their victims; now we must consider the plights of five women abandoned by their seducers.

The lives and deaths of these ladies—Dido, Hypsipyle, Medea, Ariadne, and Phyllis—were taken directly from the *Heroides*, but they could be reconciled with Jerome's ideal as well by making them virtuous in their dereliction. Hypsipyle and Phyllis, of course, presented no problem. For the former, Chaucer tones down her final curse against Medea, and concludes:

> And trewe to Jason was she al hire lyf,
> And evere kepte hire chast, as for his wif;
> Ne nevere hadde she joye at hire hert,
> But deyede, for his love, of sorowes smerte.   [1576–1579]

Phyllis's sorrow and despair at Demophoon's infidelity led her to suicide; in a sense, then, she is like Porcia, who cannot live without her husband. In Ovid, she wishes that she had remained *honesta* and not given Demophoon, though he promised to marry her, the rights of the marriage bed; and she complains that her countrymen will now scorn to marry her because she preferred a stranger (*Heroides* 2.57–60, 81–82). In Chaucer there is none of

---

19. Earlier he is a bit unjust to Pyramus, when he regrets that Thisbe "wolde ben so trewe / To truste man, but she the bet hym knewe" (799–801).

20. The legend breaks off before the conclusion to this can be drawn, but it was obviously to be a variation on the theme that women are better than men.

this, for we are to assume that she is actually married to Demophoon.[21]

Clandestine marriages are also arranged for Medea, Ariadne, and Dido. Chaucer ends the account of Medea by telling of her sorrowful rebukes against Jason, with no word of her revenge.[22] He omits all hint of Ariadne's second marriage.[23] He does say that Dido had once been the wife of Sychaeus (1005), but he omits her lamentations of infidelity to his memory, which both Virgil and Ovid make much of.[24]

The Unsung Heroines

Why did Chaucer not finish his accounts of the good ladies he had singled out? There was certainly no moral problem with Alcestis, Penelope, and Laodamia, for they were heroines praised by Jerome as well as by Ovid.[25] The well-meaning Deianira too could have been taken over intact. Hero and even Briseis could easily have been Hieronymized by means of secret marriages. Canace's morals, however, could have been rectified only by making her a cousin rather than a sister of Macareus. In the case of Hypermnestra, who married her first cousin, Chaucer was careful to point out that before the time of Christ no collateral degree of kinship beyond the immediate family created an impediment to marriage: "For thilke tyme was spared no lynage" (2602). But he apparently decided that the brother-sister incest was too central to the story to be ignored.

Of all the Ovidian heroines that Chaucer proposed to write about and did not, the most interesting is Hermione. For she and Orestes are an example of those lovers that Pandarus speaks about in the *Troilus:*

21. See below, Chap. 8.
22. See above, "Ovid as Mother Lode."
23. See above, n. 4.
24. See above, Chap. 3, and below, Chap. 8. Jerome, *Adv. Iov.* 1.43 (286) gives the account later followed by the "reformed" Boccaccio in his *De claris mulieribus:* she died upon a pyre constructed in honor of Sychaeus rather than marry the King of Libya. He wittily inverts St. Paul's dictum by saying that she considered it better to burn than to marry: "Maluit ardere quam nubere."
25. Jerome, *Adv. Iov.* 1.45 (287).

> How don this folk that seen hire loves wedded
> By frendes myght, as it bitit ful ofte,
> And sen hem in hire spouses bed ybedded?
> God woot, they take it wisly, faire, and softe,
> Forwhi good hope halt up hire herte o-lofte.
> And, for they kan a tyme of sorwe endure,
> As tyme hem hurt, a tyme doth hem cure.   [5.344–350]

The sort of complaisant attitude that Pandarus approves of here would not, of course, have been acceptable to Troilus, as it was not to Hermione, and would not be to Juliet, when her parents, unaware of her secret marriage to Romeo, set about to marry her to Paris. It is unfortunate that Chaucer did not get around to analyzing the dilemma from the strict moral viewpoint propounded in the *Legend*. Similar opportunities existed in the story of Briseis and also in that of Isolde, for Tristan fell in love with her and she with him before she was married to his uncle Mark.[26]

Once we stop talking about the protagonists of Ovid's *Heroides*, there is sometimes an obvious reason why Chaucer did not compose certain of the legends. It is a reason that holds true even for Alcestis, whose story above all he was solemnly commissioned to write:

> But now I charge the, upon thy lyf,
> That in thy legende thou make of this wyf,
> Whan thou hast other smale ymaad before.   [F 548–550]

Chaucer could not very well have told her story after all the others, because the God of Love had already told almost all there is to tell. All the known sources of the story are extremely scanty,[27] and to expand it Chaucer would have had to exercise more invention and imagination that he seemed prepared to do. The same is true of Cato's daughter Marcia. Chaucer could hardly have known more about her than the two anecdotes told by Jerome: when asked, after the death of her husband, why she did not

---

26. See Gower, *Confessio amantis* 6.470–475.

27. Chaucer could have used Hyginus, *Fables* 51, and Boccaccio, *De genealogia deorum* 13.1, but he gives his source as "Agaton," referring to Agatho, the host of the symposium at which Phaedrus tells the story of Alcestis (Plato, *Symposium* 179BC). He would not, of course, have had access to Plato's work or to Euripides's *Alcestis*. John Gower gives a short version of the story in *Confessio amantis* 7.1917–1943.

remarry, she answered that she could not find a man who preferred her to her possessions; and when asked what day she had
decided upon to end her formal mourning for her husband, she
responded, "The day I die." The moral Jerome draws from this is
that a woman who so missed her first husband would not think of
remarrying.[28] Marcia's first answer, however, with its suggestion
that she would indeed remarry if only she could find a suitable
husband, could easily temper one's estimation of her grief. One
could even surmise that, like that other widow in mourning garb,
Criseyde, she was simply happy to be free and did not relish the
idea of another husband saying "Checkmate" to her.[29]

Esther, of course, had a whole book of the Bible devoted to her,
and Jerome doubtless would have approved of her. But it is hard
to see how she suffered for her fidelity to her husband. In all
probability her appearance in the ballade was originally no more
significant than that of Absalom and Jonathan; that is, she was
simply being singled out for her outstanding meekness, as Absalom
was for his celebrated golden hair, and Jonathan for his friendli-
ness. Similarly, Lavinia is noticed for her fair body. But what has
she to offer in the matter of love and fidelity? In the *Aeneid* we
are never told of her feelings either for Turnus or for Aeneas, nor
is her opinion sought.[30] Worse still, Ovid in the *Fasti* portrays her
as overcome with a homicidal jealousy when Aeneas asks her to
show hospitality to Dido's sister Anna (3.629 ff.).

Likewise, it would be logical to conclude that the adulterous
Isolde and Helen are given a place in the ballade because of their
beauty alone were it not for the fact that the Man of Law says
that the *Legend* tells of the tears of Helen. Helen weeps for a

28. Jerome, *Adv. Iov.* 1.46 (288): "Marcia, Catonis filia minor, cum
quaereretur ab ea cur post amissum maritum denuo non nuberet, respondit
non se invenire virum qui se magis vellet quam sua. . . . Eadem cum
lugeret virum, et matronae ab ea quaererent quem diem haberet luctus
ultimum, ait, 'Quem et vitae.' Arbitror, quae ita virum quaerebat absentem,
de secundo matrimonio non cogitabat."

29. See above, Chap. 2.

30. *Aeneid* 7.55ff., 91ff., 259ff., 359ff. Later, she blushes at the mention of
her two claimants (12.64–69). The twelfth-century French romance of
Eneas does go on at great length about Lavinia's love for Aeneas and her
faithfulness to him (though it says nothing of her fair body), but there is
no indication that Chaucer was familiar with it.

good many pages in the accounts that two of Chaucer's authors give of her, namely Benoit of Sainte Maure and Guido of Le Colonne. Perhaps Chaucer toyed with the idea of rehabilitating her like Cleopatra, by describing her devotion to Paris without mentioning her first husband. If so, he must eventually have realized the implausibility of the idea. Apart from the fact that her union with Menelaus both before and after her years as Paris's wife was notorious, he would be left with little to write about.

Helen's first seizure of tears comes when she has almost reached Troy: she begins to weep uncontrollably at the thought of having left her husband, brothers, daughter, and people behind. Paris tries to console her without success. He promises to marry her, and she says that she must accept whether she wishes to or not. When they do marry, on the day after their arrival, it is done with great joy, in which Helen presumably participates.[31] Later, during the war, after a fierce battle between Paris and Menelaus, Hector praises the prowess of her two husbands ("voz dous seignors") and says it was fortunate that she was not present, for she would have experienced great fear if she loved them at all ("se vos de rien les amisseiz"). Helen replies that even though she did not see it, she has great fear of some mishap. With that she bursts into tears: "Adonc plorerent si dui ueil."[32] When Paris is killed, she laments and weeps at great length, accusing herself of being the cause of his death and of all the other bloodshed of the war.[33] It is only when she weeps at Hector's death that the theme of her two husbands is not in the forefront.[34]

31. Benoit de Sainte-Maure, *Le roman de Troie* 4639–4865, ed. Léopold Constans, SATF (Paris 1904–1912); cf. Guido de Columnis, *Historia destructionis Troiae* 7, ed. Nathaniel Edward Griffin, Mediaeval Academy of America Publications 26 (Cambridge, Mass., 1936, repr. New York 1970) 76–79. For a good analysis of the love stories in Benoit, see Rosemarie Jones, *The Theme of Love in the "Romans d'antiquité,"* Modern Humanites Research Association Dissertation Series 5 (London 1972) 43–58.

32. Benoit 11740–11752. That she wept with both eyes was no doubt a great testimony to her sincerity, for according to Benoit, when speaking of Briseida (the prototype of Criseyde) as she leaves Troy and Troilus, women who mourn weep with one eye and laugh with the other: "A femme dure dueus petit: / A l'un ueil plore, a l'autre rit" (13441–13442).

33. Benoit 22915ff.
34. Benoit 16484ff.

Polyxena, the only other of Chaucer's potentially good women that we have not yet discussed, is praised as one "that boughten love so dere." She has a curiously fragmented story in Benoit and Guido. Achilles falls in love with her without her knowledge and starts to treat for her hand. The first indication of her feelings is given when Achilles resumes fighting, thereby breaking off negotiations. This news, Benoit says, was not welcome to her, for the prospect of becoming Achilles's wife had very much pleased her.[35] Later, Hecuba encompasses Achilles's death by using Polyxena as the unconscious bait. When he is buried, a statue resembling Polyxena is placed on his tomb, and she is secretly much grieved and angry about it, since he died because of her. But she is wise and keeps her feelings to herself.[36]

Benoit's account of Polyxena's death goes back to Ovid. After the Greek victory, according to the *Metamorphoses*, she is sacrificed to appease the shade of Achilles. But she is not told that she is to die because of Achilles. Before she is killed, she speaks of her noble blood, and asks that no man touch her virgin body (13.450–469). In Benoit, Polyxena knows that she is to die because of Achilles, but she makes no reference to him. She simply says that though she does not deserve such a death, after the death of her father and brothers she has no desire to live. She takes consolation in that no child will be born of her to bastardize the lineages of which she is descended. She will not refuse her destiny; she will die with her virginity, and she dedicates her maidenhood to death.[37] In so doing, she has almost become a virgin heroine of the Hieronymian stamp: one who dies not for love but for her virginity. Guido moves her further in this direction: though she excuses herself explicitly of Achilles's death and says that she greatly lamented it, she also expresses her grief over the fact that the Greek kings and princes would allow an innocent virgin to perish in this way. Not that she has an abhorrence of death, she says, since life would now be harder to bear than death; for if she lived, she, a virgin of such great nobility, would thereby allow her maidenhead to be illicitly broken, and would suffer the untouched

35. Benoit 21227–21233; cf. Guido 26 (203).
36. Benoit 22435–22460.
37. Benoit 26475–26523.

purity of her chastity to be defiled by the hands of those less noble than she.[38] She willingly embraces death while still a virgin, she adds, and willingly sacrifices her virginity to all the gods and to death itself.

According to Chaucer's sources, then, Polyxena purchased her love dearly mainly in the sense that Achilles's love for her was the cause of her death. But it would not have been difficult for Chaucer to have transfused her with a passion similar to her lover's, and to expand upon her grief at his death (of which, like Deianira, she was the unwitting cause) and make her rejoice that she preserved her maidenhood in his memory.

Enhanced Morality, Heightened Dullness

Chaucer's original goal was to praise the kind of fidelity exemplified by the noble wives Penelope and Alcestis. To put his plan into action, he turned to two champions of married love, Publius Ovidius Naso, *magister amoris*, and Eusebius Hieronymus, *doctor ecclesiae*. In their natural state these two authors would make strange bedfellows indeed. But by combining Ovid's passion with Jerome's moral rigor Chaucer yokes them together (to use a conjugal metaphor) into a viable union—though with sacrifice on both sides. For although Ovid considered marriage to be the ideal medium of love in ideal circumstances, he by no means regarded it as an essential requirement for the exercise of love. And though Jerome admired faithful wives, he had scarcely any sympathy for love that went beyond mere loyalty. For him, love between man and woman was to be endured, not enjoyed, and was to be avoided if at all possible. If he praised wives, it was not with a

38. Guido 30 (236): "Polyxena autem, ante Achillis tumulum constituta, de morte Achillis verbis humilibus se plurimum excusavit; immo de morte eius dixit se nimium doluisse, et [etiam dolere] quod reges et principes Graecorum virginem innocentem contra iustitiam patiuntur sine culpa perire; non quod mortem abhorreat, cum vita eius esset satis durior morte sua, ut tantae nobilitatis virgo suae virginitatis claustra illicite disrumpi permitteret et sui pudoris integram puritatem pateretur per manus minus se nobilium deturpari." As is evident from the clause "cum vita eius esset satis durior morte sua," Guido uses *eius* as well as *suus* reflexively. When Polyxena says, then, that she had lamented *de morte eius* she could be referring to her own future death, were it not for the past tense of *doluisse* and the adversative force of *immo*.

view to encouraging marriage but in order to reprehend remarriage. He is fundamentally not only a misogamist, but a misogynist as well. His treatise against Jovinian was one of the great source books for medieval antifeminism. Chaucer too used it for this purpose, but only in his humorous works.

When all is said, however, it must be confessed that Chaucer's moralized Ovid, or romanticized Jerome, is disappointing. The characters are stiff and uninteresting, and the ceaselessly plaintive tone is oppressive. One of the reasons for this monotony is, of course, his excessive dependence on the *Heroides*. The lamentations of Ovid's unfortunate heroines tended to be repetitive because, as we saw, they dealt for the most part with the disastrous aftermath of love, and not with love in the making. Though Chaucer is free to tell his stories from the beginning and does so, the incubus of catastrophe rarely allows the action to leave the ground.

Chaucer's legends also suffer from the Ovidian and medieval failing of preferring quantity to quality, of producing many short and perfunctory variations on a theme instead of one or two carefully chosen and finely wrought examples. Chaucer seldom rises above his sources in this work as he did in the *Troilus*, by inventing new episodes and not merely revising the characters but radically expanding them. Instead, he departed from the sources, if at all, chiefly by way of omission and minor adjustment of unsuitable passages. Cleopatra's recollection of her marriage to Antony is a rare instance of what he could do when he wished to rely on his own genius.

Moreover, the restrictions placed upon him by the queen (Queen Alcestis or possibly even Queen Anne, Richard II's first wife)[39] almost insured that the characters would be dull. He was to write only about good women, thus giving the impression that all women are "infallible." The corollary that almost all men are traitorous knaves is just as deadly for dramatic interest. Both Ovid and Chaucer rob Dido's story of its power by failing to show her faults and Aeneas's virtues. There is no hesitation or temptation, no real decisions and no suspense. In *The House of Fame* Chaucer

39. The completed *Legend* was to be given to Queen Anne on behalf of Queen Alcestis (F 496–497).

did, at least as an afterthought, admit that there were mitigating circumstances for Aeneas's betrayal (427–432), but in the *Legend* even this small concession to human complexity is omitted.

However, even though the tales of good women that Chaucer tells are lacking in narrative power, they are extremely interesting in showing us the sort of moral bias that he brought to his authorities and the methods he used in bringing the stories up to his standards of behavior. We must remember, of course, that Chaucer imposed this task upon himself with a certain amount of mock seriousness, and that the legends are no doubt meant to reflect the irony of the Prologue to a certain extent. The dullness is deliberate, and, in the case of a virtuous Cleopatra and Medea, amusing. But nevertheless he is fundamentally sincere in his support of the morality they are made to expound.

If, then, the *Troilus* helps us understand why the legends fail to hold our interest on their own aesthetic and dramatic grounds, the legends reveal to us the ethical principles and methods that transformed Boccaccio's *Filostrato* into a truly great romance. In the Prologue to the *Legend*, as we saw, Chaucer said that his purpose in writing the *Troilus* was to encourage lovers to remain true to each other, and to beware of falseness and vice. In the *Troilus* itself he spoke badly of Diomede, who was deliberately false, but not of Criseyde, who fell through weakness. Both characters, however, served to enforce the warning against falsity and vice. The lesson was all the more impressive because Criseyde, like Troilus, was so completely honorable before she fell.

Of the means used in *The Legend of Good Women* to purify characters of doubtful antecedents, the most important for the *Troilus* is that of clandestine marriage, which will be studied later in detail. We shall find that the *Legend* provides us with a great deal of insight into the theory and practice of marriage in the Middle Ages.

Chapter 5

John Gower: Confessions of a Penitent Lover

Lust Interspersed with Lore

Chaucer's legends of good women were written in fulfillment of the penance given him by Queen Alcestis and were to be delivered to Queen Anne. A year or two after he set about this task, King Richard commissioned Chaucer's friend John Gower to "book" some new things that he could examine himself.[1] Gower decided on a *via media* between *placere* and *docere*, which would combine the *dolce* with the *utile:*

> I wolde go the middel weie
> And write a bok betwen the tweie,
> Somwhat of lust, somwhat of lore. [17–19]

Like Chaucer he decided to give his work a penitential setting. Rather than make the body of his work the result of an encounter with a confessor, however, Gower chose to prolong the encounter or act of confession itself. He too experiences a vision[2] of the God-King of Love. But the queen who appears to him is Venus, and she instructs him to go to confession to her priest Genius. He is to detail all of his sins, both in thought and in deed, as the confessor prods his conscience; and he is also to tell of all the happiness and sorrow he has experienced in love (1.138–211). He is to

1. John Gower, *Confessio amantis* Prologue 48*–53*, ed. G. C. Macaulay, EETSes 81–82 (London 1900–1901, repr. 1969). The asterisked lines appear only in the first recension (ca. 1386–1390), and not in the second (1390–1392) or third (1393).
2. It is not a dream in the strict sense, since it occurs after he wakes from a sorrowful swoon (1.121).

be examined and instructed first according to the five senses, and then according to the seven deadly vices and their subdivisions. At the end, he is absolved and given a form of penance which also is to function as a remedy against relapse.

In all of his major works except *The Canterbury Tales,* Chaucer casts himself as an interested spectator and admirer of the servants of love, but one whose personality and appearance are so ludicrous that he would have no hope of participating in a love affair himself. Gower also pictures himself basically as a no-hoper, but one who does not realize the hopelessness of his situation. He is still a would-be lover and will not learn until the end of his confession that love is not for him.[3] Chaucer assumes his humorous guise immediately and never steps out of it. But Gower not only supplies a straightforward prologue and epilogue to his work, in which he speaks in his own highly moralistic voice, but he also makes his real presence felt in the course of the poem, especially in Latin verses and sidenotes. He is in touch with his audience almost as much as George Bernard Shaw in the published versions of his plays, with their long introductions and expansive stage directions. To make clear to his readers what he is doing when he appears as a character in his work, Gower attaches this explanation: "Here as if in the person of others who are bound by love, the author pretends to be a lover, and sets about to write of their various passions one by one according to the various distinctions of this book.[4]

Gower's project, which he not only brought to completion but revised at least twice, was on a much larger scale than Chaucer's *Legend.* Apart from lengthy discourses and dialogues, approximately 150 stories or extended examples are offered by Genius to illustrate his points. Ovid is the source of one-fourth of these exempla. Only half of all the tales deal with love, however, and of

---

3. Even Ovid in the *Amores* is slightly foolish and self-depreciating in his self-characterization as a lover. Although he has a certain amount of success, he has frequent failures as well. We may also think of the general lack of success of the men in Andrew the Chaplain's dialogues.

4. *Confessio* 1.62 sidenote: "Hic quasi in persona aliorum quos amor alligat, fingens se auctor esse amantem, varias eorum passiones variis huius libri distinctionibus per singula scribere proponit."

these Ovid supplies two-fifths.[5] Clearly, then, for Gower as for Chaucer, Ovid was the great authority on love.

Trouthe and the Matrimonial Bond

Chaucer's intention in the *Troilus* and in the *Legend* was to encourage "trouthe" in lovers. It soon appears that this is also one of Genius's cardinal precepts:

> Mi sone, it sit wel every wiht
> To kepe his word in trowthe upryht
> Towardes love in alle wise.   [1.745–747]

He is warning against hypocrisy, the first subdivision of the first vice, pride; and his point is that deceit should not be employed to win love. He illustrates this principle with the story of Paulina, a married woman famous for her chastity, *castitatis famosissima*, and her seduction by Duke Mundus, who poses as a god. When she discovers his real identity, she exposes him to her husband, who turns him over to the authorities. The duke pleads love in extenuation of his "horrible sinne," and his punishment is accordingly commuted from death to exile:

> For he with love was bestad,
> His dom was noght so harde lad.   [1049–1050]

His exile is to be permanent, however, because of his deceit:

> For he his love hath so beguiled,
> That he schal nevere come ayein;
> For who that is to trowthe unplein,
> He may noght failen of vengance.   [1056–1059]

---

5. According to my count (which could no doubt be challenged in details), Genius sets forth 147 exempla, 73 of which deal with love or the lack of it. Ovid is the source for 38 stories out of the total, and for 29 of the love stories. I have not taken into consideration simple one-line references to exempla, nor summary accounts of only three or four lines. John H. Fisher, *John Gower: Moral Philosopher and Friend of Chaucer* (New York 1964) 188, seems to find a total of 172 stories (including repetitions), 72 of which deal with love. There is, however, a discrepancy in his figures: he has a total of 141 stories, not counting overlappings or repetitions; 15 stories overlap, and he counts them twice in his subtotals, which should add up to 156, whereas in fact they add up to 147. Derek Pearsall in his pamphlet *Gower and Lydgate*, Writers and Their Work 211, ed. Geoffrey Bullough (London 1969) 17, counts 133 stories in the *Confessio*.

The Middle English word "trewe," like the modern "true," has basically two meanings: the first entails the *doing or saying of what is true*, that is, consonant with fact; the second involves the state or quality of *being true*, that is, faithful to one's promise or duty. The substantive "trouthe," or "trowthe," also contains both of these meanings, but in modern English the word has split in two: "truth" bears only the first meaning, while the now rather antique "troth" has only the second meaning. The story of Paulina, "which alle trowthe weneth," and Mundus, "that alle untrowthe meneth" (925–926), might seem, at first sight, to illustrate only the violation of truth, not troth. No troth is pledged in the story except by the priests of the temple (822), and they keep it, to their shame.

In the case of most of Chaucer's villains in the *Legend*, the two meanings are clearly merged: they were not telling the truth when they pledged their troth. Criseyde, however, both spoke truly and was true to Troilus at first: "Hire herte trewe was and kynde / Towardes hym, and spak right as she mente" (4.1417–1418). Later, in the Greek camp, she began to speak untruths in denying that she was in love with anyone. This would have been permissible to her code of honor if her only purpose was to keep her love for Troilus secret; but it was reprehensible in that it opened the way to her *becoming* untrue to him. According to some critics, Troilus and Pandarus are meant to be considered culpable for the deceits and untruths they resort to to win Criseyde over in the first place. When Genius warns,

> To love is every herte fre,
> Bot in deceipte if that thou feignest
> And therupon thi lust atteignest,
> That thow hast wonne with thi wyle,
> Thogh it thee like for a whyle,
> Thou schalt it afterward repent,   [752–757]

can we not think of Troilus? Perhaps; but Genius is primarily denouncing the hypocritical and treacherous seducer:

> There ben lovers of such a sort
> That feignen hem an humble port,
> And al is bot ypocrisie,

> Which with deceipte and flaterie
> Hath many a worthi wif beguiled.   [673–677]

This description makes us think of Diomede rather than Troilus;
for Diomede is basically untrue, like Genius's hypocrite:

> For if he may have his desir
> How so falle of the remenant,
> He halt no word of covenant.   [684–686]

Troilus's untruths were pardonable since they were dictated by
his basic troth: "he mente trouthe" (2.665);[6] and Criseyde was
grateful for being thus deceived.

Troilus and Pandarus, then, could speak untruly while remaining
true. But it is obvious that such is not true of Duke Mundus: he
is not only lacking in truth but in troth as well, in the wider sense
of fidelity to one's duty as well as to one's love. Apart from the
implication that Mundus did not have any permanent commitment
to Paulina, or even any long-range plans, he was also being untrue
to the institution of marriage and untrue to Paulina in making her
violate the troth whereby she betrothed herself to her husband.
His crime goes deeper still: the full implication of her attitude of
"weening all trouthe" can be gathered from the kindred words
"trust" and "trow" (as, "I trow in God"); Mundus captured her
by resorting to sacrilege and betraying her religious belief and
trust.

When she discovers how she has been beguiled, Paulina says to
her husband:

> Helas, wifhode is lore
> In me, which whilom was honeste;[7]
> I am non other than a beste,
> Now I defouled am of tuo.   [974–977]

We shall study later the implications of her statement that she is
now befouled by two men (including, therefore, her husband).[8]
But the point I wish to make here is that fidelity in marriage is

---

6. Cf. Acontius's justification of his deceit, above, Chap. 3.
7. Cf. 868: "sche, which was al honeste."
8. Below, in the section "John's Status as a Lover," where virginity is
placed above marriage.

always commended over adultery throughout the poem both by
Genius and by John Gower, whether in his character of the lover
or *amans*, or in his own authorial person (to distinguish between
the two, I shall call the first "John," as Venus does,[9] and the second "Gower").

In Paulina's case, her marriage was violated without her knowledge or consent, but in the more usual kind of "spousebreach"
one of the spouses initiates or connives at the adultery. For instance, in the case of Aegisthus and Clytemnestra, the guilt is
mutual. When Genius says of the latter,

> She was thereof gretli to blame,
> To love there it mai noght laste,   [3.1910–1911]

the reason he gives (that is, that such love cannot last) appears,
in the context, to be a great understatement, when we consider
the terrible way in which her love ended. But if we realize the
importance of the general principle that love must be intended to
last forever, his logic will not seem misplaced.[10] However "good"
their intentions were to be true to each other, Clytemnestra and
Aegisthus could not have expected their love to last because they
committed crimes to achieve it and preserve it. By one assent,
they treacherously killed Agamemnon in his bed;

> But moerdre, which mai noght ben hedd,
> Sprong out to every mannes ere,
> Wherof the lond was full of fere.   [1920–1922]

Orestes secures the support of Phoeius, Aegisthus's former
father-in-law, who tells him

> How that Egiste in mariage
> His dowhter whilom of ful age
> Forlai, and afterward forsok,
> Whan he Horestes moder tok.
> Men sein, "Old senne, new schame":
> Thus more and more aros the blame
> Ayein Egiste on every side.   [2029–2035]

Orestes is acquitted of the guilt of matricide because Clytemnestra

---

9. *Confessio* 8.2322; in line 2908, however, she uses his full name.
10. See below, Chap. 12, in the section "Communion over Coitus."

deserved to die at the hand of her son, first of all for her adultery
and then for the "mariticide" that followed from it:

> Sche hadde wel deserved wreche,
> Ferst for the cause of spousebreche,
> And after wroghte in such a wise
> That al the world it oghte agrise,
> Whan that sche for so foul a vice
> Was of hire oghne lord moerdrice.   [2157–2162]

Adultery can never be knowingly committed without violation
of marriage troth. But, of course, troth can be pledged between
lovers before marriage, or without thought of marriage. However,
the "honest love" that leads to marriage or finds its consummation
in marriage is naturally commended over fornication in the *Confessio*. This teaching becomes most explicit in the discussion that
follows upon the tale of Rosiphilee, the girl who refuses to love
until she has a vision of the afterlife; she sees the happy condition
of women who have loved and the sad lot of one who refused to
do so (4.1240–1446). The lesson that Genius immediately draws
from this tale is that idleness should be avoided and one's time
taken up with love:

> Love is an occupacion
> Which forto kepe hise lustes save
> Scholde every gentil herte have.   [1452–1454]

By "keeping safe" one's desires or pleasures, Genius no doubt
means "insuring happiness." At this point, Gower intervenes for
the second and last time in his work to make it clear that the
sentiments expressed in the poem are not necessarily to be taken
literally. As at the beginning of the first book he said that he was
only pretending to be a lover swayed by various passions, so here
he tells us not to accept Genius's postulate as the truth, but as the
opinion of lovers: "Non quia sic se habet veritas, sed opinio
amantum."

With the warning in mind that love between man and woman
is not an essential requirement for beatitude, let us examine
Genius's further instruction. He says that if any woman wishes to
deserve Venus's "thonk" (goodwill),

> Sche mai noght thilke love eschuie
> Of paramours, bot sche mot suie
> Cupides lawe. [1469–1471]

He is distinguishing love of paramours here from love that is aimed at marriage, a distinction which, as we saw, is not found in Chaucer.[11] It has naturally been thought by proponents of the theory of courtly love that, according to the law of Cupid, love must be illicit. But Cupid as well as Venus is quite indifferent to whether love is marital or not, as is obvious from the original reaction of these gods to Rosiphilee's lack of interest in love:

> For they merveille how such a wiht,
> Which tho was in hir lusti age,
> Desireth nother mariage
> Ne yit the love of paramours,
> Which evere hath be the comun cours
> Amonges hem that lusti were. [1266–1271]

After Cupid shows her the results of sloth in love, she becomes more diligent than all others in fulfilling her duty to love ("in amoris obsequium prae ceteris diligentior efficitur"); but we are not told the direction her love took; she simply "changede al hire ferste entente" (1444).

Genius must therefore mean, not that a true follower of Venus must seek out illicit love, but that she cannot refuse it when it is proposed to her. He goes on to warn of its disadvantages:

>   Natheles
> Men sen such love sielde in pes,
> That it nys evere upon aspie
> Of janglinge and of fals envie,
> Fulofte medlid with disese. [1471–1475]

He does not advise against it because it is sinful, since he is at this point very conscious of "mi lady Venus, whom I serve" (1467).

The fact that he serves Venus, however, does not prevent him from asserting his preference for marriage, because, as stated above, Venus is as well satisfied with marriage as with love of paramours. Since lovers who intend to marry can indulge their love in perfect freedom and openness, he finds it hard to under-

11. See above, Chap. 2.

stand why any girl would not set about getting married as soon
as she can:

> Bot thilke love is wel at ese,
> Which set is upon mariage;
> For that dar schewen the visage
> In alle places openly.
> A gret mervaile it is, forthi,
> How that a maiden wolde lette
> That sche hir time ne besette
> To haste unto that ilke feste,
> Wherof the love is al honeste.   [1476–1484]

In making such a clear dichotomy between open marriage and
secret love of paramours, Genius overlooks the middle ground of
clandestine marriage, in which the love is, or can be, "all honest,"
at least for non-Christians, but must be carried on as if it were
not, until such time as it is made public.[12]

After giving his reason for preferring love of a husband to love
of a paramour, Genius proceeds to give a reason for hastening
into marriage. If he had continued his discourse as he began it, he
could have warned young girls to hurry up and find a licit match
before Cupid's law tempts them into an illicit one. But instead he
seems to take this conclusion for granted, and goes on to talk of
the procreation of children. It is obvious that he is now speaking
only of the married state, where no secrecy is necessary.[13] He says
that a maiden who delays "changing her heart" to marriage when
she is young thereby loses a year or two or three,

> Whyl sche the charge myhte bere
> Of children, whiche the world forbere
> Ne mai, bot if it scholde faile.   [1495–1497]

That is, delay of this sort might result in her bearing fewer children, thus contributing to a dangerous population decline (a real
worry in Gower's time, after the decimations of the Black Death);

---

12. On the question of clandestine marriages in Gower's accounts of
Pygmalion and his vivified statue, Jason and Medea, and Theseus and
Ariadne, see Chap. 8 below.

13. The story of Cephalus (n. 22 below) shows that secrecy is of course
naturally desired during the very act of begetting children.

furthermore, she may never be able to marry and have any children at all:

> Bot what maiden hire esposaile
> Wol taire, whan sche take mai,
> Sche schal per chance an other dai
> Be let, whan that hire lievest were.   [1498–1501]

He then tells the story of Jephthah's daughter, who laments

> That sche no children hath forthdrawe
> In mariage after the lawe.   [1569–1570]

At the end of the *Confessio*, when the Parliament or Supreme Court of lovers convenes, a special place of honor is given to the four great wives, Penelope, Lucretia, Alcestis, and Alcyone (the latter is now demetamorphosed). They are treated as empresses, for their "feith was proeved in her lyves," and they were outstanding "in essample of alle goode / With mariage (8.2605–2620).[14] Other remarkable examples previously cited by Genius could have been mentioned alongside them, especially the saintly Constance and the wife of Apollonius of Tyre.[15]

---

14. Their stories are briefly reviewed here (2621–2656), after having been given more fully earlier: 4.143ff. (Penelope), 4.2927ff. (Alcyone), 7.1917ff. (Alcestis), and 7.4754ff. (Lucretia).

15. *Confessio* 2.587ff., 8.729ff. See below, and Chap. 12, "Alla and Troilus." Laodamia, Ovid's other great wife, appears in the *Confessio* in a rather strange context. After speaking of girls like Rosiphilee and Jephthah's daughter, who were too slow off the mark, Genius begins to explain how men can avoid idleness by their prowess in arms, which makes a man worthy of love (4.1608–1644). John replies that he would rather make love than war; this is the teaching of Christ (4.1648–1770). It was Genius's teaching as well in the previous book (3.2251–2546), but Genius now justifies was as a knightly duty; and whereas he just got through blaming Ulysses for sloth, in continuing to fight at Troy instead of hastening back to Penelope (4.143–233), he now blames him for having been so much in love with Penelope as to try to avoid going to Troy in the first place (4.1815–1895), and he praises Protesilaus for ignoring the warnings of Laodamia (4.1900–1934). This teaching corresponds to the doctrine of the *Vox clamantis* 5.1ff., where Gower warns knights against letting love interfere with duty. In the *Confessio* he returns to this theme when speaking of the education of a king (7.3518–3626). Sometimes prowess in arms wins love, as in the case of Hercules and Aeneas (see below); sometimes, however, such prowess destroys love, as with Protesilaus, who lost his life in the war. In Ulysses's case, it was simply a hindrance. In Troy, Penelope's letter was necessary to rekindle his love; he could think then of nothing but her and

Marriage Neglected, Adultery Overlooked,
and Fornication Winked At

It ought to follow from what has been said that adultery should always be condemned in the *Confessio* and fornication at least discouraged. But it is not so. The reason lies in the nature of the exemplary technique, which we analyzed earlier: an exemplum is normally told to illustrate one lesson alone, without much worry about whether it contradicts earlier or subsequent lessons.[16]

Thus it is that Gower often fails to specify the marital status or intent of his characters, or to register approval of those who have marriage in mind and disapproval of those not so inclined. In his treatment of Pyramus and Thisbe, for example, he neglects to mention that the young lovers were prevented from marrying by their parents, and so he gives no reason for their need for secrecy. The point that he wishes to stress is simply that Pyramus was too rash in killing himself before making sure that Thisbe was dead (3.1331ff.). Similarly, he omits mention of Phoebus's desire to marry Daphne (1685ff.).

He does accentuate Tereus's duty as a husband (5.5551ff.) and gives details of the marriages of Jason to Medea (3247ff.) and Theseus to Ariadne (5231ff.), thus bringing out the true gravity of their crimes of infidelity. But he says nothing of the marriage of Aeneas and Dido.[17] Of Dido he merely says:

> [She] loveth Eneas so hote
> Upon the wordes which he seide,
> That al hire herte on him sche leide,
> And dede al holi what he wolde.   [4.88–91]

The last line means that she went to bed with him, as it does in the story of Phyllis and Demophoon:

---

went home without delay as soon as he could, that is, when the war was over (4.204–229). This will be contradicted later, in the sixth book, when, as we shall see, Ulysses had an active role in the affair with Circe; but no matter: Genius is teaching a different lesson here.

16. See above, Chap. 1, in the section "Exemplary Hits and Misses," and cf. the contradictions spoken of in n. 15 above.

17. The matrimonial character of Dido's union to Aeneas will be taken up in Chap. 8 below.

> As thogh it were trowthe and feith,
> Sche lieveth al that evere he seith,
> And as hire infortune scholde,
> Sche granteth him al that he wolde.   [767–770]

In Aeneas's case, there is no suggestion that he was being untrue when he made love to Dido, as there is here. Aeneas is blamed only for the vice of "lachesse" (procrastination), since, according to Genius, he had promised to return but simply did not get around to it:

> Bot he, which hadde hise thoghtes feinte
> Towardes love and full of slowthe,
> His time lette, and that was rowthe.   [118–120]

Genius offers Demophoon as an example of another subspecies of sloth, namely, forgetfulness, and according to Gower's sidenote he follows the same pattern as Aeneas: he promised Phyllis most faithfully that he would return on a certain date, and then forgot about it.[18] But as the story unfolds in verse, Demophoon rather resembles Chaucer's character, who is false from the beginning. Phyllis, of course, diagnoses the trouble as sloth without further specification, and when Demophoon hears of her suicide, he dutifully curses the said vice in himself (795–878).[19]

Hercules, like Aeneas and Demophoon, is untrue to both love and marriage but is blamed only for violating love-troth. At first his heart is set on Deianira alone, and there is no indication of his future infidelity (2.2157–2166); but Genius gives John to understand that something was lacking in him:

> The daies gon, the yeres passe,
> The hertes waxen lasse and lasse
> Of hem that ben to love untrewe:

18. "Rediturum infra certum tempus fidelissime se compromisit. . . . Sed . . . diem statutum postmodum oblitus est."

19. Gower might seem to be emulating Ovid by arranging an original metamorphosis, when he turns Phyllis into a filbert: "And after Phillis 'Philliberd' / This tre was cleped in the yerd" (869–870). But it seems likely that he drew the idea from his medieval text of the *Heroides*. See Conrad Mainzer, "John Gower's Use of the 'Mediaeval Ovid' in the *Confessio amantis*," *Medium aevum* 41 (1972) 215–229, esp. 223.

> This Hercules with herte newe
> His love hath set on Eolen.[20]   [2259–2263]

It must not be thought that Gower deliberately suppressed the fact that Hercules and Deianira were married, out of some thematic purpose; for at Hercules's next appearance we are told of his courtship of Deianira: he seeks her love, and so naturally speaks to her father about marrying her. The father agrees, on condition that he defeat her present fiancé, the giant Achelons (4.2060–2074). The episode is related as an example of "hou love and armes ben aqueinted" (2147). When Aeneas and Turnus fight over Lavinia, however, her love is specified as the goal and prize, and no mention is made of the marriage which was in fact their aim (4.2183–2189).

When Hercules appears in yet a third exemplum, he is with Iole, "which was the love of his corage" (5.6809), but now there is no word of Deianira, whether as his wife or merely as his former love, nor is there any word of condemnation for his present love. Genius has a different lesson to teach: the inadvisability of stealth. Once again it is not Hercules who bears the brunt of the cautionary tale, but Faunus, who tries to steal into Hercules's place in bed with Iole.

In defense of Gower's failure to specify the nature of the love affairs that Genius retails, one could say, at least in certain cases, that it prevents the reader from being distracted from the specific moral being urged at the moment. When Genius in the same breath condemns Agamemnon for supplanting Achilles as Brexeida's lover and Diomede for supplanting Troilus as Criseyde's lover (2.2451–2458), he does not have to enter into the morality of the original unions. In the case of Troilus, Gower is quite obviously relying on Chaucer's story, or perhaps on Chaucer's copy of Boccaccio's *Filostrato*, whether in the original Italian or

---

20. The story of Jason is similar. At first, "Al was Medea that he thoghte"; but later Genius blames him for swearing "an oth which is noght soth" (5.3407, 4224). Jason took his oath "for sikernesse of mariage" (3483), but afterward they are spoken of only as lovers: "Togedre ben these lovers tho / Til that thei hadden sones tuo" (3937–3938), and: "Thus Jason, / As he that was to love untrewe, / Medea lefte and tok a newe" (4196–4198).

in the French translation, for only these versions refer to Troilus's
lady as Criseida rather than Briseida. As we have seen and shall
see further, there is a great difference in the moral tones set by
Boccaccio and Chaucer. But Gower did not have to commit himself to either view, or formulate one of his own.[21] Similarly, in the
tale of Geta that follows, he has only to say that "the lusti faire
Almeene / Assured was be weie of love" to him (2.2467–2468),
without specifying whether the surety involved a matrimonial
contract or not. We are not to worry, then, whether there is
anything morally offensive about Geta's habit of lying "abedde al
warm" with her, "naked in hir arm" (2485–2486), but are simply
to join Genius in blaming Amphitrion for tricking his way into
Geta's place.[22]

Sometimes, however, the circumstances of the stories are such
that it is difficult to avoid raising a moral eyebrow at the resulting
incongruities, even though we might wish to applaud the general
lesson. For example, we are invited to look with satisfaction upon
Philemenis, who, for taking the trouble of bringing the body of
the Amazon queen Penthesilea back to her native land, "wan of

21. Genius returns later to Troilus and Achilles (though Achilles's love
this time is Polyxena) to mark them out, along with Paris, as examples of
sacrilegious lovers, whose loves go wrong because they began them in
temples (5.7505–7602).

22. Other examples of loves not specified as either marital (aimed at marriage, or within marriage) or nonmarital (premarital, extramarital, anti-
marital) are those of Acis for Galatea (2.104ff.); Penthesilea for Hector,
with no mention of Andromache (4.2135ff.); Cephalus for Aurora (4.3187ff.);
Iphis for Anaxarete (4.3515ff.); and Achilles for Deidamia (5.2961ff.).
According to Ovid, Cephalus, happily married to Procris, scorns the love
of Aurora (*Meta.* 7.704ff.), and elsewhere he says that if Aurora had
Cephalus in her arms as she desired, she would cry out, "Lente currite,
noctis equi!" (*Amores* 1.13.39–40). Gower, however, portrays Cephalus as a
willing lover and gives him a charming *alba* (see Lewis 205), in which he is
the one who wishes the night to delay. Genius presents him as an illustration
that love and sleep do not go together; Cephalus prayed
> So that he mihte do the lawe
> In thilke point of loves heste,
> Which cleped is the nyhthes feste,
> Withoute slep of sluggardie. [4.3253–3258]
According to Cephalus himself, love-making seeks silence and darkness
(3201–3207); but apart from this, he also prays that he may beget children
(3238–3252).

love in special / A fair tribut for everemo." Well and good; but
the terms of the tribute were that Philemenis and his heirs were
to be given three girls every year in perpetuity. While we might
agree, therefore, that "with his travail his ese he boghte" (4.2148–
2182) we could easily object that gathering a harem in this way
does violence to some of the other principles that Genius expounds.

Again, when Babio is presented as an object lesson against the
danger of miserliness, we can appreciate why Viola, the "love at
his menage," should want to go off with Croceus, who is not
miserly; it is "riht as it scholde be" that Babio should be punished
for his behavior (5.4808–4862). But is it entirely right and in accord with "trouthe" for Viola to change lovers so easily? Or, let
us take the case of the steward of the King of Apulia. He married
his wife in the first place not for love but for money, and then,
in order to get more money, shamefully arranged for her to be
the "lusti womman" required to cure the king's rather peculiar
ailment. We rejoice, of course, when the steward is found out
and punished with exile. But it does seem a bit inappropriate for
the king to marry the wife himself (5.2643–2825). After all, her
husband liveth.

If Gower had been truly interested or concerned to make all
of his examples exemplary on all points, he could have done so
with a certain amount of adjustment, manipulation, qualification,
or selectivity. For instance, in the last-cited tale, though the
steward's marriage was not "true" to begin with, in the sense that
he did not marry his wife for a worthy motive, it was legally and
morally binding upon her.[23] But Gower could easily have cleared
her of her onerous obligation by sending the steward to an early
death. The fact that he did not do so shows either that he did not
think of it, or, perhaps more likely, that he did not think it necessary, since he clearly and directly sets forth his views on marriage
elsewhere in the poem.

Even when he speaks of man's duty to be satisfied with only
one partner, he does not always do so in explicit terms of marriage

23. See below, Chap. 10 and Chap. 11, for discussion of the motives for
marriage.

alone. An example is Genius's characterization of the "delicate" man:

> For though he hadde to his hond
> The beste wif of all the lond,
> Or the faireste love of alle,
> Yit wolde his herte on othre falle
> And thenke hem mor delicious
> Than he hath in his oghne hous.   [6.667–672]

There is, of course, no reason to assume that a man's "fairest love" cannot also be his wife, especially since she is living in his house. Gower has obviously not heard of the rule that love cannot exist within marriage, and he takes no special precaution against being misunderstood on the point. But earlier, in a similar discussion, he specified that he was speaking of wayward husbands who go after other women: "Hic ponit exemplum contra istos maritos qui ultra id quod proprias habent uxores ad novae voluptatis incrementum alias mulieres superflue lucrare non verentur." The exemplum in question is that of Echo, who is punished for acting as a bawd for Jupiter (5.4583 ff.).

Nature, Reason, and Incest

Eventually Genius explains the one-to-one rule of human love as a requirement of the law of nature, and states it in terms of marriage. The male is made for the female, he says, but when one desires many,

> That nedeth noght by weie of kinde.
> For whan a man mai redy finde
> His oghne wif, what scholde he seche
> In strange places to beseche
> To borwe an other mannes plouh,
> Whan he hath geere good ynouh
> Affaited at his oghne heste,
> And is to him wel more honeste
> Than other thing which is unknowe?   [7.4217–4225]

Earlier he had condemned Ulysses's affair with Circe whereby Telegonus was *genitus contra naturam*, that is, "gete in sorcerie," after he had won her love "amiss" with similar magical means (6.1768–1781). But even though immediately after the birth of the child Genius spoke of Penelope, "a betre wife ther mai non be," and recounted "hou many loves sche forsok" (1472–1476), he did not choose to condemn Ulysses's adultery as *contra naturam;* only later do we find that all adultery falls under the same censure.[24]

By "nature" Gower sometimes means the mating instinct, which is, at times, in opposition to itself. In Ovid's story of Iphis, the young girl reared as a boy and married to another girl, Genius says:

> Nature, which doth every wiht
> Upon hire lawe forto muse,
> Constreigneth hem, so that thei use
> Thing which to hem was al unknowe.   [4.484–487]

But homosexual love of this sort, even though inspired by nature, is unnatural. Cupid sees this, and because of their great love for each other takes *supernatural* measures to rectify the situation:

> [He] let do sette kinde above,
> So that hir law mai ben used,
> And thei upon here lust excused.[25]   [490–492]

In the following lines, Genius describes the fundamental opposition between love and the unnatural:

> For love hateth nothing more
> Than thing which stant ayein the lore
> Of that Nature in kinde hath sett.
> Forthi, Cupide hath so besett
> His grace upon this aventure
> That he, acordant to Nature,
> Whan that he syh the time best,
> That ech of hem hath other kest,
> Transformeth Iphe into a man.   [493–501]

The result is a natural love that involves no sin against nature:

24. The story of Nectanabus (6.1782ff.) is similar to the story of Ulysses: he commits adultery by trickery and thus becomes the father of Alexander the Great. But his adultery is not condemned, nor his lack of "trouthe" (as in the similar story of Mundus), but only his use of sorcery.

25. Similarly, in the case of Pygmalion, who invokes supernatural aid, we see "that worde mai worche above kinde" (4.438); and we learn the important lesson that "the God of Love is favorable / To hem that ben of love stable" (443–444).

> Whereof the kinde love he wan
> Of lusti yonge Iante his wif;
> And tho thei ladde a merie lif,
> Which was to kinde non offence.   [502–505]

It is worth noting that in the rubric Gower tells a much different story. After Iphis was married at the usual age, since she did not have the wherewithal to pay the marital debt ("debitum suae coniugi unde solvere non habuit"), she called upon the gods for their help. They took pity on her and completely changed her sex, because of the desire of nature ("ob affectum naturae").

In a rather similar case, Achilles is reared as a girl and shares the bed of a girl, Deidamia. Eventually the predictable occurs; for when one's nature wishes to assert itself ("wher kinde wole himselve rihte"), there is no stopping it. Nature (the female personification of nature, I take it) stirs them to love:

> Nature, which mai noght forbere,
> Hath mad hem bothe forto stere:
> Thei kessen ferst, and overmore
> The hihe weie of loves lore
> Thei gon, and al was don in dede,
> Wherof lost is the maydenhede.   [5.3063–3068]

Where Chaucer would doubtless have arranged a marriage between the two, Gower characteristically passes on without bothering to specify the morality of their pursuit of nature and love.

At the beginning of the first book, Gower states that he intends to write about that love to which not only man but all living things are *naturally* subject ("de illo amore, a quo non solum humanum genus sed etiam cuncta animantia naturaliter subiciuntur"). And because many lovers are often stimulated by the passions of desire more than they should be ("ultra quam expedit"), he has divided his book according to these passions.

Though both men and animals are naturally bound by love, there is a difference between them, as is clear from the example of Tiresias, who was punished for interfering with the coupling of two serpents. For, as Genius says,

> More is a man than such a beste.
> So mihte it nevere ben honeste
> A man to wraththen him to sore

> Of that an other doth the lore
> Of kinde, in which is no malice,
> Bot only that it is a vice.

That is, no vice can exist without malice, and malice requires reason. But man, in spite of his reason, is apt to be drawn by nature into love even against his will:

> And thogh a man be resonable,
> Yit after kinde he is menable
> To love, wher he wole or non.   [3.383–391]

The tale of Tiresias is told to caution John against judging lovers too harshly, and to teach him to sympathize with the natural pressures upon them that sometimes bring them into conflict with the dictates of reason. The preceding story, of Canace and Macareus, teaches the same lesson, which is directed against their father, King Aeolus (Gower frequently dedivinizes Ovid's gods). He is blamed for reacting with "an excessive melancholy of fury" because he did not understand how irresistibly concupiscence affects youth ("intolerabilis iuventutis concupiscentia"), or, as Genius puts it, "how maistrefull love is in yowthe" (3.212).

Canace and Macareus, brother and sister, grow up together uneventfully until they reach puberty, that is,

> Til thei be growen up alofte
> Into the youthe of lusti age.

This is the stage at which "kinde," in the sense of the mating urge, makes itself felt in a youth:

> Whan kinde assaileth the corage
> With love and doth him forto bowe,
> That he no reson can allowe,
> Bot halt the lawes of nature.   [152–157]

Genius will later clarify the distinction between the laws of nature and the laws of reason, after telling the story of Tobias and Sara:

> For God the lawes hath assissed
> Als wel to reson as to kinde,
> Bot he the bestes wolde binde
> Only to lawes of nature;
> Bot to the mannes creature

God yaf him reson forth withal
Wherof that he nature schal
Upon the causes modefie,
That he schal do no lecherie,   *Nota.*
And yit he schal hise lustes have.
So ben the lawes bothe save
And every thing put out of sclandre. [7.5372–5383]

Gower considered this conclusion so important that he drew
attention to it in the margin when he revised his poem.[26] We shall
return to discuss it more fully later, in Chapter 11, when we take
up the question of the morality of sexual delight within marriage.
But here I wish only to ascertain the limits of the law of nature
when contrasted with reason. We have seen nature impel two
girls to a homosexual love, which however was something that
love hated, because it was contrary to the dictates of that which
Nature had established in nature. Love in that case was discrimi-
nating; when Cupid "saw" the right time, he transformed Iphis's
sex. But in the case of Canace and her brother, the sightless Cupid
is at work, and he takes no pains to modify nature "upon the
causes" according to the law of reason:

For whom that Love hath under cure,
As he is blind himself, riht so
He makth his client blind also. [3.158–160]

The law of nature in question here, then, is the "unmodified"
instinct that man shares with beasts, an instinct that takes no
notice of person, number, or gender; the persons may be inti-
mately related by blood, like Canace and Macareus; they are not
restricted to one mate (Paulina, we recall, said she was like a
beast for having had intercourse with two men); and they may
even be impelled to others of the same sex. Nature teaches Canace
and Macareus how to perform the act of coitus, and, in the due
course of Nature's law, Canace becomes pregnant. As Gower puts
it in his rubric, Cupid amorously pierced the desires of their
hearts with a flaming dart, so that with Nature's help ("Natura
cooperante") Canace was made pregnant by her brother and gave
birth.[27]

26. The *nota* appears in the revised first recension (MS A) and in the
third recension (MS F).
27. Nature performs a similar function in bringing the pregnancies of Lot's

When, therefore, Nature is described as

> sche which is Maistresse
> In kinde and techeth every lif
> Withoute lawe positif,
> Of which sche takth nomaner charge,
> Bot kepth hire lawes al at large,   [170–174]

we must not interpret the positive law as the arbitrary disciplinary law (as opposed to the moral law) of the Church, though this is how Gower uses the term in the Prologue.[28] Rather, the positive law must be taken as the equivalent of the moral law itself, of nature informed by reason. This reading is confirmed in the discussion of the morality of kinship marriage in the last book of the *Confessio:* Mankind had its origin from a single couple, Adam and Eve, who of course were virgins to begin with. They were ashamed at first until "Nature hem hath reclamed / To love and tauht hem thilke lore," so that, like Canace and Macareus, they first kissed and then "thei don that is to kinde due, / Wherof thei hadden fair issue," namely, two sons, Cain and Abel. Then "Nature so the cause ladde" that Eve also produced two daughters, and from these four siblings mankind was to multiply.

> Forthi, that time it was no sinne
> The soster forto take hire brother,
> Whan that ther was of chois non other.   [8.68–70]

The principle involved here, Genius says, is that "nede hath no lawe," and this need lasted through the second age of the world.

Genius's account of the transition to the time when brother-sister marriage was no longer practiced is somewhat elliptical, and I have taken the liberty of filling in the ellipses (as I see them). The children of Noah so multiplied that they formed seventy-two nations throughout the world;

> Bot as Nature hem hath excited,
> They token thanne litel hiede [of kindred];
> The brother of the sosterhiede [continued]

daughters to term (8.232–234). Cf. also Constance's conception of a child: "The hihe maker of nature / Hire hath visited in a throwe" (2.916–917).

28. "Holy cherche" by means of "here lawe positif / Hath set to make werre and strif / For worldes good, which may noght laste" (Prologue 246–249). Cf. the discussion in Fisher, *John Gower* 159–161.

> To wedde wyves, til it cam
> Into the time of Habraham.
> Whan the thridde age was begunne,
> The nede tho was overrunne,
> For ther was people ynouh in londe.
> Thanne ate ferste it came to honde,
> That sosterhode of marriage
> Was torned into cousinage,
> So that after the riht lyne
> The cousin weddeth the cousine.   [90–106]

This practice of kinship alliance was commonly practiced, he says, until Christ was born,[29]

> Bot afterward it was forbore
> Amonges ous that ben baptized.   [142–143]

This corresponds to what Chaucer says in the legend of Hypermnestra[30] and to the general teaching of the canonists and theologians of the time. Genius in fact cites canon law (specifically the decretal of Pope Innocent III in the Fourth Lateran Council of 1215)[31] as forbidding marriage between first, second, and third cousins:

> For of the lawe canonized
> The pope hath bede to the men
> That non schal wedden of his ken
> Ne the seconde ne the thridde.
> Bot thogh that holy Cherche it bidde,
> So to restreigne mariage,
> Ther ben yit upon loves rage
> Full manye of such nou aday
> That taken wher thei take may.   [144–152]

Until now, Genius has been talking of marriage, and it could be thought that he is now castigating those who are presumptuous

29. In the course of his account he mentions that Jacob married *two* of his first cousins (121–122); but Gower nowhere enters into the theological explanations that were commonly given for the use of polygamy in the Old Testament.

30. See above, Chap. 4.

31. The decretal referred to, *Non debet* (X 4.14.8), actually relaxed the range of prohibited degrees from the seventh (sixth cousins) to the fourth (third cousins). Gower also cites Roman civil law; see *Confessio* 2.83 and Macaulay's note.

enough to attempt marriage within the forbidden degrees of consanguinity and affinity. But it soon becomes evident that he is
speaking instead of men who have no matrimonial intentions at
all, for he includes those who lust after persons with religious
vows of celibacy:

> For love, which is unbesein
> Of alle reson, as men sein,
> Thurgh sotie and thurgh nycete,
> Of his voluptuosite
> He spareth no condicion
> Of ken ne yet religion. [153–158]

He has returned, then, to the idea that incestuous love is contrary
to reason, and he goes on to say that it operates on the level of
beasts: like a cock among the hens or a stallion let out to stud, it
takes whatever is nearest at hand. "Such delit," needless to say, "is
forto blame" (159–165).

Macaulay therefore is mistaken when he says: "Gower's view
is that there is nothing naturally immoral about an incestuous
marriage, but that it is made wrong by the *lex positiva* of the
Church."[32] Gower's view is the received theological one, that
brother-sister marriage was sinless when the world was thinly
populated, and that it became sinful when the population increased, long before the Church came into existence. The divinely
prohibited degrees detailed in Leviticus 18 and 20, which effectively restricted kinfolk closer than first cousins from marrying,
was considered part of the moral law binding on all men.[33] Positive law by definition is contrasted with natural law.[34] Natural
law usually includes the moral law, but Gower makes it clear
that for him, at least at times, it does not. Rather, natural law is
the same law that God has given to men and animals alike; and

---

32. Note to *Confessio* 3.172.

33. See my article "Canonical Implications of Richard III's Plan to Marry
His Niece," *Traditio* 23 (1967) 269–311; also, "Kinship, Incest, and the Dic-
tates of Law," *American Journal of Jurisprudence* (formerly *Natural Law
Forum*) 14 (1969) 69–78.

34. Cf. *Cursor mundi* 9433–9450, cited under "positive" in the Oxford
English Dictionary: The first law was called "of kind"; "The tother has
'positive' to nam." And: "The laghes bath he than forlete, / Bath naturel and
positif."

positive law in this context refers to the law of reason that God has given only to men.

In the days when men had no other choice than to "take" their sisters, it was a matter of "wedding wives of the sisterhood." Later, when the world is populated, a man who takes his sister has no thoughts for marriage, but simply "takth what thing comth next to honde." As we have seen, it is not always significant when Gower fails to mention marital intent, but it is surely meaningful in the case of Canace, when he omits Macareus's determination to marry her, which Ovid speaks of.[35] Also significant is his characterization of their action as a fall and a misdeed. They were so bewitched by Nature that they were like the blind leading the blind, who feared nothing until they fell, or like a bird lured into a snare by bait,

> So that thei felle upon the chance
> Where witt hath lore his remembrance.   [3.187–188]

Canace tells her father, "That I misdede, yowthe it made"—her youthfulness tempted her to wade into the water without perceiving the danger (227–229).

It must be admitted, however, that Gower follows Ovid in making Canace unrepentant of her love for her brother (288–290); and when Genius draws the moral against wrath, he says that everyone should "have / Reward[36] to love and to his miht, / Ayein whos strengthe mai no wiht," and goes on to speak of the absolute irresistibility of nature when it constrains a man to love (342–359). But the conclusion that we should draw from this is simply that Gower has once again let his confessor run away with himself; by overenforcing one lesson he damages another. A certain amount of discretion is required on the part of his reader to cut through the rhetoric and piece together a moderate and accurate statement of his position without having to resort again to his caution that Genius is not speaking the truth but merely the opinion of lovers.

Duke Mundus was described as being unable to help himself when tempted:

35. See above, Chap. 3.
36. "Reward" in this context means "regard."

> Bot yet he was noght of such myht
> The strengthe of love to withstonde
> That he ne was so broght to honde,
> That malgre wher he wole or no,
> This yonge wif he loveth so, [1.786–790]

and so on.[37] Mundus, however, did not avoid blame, as we have seen; but he pleaded the force of love, and his punishment was diminished. As Genius says after the Canace story, one's "reddour" or harshness should be restrained toward one who is forced to obey nature (3.347–350). But Genius is ashamed of Cupid when he is blind, and of Venus when she is unwise (5.1382–1417). Love in such circumstances leads even to the worst kind of incest, that between mother and son, and to promiscuity; for "every womman mihte take / What man hire liste, and noght forsake / To ben als comun as sche wolde," according to the law that Venus established (1426–1429).

The ultimate lesson, then, is that whenever love occurs in circumstances other "than it is of the lawe set," that is, *posited* by positive law, it is cause for repentance. When "lust of love excedeth lawe, / It oghte forto be withdrawe," especially in the matter of kinship (8.250–266). At this point (in the last book) Genius has just given two examples of brother-sister incest which admitted of no mitigation. When Caligula oppressed his three sisters, God in his wrath bereft him of life and empire; when Ammon lay with his sister Thamar "ayein kinde," the sin was avenged by his brother Absalom, who put him to death with his own hand. "Thus th'unkinde unkinde fond"—that is, an unnatural deed had an unnatural end (199–222). Genius has also given an instance of father-child incest, the case of Lot and his two daughters, who were punished in their descendants (223–246); and he adds another, that of King Antiochus and his daughter, in his last exemplum, the story of Apollonius of Tyre (271ff).

37. Cf. the man born under the influence of the planet Venus:
> He is so ferforth amourous,
> He not what thing is vicious
> Touchende love, for that lawe
> Ther mai no maner man withdrawe,
> The which Venerien is bore
> Be weie of kinde. [7.791–796]

The account of Apollonius's adventures is preceded by a pair of Latin distichs, which sum up Genius's, and presumably Gower's, teaching on the morality of love:

> Omnibus est communis amor; sed et immoderatos
> Qui facit excessus, non reputatur amans.
> Sors tamen unde Venus attractat corda, videre
> Quae rationis erunt non ratione sinit.

That is, "Love is common to all men; but one who commits immoderate excesses is not considered a lover. But the occasion by which Venus entices the heart does not permit one to see by his reason what is in accord with reason." The immediate inspiration of these lines is no doubt the incestuous love of King Antiochus, but the second couplet seems to apply to all human sexual love: there is indeed a rational basis to it, but it is often, or perhaps always, beyond the scope of human reason completely to understand or control it. This uncertainty or ambiguity about the relationship of sexuality to our rational standards is often a matter of concern in the *Confessio,* and it may help to explain some of the rather elusive reasoning of Genius (a character who has a complicated history as a sexologist) in glossing stories of irregular sexual happenings.[38]

Apollonius's life produces the following moral:

> Lo, what it is to be wel grounded:
> For he hath ferst his love founded
> Honesteliche as forto wedde,
> Honesteliche his love he spedde
> And hadde children with his wif,
> And as him liste he ladde his lif.   [1993–1998]

No matter that fifteen years of horrendous ordeals intervened between the time of his marriage and his enjoyment of it in peace; the "sentence" is good. As for Antiochus, who "sette his love unkindely," he was struck down by lightning; he thus "for his lust hath his penance" (2004–2008).

---

38. For this idea I am indebted to Professor Winthrop Wetherbee. We shall consider Gower's attitude toward sexuality further in Chap. 11 and Chap. 12 below.

John's Status as a Lover

At the end of his instruction Genius says that the story of
Apollonius can teach John "what it is to love in good manere."
He urges him, accordingly, to abandon all love that is not in ac-
cord with reason:

> For elles, if that thou descorde,
> And take lust as doth a beste,
> Thi love mai noght ben honeste.
> For by no skile that I finde
> Such lust is noght of loves kinde. [2024–2028]

Which is to say, for man unreasonable love is unnatural. John
answers that he is not guilty of any such deviations from reason:

> In this point, miself aquite
> I mai riht wel, that nevere yit
> I was assoted in my wit
> Bot only in that worthi place
> Wher alle lust and alle grace
> Is set, if that Danger ne were. [2034–2039]

He is asserting, therefore, that his love is honest; and since honest
love means marriage, he would marry her if only she could cease
being "dangerous" and accept him.

Some of the proponents of courtly love have assumed that
Gower portrayed himself as pursuing an adulterous affair. But,
as is admitted in the book of essays in honor of C. S. Lewis cited
in the Introduction above, "Nowhere is there any hint that [his
mistress] is married, still less is there any suggestion that Amans
is: he is as 'innocent' as his antecedent in the *Roman* [*de la Rose*],
and she, like the *amie* in the *Roman*, is a *damoisele* and a *pucele*."[39]
In fact, as we have seen, John's matrimonial intentions were admitted by W. G. Dodd, who was among the first to treat him as a
courtly lover.[40]

The question of John's freedom to marry arises in the fifth book,
when Genius says to him:

> Forthi, if evere it so befalle
> That thou, mi sone, amonges alle

39. J. A. W. Bennett, "Gower's 'Honeste Love,'" in Lawlor 112.
40. See above, Introduction.

> Be wedded man, hold that thou hast;
> For thanne al other love is wast;
> O wif schal wel to thee suffise.
> And thanne, if thou for covoitise
> Of love woldest axe more,
> Thou scholdest don ayein the lore
> Of alle hem that trewe be.

John answers,

> Mi fader, as in this degre
> My conscience is noght accused.   [5.4653–4663]

Strangely enough, however, he goes on to explain himself as being innocent of using bawds to acquire love: "For I no such brocage have used, / Wherof that lust of love is wonne" (4664–4665), a point on which Genius had already expressed himself satisfied (4568–4571).

It might be thought, then, that John is being evasive about his marital status. But he had no way of knowing that adultery was supposed to be a prerequisite for true love; for this doctrine, which is not contained even in the *Ars honeste amandi,* did not see the light of day until the nineteenth or twentieth century. John is vague, then, because he has no pressing reason to be specific.

He is a bit more specific, however, when he responds to Genius's discourse against love-delicacy, quoted above. Genius spoke of a man who had the best wife or the fairest love (who, we deduced, was also his wife).[41] John answers that he is not guilty of the fault described:

> For if I hadde such a wif
> As ye spake of, what scholde I more?
> For thanne I wolde neveremore
> For lust of eny wommanhiede
> Myn herte upon non other fiede.
> And if I dede, it were a wast.
> Bot al withoute such repast
> Of lust, as ye me tolde above,
> Of wif, or yet of other love,
> I faste, and mai no fode gete.   [6.692–701]

41. Above, at the end of the section "Marriage Neglected."

Genius takes him at his word, and so must we.

Since, then, Genius accepts that both John and his lady are basically honest in their intentions, he directs John to give his lady the benefit of the doubt and assume that it is somehow not honorable for her to respond to his advances at the present time:

> For it mai be that thi desir,
> Thogh it brenne evere as doth the fyr,
> Per cas to hire honour missit,
> Or elles time com noght yit,
> Which standt upon thi destinie;

for, he says, "noman hath his lustes alle" (5.5211–5218).

At the end, when John asks Genius for his "whole counsel" as to what would be best for him, Genius declares that he will leave aside all other trifles and come straight to the truth:

> Forthi, to speken overmore
> Of love which thee mai availe,
> Tak love where it mai noght faile.
> For, as of this which thou art inne,
> Be that thou seist it is a sinne,
> And sinne mai no pris deserve,
> Withoute pris and who schal serve,
> I not what profit myhte availe.   [8.2084–2091]

Since, therefore, John himself "says"[42] his love is a sin, and since he does not admit to adulterous desires, his guilt must lie in what he has confessed.

Though Genius normally quizzed him on matters of sin and vice, John's responses were in keeping with his original instructions: he told all the happiness and sorrow that he had experienced in love both in thought and in deed. In general, his record was commendable, from the viewpoint of honest love. Most of his faults arose from his frustration at receiving no response to his advances, but these faults were largely the merest peccadilloes.

42. Macaulay lists the form *seist* as meaning only "sayest"; the form for "seest" is *sest*. "Be that" at the beginning of the line could be read as a prepositional phrase, so that the line would mean, "From what you say, it is a sin." But the sentence as a whole seems to call for a conjunction: "Since you say it is a sin, I know not what profit it might bring." This is the interpretation given by Hans Kurath and Sherman M. Kuhn, *Middle English Dictionary* B.3 (Ann Arbor 1958, repr. 1970) 793: *bī* conj. 3.

A stern moralist would no doubt find the mortal sin of *delectatio morosa* in his desires to be in bed with his lady;[43] but when John asks Genius to decide whether he deserves a penance for wishing to steal love in this way, Genius simply responds that it would be better to avoid such stealth, for "thogh it be for a time swete, / At ende it doth bot litel good" (5.6696–6703).

Genius's advice here does, however, correspond to the second of the two reasons he gives in his final counsel to avoid human love altogether. The first reason, as we saw, is that John's present love is sinful and therefore profitless. The second is that such love will eventually fail. Even if John should attain his desires, it would all come to an end in time, and therefore finish in sorrow:

> And sett thou myhtest lust atteigne;
> Of every lust th'ende is a peine,
> And every peine is good to fle. [8.2095–2097]

Genius goes on to warn him against misruling his kingdom, that is, himself (2106–2125). This counsel corresponds to advice he gave earlier, after John had confessed to a desire to enjoy the delicacies and delights of love: he should not be "to sore delicat, / Wherof that thou reson excede" (6.960–961). For, Genius says,

> The bodely delices alle
> In every point, hou so thei falle,
> Unto the soule don grievance. [967–969]

Or, as the sidenote puts it, "Deliciae corporis militant adversus animam."

The upshot of this earlier counsel was that John was to love his lady according to reason. Now, however, he is told that reason requires him to withdraw from that love entirely,

> For Love, which that blind was evere,
> Makth all his servantz blinde also. [2130–2131, cf. 2104–2105]

But we know that Love is not always blind; in the story of Iphis, Cupid saw what was unnatural and did something about it. Again, when lovers like Mundus use deceit to achieve their desires, "Love hath cause to be wroth" (1.1204).

Blind Love in the case of Canace and her brother was charac-

43. *Confessio* 4.2884–2888, 3276–3281; 5.6652–6681.

terized as following the law of Nature instead of reason. Now,
Genius contrasts the law of reason with the law of will:

> My sone, and if thou have be so [i.e., blind],
> Yit is it time to withdrawe,
> And set thin herte under that law
> The which of reson is governed,
> And noght of will.   [8.2132–2136]

Once again the "reason" is that "every lust is bot a while" (2139).
Genius concludes by saying:

> I can do to thee nomore
> Bot teche thee the rihte weie:
> Now ches if thou wolt live or deie.   [2146–2148]

The confessor's life-or-death alternative could be interpreted
as assessing John's love as mortally sinful. But we must make al-
lowances for rhetorical exaggeration in this kind of spiritual
exhortation, as we shall see when discussing the ending of *Troilus
and Criseyde*.[44] It is similar, in fact, to the kind of exaggeration
that lovers use. John, for instance, once declared that he would
stop at nothing to get rid of Danger:

> Thus wolde I wonde for no sinne,
> Ne yit for al this world to winne.   [3.1569–1570]

Yet elsewhere he often asserts that there are certain sins that he
would never commit, even to gain his lady's love.[45]

We know, too, according to Genius's doctrine, that if the passion of love can be restrained, the love can merit heaven. The
widow Constance, for instance, when she married King Allee,
obviously had such passion to some extent, but she kept it under
control:

> Bot for no lust ne for no rage
> Sche tolde hem nevere what sche was.   [2.910–911]

And when she died, God "fro this worldes faierie / Hath take hire
into compaignie" (1593–1594) as a reward for her well-ordered
love:

44. Below, Chap. 12.
45. Consider, for instance, his denial that he has ever used love-brokerage,
quoted above.

> And thus the wel meninge of love
> Was ate laste set above.   [1599–1600]

Furthermore, love between man and woman is not profitless on earth, if it is the right sort of love:

> For evere yit it hath be so,
> That love honeste in sondri weie
> Profiteth, for it doth aweie
> The vice, and, as the boeks sein,
> It makth curteis of the vilein,
> And to the couard hardiesce
> It yifth.   [4.2296–2302]

It is, in fact, assimilated to the supernatural love of charity, of which St. John said, "Who loveth noght is hier as ded" (2320–2325). Gower calls attention to the importance of this point: "Nota de amore caritatis, ubi dicit, 'Qui non diligit, manet in morte.' "[46]

This is not to say that "honest love" is the best way to live on earth and to get to heaven. Genius once admitted that

> Virginite is forto preise,
> Which, as th'Apocalips recordeth,
> To Crist in hevene best acordeth.   [5.6388–6390]

And in the headnote to this section Gower said that as the rose surpasses thorns, virginity surpasses fleshly marriage:

> Sic sibi virginitas carnis sponsalia vincit,
> Aeternos foetus quae sine labe parit.

The reason given, that spouses of heaven give birth to eternal offspring without taint, suggests that marital love always involves some sin or imperfection. He may, of course, simply be referring to the *labes originalis* that is passed on to all children, but more likely he is referring to some lack of perfection in the spouses themselves, perhaps the sort of thing that Reason speaks of in Machaut's *Judgment of the King of Bohemia:*

> Mais il n'est ame,
> N'homme vivant qui aimme si sans blame,

46. Citing 1 John 3.14.

> S'il est tapez de l'amoureuse flame,
> Qu'il n'aimme mieus assez le corps que l'ame.

The reason why such a one loves the body more than the soul is that the love is basically carnal and contrary to the soul:

> Pour quel raison?
> Amour vient de charnel affection,
> Et si desir et sa condition
> Sont tuit enclin a delectation.
>   Si ne se puet
> Nuls, ne nulle, garder qui amer vuet
> Qu'il n'i ait vice ou pechié; il l'estuet,
> Et c'est contraire a l'ame qui s'en duet.
>   Et d'autre part,
> Tout aussi tost com l'ame se depart
> Dou corps, l'amour s'en eslonge et espart.[47]

But it is only purely carnal love that leaves the soul at death, not that which is guided by reason and informed by charity. Such love, by Genius's own previous admission, is possible even between man and woman. However, perhaps because of the dangers and difficulties of achieving it, he chooses not to acknowledge even the possibility of its existence in his final counsel.

The Remedy of Love

We have seen that by modifying the God-given law of nature by the God-given law of reason, a man could avoid lechery and still enjoy the delights of physical love, but that anyone who is immoderate and goes to excess, "non reputatur amans."[48] This is the final sentence on John. Throughout the long dialogue with Genius, he has been identified in the margin as Amans; but now he is told that he does not have what it takes. In his case, then, the verdict is dictated not by excess but by defect.

47. Guillaume de Machaut, Le jugement dou roy de Behaingne 1704–1718 (Oeuvres 1.121); emphasis mine. Cf. above for Paulina's implied conclusion that even marital sex involves defilement. For discussions of the view that sexual delight could never be experienced without sin, see below, Chap. 10 and Chap. 11.
48. Bennett, "Gower's 'Honeste Love'" 118 seems to diagnose John's sin as mainly potential rather than actual: "Lovers' malady destroys Reason (which in Gower always connotes 'measure' and restraint). To persist in it, says Genius, is a sin."

When the dramatic form of the confessional dialogue, with its marginal cues, comes to an end, John resumes his role as narrator. He says that his reason agreed with Genius's judgment, but that his will took no notice of it. He acknowledged the truth of the confessor's extreme view that reason and love never go together:

> Yit myhte nevere man beholde
> Reson, wher love was withholde [i.e., kept in service];
> Thei be noght of o governance.   [8.2197–2199]

Deflated of their hyperbole, these lines mean only that it is very difficult for love always to be kept in bounds by reason. This more moderate manner of assessing love is verified later by Venus —who is not now the incestuous and promiscuous goddess that Genius once described, but represents love thoroughly modified by reason. Only a few holy men, she says, can go against Nature and Nature's law by practicing virginity. There are, however, a good many who go against her and her office in a much different way, by taking delight in various vices, and Nature has often lamented because of it.[49] Venus's own court also disdains this kind of love, and ever shall:

>   for it receiveth
> Non such that kinde so deceiveth.
> For al onliche of gentil love
> Mi court stant alle courtz above
> And takth noght into retenue
> Bot thing which is to kinde due,
> For elles it schal be refused.
> Wherof I holde thee excused.   [2343–2350]

She concludes therefore by acquitting John of indulging in any vice that is against nature.

The presence of incestuous, adulterous, and bewitching lovers in John's subsequent dream of Cupid's court[50] might lead us to think that Venus is speaking of a very low level of natural law,

49. "Wherof that sche fullofte hath pleigned" (2341). Gower is no doubt referring here not only to the Nature of the *Roman de la Rose*, but also to that of the *Roman's* source, Alan of Lille's *De planctu Naturae*.

50. *Confessio* 8.2500ff. (Tristan and Isolde, Lancelot and Guinevere, Jason and Creusa, Hercules and Iole, and others), 2587 (Canace), 2599 (Circe and Calypso). On the nature and function of this dream, see below.

one that is satisfied by the minimum requirement of heterosexuality. But she takes reason as her criterion of what is natural: her medicine for John may not be of the sort that he wishes, but it is the kind of remedy dictated "be reson," and "acordant unto loves kinde" (2367–2371).

John is hoping for a "remedy" of love in the homeopathic medieval sense of the word, whereby the pains of love are cured by attaining one's beloved. But Venus has the more radical Ovidian cure of total abstinence in mind.

At this point in his narrative, John rails against Venus and attributes to her qualities frequently possessed by Cupid and Fortune: she is lawless, blind, and capricious, and often rejects true men and rewards the untrue. But he admits that this is a partial view: "as to me siemeth" (2377–2386). Her own words make it clear that she is still being perfectly rational, though capable of irrationality. She says, half-mockingly, perhaps divining his unspoken criticism of her,

> Thow wost wel that I am Venus,
> Which al only my lustes seche.
> And wel I wot, thogh thou beseche
> Mi love, lustes be ther none
> Whiche I mai take in thi persone.   [2398–2402]

She reiterates Genius's advice, but now with more point:

> Betre is to make a beau retret;
> For thogh thou myhtest love atteigne,
> Yit were it bot an ydel peine,
> Whan that thou art noght sufficant
> To holde love his covenant.   [2416–2420]

Like Iphis, John does not have the means to pay the marriage debt; and to underline the fact of his impotence, she says,

> I wot and have it wel conceived
> Hou that thi will is good ynowh;
> Bot mor behoveth to the plowh,
> Whereof the lacketh, as I trowe.   [2424–2427]

Her advice, then, is that he act his age:

> Forthi, mi conseil is that thou
> Remembre wel hou thou art old.   [2438–2439]

The headnote expresses her judgment in even more convincing terms: Nature does not give to December what May possesses ("sicut habet Maius non dat Natura Decembri"). It is fitting (that is, reasonable) for those whom white old age has touched to preserve themselves in chastity ever after:

> Conveniens igitur foret ut quos cana senectus
> Attigit, ulterius corpora casta colant.

After he hears Venus's pronouncement, John swoons, and in his swoon he thinks he sees a great assembly, like a parliament of lovers, who come to discuss his case. They are divided roughly into the young and the old, though the former group contains such seasoned practitioners as Penelope and Ulysses. The older ones show the greater interest in him, and they enter into a theoretical dispute over the nature of love in the aged. Some say that there is no reason why an old man should be afflicted with such pains unless he foolishly brought them on himself. But others maintain, and their opinion is awarded a *nota* in the margin, that "the wylde loves rage / In mannes lif forberth non age." Only a saint by the grace of God can be delivered from it (2440–2779).

Cupid performs this service of liberation for John in his vision. The god is once again said to be blind, but he acts with the full advice of his mother Venus. He removes from John's heart his "fiery lancegay," identified in the sidenote as the dart of his *concupiscentia*. To prevent him from dying, Venus anoints his heart, temples, and reins—a sort of extreme unction or sacrament of the sick. She gives him a mirror whereby he can literally see how old he is. He finally realizes that he is in the winter of his years (2784–2857).

He then wakes from his swoon, and finds only Venus and Genius there, as before. Perhaps, then, his vision of lovers was only a dream inspired by Genius's endless exempla. But if so, it had the effect of curing him. When Reason (a male personification who must have been waiting in the wings) hears it said that love's rage was gone from John, he comes and removes the folly of the "unwise fantasy" that he was wont to complain about. Venus is amused by it all, and John assures her that he will follow her advice (2858–2878).[51]

51. According to the sidenote, after Cupid has removed his fiery dart,

John asks Genius for absolution and is granted full pardon, without penance: a sign, perhaps, that his sin of love was not very serious. But it may well be that he is indeed assigned a penance, not by Genius but by Venus, when she gives him a set of black prayer beads on which he is to pray "for the pes, / And that thou make a plein reles / To love" (2889–2915). Since he has already received full pardon for his sins, the "full release" would be a plenary indulgence or remission of the temporal pains due to the sins. Or it could mean simply that he is to pray for complete liberation from his servitude to Love, for she goes on to characterize Love as taking little heed of the needs of old men, when "the lustes ben aweie." She explains once again that this is the reason why he is not to follow the laws of nature:

> Forthi, to thee nys bot o weie,
> In which let reson be thi guide.

He is to leave her court and confine himself to the study of moral virtue in his own library. For when one is not able to catch the game, "it were a thing unreasonable" to go hunting (2915–2933).

An End of All His Work

After bidding John farewell, Venus, the Queen of Love, like the Blessed Virgin Mary, is assumed into heaven, and Genius too departs, presumably in a more pedestrian way (2940–2951). In the original version, however, Venus first entrusts John with a commission for Chaucer, who is likewise in his old age. He is to have "his testament of love" made, just as John has made his confession "above" (presumably referring to the written text of the *Confessio*). Then Venus catches her way straight up to heaven, and John catches his way straight home, where he is determined to pray on his beads "for hem that trew love fonde," during the rest of his life, "upon the poynt which I am schryve (2941*–2970*).

Readers have long been puzzled as to why Gower omitted the lines about Chaucer in his revision of the poem.[52] An answer sug-

---

Venus leaves him because there is no more heat in him. Personified Old Age then acts as the physician: calling upon *Ratio*, *Senectus* restores the interior man, previously infatuated by love, to health of mind. No notice is taken in this process of John's awakening from his swoon.

52. Macaulay, Introduction xxvii–xxviii, suggests a very simple, practical

gests itself when we consider the whole context of the reformed passage. After seeing both Venus and Genius depart, and realizing that he is completely without help, John does not immediately go home, but stands for a while where he is, in a daze, sorrowing to think that he has so wasted his time. Then he smiles and thinks of his black beads and the purpose for which they were given him. He resolutely turns his back on his former life and goes home, intending to give himself over entirely for the rest of his life to pray "uppon the point that y am schryve" (2951–2970).

This ending is clearly more in keeping with the conversion from the foolishness of love that he has undergone. Now he no longer prays for "those who attempt true love" (or "those whom true love found"), and his prayers are directed only toward the matter that has been confessed and forgiven. He cannot now be concerned, nor would Venus wish him to be, with running errands for her and involving Chaucer in the writing of more love poetry. Chaucer too is old now, and should, like John, give up his interest in love. Perhaps, however, this is the meaning of the commission: Chaucer is to "sette an ende of alle his werk" on behalf of Love by bequeathing it all to Love in his last will and testament (which is to be "recorded" in Venus's court), and then have nothing further to do with love. But since Chaucer is to make his testament "as he which is myn owne clerk" (2950*– 2957*), it seems more likely that Venus intended him to spend the rest of his days on earth writing about love, and that it was for this reason that Gower brought himself to omit the passage in the second edition.

When John the Lover's account of his experience is brought to an end, Gower again emerges in his own person of poet and moralist. At the end of this epilogue, however, he discusses the main subject matter of the *Confessio*. His Muse informs him, he says, that it is better for him to write no more of love. In the original version, where he leaves his autoprotagonist still con- cerned about true lovers, he goes on to say that making love poetry is quite fitting for one who has received his mate from

---

explanation: the lines were sacrificed in order to make room for the longer revised conclusion, which had to fit on the same page of the manuscript.

Love, for he has what he wishes. "But where a man schal love
crave / And faile, it stant al otherwise," and it is best to give up.
He is obviously speaking of himself, whom he has just described
as "feble and old" (3070*–3087*).

Gower has obviously reverted here to his persona of John the
also-ran lover. In revising the poem, however, he eliminates this
inconsistency, and makes no reference to his own incapacity for
love. Instead he describes the dangers of love in a general way,
and hearkens back to the dichotomy between reason and the law
of nature: he will write no more of love,

> Which many an herte hath overtake
> And ovyrturned as the blynde
> Fro reson in to lawe of kynde,

and so on (3144–3151). He resumes the original text with the
farewell to love: Love is such, he says, that no one can fully
delight in it (which goes contrary to what he said in the first
version about the man with his mate who "hath that he wolde
have"); for it is either lacking in some way or another, or it goes
to excess (3152–3161).

He contrasts this imperfect love with the love reinforced by
charity. We have seen (especially in the case of Constance), and
shall see later, that love between man and woman need not be incompatible with charity. But because of love's dangers and fail-
ings, such is often assumed to be the case—particularly at the end
of treatises of spiritual instruction, when one is to be left looking
at the shortest way to heaven. The love, then, which is "withinne
a mannes herte affermed / And stant of charite confermed" requires no repentance and entails no retribution. Rather, it dis-
charges one's conscience and is beneficial in all circumstances;

> Forthi, this love in special
> Is good for every man to holde,
> And who that resoun wol beholde,
> Al other lust is good to daunte.   [3106*–3109*]

Or, to put it all in another way (as Gower does in his revision, lest
perhaps we be distracted at this point by a hint that with a bit of
reasonable moderation, and repentance for the occasional excess,
the two loves could go together):

> Such love is goodly forto have,
> Such love mai the bodi save,
> Such love mai the soule amende. [3165–3167]

He concludes with a prayer that God send us such love and the grace necessary to attain endless joy in heaven, "wher resteth love," and all peace (3168–3172, cf. 3110*–3114*).

In his final rubric describing the *Confessio,* Gower said in the first version that it was basically about love and the conditions of lovers. But in keeping with his revisionist policy of greater severity toward love at the end of his work, the second-edition rubric says that it is about love and the infatuated passions of lovers. We must not, however, allow this concluding description to make us forget that the treatise also marks out a *via media* of honest love,

> That alle lovers myhten wite
> How ate laste it shal be sene
> Of love what thei wolden mene. [8.2000–2002]

PART III

Clandestine Marriage

Hymeneüs et Juno m'oie,
Qu'il veillent a noz noces estre.
Je n'i quier plus ne clerc ne prestre,
Ne de prelaz mitres ne croces,
Car cist sunt li vrai dieu des noces.

(May Hymenaeus and Juno hear my prayer, and deign to be present at our marriage; I wish for nothing more, neither cleric nor priest nor a bishop's miter and cross; for they are the true gods of marriage.)

—Jean de Meun, *Roman de le Rose* 20986–20990

Acciò che niuna cagione mai, se non morte, potesse questo lor dilettevole amor separare, marito e moglie segretamente divennero.

(In order that no other cause than death could separate this delightful love of theirs, they secretly became man and wife.)

—Boccaccio, *Decameron*, 4.6.9

Chapter 6

Ecclesiastical Precept
and Lay Observance

The Law

Church law in the Middle Ages was chiefly embodied in two great collections, the *Concordance of Discordant Canons* of Gratian of Bologna (ca. 1140) and the *Decretals of Gregory IX* (1234). These volumes, together with four later but much smaller collections (the *Sext*, the *Clementines*, the *Extravagants of John XXII*, and the *Common Extravagants*), made up the *Corpus of Canon Law*, the "law canonized" by the pope, as John Gower puts it.[1] Special legislation for England was enacted by the papal legates Cardinal Otto of Tonengo and Cardinal Ottobono Fieschi in the thirteenth century.[2] In addition, various constitutions were issued by synods of the English provinces from time to time, or by individual bishops. The legatine constitutions of Otto and

1. *Confessio amantis* 8.144–145; see above, Chap. 5. The most modern edition of the *Corpus iuris canonici* is Emil Friedberg's (Leipzig 1879–1881, repr. Graz 1959). For the Ordinary Gloss to the various collections, one must rely either on manuscripts or on the unreliable text of the edition of the *Corpus* issued under Gregory XIII, Rome 1582, or one of its numerous reprints. I have used principally the copy of the Paris 1585 edition kept in the reading room of the Vatican Library, and secondarily the Lyons 1606 edition at U.C.L.A., which corresponds to the Vatican copy in all particulars that I have checked. The *Decretals of Gregory IX* is usually abbreviated by the letter "X" (i.e., "Extra.," meaning "Decretales extravagantes," that is, falling outside of Gratian). For this and other information on the interpretation of canon-law texts, see G. Mollat, "*Corpus iuris canonici*: Manière de faire citations," in R. Naz, *Dictionnaire de droit canonique* 4 (Paris 1949) 643–644.

2. See Agostino Paravicini Bagliani, *Cardinali di curia e "familiae" cardinalizie dal 1227 al 1254*, Italia sacra 18 (Padua 1972) 86, 364. Otto's legateship was from 1237 to 1241 and Ottobono's from 1265 to 1268.

Ottobono were given an authoritative gloss about 1335 by John
Acton, Official (that is, Judge) of the Court of York, and the pro-
vincial constitutions were systematized and glossed by William
Lyndwood, Official of the Court of Canterbury in London, in his
Provinciale (1422–1430).[3]

Gratian's *Concordance* differs from the rest of the *Corpus* in
that it was not issued by papal authority; it was simply the result of
an outstanding jurist's attempt to bring coherence to the varied
judgments of the Fathers, councils, and popes on matters of law
and morality. But it attained such high regard in its own right that
it was usually referred to as the *Decretum* (in English, the *Decree*); it is twice cited in this way in Chaucer's *Parson's Tale*.[4]

Gratian begins his work of harmonizing diverse traditions on
clandestine marriage by introducing the canon *Aliter*, supposedly
a pronouncement of Pope Evaristus but in reality one of the
forged decretals of Pseudo-Isidore. According to this canon, a
marriage is not legitimate unless permission is sought from those
who seem to be the woman's guardians; she must also be betrothed by her parents, and given a dowry in accord with the
laws; she must be blessed by the priest at the proper time according to custom; she must be accompanied by the usual bridesmaids,
and handed over at the appropriate time and solemnly received by
the groom. Finally, the couple must devote the first two or three
days of their married life to prayer and preserve their chastity
during this time. Otherwise, the union is presumed not to be
marriage but rather adultery, concubinage, debauchery, or fornication, unless they intend (to marry) of their own will, supported
by legitimate vows.[5]

3. The Oxford 1679 edition of the *Provinciale* also contains the legatine
constitutions and Acton's *Glossemata*, as well as an appendix of the major
provincial and episcopal constitutions arranged in chronological order
(Lyndwood arranges them according to the five books of the *Decretals of
Gregory IX*). For Acton and Lyndwood, see A. B. Emden, *A Biographical
Register of the University of Oxford to A.D. 1500* (Oxford 1957–1959) 11–
12, 1191–1193.

4. *Parson's Tale* 931, 941; cf. *Melibee* 1404. Gower also cites the *Decree:
Miroir de l'omme* 17425 and 17518. See below, Chap. 11 nn. 2, 25.

5. Gratian 2.30.5.1 (that is, part 2, cause 30, question 5, canon or chapter 1:
Aliter), Friedberg 1.1104. See Friedberg's first note to this canon for the
reference to Pseudo-Isidore. The final requirement listed in the canon, that

Five more canons are brought up, reinforcing or adding to the requirements of *Aliter;* and Gratian sums up these authorities as holding that occult weddings are prohibited and should be considered "infected."[6] But then, after two canons on the significance of the ring and the veil in the marriage service, he enters the objection that many deeds which are prohibited become valid *ex postfacto.* For instance, persons bound by vows of chastity are forbidden to marry, but if they do marry they must stay married. So too clandestine marriages are against the law, but once contracted they cannot be dissolved; and this is what Pope Evaristus meant by his concluding statement in *Aliter.*[7] Gratian then introduces the canon *Si quis divinis* from civil law, which prescribes that if anyone swears to a woman while touching the Bible, or while in an oratory, that he will hold her as his legitimate wife, she is to be his wife whether or not any dowry or written agreement has been arranged.[8]

Gratian's final judgment, then, is that secretly contracted marriage is not denied to be a marriage nor is it ordered to be dissolved if it can be proved by the admission of both parties. Such a marriage is forbidden, however, because if one of the parties changes his mind and denies it, the affirmation of the other party cannot be accepted in court.[9] It must be proved by witnesses, and witnesses can only testify as to what has happened in their presence. It is obvious, then, he says, that clandestine marriages are prohibited because they open the way to adultery (we should rather say "bigamy"); for one or both of the spouses can deny the marriage and marry anew with impunity.[10]

In the Ordinary Gloss to Gratian, compiled by John Teutonicus around the year 1215, the question of the presumption against marriage in *Aliter* is taken up: "Is it not true that to establish marriage it is enough to prove that a man has taken a woman with

---

of devoting a *biduum* or *triduum* to prayer, is obviously inspired by the Vulgate version of the story of Tobias and Sara; see below, Chap. 11.
6. Gratian 2.30.5.6 *post* (that is, Gratian's own remark after canon 6).
7. Gratian 2.30.5.8 *post.*
8. Gratian 2.30.5.9 (*Si quis divinis*),
9. Gratian 2.30.5.9 *post.*
10. Gratian 2.30.5.11 *post,*

the intention of having her forever, even though nothing else is said? . . . And in the union of a free woman marriage is presumed rather than concubinage. . . . For if the man does not explicitly say that he wants her as his concubine, as long as the woman is *honesta*, he shall possess her as his legitimate wife." This legal presumption in favor of marriage is reconciled with *Aliter's* presumption against it by saying that the canon is warning against the danger to one's soul.[11] The implication is that Pope Evaristus is indulging in the exaggerated rhetoric of spiritual counsel.[12]

The Gloss goes on to say that civil law is more severe than canon law; for (as we saw from *Si quis divinis*) it requires a man to say explicitly that he is taking the woman as his legitimate wife; otherwise there is no marriage. The Gloss concords this discord by saying that when the union is between unequal persons, the presumption is against the marriage unless dowry has been arranged and other circumstances, such as the showing of marital affection, are taken into consideration.

In the third canon that Gratian alleges against clandestine marriage, *Nostrates*, Pope Nicholas I informs the Bulgarians of various ceremonies connected with the celebration of marriage in the West. He ends by saying that there are other details as well which have slipped from his memory. "But we do not say that it is a sin if all of these things are not observed in the nuptial pact."[13] The Gloss takes him at his word, but adds the opinion of the stern Cardinal Huguccio, Bishop of Ferrara (d. 1210), that it is a sin to omit the solemnities if they can be performed.[14]

The *Decretals of Gregory IX*, compiled by the Spanish Do-

---

11. Ordinary Gloss to Gratian 2.30.5.1 (*Aliter*) v. *contubernia*: "Sed nonne in matrimonio sufficit probare quod aliquis eam receperit eo praetextu ut eam perpetuo haberet, licet aliud non sit dictum? . . . Et in liberae mulieris coniunctione potius praesumitur matrimonium quam concubinatus. . . . Nam cum quis non protestatur se velle habere aliquam ut concubinam, dummodo honesta sit mulier, habebit eam ut legitimam. . . . Solutio: canon considerat periculum animae . . . et ideo potius iudicat esse fornicationem quam matrimonium." I have omitted the laws cited at each stage of the Gloss's argument.

12. See above, Chap. 5 and below, Chap. 12.

13. Gratian 2.30.5.3 (*Nostrates*).

14. Ordinary Gloss to Gratian *ibid*. v. *non interveniant*.

minican Raymond of Pennafort at the pope's command, is divided into five books, the fourth of which is given over entirely to the laws on marriage. The first decretal, *De Francia*, of the first title, *De sponsalibus et matrimoniis*, specifies, in effect, that marriage is brought about by the consent of the man and woman alone.[15] That is, no other requirements or ceremonies are necessary for validity.

The third title of the fourth book, *De clandestina desponsatione*, contains only three chapters or decretals, which for the most part recapitulate Gratian's teaching. The first, *Si quis clam*, stipulates that if one of the parties to a secret marriage denies it, the burden of proof is on the one who asserts it. The second, *Quod nobis*, provides that if both spouses admit the clandestine marriage, the Church is bound to ratify it as if it had been contracted in the sight of the Church from the beginning.[16] The third, *Cum inhibitio*, is one of the decrees of the Fourth Lateran Council, issued by Innocent III in 1215. It confirms earlier prohibitions against clandestine marriage and specifies that those who enter into such unions are to be given a fitting penance. Even greater publicity than before is to be given to marriages: notices of forthcoming unions are to be posted in church, so that any impediments to them might be made known.[17] In England, these notices, or banns, were to be published on three successive Sundays or feast days before the wedding was to take place.[18]

In 1329, Archbishop Simon Mepham of Canterbury ordered that the decretal *Cum inhibitio* be made known to all the faithful. Priests who participated in marriages before the publications of banns or outside of the proper parish were to be suspended from their duties, and the spouses themselves given due punishment

15. X 4.1.1 (*De Francia*), Friedberg 2.660. The headnote for this "chapter" reads: "Matrimonium solo consensu contrahitur, nec invalidatur si consuetudo patriae non servetur."

16. X 4.3.1 (*Si quis clam*) and 2 (*Quod nobis*).

17. X 4.3.3 (*Cum inhibitio*).

18. See the constitution of Walter Reynolds, Archbishop of Canterbury, at the provincial synod of Oxford held in 1322, Lyndwood 4.1 (270–271 and appendix 39–40); reprinted in David Wilkins, *Concilia Magnae Britanniae et Hiberniae* (London 1737) 2.513.

("poena debita percellendo").[19] In 1342, in his constitution *Humana concupiscentia*, Archbishop John Stratford of Canterbury imposed a penalty of *ipso facto* excommunication upon those who forced priests to solemnize (that is, conduct a wedding service for) clandestine marriages, and ordered these and other excommunicates to be regularly denounced and to receive the other penalties set for those who celebrated a marriage clandestinely.[20]

The upshot of this legislation was that all marriages not performed in church after a proper publications of banns were considered clandestine, whether they were witnessed or not; and while they were regarded as valid, if there were no impediments, they were severely forbidden.

The Practice

What effect did these rules against clandestine marriage have upon the English people at large? One way of answering this question is to see how often violations of the prohibition against secret marriage came to the attention of the authorities.

Ordinarily there were two main courts concerned with ferreting out clandestine unions: the bishop's consistory and the court of the archdeacon.[21] We know from Chaucer that there was a certain amount of competition or overlapping between these two courts:

> For er the bisshop caughte hem with his hook,
> They weren in the erchedeknes book.
>   [*Friar's Tale* 1317–1318]

In his study of the marriage cases that came before the consistory court of Ely during the first part of the reign of Bishop Thomas Arundel (1374 to 1382), Michael Sheehan has shown that clan-

---

19. Constitution of the provincial synod held at St. Paul's, London, Jan.-Feb. 1328/29; Lyndwood 4.3.1 (273–274; app. 41–43); Wilkins 2.554.

20. Issued at the provincial synod of London, 1342; Lyndwood 4.3.2 (274–276; app. 47). For a discussion of the text and its meaning see my article "Clandestine Marriage and Chaucer's *Troilus*," *Viator* 4 (1973) 435–457, esp. 438 n. 15.

21. See Michael M. Sheehan, "The Formation and Stability of Marriage in Fourteenth-Century England: Evidence of an Ely Register," *Mediaeval Studies* 33 (1971) 228–263, esp. 232–233.

destine marriages figured prominently in the register. One-fourth of all the cases heard were matrimonial, and nine-tenths of the matrimonial cases in which details are given (specifically, 89 out of 101) involved clandestine unions.[22] I have made a similar study of the consistory court of Rochester for the year and a half immediately preceding the arrival of the Black Death,[23] and I find a nearly identical proportion of such cases. Out of the 190 actions or trials recorded, in at least 55 of them (therefore 29 per cent) the marriage bond was being asserted or called into question; and 46 of the 52 detailed matrimonial cases (therefore 88 per cent) turned on clandestine unions.

The archdeacon of Ely's records have not been preserved, but Father Sheehan concludes that similar matters must have appeared frequently before his court. Chaucer describes the activity of the archdeacon in Friar Hubert's home region:

> [He] boldely dide execucioun
> In punysshynge of fornicacioun,
> Of wicchecraft, and eek of bawderye,
> Of diffamacioun, and avowtrye,
> Of chirche reves, and of testamentz,
> Of contractes and of lakke of sacramentz,
> Of usure, and of symonye also.
> But certes, lecchours dide he grettest wo;
> They sholde syngen if that they were hent;
> And smale tytheres weren foule yshent,
> If any persoun wolde upon hem pleyne.
> [*Friar's Tale* 1303–1313]

The record of the Official of Rochester shows a similar preoccupation with lechery: fornication is mentioned explicitly in two-thirds of all the *ex officio* charges (77 out of 127).[24] And unlawful

22. *Ibid.* 234, 250.

23. *Registrum Hamonis Hethe diocesis Roffensis, A.D. 1319–1352*, ed. Charles Johnson, Canterbury and York Society (Oxford 1948) 911–1043: Acts of the Consistory Court, 9 April 1347 to 4 November 1348.

24. *Ex officio* inquisitions (that is, trials) are initiated by the judge himself, on the basis of a usually anonymous complaint. See R. Naz, "Inquisition," *DDC* 6.1418–1426. Such inquisitions are distinguished from instance cases, that is, trials in which a party brings a formal suit against another party, e.g., a parson complaining of insufficient tithes (to use the example given by Chaucer in the last two lines cited above). At least 39 of the 63 instance cases at Rochester were over debts or property claims.

intercourse of all kinds, including adultery, grave fornication (where a priest is one of the delinquents), incest (intercourse between cousins or affines),[25] and bigamy, is involved in at least 124 of the 190 cases. Convicted delinquents were usually made to "sing" by being whipped three times around the church and sometimes another three times around the marketplace.

It would be surprising, given this identity of interests, to find no reference, in Chaucer's list, to the archdeacon's concern for uncovering and regularizing clandestine marriages. But such a reference is to be had in the word "contractes." The only contracts designated as such in all the cases of the Rochester tribunal are marriage contracts. Suspected offenders are summoned "upon a matrimonial contract" (5 cases) or "upon fornication and matrimonial contract" (14 cases).[26] Furthermore, in one-third (16 out of 48) of the cases in which fornication was charged between marriageable couples, a matrimonial contract was either admitted by both partners or alleged by one and denied by the other.

The Sanctions

There is one striking difference between the way in which clandestine spouses were treated at Rochester and at Ely. In the latter diocese they were assigned no punishment but simply required to undergo a church wedding.[27] At Rochester, on the contrary, they were not only required to marry publicly but were also usually punished by a public whipping, whether they confessed to "fornication and matrimonial contract" or "matrimonial contract followed by intercourse"; but there are enough instances of both kinds of offenders who received no penance to show that

25. Cf. Gower's attack upon those who indulge in this kind of canonically prohibited incest (above, Chap. 5). There are, of course, many instances in which persons so related have attempted to enter marriage. When such kinship is brought to light, they are required to separate (that is, the marriage is declared null), whether they were previously aware of such impediments or not. It should be remembered that affinity was contracted not by marriage but by intercourse, whether in or out of marriage. Thus a man would be forbidden to marry the blood relatives of any woman he lay with.

26. E.g., "Citati super fornicatione ut dicebatur commissa, ac etiam super contractu matrimoniali inter eosdem ut dicebatur inito" (Rochester Register 937).

27. Sheehan 250–251.

the decision was completely at the discretion of the judge. In one case, a man contracted marriage with one woman, but did not consummate it, and then bigamously contracted and consummated marriage with another woman. He was ordered to solemnize the union with the first, and all three were to be whipped, even the woman whose only offense was the secret contract.[28]

In most of the cases at Rochester in which intercourse followed the contract, the spouses were required to take an oath abjuring the sin of further intercourse until the public wedding. Though such postmarital intercourse is never called fornication, it is regarded as a whippable offense, and it was considered a serious matter by the two prominent English canonists who discussed the subject, John Burgh and William Lyndwood. Lyndwood, as we saw, was Official of Canterbury under Archbishop Chichele (ca. 1417–1431), and Burgh also had ecclesiastical jurisdiction when he was Chancellor of the University of Cambridge (1384–1386). Burgh follows the opinion regarding it as a mortal sin in those regions (like England, of course) where the nuptial blessing is customary,[29] though later he somewhat qualifies this judgment.[30]

---

28. Rochester Register 937–938. In the only two other cases in which there is a clandestine contract and no intercourse, no penance was given (932–933, 969). See also below, Chap. 8. The judge's discretionary powers in this matter are specified by Lyndwood 4.3.1 (274), commenting on the words *poena debita* of Archbishop Mepham (above, n. 19): "Erit arbitraria, cum non exprimatur."

29. Iohannes de Burgo, *Pupilla oculi* 8.5.A (Paris 1527) sig. [v viii^v]. One Cambridge MS of the *Pupilla* is dated 1380 and another 1385; see A. B. Emden, *A Biographical Register of the University of Cambridge to 1500* (Cambridge 1963) 107. In the conclusion just cited, Burgh is following the authority of "William," referring either to William of Montlauzon's *Sacramentale* (ca. 1319) or William of Rennes's *Gloss on the Summa of Raymond of Pennafort* (ca. 1250), both of which works he cites specifically elsewhere.

30. Burgh 8.5.M: If after the marriage is contracted but before the solemnization the bride believes that her husband desires to consummate the marriage, she is excused from sin if she admits him to carnal copula, unless there is some evident sign that he is merely trying to seduce her and does not really intend marriage (Burgh would suspect such fraud if there were a great disparity of condition, nobility of race, or fortune between the spouses). He cites Thomas Aquinas, *In Sent.* 4.28.1.2 ad 3, for the opinion that even the husband commits no sin by such preliminary consummation. But according to William, Burgh adds, in regions where it is customary to have the nuptial blessing beforehand, a bride who admitted her husband to

Lyndwood indicates that those who anticipate the wedding in this way are to be given a heavy penalty when their action is brought to light in court, because they have contemned the custom of the Church.[31]

Similarly, Lyndwood is very severe on those who enter into a clandestine contract, whether or not they consummate it with intercourse. They are to be punished if they have acted out of contempt for the Church's statute. And in fact he holds with those who interpret Archbishop Stratford's constitution as imposing excommunication upon all participants in secret marriages.[32] Burgh, however, who was writing as a resident of the diocese of Ely during Bishop Arundel's tenure, restricts the excommunication to those who force the blessing of a secret marriage (5.21. ab). Though he admits that it is forbidden to marry secretly (8.4.A-B), he does not discuss the gravity of the offense, and in fact he seems to take for granted that marriage is normally contracted some time before the actual solemnity.[33]

There are, according to Burgh, basically two kinds of clandestine consent; (1) before witnesses, but without ecclesiastical solemnity; (2) without solemnity or witnesses. In the first case, the legal presumption is in favor of the marriage. (But it is clear both from canon law and the practice of the Rochester tribunal that a minimum of two witnesses is necessary to prove the marriage in court if one of the parties denies it.)[34] In the second instance, true though not presumptive matrimony results. When such a marriage comes to the priest's attention, he is to urge the couple to contract anew and publicly, and to do penance, for they have scandalized the Church (8.4.B). This advice characterizes the pastoral rather than the forensic approach to the problem. The marriage can be made public of the spouses' own volition, and

---

carnal copula would sin mortally if she did so without a dispensation of the Church and without a just cause.

31. Lyndwood 4.3.2 v. *statutis a iure* (276).

32. *Ibid.* 4.3.1 v. *poena debita* (274); 4.3.2 v. *praedictorum* (276). See above, n. 20.

33. See 8.5.A, cited below (n. 38).

34. See Johnson's introduction to the Rochester cases (Register 913), and cf. Lyndwood 4.3.2 as cited below (n. 39).

they will no longer be liable to appear in court or to be given a judicial penalty.

John Acton, who as we have seen was also an ecclesiastical judge, makes an important distinction: it is a mortal sin to contract marriage in such a way that the Church would be left uncertain of the union, thereby opening the way to bigamy. But if there is some just cause for delaying or omitting some formality, no sin is committed.[35]

The discrepancy, therefore, that we have noticed between the courts of Rochester and Ely in punishing or not punishing clandestine spouses is probably not to be attributed to a general relaxation in the latter part of the fourteenth century. Rather it should simply be put down to differences of place, time, and circumstances (especially the attitudes of particular judges).

Private Contract Leading to Public Wedding

No doubt a vast number of technically clandestine marriages never came to the attention of the authorities for the simple reason that they were eventually made public as a matter of course. It must have been a fairly common practice for couples to pledge themselves to each other *per verba de praesenti* when they finally decided on the match, and then to go through the formalities of the banns and church service as time permitted.[36] Church weddings were not allowed during a good part of the year: from the beginning of Advent to the octave of the Epiphany, from Septuagesima Sunday to the first Sunday after Easter, and from the Rogation Days to the seventh day after Pentecost.[37]

When John Burgh discusses the two-month period of grace given to all newly-married spouses (during which time they can refuse intercourse and even dissolve the marriage, if no intercourse has occurred, by entering a religious order), he includes among the reasons for it the following: "in order to allow for an interval to make ready what is necessary for the solemnization of

---

35. Iohannes de Athon, *In constitutiones legitimas Angliae glossemata*, Constitution of Cardinal Otto, title 13 v. *non subiaceat* (106).

36. Sheehan 239 gives evidence of such a sequence of events at Ely.

37. See Lyndwood 4.3.1 v. *solemnizationem* (274).

the wedding."³⁸ He thereby indicates that private marriage of this sort was a widespread and accepted custom.

In fact, not even Lyndwood would consider such a preliminary marriage contract to be sinful (were it not for Archbishop Stratford's dubiously applicable censure), as long as there were a minimum of two witnesses present, and provided the solemnization followed as soon as possible.³⁹ Such a private contract can almost certainly be seen in the well-known Arnolfini portrait of Jan van Eyck in the London National Gallery, in which the two witnesses are reflected in the mirror in the background.⁴⁰

According to Hostiensis (Henry of Suse, Cardinal of Ostia, d. 1271), whom Lyndwood follows in his classification and assessment of clandestine marriages, marriages performed without the publication of banns are also clandestine and forbidden. But he goes on to ask if this is true in a case where the marriage is known to the whole country—for instance the marriage negotiated with

38. "Ut interim possint praeparare ea quae necessaria sunt ad nuptiarum solemnizationem" (8.5.A).

39. Lyndwood 4.3.2 v. *clandestina* and *statutis a iure* (276).

40. See Erwin Panofsky, "Jan van Eyck's *Arnolfini* Portrait," *Burlington Magazine* 64 (1934) 117–127; *Early Netherlandish Painting* (Cambridge, Mass., 1953) 201–203. The painter identifies himself as one of the witnesses in a "graffito" in legal script on the wall over the mirror: "Johannes de Eyck fuit hic. 1434." See Martin Robertson's letter on p. 297 of the *Burlington* volume cited above for other Latin graffiti of the "Kilroy was here" pattern. It should perhaps be noted that Panofsky does not adequately prove his case in all the details that he alleges. He has consulted only general encyclopedias and dictionaries for his evidence of marriage rites, and has not inquired into specific practices in the Low Countries during the fifteenth century, or in Paris or Lucca, the respective birthplaces of the bride and groom. He refers, for instance, to various meanings and uses of bridal candles in Europe but offers no specific evidence to prove that the candle in the painting falls into one of these traditions. Worse still, in his article he says that "the forearm raised in confirmation of marriage was called the *fides levata*" and refers to Du Cange's *Glossarium;* but Du Cange offers only a nonmatrimonial finger-lifting: "Ipse Georgius promisit sibi quod nullum faceret malum, levando fidem sive digitum." In his book, Panofsky even suggests that the matrimonial *fides levata* was a requirement of canon law, but he can refer only to modern legal practice. The usual custom in the Middle Ages (as in the Sarum Manual) was that the right hand of one spouse be joined to the right hand of the other during the exchange of promises. Panofsky believes that this *dextrarum iunctio* is an absolute essential to the marriage (whereas in fact the only absolute essential is the exchange of consent), and considers the left-right handclasp of the painting to be its equivalent.

King Louis IX of France when he besieged Avignon. He accepted Lady Margaret, daughter of Count Raymond of Provence; and Count Raymond also married another daughter, Eleanor, to Henry III of England. "Are those marriages to be called clandestine, because that solemnity was not then observed? It seems not, since there is no obligation to make what is already certain more certain." In the cases instanced, says Hostiensis, Pope Gregory IX himself approved the marriages. But even today, he continues, it is not the custom for banns to be published for the marriages of magnates—counts, marquises, and the like—and this is acceptable, since it is not necessary to have banns when the wife is publicly summoned from remote parts. In such circumstances the marriage can be contracted in the face of the Church, and the sense of *Cum inhibitio* will not be offended.[41]

Giles Bellemère, Bishop of Avignon, writing in 1398, repeats this opinion of Hostiensis that banns are not necessary when the bride is publicly summoned from afar. Normally, however, it is a mortal sin to omit the banns without cause and in full awareness of the law, especially in those places where the rule is commonly observed. But no such guilt is incurred when there is some special reason for the omission; for example, one or both of the parties may be advanced in age, and the ceremony would embarrass them; or a *nobilis* marries an *innobilis*, and they fear the former's parents; or they have long lived as man and wife, and it would shame them now to undergo the solemnity of banns and nuptial blessing. He then goes on to discuss whether the bishop or even a lesser prelate can give dispensations in the matter; and he also brings up the opinion that kings, princes, and knights who marry without banns do not sin mortally if it is not customary for banns to be published for their marriages.[42]

The fact that Lyndwood does not exempt the nobility from

---

41. Hostiensis, *Summa aurea* 4, De matrimoniis, § Quot modis dicantur sponsalia clandestina (Lyons 1568) 296v.

42. Aegidius Bellemère, *Super Decretales Gregorii IX lecturae* 4.3.3 (*Cum inhibitio*), Vatican MS Ross. 832, f. 123rb-va. Cf. Henri Gilles, *La vie et les oeuvres de Gilles Bellemère* (Paris 1966) 1–159, esp. 126; reprinted with renumbered pages from *Bibliothèque de l'École de chartes* 124 (1966) 30–136, 384–431 (see esp. 398).

banns may be an indication that such omission was not an English practice. In later times, at least, it seems to have been the custom to obtain the bishop's permission, if we can judge from the dispensation given by Archbishop Cranmer enabling Henry VIII to marry Catherine Parr without banns.[43] That such dispensations could be given two centuries earlier in England is implicit in Archbishop Mepham's constitution, which indicates that the penalty of suspension for solemnizing a clandestine marriage (or performing a clandestine solemnization) applies only to a priest who, like Friar Lawrence in *Romeo and Juliet*, acts without the permission of his ordinary.[44]

Further specifications of the law will be noted in the chapters to follow. But we have seen the basic theory, which is quite simple. Marriage was made by the consent of the bride and groom. No other permission, authorization, witness, minister, ceremony, or action was required for the marriage to take effect. Many such accessory provisions were insisted upon by the law, and delinquents were liable to be punished if detected, but a simple marriage of consent remained intact in the eyes of the law, no matter which of its other provisions were left unobserved.

43. *Letters and Papers, Foreign and Domestic, of the Reign of Henry VIII*, ed. J. S. Brewer *et al.* (London 1856–1929) vol. 18 no. 854 (10 July 1543).

44. See the constitution cited in n. 19 above.

Chapter 7

The Witness of Literature: In Which the Foregoing Chapter Is Confirmed by Sundry Examples

Ante-Trent and Anti-Trent

The first thoroughgoing analysis of clandestine marriage and its importance for literature is, to my knowledge, that of Justina Ruiz de Conde, in her study *El amor y el matrimonio secreto in los libros de caballerias.* In the course of her discussion, as we saw earlier, she questions the validity of the courtly-love bias against marriage; she concludes that in France there was, on the contrary, a general bias in favor of marriage, and that in Spain the matrimonial bias was, for all practical purposes, absolute.[1] One way of indulging this bias while also allowing for the secrecy and intrigue so dear to the romantic spirit was to bring the lovers together in clandestine unions; instances of this expedient can be found in two medieval romances, *Tirant lo Blanch* and *Amadís de Gaula.*

The English popular romances of the Middle Ages have been subjected to a similar analysis by Donnell Van de Voort and Margaret Gist, though without a full understanding of the laws and traditions involved. But Gist seems basically correct when she concludes that the romances show little interest in the legal niceties of the contracting of marriage: lovers are normally bound only by the dictates of love and not by those of canon law.[2]

---

1. Justina Ruiz de Conde, *El amor y el matrimonio secreto en los libros de caballerias* (Madrid 1948) 122, 153–155.
2. Gist 27–29; cf. Van de Voort 26–30, 99–106.

Cervantes's use of clandestine marriage has also been examined,[3] and Shakespeare has inspired similar studies. There are two secret contracts of marriage in *Measure for Measure*, and *Romeo and Juliet* centers on a clandestinely solemnized marriage.[4] John Webster's *Duchess of Malfi* also deals with a secret marriage. The Duchess says to her lover:

> I have heard lawyers say, a contract in a chamber
> *Per verba de praesenti* is absolute marriage.

No specific words of marriage in the present tense follow,[5] but their intention is clear, and that is enough:

> We now are man and wife, and 'tis the Church
> That must but echo this.   [1.3]

By the time of Shakespeare and Cervantes, a great change had occurred in the Catholic law on marriage. At the Council of Trent, after much debate, clandestine marriage was declared invalid. Thenceforth, unless a union was properly blessed by a priest and performed in the presence of two other witnesses, it had no binding force. But the new law applied only in regions where the Tridentine decrees were promulgated—not, therefore, in Protestant or schismatic countries.[6]

3. Robert V. Piluso, *Amor, matrimonio, y honra en Cervantes* (New York 1967) 63–113. I owe this reference to James F. Burke via John Leyerle.

4. A similar marriage occurs in *Twelfth Night* between Olivia and Sebastiano, and in *Much Ado about Nothing* 4.1.49–51 Claudio describes the practice of secret contract followed by intercourse:

> If I have known her,
> You will say she did embrace me as a husband,
> And so extenuate the 'forehand sin.

The laws and practices of Shakespeare's time are best set forth by Ernest Schanzer, "The Marriage-Contracts in *Measure for Measure*," *Shakespeare Survey* 13 (1960) 81–89.

5. It seems that all marriages in Elizabethan and Jacobean drama were clandestine in the sense that they were all held offstage; at least I cannot think of any onstage examples, apart from the practice wedding between Orlando and the disguised Rosalind in *As You Like It* 4.1. I do not know if there was some law or custom prohibiting religious ceremonies from being enacted on the stage.

6. See George H. Joyce, *Christian Marriage*, ed. 1 (London 1933) 122–128.

In England, Henry VIII had attempted in the year 1540 a some-what similar reform in order to ensure the dissolution of his marriage to Anne of Cleves and the validity of his new marriage to Catherine Howard. The law of precontracts declared that a marriage contracted but not solemnized and consummated could not be alleged as an impediment to another marriage which was so solemnized and consummated. In effect, the second marriage dissolved the first. But the law was found unworkable, and was repealed shortly after Henry's death.[7]

In Chaucer's time, of course, there was no question about the law: secret marriage, though valid, was prohibited; the prohibition was well known and freely violated, and at least certain categories of clandestine spouses were frequently punished. Let us look now at the works of Chaucer and of some of his predecessors, in order to get some idea of the variety possible in the contracting of matrimony.

The marriage of January and May sets the standard, with its preliminary financial arrangements and full-blown church wedding.[8] Banns are not mentioned, but they can be presumed. The Wife of Bath's five marriages must have been quite similar.[9] In a tale of earlier times, we are told that Jesus mercifully made King Alla marry the widow Constance "full solemnly";[10] and in the interestingly chaste marriage of St. Cecilia, we may take it from her robe of gold and the playing of the organs that hers too was a solemn wedding.[11]

Only in the case of Walter and Griselda, among Chaucer's Christian marriages, can any deviation from the canonical norm be noticed. True, Walter does request Griselda from her father, in accord with the canon *Aliter*. Then, however, after she agrees to his condition that she obey him in all things, he takes her outside

7. I treat this matter fully in a book on the matrimonial trials of King Henry VIII, which I hope to publish soon.

8. *Merchant's Tale* 1691–1709.

9. *General Prologue* 460; *Wife of Bath's Prologue* 4–6, 212, 627–631. In marrying Jankyn within a month of her fourth husband's death, she was, we know, acting on the largess of canon law. See above, Chap. 1, n. 19.

10. *Man of Law's Tale* 691. About her first marriage we are told only of the formal betrothal (233–244).

11. *Second Nun's Tale* 130–134. See below, Chap. 11, n. 26.

and announces to the people, "This is my wyf." By this declaration and by Griselda's tacit consent they are married. Nothing further is added to the bond when, after Griselda is adorned in the clothes and jewelry prepared for the wedding, Walter espouses her with a ring.[12] Or, if he had said nothing before, and simply put the ring on her finger in silence, they would still be considered married. According to John Burgh, if this sort of "subarrhation" (bestowal of the spousal *arrha*, or pledge) is made directly between the spouses, it is presumed to be a marriage, whether or not words of mutual consent have been spoken. For, as Burgh says, it makes no difference whether one declares his will by word or by deed. But if the subarrhation is performed by one of the parents, then only betrothal is to be presumed.[13]

In describing Walter's marriage as he does, Chaucer is simply following Petrarch, his source, who sums up the scene, after Walter leads Griselda to his palace, as *nuptiae ad hunc modum celebratae*. The French translation, which Chaucer also used, seems to specify on the contrary that the *nuptiae* followed: "Et furent faites les nopces, et passa le jour moult joyeusement et liément."[14] Chaucer simply says that they all spent the day in revel.

Marriage and Marriage-Feast in the *Decameron*

Petrarch in his turn was drawing on the last tale of the *Decameron*, where the marriage contract is entered into in a much more explicit and formal fashion. Well before the day of the marriage, Gualtieri secretly arranged the matter with Griselda's father (10.10.9). On the day appointed he comes and breaks the news to Griselda. After receiving her promise of complaisance to his will, he leads her outside, has her changed into her bridal garments, and announces to the people that this is she whom he *intends* to marry, if she will have him. He turns to her and says: "Griselda, vuo'mi tu per tuo marito?"

12. *Clerk's Tale* 253–387.
13. Burgh 8.2.C.
14. Petrarch, *Epistolae seniles* 17.3; for both the Latin and French texts, see the edition of J. Burke Severs in W. F. Bryan and Germaine Dempster, *Sources and Analogues of Chaucer's Canterbury Tales* (New York 1941, repr. 1958) 306–307.

She answers, "Signor mio, sì."
He then says, "E io voglio te per mia moglie."
Boccaccio adds, "E in presenza di tutti la sposò."
Gualtieri then has her brought to his dwelling, where the wedding celebration takes place: "Quivi furon le nozze belle e grandi, e la festa non altramenti che se presa avesse la figliuola del re di Francia" (17–23).

For Boccaccio, *nozze* and *festa* seem to be almost synonymous: the *nozze* are the festivities that follow upon marriage, or, more specifically, the wedding banquet. In the previous *novella*, Messer Torello's wife is already married ("è rimaritata") and has on the bridal crown and rings before the *nozze* begin. Torello has persuaded the abbot to accompany him to "queste nozze," even though religious like him are not accustomed to go to such banquets, "così fatti conviti" (10.9.96, 99, 111). The *nozze* normally take place in the new husband's home.[15]

In Boccaccio's usage, then, the term *nozze* is only connected by implication to the actual contracting of marriage, whether the marriage is contracted with or without witnesses, or with or without church services. The word for the actual act of marrying is *sponsalizie* (or *sposalizie*) or the verb *sposare*. These meanings are very clearly illustrated in the story of the King of England's daughter, who, while traveling to Rome disguised as an underaged abbot-elect, falls in love with young Alessandro. One night she reveals to him her sex and her love, and says that she wishes him for a husband. He agrees; and thereupon, sitting up in bed, before a table bearing a picture of Christ, she puts a ring in Alessandro's hand and has him take her as his wife: "Postogli in mano uno anello, gli si fece sposare" (2.3.33–35). As we shall see later, this means that Alessandro put the ring back on her finger.[16]

The princess of this *novella* was being sent to Rome to be married by the pope to the old King of Scotland. When she reaches her destination and comes into the pope's presence, she first explains her reluctance to be married to the man her father chose for her. Her reason for coming before him now, she says, is totally different from that for which she was sent; she desires

15. *Decameron* 2.10.7, 5.4.49; cf. 5.5.40, 5.6.42, 5.7.52.
16. See below, Chap. 9.

through him to make public the marriage she has contracted with Alessandro in the presence of God alone: "si acciò che per voi il contratto matrimonio tra Alessandro e me solamente nella presenza di Dio io facessi aperto nella vostra e per consequente degli altri uomini" (40). The pope can obviously do nothing but agree, and he has the marriage celebrated anew with solemnity; and then, after a magnificent wedding banquet, he sends them away with his blessing: "Quivi da capo fece solennemente le sponsalizie celebrare; e appresso, le nozze belle e magnifiche fatte, colla sua benedizione gli licenziò" (44).

This is the only instance in the whole of the *Decameron* where Boccaccio gives any indication of a marriage celebrated with the usual church solemnities. In other *novelle*, the matrimony is either effected on the spot, as soon as it is decided upon, or, if it is planned in advance, it simply takes place with no indication of circumstances.

Thus, in the story of the "Goatherdess," Giannotto and a sixteen-year-old widow fall in love and are discovered *in flagrantibus;* Currado, the girl's father, puts them in prison, but when he learns that Giannotto is nobly born, he offers him the chance of marrying her. Giannotto, who says he desired to do so from the beginning but feared refusal, agrees; and the couple marry immediately in the father's presence: "I quali, nella presenzia di Currado, di pari consentimento contrassero le sponsalizie secondo la nostra usanza" (2.6.57). Thenceforward, Currado speaks of Giannotto as his daughter's husband (*marito*) and of himself as father-in-law (*genero*); and after announcing the new alliance (*parentado*), he orders a great *festa* to be made (58–60, 69). Soon after, Giannotto's brother Scacciato is also married. Messer Guasparrino gives his eleven-year-old daughter to him as his wife, together with a great dowry ("con una gran dote gli diè per moglie"), and a *gran festa* follows (74–75). The canonical minimum age for marriage was fourteen for boys and twelve for girls, unless puberty was reached earlier (*nisi malitia aetatem supplet,* "unless malice makes up for the age," as the canonists pleasantly put it).[17] We have the word of Boccaccio's contemporary Fran-

17. See W. Onclin, "L'âge requis pour le mariage dans la doctrine canoni-

cesco de Buti that girls were married even at ten years of age: "Maritansi oggi di dieci anni."[18]

In the story of the "Nightingale," another couple are caught in bed together, and the boy, Ricciardo, is given the choice of immediate death or immediate marriage: "acciò che tu tolga a te la morte e a me la vergogna, prima che tu ti muova, sposa per tua legittima moglie la Caterina." He readily accepts marriage, and the girl's father gives him one of his wife's rings; thereupon, without getting up from the bed, in the presence of both her parents, the boy marries her: "Per che, messer Lizio, fattosi prestare a madonna Giacomina uno de' suoi anelli, quivi, senza mutarsi, in presenzia di loro, Ricciardo per sua moglie sposò la Caterina." A short time later, as was fitting, he married her again in the presence of friends and relatives, and brought her home for the further festivities: "Pochi dì appresso, sì come si convenia, in presenza degli amici e de' parenti, da capo sposò la giovane, e con gran festa se ne la menò a casa e fece onorevoli e belle nozze" (5.4.43–49).

In the last two *novelle* discussed, the lovers did not marry until the parents approved and actually forced the issue. Legally, however, parental approbation was not essential, and they could have married even against the fathers' wishes. In another story, it is to prevent such an occurrence that young Girolamo, who has just turned the canonical age of fourteen, is sent away; he is in love with the tailor's daughter, and his parents fear that he might

que médiévale," *Proceedings of the Second International Congress of Medieval Canon Law*, ed. S. Kuttner and J. J. Ryan, Monumenta iuris canonici, series C, subsidia 1 (Vatican City 1965) 237–247. Cf. *Wife of Bath's Prologue* 4–6: "Sith I twelve yeer was of age . . . Housbondes at chirche dore I have had fyve."

18. Commentary on *Paradiso* 15.105, cited by Branca in connection with the eleven-year-old bride of Boccaccio's *novella* (2.6.74 n. 5). But Branca refuses to take this testimony literally. He believes for some reason that the canonical age for girls was fifteen (note on 2.6.35); elsewhere, however, he acknowledges fourteen as the limit (4.3.9 n. 6); and in still another place he says that girls were *da marito* ("ready for a husband"; see 5.4.6) at the age of twelve, and that the *nozze* usually took place between the ages of fourteen and eighteen (*Decameron* intro. sentence 49 n. 7). Branca has no conception of clandestine marriage and is under the mistaken impression that *nozze* includes the meaning of marriage and that *sposare* refers only to betrothal (see his notes to 2.3.35, 5.3.53, 5.4.46).

secretly marry her: "Per avventura egli la si prenderà un giorno, senza che alcuno il sappia, per moglie" (4.8.8).

In another tale, which we have discussed earlier,[19] the lovers Andreuola and Gabriotto secretly marry ("marito e moglie segretamente divennero"). As with the King of England's daughter, the marriage is effected by means of a ring, given by Gabriotto to Andreuola ("quello anello medesimo col quale da Gabriotto era stata sposata"). The reason for their secrecy is inferable from the circumstances: Andreuola is the daughter of a *gentile uomo*, and Gabriotto is *di bassa condizione*. After Gabriotto's tragic death, Andreuola's father asserts that he would have accepted *tal marito*, and he grieves that she kept him hidden from him because of her lack of confidence in him (4.6.8–9, 29, 40).

The words *sposare* and *sponsalizie* correspond to the Latin terms *desponsare* and *sponsalia*. Boccaccio, who had once made a formal study of canon law, was well aware that the same terms could be applied to betrothal (*sponsalia per verba de futuro*) and to marriage (*sponsalia per verba de praesenti*), and that sometimes the precise meaning could be determined only from the circumstances of the case. The same is true of the Italian terms, as can be seen from the eighth *novella* of the last day. Gisippo has arranged to marry Sofronia, but before the match is brought to fulfillment he discovers that his friend Tito has fallen in love with her. Gisippo speaks of "Sofronia a me sposata"; she is his spouse, and he awaits the wedding feast: "Egli è vero che Sofronia è mia sposa e che io l'amava molto e con gran festa le sue nozze aspettava" (10.8.26, 30). But it becomes evident that he is only engaged to her, and that even after the *nozze* have been celebrated at his house the marriage has not yet occurred. This sequence is irregular, to say the least, and perhaps it was for this reason that Boccaccio gave it an antique rather than a contemporary setting (it takes place in the time of Octavian). The exchange of marriage promises is made only that night following the *nozze*, when Sofronia is in bed with the man she presumes to be Gisippo. But Gisippo has arranged to let Tito take his place in the dark, and it is he who asks if she wishes to be his wife. She, thinking him to

19. See above, Chap. 2.

be Gisippo, says yes. Tito then slips a ring on her finger and voices his own consent: "E io voglio esser tuo marito." And thereupon the marriage was consummated ("E quinci consumato il matrimonio"), and Tito enjoyed himself immensely (46–49).

Such a marriage was not valid, of course, technically speaking, because of the *error personae*. When Sofronia discovers her error, however, she does not think in technical terms; she believes herself to be Tito's wife, but refuses to have anything to do with him. Tito then sets about justifying himself to her, in the presence of her relatives and the relatives of Gisippo. He admits that he practiced deceit, but points out that he came to her not as a lover but as a husband: "Non come amante ma come marito i suoi congiugnimenti cercai." He did not approach her until he had married her with the customary words and with a ring ("con le debite parole e con l'anello l'ebbi sposata"; now the word *sposare* has its usual present force). The relatives are persuaded to go along with Tito, and they give Sofronia to him; she makes a virtue of necessity and transfers her love for Gisippo to Tito (79–81, 89). At this point her marriage becomes canonically valid.

Another story with a somewhat similar plot is also given a classical setting. Arrangements have been made for two girls to marry two brothers; troth has been pledged ("promessa fede"), and on the day set for the festivities ("pattovite nozze"), the brides ("spose") enter the home of their husbands ("mariti") for the first time. As they are seated at the meal, they are kidnaped by two other men and are married to them instead: "e sposate le donne e fatta la festa grande" (5.1.25, 33, 61–70).

Motives and Methods

In the course of Tito's self-defense, he enters into a discussion of clandestine marriage which reflects the conditions of Boccaccio's own time. Some might object, says Tito, not to him as a husband but to the manner in which he became a husband—secretly and furtively, without the knowledge of friend or relative. He admits that this frequently happens, and he speaks of those women who have taken husbands against the will of their fathers, and those who have eloped with their lovers and have been paramours before they became wives, and those who have not sought marriage until they had to, after becoming pregnant or giving birth to children. But such was certainly not the case with Sofronia.[20]

John Andreae of Bologna, the most authoritative canonist in the fourteenth century, repeats what Hostiensis says about rich and noble girls who are frequently seduced and secretly married (presumably for their rank and money). But Andreae, who was a married man himself, and whose daughter Novella, according to a "charming tale," had the brilliant mind of an Heloise, seems to think that it is primarily the delights of furtiveness that lead couples to clandestine marriage.[21] Also, as can be gathered not only from the canonists but from historical and literary examples as well, secret marriage was a ready means for men to obtain their way with women (often of a lower class than themselves) whom they had no intention of really marrying. We shall see that the misadventures of the classical heroines like Dido and Medea were habitually recast in this pattern.

Cardinal Otto of Tonengo and John Acton give still another motive for clandestine marriage: clerics in minor orders often marry in this way in order to continue in their benefices, which would be removed from them if their change of status came to light.[22] Then, too, of course, there were countless couples who married without banns or without witnesses because they were not free to enter into a valid marriage in the eyes of the Church;

20. "Saranno forse alcuni che diranno non dolersi Sofronia esser moglie de Tito, ma dolersi del modo nel quale sua moglie è divenuta: nascosamente, di furto, senza saperne amico o parente alcuna cosa. E questo non è miracolo, né cosa che di nuovo avvenga. Io lascio stare volentieri quelle che già contra a' voleri de' padri hanno i mariti presi, e quelle che si sono con li loro amanti fuggite, e prima amiche sono state che mogli, e quella che prima con le gravidezze e co' parti hanno i matrimoni palesati che con la lingua, e hagli fatti la necessità aggradire: quello che di Sofronia non è avvenuto" (10.8.72–73).

21. Andreae, *Novella* on X 4.3 (see above, Chap. 2 n. 28 for a citation of part of this passage). Cf. Stephen Kuttner, "Joannes Andreae and His *Novella* on the *Decretals of Gregory IX,*" *The Jurist* 24 (1964) 390–408. (Andreae named his commentary after his mother and perhaps after his daughter.)

22. *Constitutio domini Othonis* title *De uxoratis a beneficiis amovendis,* and John Acton, *Glossemata* 38–39, both included in the Oxford 1679 ed. of Lyndwood.

perhaps one of them was already married, or there was an impediment of blood (consanguinity), affinity, public honesty, or some such between them. Archbishop Stratford's *Humana concupiscentia* was directed primarily against such unions, especially when the impeded couples moved to strange parishes and had their fictitious marriages openly celebrated.[23]

Chaucer's Antony would fit under this canonical rubric of entering an invalid marriage or an illegal equivalent to marriage,[24] and perhaps the same notion can help us to understand the situation of lovers like Lancelot and Guinevere and Tristan and Isolde, who pledge fidelity to each other almost as if they were married. Tristan has been associated with the theme of "the man with two wives," such as is found in Marie de France's *Eliduc* and *Lefresne*.[25] This means, of course, that the Irish Isolde is to be regarded somehow as Tristan's first wife, and that she, accordingly, should be found to exemplify a theme of "the woman with two husbands." Unlike Guinevere, her love for Tristan preceded her marriage to Mark, and their declaration of love for each other had at least all the potentialities of a clandestine marriage. When these stories were first elaborated, of course, the rules and concepts of canon law were still in the process of formation. For instance, only with Alexander III (1159–1181) did the popes begin to hold with the Parisian theologians that a nonconsummated marriage was not dissolved by a subsequent consummated marriage.[26]

23. In Lyndwood app. 47. The whole of Title 7 in Book 4 of the *Decretals* is given over to the question of bigamous marriages: *De eo qui duxit in matrimonium quam polluit per adulterium*. In general, a married man who remarries and conceals his first marriage from his second wife is required to stay married to the latter after his first wife's death, whether he wants to or not. But if the second wife knows about the first wife, she is forbidden to stay married to him or to remarry him after the first wife's death. The same provision is made in the allied Title 4, *De sponsa duorum*, chap. 2, *Accepisti* (X 4.4.2).

24. See above, Chap. 4.

25. See Gaston Paris, *La poésie du moyen âge* 2 (Paris 1895) 109–130 for "La légende du mari aux deux femmes," and Helaine Newstead, "The Origin and Growth of the Tristan Legend," *Arthurian Literature in the Middle Ages*, ed. R. S. Loomis (Oxford 1959) 129, 131–132, for application of the theme to Tristan.

26. X 4.4.3: In the title *De sponsa duorum* the decretal *Licet praeter solitum* of Alexander III (Roland Bandinelli), pupil of Gratian and first of the

Therefore authors like Thomas and Chrétien or even Gottfried von Strassburg could hardly be expected to yield easily to a technical canonical examination. But, as Van de Voort shows, there is some indication in Thomas's version (according to Bédier's reconstruction) that Tristan's parents are considered clandestinely married; furthermore, Tristan is aware of the obligation imposed by marriage to pay the marital debt, when he marries Isolde of the White Hands.[27] In *Partonopeus de Blois*, a romance composed around 1190, Partonopeus and the mysterious Melior often sleep together after they have agreed that they will eventually marry (1473–1475), without assuming that they are actually married, even though Pope Alexander III had recently decreed that betrothal followed by copula constituted marriage.[28] However, in keeping with other romances of this period, like *Floire et Blancheflor*, they do not seem to advert to the sinfulness of premarital intercourse.[29] Partonopeus later marries someone else, but he escapes from this union just in time, in his opinion: he did not consummate the marriage, and therefore considers himself still free to marry Melior (4167–4173). Another example, this time in a non-Christian setting, can be seen in the fifteenth-century ro-

---

lawyer popes. At the end of his decree he admits that others hold a different view, and that an opposite judgment had been made by certain of his predecessors. Both Gratian and Alexander himself (in the *Summa Rolandi*) were among those who held the opposing view. The opinion that consent alone made a marriage indissoluble was reinforced ca. 1200 by Innocent III in his decretal *Tuas dudum* (X 4.4.5), where he disallowed contrary customs. When Raymond of Pennafort edited Alexander's decree for the *Decretals*, he omitted his statement that "some hold a different view," and he eliminated as well Alexander's stipulation that a priest, or even a notary where customary, had to be present at the first marriage, along with suitable witnesses. See Friedburg 2.680–681 (the italicized phrases were omitted by Raymond). Cf. Joyce, *Christian Marriage* 57–65.

27. Van de Voort 34–35, 76–77. See *Le roman de Tristan*, ed. J. Bédier, SATF (Paris 1902–1905) 1.19–22, 266–283. The latter passage, from the Sneyd Fragment of Thomas's poem, is also edited by Bartina H. Wind, *Les fragments du roman de Tristan*, Textes littéraires français 92 (Geneva 1960).

28. *Partonopeus de Blois*, ed. G. A. Crapelet (Paris 1834). Cf. the English version, ed. A. Trampe Bödtker, EETSes 109 (London 1912). See Alexander III's decretals *Veniens* and *De illis autem* (X 4.1.15 and 4.5.3); cf. Joyce, *Christian Marriage* 88.

29. *Li romans de Floire et Blancheflor*, ed. Felicitas Krüger, Romanische Studien 45 (Berlin 1938) 107–108, 221–224.

mance *Generides*, which is undoubtedly based on a lost French original. The heroine, Clarionas, was abducted and married to King Gwynan of Egypt. But fortunately it was a stipulation of Egyptian royal marriages that the king and his bride should remain "chaste" until the wedding feast was over, and Sir Generides was able to rescue her in good time and marry her himself.[30]

Let us consider another case, that of Chrétien's *Cligés*. He, when not yet fifteen years old, falls in love with Fenice, the girl who has been pledged to marry his uncle Alis, in spite of the latter's vow never to marry. Without speaking a word, the two young people give their hearts to each other. Fenice realizes that her situation is like that of Isolde, but unlike Isolde she determines to avoid consummating her marriage to Alis. She feels that it is wrong to give her body to one man when her heart belongs to another. She also knows that it is wrong for Alis to marry her at all, since he cannot do so without perjuring himself.[31] For all this, however, she does not come to the conclusion that her marriage to Alis would be invalid. Her father has given her to him, and she does not dare to resist (3128–3129); therefore, she goes through with the wedding. Accordingly, when she explains to Cligés that her dedication of her body and heart to him antedated her marriage to Alis, and that she is not really Alis's wife ("dame") but is still a virgin ("pucele"), she does not thereby conclude that she will be truly married to Cligés if he can take her away from Alis. Instead, she simply considers it the next best thing to marriage. She even cites St. Paul's advice to those who

30. There are two English versions of the romance, one in couplets, ed. Frederick J. Furnivall, Roxburghe Club (Hertford 1865), and another in seven-line stanzas, ed. W. Aldis Wright, EETS 55, 70 (London 1878). Cf. Derek Pearsall, "*The Assembly of Ladies* and *Generydes*," *Review of English Studies* 2.12 (1961) 229–237. The situation described above is brought out most clearly in the coupleted version, lines 6805ff., but see also the stanzaic version, lines 4215ff. At the time of her forced marriage, Clarionas was already "strongly engaged" to Generides (see below, Chap. 9).

31. *Cligés* 2724–3147, ed. Alexandre Micha, CFMA 84 (repr. Paris 1970). According to canon law, at least from the time of Alexander III, only solemn vows of religion or major orders (those of subdeacon, deacon, and priest) invalidate a subsequent marriage. So by this standard Alis's marriage would be valid but illicit, like clandestine marriage. See above, Chap. 6, for the same position in Gratian; and see the decretals under X 4.6 (*Qui clerici vel voventes matrimonium contrahere possunt*).

are unwilling to remain chaste; but instead of repeating his conclusion ("let them marry"), she leaps to an equally Pauline conclusion in a different context: that they should act wisely and
without giving cause for blame (5173–5269).[32] When Fenice and
Cligés live together secretly in their tower and sleep together
naked, we have no reason to doubt, as we do in the case of Perceval,[33] that there is sexual intercourse between them, or to think
that Fenice has not fulfilled her promise to give Cligés her body.
But until Alis dies, she remains only his *amie;* thereafter she becomes his *dame* as well as his *amie* (6362–6363).

Spousals Future and Present, Private and Publicized, Conditioned and Fulfilled

Chaucer was not acquainted with the *Decameron,* but he did
know and use some of Boccaccio's other works. The *Filocolo* and
the *Teseida* are particularly interesting for their treatment of
marriage. We shall consider a bit later Chaucer's use of the clandestine marriage between Florio and Biancifiore in the *Filocolo,*
but here let us look at the story of Tarolfo, the source for *The
Franklin's Tale.* The knight and lady who correspond to Arveragus and Dorigen are nameless in *Filocolo.* Of the knight's courtship and marriage it is said only that he loved the lady with the
most perfect love, and married her: "il quale, di perfettissimo
amore amando una donna nobile della terra, per isposa la prese"
(4.31.2). Chaucer elaborates upon the love-service Arveragus paid
to Dorigen and upon the understanding of mutual love with which
they married.[34] But what interests us here is that he describes
them as entering into a marriage contract with no witnesses whatever. Dorigen says to Arveragus, "Sire, I wol be youre humble
trewe wyf" (758).

The word "wol," that is, "will," like the Latin *volo,* is ambiguous. Sometimes it is primarily an expression of present intention:
"I will to be your wife here and now"; and sometimes its main
force is future: "I will become your wife." The difference is

32. See 1 Cor. 7.9, 10.32; Eph. 5.15.
33. See *Perceval* 1964–2069, ed. William Roach, Textes littéraires français
71, ed. 2 (Geneva 1939).
34. See above, Chap. 2.

crucial, for a mere betrothal could be easily broken, whereas a contract in the present tense was indissoluble, even though no cohabitation or intercourse followed.[35] As a result, the precise meaning of this and similar expressions was apt to be debated in court. Michael Sheehan adduces the example of Margery Paston and her clandestine union with Richard Calle. When summoned before the bishop, she was asked whether the words she spoke constituted marriage or not. She answered by repeating what she had spoken, "and said if tho words made it not sure, she said boldly that she would make it surer ere than she went thence; for she said she thought in her conscience she was bound, whatsoever the words wern."[36]

In Dorigen's case, her present intention seems clear from her next words: "Have heer my trouthe, til that myn herte breste." At any rate, Chaucer does not bother to go into subsequent formalities, simply saying, "Thus been they bothe in quiete and in reste." But presumably they made their marriage public, however that was customarily done in the vaguely pre-Christian setting of the story; for they lived together publicly as man and wife.[37]

When Cleopatra recalls the terms of her wedding covenant with Antony in Chaucer's *Legend*,[38] "that blisful houre" when she "swor to ben al frely youre" is no doubt meant to conjure up a solitary lovers' exchange of vows, like that of Arveragus and Dorigen. It would be at this point that "she wax his wif" (615), and "the weddynge and the feste" (616) would have followed in due course.

Similar situations can be seen in Chrétien's *Yvain* and *Cligés*. In the former, Yvain and Laudine first agree to each other:

> *Yvain:* Toz a vos m'otroi.
> *Laudine:* Sachiez donc, bien acordé somes.
> *Chrétien:* Einsi sont acordé briemant.

35. See below, Chap. 10 n. 3, for exceptions to this rule.
36. Sheehan 246 n. 67, citing Norman Davis, *The Paston Letters* (London 1963) 182; for Margery Paston, see also Ann Haskell, "The Paston Women on Marriage in Fifteenth-Century England," *Viator* 4 (1973) 467. Sheehan 245–247 discusses the ambiguity of *volo*, as does Burgh 8.3.C.
37. The pagan setting is established in line 1293: "As hethen folk useden in thilke dayes."
38. See above, Chap. 4.

Laudine makes clear her matrimonial intention: her barons have authorized her to take a husband ("mari a prandre m'otroient"), and she accordingly gives herself to him *per verba de praesenti:*

> Ci meïsmes a vos me doing;
> Qu'a seignor refuser ne doi
> Buen chevalier et fil de roi.

Chrétien considers it a *fait accompli:*

> Ore a la dameisele fet
> Quanqu'ele voloit antreset.[39]

When they come before the barons to discuss the matter, we are told that the barons wish that they were already pledged to each other and that Laudine had given him her hand, and so could marry him today or tomorrow:

> Car l'eüst il ore afiëe,
> Et ele liu de nue main,
> Si l'esposast hui ou demain!   [2066–2068]

When, after some pretended hesitation, Laudine agrees to the match, she gives herself to him in their presence, and he receives her from the hand of one of her chaplains:

> Veant toz ses barons se done
> La dame a mon seignor Yvain:
> Par la main d'un suen chapelain
> Prise a Laudine de Landuc,
> La dame. [2148–2152]

This is the first time her name has been mentioned. According to *Erec and Enide*, a wife is not married until called by her proper name:

> Qu'altremant n'est fame esposee,
> Se par son droit non n'est nomee.[40]

Perhaps this was a precaution against the sort of *error personae* that Sofronia was victim of.

---

39. *Yvain* 2029–2050, ed. T. W. B. Reid, text of W. Foerster (Manchester 1942, repr. 1967).
40. *Erec et Enide* 1975–1976, ed. Mario Roques, CFMA 80 (repr. Paris 1970).

It is doubtless an unanswerable academic question whether Chrétien considered the private agreement between Yvain and Laudine, and the public repetition of it, to be an actual marriage contract or simply a betrothal. It makes no difference to the story, of course, since the wedding and wedding festivities (to give the Boccaccian distinction to *esposer* and *noces*) occur that very day:

> Le jor meïsme sanz delai
> L'esposa et firent les noces.
> Assez i ot mitres et croces,

and so on; the celebration lasts until evening:

> A ses noces bien le servirent,
> Qui durerent jusqu'a la voille.   [2154–2171]

In *Cligés*, Arthur's queen (presumably Guinevere)[41] lectures Alexander and Soredamours on love: they are not to seek mere gratification ("volanté") in their love, but should seek to be honorably joined in marriage, for so, she believes, their love will long endure. If they agree, she herself will effect the marriage:

> Se vos en avez boen corage,
> J'asanblerai le mariage.   [2271–2272]

Alexander responds that whether or not Soredamours will pledge herself to him, he pledges himself wholly to her:

> S'ele di li rien ne m'otroie,
> Totevoies m'otroi a li.   [2290–2291]

She, of course, reciprocates: "A lui s'otroie an tranblant" (2296). The queen gives them to each other ("fet de l'un a l'autre don," 2303) in rather definitive terms:

> Qui qu'an face chiere ne groing,
> L'un de vos deus a l'autre doing.
> Tien tu le tuen, e tu la toe.

And Chrétien speaks as if possession is complete:

> Cele a le suen, et cil la soe,
> Cil li tote, cele lui tot.   [2307–2311]

41. She is named in *Erec, Yvain,* and *Lancelot,* but not in *Cligés*.

As in *Yvain*, the wedding takes place that very day, after Arthur
and Gawain have agreed to it:

> Firent au los et a otroi
> Mon seignor Gauvain et le roi,
> Le jor firent lor esposailles. [2313–2315]

Boccaccio's *Teseida delle nozze d'Emilia* deals with two solemnly performed wedding services, or *sponsalizie*, but with only
one celebration, or *nozze*. For after the ceremonies of Emilia's
wedding to Arcita, "the days of their *nozze* were postponed"
(*prolungati*) until Arcita should be completely recovered.[42] Unfortunately, Arcita died shortly thereafter, and, to make a long
story short, after some days of mourning, it was decided before
an assembly of the kings who had come to the fatal tournament
that his widow Emilia should now marry Palemone. A day was
set for the *sponsalizie*, which took place in due course at the temple
of Venus, whither the priests carried a beautiful image of Hymenaeus (12.18–49). Since we are told that no rings were yet on
her fingers when Emilia came to the temple (62), we can assume
that Palemone gave her rings during the services. As at Arcita's
wedding, where the customary sacrifices were offered ("sacri-
ficii fatti degnamente / Sì come egli erano in quel tempo usati,"
9.83), the priests made their oblations and followed the Athenian
custom of invoking the aid of Hymenaeus and Juno:

> E con voci pietose fu chiamato
> L'aiuto d'Imeneo, sì come fare
> Era usato in Attene a la stagione,
> E dopo quel l'altissima Giunone. [12.68]

Then Palemone and Emilia exchanged vows before the altar in the
presence of all the kings, and finally, as was fitting, they kissed:

> E poi in presenza di quella santa ara
> Il teban Palemon gioiosamente
> Prese e giurò per sua sposa cara
> Emilia bella, a tutti i re presente.
> E essa, come donna non già gnara,

---

42. *Teseida* 9.82–83, ed. Alberto Limentani (*Opere* 2).

> Simil promessa fece immantanente.
> Poi la basciò, sì come si convenne,
> E ella vergognosa sel sostenne. [69]

Thereupon everyone returned to the palace for the celebration of the *nozze*. The fifth hour of the day had already come when they sat down to eat. There was music, dancing, and games. The bridal chamber and bed were richly appareled, as was fitting for such a great marriage ("a così altiera Isponsalizia"). Invoking Juno, Emilia entered the room with Palemone, where the marriage was consummated seven times over. The next day the festivity recommenced, and continued for several more days (70–80).

In his shortened version of the story, Chaucer cuts down the marriages to the bare canonical essentials. In Boccaccio, Teseo promised Emilia in marriage to the winner of the tournament (5.98–102). Emilia, out of modesty, said nothing at the time but made her consent clear later: if she had to marry, she preferred the one who desired her most (7.85); and when Arcita gained the upper hand, she fastened her love on him, and it was kindled no more for Palemone (8.124). By this sequence of events, which Chaucer follows,[43] Emilia would be considered to have married Arcita *sub conditione*, and when the condition was fulfilled she was justified in thinking herself already married to him:

> E già d'Arcita si dice sposata,
> E già li porta non usato amore
> Occultamente, e già spessa fiata
> Priega l'iddii per lo suo signore; [8.127]

and she is justified in calling him her lord ("O signor mio") and husband ("O dolce sposo") before anything more is said or done (9.27). Arcita, however, desires her to be united to him more formally and Teseo determines to have them solemnly married after the traditions of their forebears (9.81–82).

Chaucer's Arcite, on the other hand, is content with the implicit but real contract, as is evident from his words to Emily on his deathbed: "Allas, myn hertes queene! Allas, my wif!" (2775). Theseus later confirms his assumption of marriage by referring to Emily as his wife (3062). When, therefore, Arcite says to Emily

---

43. *Knight's Tale* 1841–1861, 2323–2325, 2680.

that she should marry Palamon, "if that evere ye shul ben a wyf"
(2796), we must add an "again" to his meaning, or an "indeed,"
understanding him in the sense of Arcita's words to Teseo, that he
leaves his love for Emilia *infinito*, "unconsummated" (10.18).

As for Emily's marriage to Palamon, when it is agreed upon in
full assembly, the bond is effected immediately ("anon") by a
simple handclasp:

> Thanne seyde he thus to Palamon the knight:
> "I trowe ther nedeth litel sermonyng
> To make yow assente to this thyng.
> Com neer, and taak youre lady by the hond."
> Betwixen hem was maad anon the bond
> That highte matrimoigne or mariage,
> By al the conseil and the baronage.   [3090–3096]

A clandestine conditional contract of marriage can be seen in
John Gower's tale of Florent (*Confessio* 1.1551ff.), who pledged
his troth to marry an ugly old woman if she would help him out
of his plight. When she fulfills the condition, he dutifully keeps
his troth, but without revealing his obligation to anyone but the
members of his household. She was prepared for the wedding
service, in accord with the laws of the time (1746), but it took
place at night; Gower does not specify whether this too was in
accord with the law—it was, of course, against Church law.[44] The
requirement of paying the matrimonial debt, however, certainly
was a part of the law:

> Bot yit for strengthe of matrimoine
> He myhte make non essoine,
> That he ne mot algates plie
> To gon to bedde of compaignie.   [1777–1780]

Spousals Inadvertent and Convalescent, Alleged and Proved, Bigamous and Uncanonical

In Chaucer's version of the same story, the knight does not
realize what will be required of him when he pledges his troth to
do whatever the Loathly Lady wishes of him. When she succeeds

44. Lyndwood 4.1 (271) on the constitution of Archbishop Reynolds, at
the words: "Matrimonium, sicut alia sacramenta, cum honore et reverentia
de die et in facie ecclesiae . . . celebretur."

in saving his life at the court of King Arthur's queen, she does not trust him to fulfill his pledge on his own, but immediately enters a plea before the queen and demands that he marry her. Her suit is granted, and he is accordingly ordered to solemnize and consummate the marriage:

> The ende is this, that he
> Constreyned was, he nedes moste hire wedde,
> And taketh his olde wyf, and gooth to bedde.
> [*Wife of Bath's Tale* 1070–1072]

Like Florent, he arranges for a clandestine service, no doubt with the dispensation of the king or queen; for the Church does not yet seem to be established in Chaucer's "olde dayes of the Kyng Arthour," in spite of the fact that the Loathly Lady can allude not only to Christ but to Dante as well. But unlike Florent he waits until morning:

> For prively he wedded hire on the morwe,
> And al day after hidde hym as an owle.   [1080–1081]

By prolonging the clandestinity throughout the day, he was relieved of the trouble and embarrassment of postnuptial celebrations.

A literary example of a matrimonial court case in Christian times can be seen in the tale of "The Wife with Three Husbands," from the *Cent nouvelles nouvelles,* a collection compiled between 1456 and 1461 and attributed to Antoine de la Sale. A certain *chaperon fourré* ("furred hood," that is, a jurist) of the Paris Parlement or Supreme Court falls in love with a shoemaker's wife and carries on an affair with her. Eventually he promises, in the presence of three or four witnesses, to marry her if her husband should die. The husband does die, and the jurist receives the widow into his home and renews his promise. Whether or not the promise is still in the future tense would not matter from the viewpoint of the law, of course, for the intercourse that follows would automatically convert the future into the present tense. When, therefore, the lady presses the jurist to make good his promise to marry her, either she does not know her canon law (which is perhaps unlikely in light of subsequent events), or she is speaking about a public wedding or acknowledgment of their marriage. The *chap-*

eron replies that since he is a man of the Church and possesses benefices, he cannot marry; the promise he made her was invalid, and was simply a ruse to win his way with her. He brings an end to the affair, so he thinks, by marrying her off to a barber.

Later, he secretly negotiates for the hand of a rich burgher's daughter. A day is set for the wedding, and he disposes of his benefices. He turns out to be only a tonsured cleric; as we have seen, even clerics in minor orders could marry, but they could not legally retain their benefices. News of these matters eventually spread all over Paris; normally, of course, the impending wedding would be published in the banns unless the bishop granted a dispensation from the formality. The reaction of the *chaperon's* former paramour is that envisioned by the law. She lodges a formal complaint before the bishop's consistory claiming the jurist as her husband. She produces witnesses to his conditional promise of marriage and establishes that she lived with him for a year after her first husband's death. The bishop therefore annuls her marriage to the barber and declares her the wife of the *chaperon fourré*, since he had had carnal knowledge of her after the aforesaid promise.[45] If, however, he had actually entered into an unconditional *de praesenti* contract with her while her first husband was still alive, he would have been safe; for when both man and woman are conscious parties to a bigamous marriage, the union can never be regularized, according to the law.[46] As it was, the wife was simply providing for the future, like the Wife of Bath and the cleric Jankyn:

> I spak to hym and seyde hym how that he,
> If I were wydwe, sholde wedde me.
>   [*Wife of Bath's Prologue* 567–568]

Father Sheehan has recounted a good many cases similar to that of the *chaperon fourré* from the diocese of Ely during Chaucer's time; and one of Chaucer's own Canterbury tales set in the same diocese (parish of Trumpington) illustrates the ease with which a clandestine contract could be made. When the Cam-

45. *Les cent nouvelles nouvelles* 67, ed. F. P. Sweetser (Geneva 1966). I wish to thank John Leyerle for bringing this story to my attention.
46. See above, n. 23.

bridge cleric Aleyn takes his leave of Malyne, the miller's daughter, he says, "Everemo, wher so I go or ryde, / I is thyn awen clerk, swa have I seel" (*Reeve's Tale* 4238–4239). With one small slip of the tongue he would have been bound to the girl for his life, if she had responded. In fact he said enough as it was, according to the Ordinary Gloss to Gratian.[47] A very commonly used formula of marriage was simply "I take you as mine," with no further specification of the relationship. This is the form cited by Pope Alexander III in his decree on the indissolubility of unconsummated marriages,[48] and the one used by John Burgh in his discussion of the marriage contract (8.3.A). It was also sometimes dictated to recidival fornicators in court. According to the synod of Winchester in 1308, after the same sinners have been found out in court for the third time they are to make a conditional contract of marriage, without oath but recorded in writing, in the following manner:

He: Ego exnunc accipio te in meam, si de cetero carnaliter te cognoscam.

She: Et ego accipio te exnunc in meum, si de cetero fuero a te carnaliter cognita.[49]

The Rochester consistory records provide one example of such a contract "convalescing" upon a further relapse (945–946); in two other cases the recidival copula was successfully denied by one of the parties, and the couples were dismissed (946, 998). But matrimony remained for them precariously imminent.

The situation described in *The Reeve's Tale,* then, shows not only how easily a clandestine contract could be made but also how easy it would be for a misunderstanding or dispute to arise later over whether such a contract actually had been made. Malyne might perhaps honestly have thought that Aleyn pledged himself as a husband, or her father might have thought it in his interest for her to say so, in spite of the cleric's inferior social status.

47. Above, Chap. 6.
48. X 4.4.3 (*Licet praeter solitum*): *He:* "Ego te accipio in meam." *She:* "Ego te accipio in meum." See n. 26 above.
49. Appendix to Lyndwood 37. The formulas used in the Bishop of Ely's court specified "in uxorem meam" and "in virum meum" (Sheehan 255 n. 105).

Symkyn could even claim to be a witness of sorts. John and
Symkyn's wife in the adjacent bed are two other possible witnesses. Alternatively, if Symkyn had been able to retain his hold
on Aleyn's Adam's apple, he might have arranged a marriage
contract on the spot. Father Sheehan has described one such clandestine "shotgun marriage" that took place elsewhere in Cambridge-
shire at this time, and we have seen two examples recounted in the
Decameron.[50] If, however, her parents were unwilling to support
her claim to be the clerk's wife, she would be in the same position
as her fellow townswoman Mariot Foot when summoned before
the Bishop of Ely's court: "She said that she was married to John
but that there was no way of proving it."[51]

The ability of Malyne's priestly grandfather, the parson of
Trumpington, to settle his estate on her (3943, 3977–3986) can
give us an insight into another kind of illegal union: the marriage-
equivalent between a priest and his "uncanonical wife," the sort
of relationship that the Parisian jurist of the *Cent nouvelles nouvelles* claimed to have entered. For even though such unions were
not recognized as valid marriage, they could be entered upon in
such a way as to be legally binding from a financial point of view.
An instance of such a practice came to the attention of the Bishop
of Pamiers in the French Pyrenees in the first part of the fourteenth century during the course of an inquisition into the
alleged heretical views of one Béatrice de Lagleize (that is, "de
l'Église"). According to a priest who "proposed" to her, the
priests of the neighboring Spanish diocese of Urgel openly committed themselves to their concubines in almost the same way that
laymen married their wives: they received a dowry from the
women, and any children born of the unions were to inherit the
goods of both father and mother. The priests promised the
women that they would keep them as long as they lived and
provide for their needs. *Nuptiae et omnia alia* were duly performed, with the exception of the sacramental words of matrimony which were normally spoken in a true marriage.

Béatrice took the priest up on his offer, and they went to Spain
together for the purpose. When they arrived at a certain town,

50. Sheehan 259 n. 126; *Decameron* 2.6 and 5.4.
51. Sheehan 252–253, testimony of "Mariota Foot de Trumpiton."

they went before a notary, and Béatrice gave the priest a dowry of thirty pounds, and he in turn pledged all his goods to her and said that any children to be born of them would be their heirs; he also promised to provide for her and keep her in sickness and in health. Public instruments were made of this transaction by the local priest. But her priest made no further oaths to her, nor did he marry her in any other way.[52]

Such, then, are some, but by no means all, of the possible ramifications of the Church's complex laws on marriage and their implications for literature. Most of the difficulties and much of the intrigue arose from the stunning ease with which marriage could be made. It was supposed to be licensed; but, at bottom, it need not be. The authorities were fighting a losing battle in their efforts to keep marriage public and aboveboard. Until such time as the license was made an absolute and necessary requirement, the law would continue to be successfully flouted.

52. *Le registre d'inquisition de Jacques Fournier, évêque de Pamiers (1318–1325)*, ed. Jean Duvernoy, Bibliothèque méridionale 2.41 (Toulouse 1965) 1.252–253: testimony of the implicated priest, Barthélemy Amilhac. Bishop Fournier later became Pope Benedict XII (1334–1342).

Chapter 8

Ovid's Heroines Regularized

Medea

In the course of the last chapter we have seen two or three examples in Chaucer of secret marriage contracts which are eventually made public and permanent in the eyes of society (*The Franklin's Tale, The Wife of Bath's Tale, The Legend of Cleopatra*). But Chaucer also provides examples of clandestine marriages in which the chief fear of the medieval legislators was realized: the women were seduced by a declaration of marriage and then abandoned. As may be supposed, all of the women involved are Ovidian heroines.

It was only natural for a systematic medieval mind to interpret classical accounts of love affairs as clandestine marriages in accord with canon law, where the circumstances warranted. Such circumstances, for instance, can be found in the story of Pygmalion: he prays for a wife (*coniunx*) like his statue. Venus vivifies the statue and is present at the marriage she has made: "Coniugio quod fecit adest dea" (*Metamorphoses* 10.274–295). Since the goddess herself intervenes to effect the marriage, it is perhaps not precisely clandestine on the medieval model;[1] but Jean de Meun takes the hint to elaborate a form more in keeping with contemporary practice: before the statue comes to life, Pygmalion put a gold ring on her finger and speaks the *verba de praesenti*, supplying a like sentiment on her part; he calls on the gods of marriage to hear him and be present at his wedding, and he desires no other minister or service:

1. Cf. Gower, who simply says that Venus heard Pygmalion's prayer and transformed the statue: "Lo, thus he wan a lusti wif, / Which obeissant was at his wille" (*Confessio* 4.424–425).

Anelez d'or es doiz le boute,
Et dist con fins leaus espous:
"Bele douce, ci vos espous
Et deveign vostres, et vos moie.
Hymeneüs et Juno m'oie,
Qu'il veillent a noz noces estre.
Je n'i quier plus ne clerc ne prestre,
Ne de prelaz mitres ne croces,
Car cist sunt li vrai dieu des noces."

[*Roman de la Rose* 20982–20990]

Later, after the statue has come to life, he renews his pledge to her once he finds that what Venus says is true, and she responds:

Por ce que c'est chose seüre,
A lui s'otroie volantiers
Con cil qui siens iert touz antiers,
A ces paroles s'antr'alient.   [21132–21135]

An even better example can be seen in the story of Medea's romance with Jason. In the *Metamorphoses,* she is portrayed as convincing herself to help Jason by saying that she will make him pledge his troth beforehand and swear to the covenant by the gods. "Et dabit ante fidem, cogamque in foedera testes / Esse deos." Later on the marriage will be solemnized: "Te face solemni iunget sibi" (7.46–49). She visualizes some of the dangers ahead when she flees with him, but says she will fear only for her husband: "Metuam de coniuge solo." But then she has a revulsion of feeling—how can she call her guilty action a marriage: "Coniugiumne vocas speciosaque nomina culpae / Inponis, Medea, tuae?" (68–70).

When she sees Jason again, her love for him overcomes all hesitation, especially when he grasps her by the right hand (an integral part of the formal Christian wedding service)[2] and promises marriage ("promisitque torum"). He swears deep oaths that he will fulfill his promises (89–97). Her recollection in the *Heroides* of this momentous event is similar. There was the *dextrarum iunctio* ("dextrae dextera iuncta meae") and the solemn oaths that he would never have any bride but her; he invoked

---

2. Sarum Manual 47: "Teneat eam per manum dexteram in manu sua dextera et sic det fidem mulieri per verba de praesenti." The bride does the same in her turn. Cf. above, Chap. 6, n. 40.

Juno, who is in charge of the sacred rites of marriage: "Conscia sit Iuno, sacris praefecta maritis" (12.72–90). All of his promises, however, are projected toward the future; and though Ovid calls Medea Jason's *coniunx* as he sails away with her (*Meta.* 7.158), it is hard to be confident that he considers them man and wife without further ado.

When Benoit of Sainte Maure treats this story in his *Roman de Troie*, Jason swears twice to marry her, first *per verba de futuro:*

> Sor toz les deus vos jurereie
> E sor trestote nostre lei
> Amor tenir e porter fei;
> A femme vos esposerai,
> Sor tote rien vos amerai;
> Ma dame sereiz e m'amie.
> De mei avreiz la seignorie. [1430–1436]

Then, later, Medea directs him to place his hand on an image of Jupiter and swear an oath *per verba de praesenti:*

> E sor l'image jureras
> A mei fei porter e tenir,
> E mei a prendre senz guerpir;
> Leial seignor, leial amant
> Me seies mais d'ore en avant.

Jason does so, and thereby perjures himself:

> Jason ensi li otreia,
> Mais envers li s'en parjura. [1630–1636]

He has not really consented to marriage, then, but in law he would be considered married; and in conscience he would be bound to give true consent. Furthermore, by consummating the contract that night ("Cele nuit la despucela"), he would be automatically married to her even without his second oath in the present tense (1625–1648).

Benoit composed his romance just after the midpoint of the twelfth century. When, in 1287, well over a hundred years later, the Sicilian lawyer and judge Guido of Le Colonne (i.e., Terranova or Gela) turned it into Latin prose, Jason's commitment

became still clearer. Even his first promise has an immediate ring
to it: "Me in virum vobis humiliter et devotum sponsum expono."
Then Medea has him bind himself to her as his wife by divine and
human law from this hour onward: "Iurabis divini et humani iuris
ab hac hora me in tuam consortem accipies" (21–24).

Chaucer, who had all of these accounts at his disposal, followed
the medieval versions in making the mechanics of the clandestine
marriage quite obvious. The *sponsalia de futuro* are followed by
an explicit *matrimonium de praesenti* before the union is consummated:

> They been accorded ful bytwixe hem two
> That Jason shal hire wedde, as trewe knyght;
> And terme set, to come sone at nyght
> Unto hire chambre and make there his oth
> Upon the goddes, that he for lef or loth
> Ne sholde nevere hire false, nyght ne day,
> To ben hire husbonde whil he lyve may,
> As she that from his deth hym saved here.
> And hereupon at nyght they mette in-feere,
> And doth his oth, and goth with hire to bedde.
> [*Legend* 1635–1644]

Perhaps it could be maintained that the line "As she that from
his deth hym saved here" constituted a condition in the contract.
Gower is quite explicit. Medea first conditions her aid upon his
response:

> If thou wolt holde covenant
> To love, of al the remenant
> I schal thi lif and honour save.
> [*Confessio* 5.3449–3451]

Jason agrees:

> Al at your oghne wille,
> Ma dame, I schal treuly fulfille
> Youre heste, whil mi lif mai laste.   [3453–3455]

Later they both become more specific:

> For sikernesse of mariage
> Sche fette forth a riche ymage
> Which was figure of Jupiter,
> And Jason swor and seide there,

> That also wiss God scholde him helpe,
> That if Medea dede him helpe
> That he his pourpos myhte winne,
> Thei scholde nevere parte atwinne,
> Bot evere whil him lasteth lif,
> He wolde hire holde for his wif.[3]   [3483-3492]

A conditional marriage contract made *per verba de praesenti*, if it were not consummated, would automatically convalesce as soon as the condition is fulfilled. The same is true of a conditional contract with a definite time limit for fulfillment, like that of Emily and the winner of the tournament in *The Knight's Tale*. But since Jason consummated his contract by intercourse before the condition was fulfilled, it would be presumed in law that he had waived his condition and the marriage would become fully binding, even if the contract had been a mere betrothal (that is, *de futuro*).[4]

An example can be seen in a couple summoned to the Rochester consistory on a charge of fornication and (clandestine) matrimonial contract. They admitted having intercourse, as well as a promise that the man would marry the woman if her parents consented. But since intercourse followed upon this promise, and the court found no reason why they should not be considered man and wife, it was so pronounced, and they were ordered to have the marriage solemnized.[5]

Of course, if some impediment were found to exist between a couple, intercourse would not affect the conditional contract. Such was the case with the shoemaker's wife in the *Cent nouvelles nouvelles*, who continued to carry on in bed with her jurist friend, after his promise to marry her, while her husband was still alive. By medieval standards, at least in Chaucer's presentation, Jason is in precisely this position, for he still has another wife, Hypsipyle. But since Medea is unaware of her existence, Jason would

3. Cf. the sidenote: "in amorem et coniugium Medeae . . . iuramento firmius se astrinxit," that is, "He firmly bound himself by oath in love and marriage to Medea."
4. See Alexander III's decretal *De illis* in the title *De conditionibus appositis in desponsatione vel in aliis contractibus* (X 4.5.3).
5. Rochester Register 967. No penance was given. A similar case is so decided in Innocent III's decretal *Per tuas*, X 4.5.6.

be estopped by law after Hypsipyle's death to use his first marriage as an excuse for abandoning Medea.[6]

Dido

Dido is perhaps the most interesting of the classical heroines for the present discussion, because of the ambiguity of her position both in Virgil and in Ovid. The union between Dido and Aeneas is effected in absolutely clandestine circumstances, and the two parties put a diametrically opposite interpretation upon the event. Dido claims that their union constitutes marriage, and Aeneas denies it. Virgil seems eventually to side with Aeneas, in a line that we saw Ovid imitate in Medea's letter: "Coniugium vocat, hoc praetexit nomine culpam" (that is, "Marriage is her name for it—with this word she concealed her guilt," 4.172). In the previous line Virgil distinguishes this pseudo marriage, or mere allegation of marriage, from the one-sided love with which she had been enflamed: "Nec iam furtivum Dido meditatur amorem" ("It is not a secret love Dido now practices").[7] But Virgil himself has just spoken of their union as a wedding:

> Prima et Tellus et pronuba Iuno
> Dant signum; fulsere ignes et conscius aether
> Conubiis, summoque ulularunt vertice Nymphae. [166–168]

(First Earth and Juno, matron-of-honor, give the sign; the lightning flashed and the heavens were witness to the wedding, and from the mountain-top the nymphs sent up the ritual cry.)

Furthermore, as Gordon Williams points out (380–381), Dido is not to be judged as subjectively guilty of entering an illicit union, for "Virgil always portrays Dido as really convinced that she is married to Aeneas." He also says that Ovid's portrayal of Dido in

6. See above, Chap. 7, n. 23; and cf. John T. Noonan, Jr., *Power to Dissolve: Lawyers and Marriages in the Courts of the Roman Curia* (Cambridge, Mass., 1972) 206.
7. Apart from the Loeb edition of the whole *Aeneid*, see the editions of the fourth book by Arthur Stanley Pease (Cambridge, Mass., 1935) and R. G. Austin (Oxford 1955). I use the translations of Gordon Williams in his study of Dido's alleged marriage in *Tradition and Originality in Roman Poetry* (Oxford 1968) 374–387. Williams (374–375) finds the model for the episode in the story of Medea and Jason in the *Argonautica* of Apollonius Rhodius.

the *Heroides* is similar, but we shall see reasons to qualify that judgment later.

According to Williams, Dido's guilt lies in other directions: she is heedless of her good name, she neglects her queenly duties, and, most of all, she is disloyal to the memory of her first husband, Sychaeus. She has violated the Roman ideal of the *univira*, the woman dedicated to one husband. When such a woman marries for the first time, it is to be the last time as well, for the bond of wedlock was considered to be eternal (378, 384). It was this ideal that St. Jerome inherited and recommended in his accounts of valiant widows like Porcia and Dido (in his version of her story, we remember, Dido killed herself on Sychaeus's pyre rather than marry for a second time).[8]

If, then, Dido is sincere in thinking that she has married Aeneas, how can Aeneas so strenuously deny it? He says, "Nec coniugis umquam / Praetendi taedos, aut haec in foedera veni" ("Neither did I hold forth a bridegroom's torch, nor make such vows," 4.338–339). Williams finds the explanation in Roman marriage practice. For in addition to the normal ceremonial wedding, another form had evolved, "one which was probably far the most frequent in real life. It was a free marriage (that is, the wife did not become a possession in the control of her husband), for which no ceremonial was needed; what was needed was simply the consent of both parties that it was marriage, and this consent did not create obligation (as in a contract), but only a status." And: "What distinguished marriage from cohabitation was consent and *affectio maritalis*" (382).

He goes on to explain the ambiguity that could result from such a practice (compare our discussion of *The Reeve's Tale* in the last chapter): "This clearly leaves a possible area of doubt, misunderstanding, and misinterpretation between the two parties, and it is precisely in this area that Virgil wishes his reader to imagine that the relationship of Dido and Aeneas is set." According to Dido, there was a *dextrarum iunctio*, and *fides* was given, as she thought, "per conubia nostra, per inceptos hymenaeos" (4.305–316, 597). Even objectively speaking, Dido might be accurate in

8. Above, Chap. 4 n. 24.

her memory of the event, and yet Aeneas need not be subjectively bound to her. For "it is impossible to imagine lovers who do not make statements and promises, which, regarded in cold blood, are ambiguous and probably go further than the speaker intended."

Williams recapitulates his argument in terms that I could use for my interpretation of *Troilus and Criseyde:* "It is in this area of ambiguity that Virgil [Chaucer] has set his drama, and he could reasonably rely on Roman [English] readers to plot the range of ambiguity within the institutions which they knew. Marriage could exist without ceremony and formality, simply by the consent of both parties" (382–383).

It seems to me, however, that one difficulty has been over-looked in this reading of the *Aeneid:* no evidence is cited to show that the Roman free marriage could be, or ever was, entered into in the complete absence of witnesses.[9] (Juno, Tellus, and the nymphs hardly count; they, like God, cannot be called upon as helpful witnesses *in foro externo.*) Perhaps it was for this reason that Ovid considered the marriage illegitimate:

> Et tamen ille tuae felix *Aeneidos* auctor
> Contulit in Tyrios arma virumque toros,
> Nec legitur pars ulla magis de corpore toto
> Quam non legitimo foedere iunctus amor.

(Yet the fortunate author of the admired *Aeneid* brought his "arms and the man" to a Tyrian bed, and no part of the whole work is more read than the love that was united by no legal compact.)[10]

In these lines, Williams says, "the attitude of an observer of Aeneas is nicely caught." Ovid is, in fact, one of the Roman

9. To support his description of free marriage, Williams does no more than refer to P. E. Corbett, *The Roman Law of Marriage* (Oxford 1930) 90ff., but Corbett does not discuss the sort of clandestine union Williams has in mind. It should be noted, by the way, that free marriage was not the same thing as *usus*. By *usus* a woman becomes equivalently married after a year of cohabitation with a man; the eventual marriage, however, is not the free form, but rather the *manus* form, whereby the man acquires rights over her (Corbett 85–90). Similarly, common-law marriage in the modern sense is to be distinguished from the medieval clandestine marriage, which is formed by consent, not by cohabitation. The consent, as we shall see in the next chapter, can be exchanged even by letter or by proxy.

10. *Tristia* 2.533–536; the translation is by Williams (386).

readers that Williams appeals to, and one who claims to be speaking for many others, though Williams warns us that he is "exaggerating for his own purposes." We shall see, however, that long before his sad exile Ovid had had several other opportunities for describing a clandestine free marriage, and he did not take them.

Even Dido in the *Heroides*, though she calls herself Aeneas's deceived *coniunx* (7.69), is perhaps only speaking of what she should be by right. Later she says that she will be content to be his "hostess" rather than his bride, if he is ashamed to have her as a wife: "Si pudet uxoris, non nupta, sed hospita dicar" (167). She asks him to delay (she is writing to him before he has left Carthage), and appeals to the *hope* she has of marriage: "Pro spe coniugii tempora parva peto" (178).

If, then, there is some doubt about the way marriage worked in Roman times, there is no such doubt regarding the Middle Ages. Though clandestine marriage was declared illegitimate by papal law, it was valid by divine law and accepted as such by all Christians, popes incuded. The ambiguity of the fourth book of the *Aeneid* still remained, of course, but invariably the medieval authors took Dido's side of the argument. Dante even cites as proof of the marriage the lines in which Virgil accuses her of using the name of marriage as a cover-up for her guilt:

> Quod fuerit coniunx, idem noster poeta vaticinatur in quarto.
> Inquit enim de Didone:
>> Nec iam furtivum Dido meditatur amorem:
>> Coniugium vocat; hoc praetexit nomine culpam.[11]

In one of Machaut's poems, Peace recounts Dido's tragedy and condemns Aeneas for having pledged his faith that she would be his wife; he falsely called her his lady and sovereign mistress:

> Dydo, roïne de Cartage,
> Ot si grant dueil et si grant rage
> Pour l'amour qu'elle ot a Enée,
> Qui le avoit sa foy donnée
> Qu'a mouillier l'aroit et a femme;
> Et li faus l'appelloit sa dame,

---

11. Dante, *De monarchia* 2.3.15, ed. Società dantesca italiana, *Opere* (Florence 1921) 375. This passage was pointed out to me by Thomas Hahn.

> Son cuer, s'amour, et sa deesse,
> Et sa souvereinne maistresse.[12]

In *The House of Fame*, Chaucer is somewhat ambiguous: Dido became Aeneas's love, "and let him doo / Al that weddynge longeth too." She "made of him shortly, at oo word, / Hyr lyf, hir love, hir lust, hir lord . . . Wenynge hyt had al be so / As he hir swor" (243–263). But in *The Legend of Good Women* he is more explicit: She "tok hym for husbonde, and becom his wyf / For everemo, whil that hem laste lyf" (1238–1239).

Later, Dido seems to say that the promise on Aeneas's part was directed toward the future: "Have ye nat sworn to wyve me to take?" (1304), and: "So ye wole me now to wive take / As ye han sworn" (1319–1320). But at the same time she calls herself his wife: "Ye wole nat from youre wif thus foule fleen?" (1307). No doubt, then, we are to take her words to refer to a public acknowledgment of her as his wife, or to a solemn wedding service. For even if his promise had been *per verba de futuro*, it would have already undergone the conversion expressed in the well-known equation, *Betrothal* + *Copula* = *Marriage*.

Ariadne, Phyllis, Hypsipyle

Of course, Chaucer would not have to take great pains to make himself understood in a matter that was of such everyday occurrence as clandestine marriage. In *The House of Fame*, for instance, when treating briefly of the story of Ariadne and Theseus, he says simply that Theseus entered into a conditional marriage contract of the sort that Jason made to Medea:

> He had yswore to here
> On al that ever he myghte swere,
> That, so she saved hym hys lyf,
> He wolde have take hir to hys wif. [421–424]

Chaucer says nothing about the keeping of the contract, but why should he? The sequel was obvious enough.

Even when he develops the story more at leisure in *The Legend of Ariadne*, he is hardly more detailed in the matter. Theseus at

12. Machaut, *Le jugement dou roy de Navarre contre le jugement dou roy de Behaingne* 2095–2102 (*Oeuvres* 1.209).

first says nothing of love or marriage, but simply promises to
serve Ariadne perpetually as her page. She responds delicately,
"Yit were it betere that I were youre wyf" (2089). She does not
ask him to swear to marry her, if we are to take her literally—he
is only to swear that he will marry his son to her sister Phaedra.
But instead he proceeds to swear that he has loved her for many
years, and he goes on to pronounce *verba de praesenti:*

> Upon my trouthe, I swere, and yow assure
> This sevene yer I have youre servaunt be.
> Now have I yow, and also have ye me,
> My dere herte, of Athenes duchesse!   [2119–2122]

With these words, the conditional contract of marriage between
Theseus and Ariadne is concluded. Ariadne does not respond in
kind; she has already expressed her matrimonial intentions. Instead
she says softly to her sister,

> Now be we duchesses, bothe I and ye,
> And sekered to the regals of Athenes.   [2127–2128]

It is ironic, of course, that they are "secured" to the same man
and will both be married to him in turn. Literally, however,
Theseus is acting as the spokesman for his son, as was normal, and
betrothes him to Phaedra. His own marriage convalesces as soon
as the condition of his rescue is fulfilled, which it is in short order:

> And every poynt was performed in dede,
> As ye han in this covenaunt herd me rede.   [2138–2139]

Accordingly, Chaucer can call Ariadne Theseus's wife: Theseus
filled the barge with "his wyves tresor," and then "tok his wif,
and ek hir sister," and stole away (2150–2154).

In Gower's treatment of the story, Theseus manages to win
Ariadne over and deflower her. The method he uses is that standard ploy of the seducer, a promise of marriage:

> Theseus in a prive stede
> Hath with this maiden spoke and rouned,
> That sche to him was abandouned
> In al that evere that sche couthe,
> So that of thilke lusty youthe
> Al prively betwen hem tweie
> The ferste flour he tok aweie.

For he so faire tho behihte
That evere, whil he live mihte,
He scholde hire take for his wif,
And as his oghne hertes lif
He scholde hire love and trouthe bere;
And sche, which mihte noght forbere,
So sore loveth him ayein,
That what as evere he wolde sein
With al hir herte sche believeth,
And thus his pourpos he achieveth,
So that, assured of his trouthe,
With him sche wente, and that was routhe.
                              [*Confessio* 5.5376–5394]

The "for" in the line "for he so faire tho behihte" shows that his promise of marriage came before he "took away the first flower."

In the Latin note, Gower speaks of Theseus as promising marriage in a most certain manner: "sponsalia certissime promittens." The words *promise* and *behote*, like the Latin *promittere*, can have an immediate as well as a future significance, as the meanings "assure," "dedicate," and "vow" make clear. We have already seen that the word *sponsalia*, "spousals," can mean "marriage" as well as "betrothal," and in fact the former is the usual meaning, as is evident, for example, from the Sarum order for effecting marriage: *Ordo ad faciendum sponsalia;*[13] and we have seen Gower use it in the same sense.[14] He goes on, indeed, in this note to say that the ungrateful Theseus, having arrived in Athens, crowned Phaedra, now married to him: "sibi sponsatam."

As for Ovid's accounts of Ariadne, he has her recall, like Medea and Dido, a *dextrarum iunctio* and a pledge of faith: Theseus's *dextera* was *crudelis*, his *fides* a *nomen inane* (*Heroides* 10.115–116). Like Dido, she may consider herself married in effect or by right to Theseus: she calls him a *vir periurus* (76). But, as we know, the word *vir* is ambiguous, and Showerman in the Loeb translation cannily renders it as "mate." In the *Metamorphoses*, Ovid simply refers to Ariadne as Theseus's *comes*, "companion" (8.175).

13. Sarum Manual 44.
14. Cf. Tereus's "espousaile" (5.5815); "Sibi virginitas carnis sponsalia vincit" (5.6358 *post*); the "spousailes" of Apollonius (8.975).

Paris is another seducer who promises marriage, except that he
is sincere in his promise (as we have seen, the fact that both he
and Helen are already married does not prevent their remarriage).[15] But it is quite clear that the marriage is to take place in
the future—the hour of marriage will repair the present sin:
"Nunc ea peccemus quae corriget hora iugalis" (*Heroides* 16.297).
If she will let him come to bed with her, he will swear to marry
her according to her own wedding service:

> Te mihi meque tibi communia gaudia iungant;
>   Candidior medio nox erit illa die.
> Tunc ego iurabo quaevis tibi numina, meque
>   Adstringam verbis in sacra vestra meis.   [319–322]

(Let mutual delights join you to me, and me to you; brighter
than mid of day will that night be. Then I will swear to you
by whatever gods you choose, and bind myself by my oath to
observe the rites of your choice.)

Demophoon's approach was similar, as Phyllis tearfully recalls:

> Iura, fides ubi nunc, commissaque dextera dextrae,
>   Quique erat in falso plurimus ore deus?
> Promissus socios ubi nunc Hymenaeus in annos,
>   Qui mihi coniugii sponsor et obses erat?   [2.31–34]

(The bonds that should hold you, the faith that you swore,
where are they now?—and the pledge of the right hand you
placed in mine, and the talk of God that was ever on your
lying lips? Where now the bond of Hymen promised for years
of life together—promise that was my warrant and surety for
the wedded state?)

In his oaths he referred to the solemnities of the marriage rite: he
swore "by Juno, the kindly ward of the bridal bed, and by the
mystical rites of the goddess who bears the torch" (41–42).

Phyllis now regrets the shameful way in which she included
the use of the marriage bed in her hospitality to Demophoon:
"Turpiter hospitium lecto cumulasse iugali / Paenitet" (57–58).
And though, like Dido in speaking of her union to Aeneas, she
refers to the loss of her virginity as a kind of marriage, she is no

15. See above, Chap. 3.

doubt being ironical. For she says that the fury Tisiphone was matron of honor at that bridal: "Pronuba Tisiphone thalamis ululavit in illis" (115–117). Just so, when Dido was in the cave with Aeneas, she thought that the nymphs had raised the marriage cry, but instead it was the Furies foretelling her fate (7.95–96).

Once again, it is understandable that a medieval audience would consider Phyllis's marriage to have been effected immediately. When Chaucer tells her story, he says that Demophoon followed the same path as did "his false father, Theseus":

> For unto Phillis hath he sworen thus,
> To wedden hire, and hire his trouthe plyghte.
> [*Legend* 2465–2466]

After consummating the union (he "doth with Phillis what so that hym leste"),

> He seyde, unto his contre moste he sayle,
> For there he wolde hire weddyng aparayle,
> As fel to hire honour, and his also.   [2472–2474]

He was speaking, of course, in Chaucer's intention, of solemnizing the clandestine contract by which he was already fully bound.

Finally, in *The Legend of Hypsipyle*, Chaucer describes another seduction, which has at least some of the aspects of a clandestine courtship. Hercules acts as Jason's go-between,

> And Jason is as coy as is a mayde:
> He loketh pitously, but nought he sayde;
> But frely yaf he to hire conseyleres
> Yiftes grete, and to hire officeres.   [1548–1551]

When he eventually marries her, he no doubt does so openly, or at least has a public wedding, whether or not a secret contract has preceded it:

> The somme is this, that Jason wedded was
> Unto this queen, and tok of hir substaunce
> What so hym leste, unto his purveyaunce,
> And upon hire begat he children two.   [1559–1562]

In Ovid, Hypsipyle makes a point of saying that theirs was not a furtive affair: "Non ego sum furto tibi cognita." To Chaucer as well as to Ovid this would mean that no intercourse had taken place before the wedding.[16] In her *ubi sunt* lament, she can appeal not only to his plighted word ("Ubi pacta fides?") but also to the bonds of marriage and the wedding torch ("Ubi conubialia iura / Faxque?"). Juno was truly at her wedding as *pronuba,* and Hymen too was present, crowned with wreaths. But she admits that it was neither Juno nor Hymen who carried the torches, but the fury Erinys (6.41–46).

Chaucer gives his impressions of what a pagan wedding contract and solemnity must have been like in his *Legend of Hypermnestra.* The fathers of Hypermnestra and Lynceus see fit to arrange a marriage between their children,

> And casten swich a day it shal be so,
> And ful acorded was it utterly.
> The aray is wrought, the tyme is faste by,
> And thus Lyno hath of his fader's brother
> The doughter wedded, and ech of hem hath other.
> The torches brennen, and the laumpes bryghte;
> The sacryfices ben ful redy dighte;
> Th'encens oute of the fyre reketh sote;
> The flour, the lef is rent up by the rote
> To maken garlondes and crounes hye.
> Ful is the place of soun of minstralsye
> Of songes amorous of maryage,
> As thylke tyme was the pleyne usage.   [2605–2617]

The last line shows that Chaucer was well aware of certain differences between pagan and Christian marriage and that he took pains to specify these differences. We have seen, however, that on one point he recognized no difference: the validity of clandestine marriage.

16. *Heroides* 6.43; see Arthur Palmer's note on this line in his edition (Oxford 1898).

Chapter 9

Filocolo and Troilus

The Frontiers of the Romance of Marriage

Apart from being well aware that clandestine marriage, though valid, was forbidden by Church law, Chaucer would doubtless have been convinced that pre-Christians were under no such restriction and that only later

> it was forbore
> Amonges ous that ben baptized;
> For of the lawe canonized
> The pope hath bede to the men
> That non schal wedden [in a den],

as John Gower might have put it.[1] The basis for such a conviction is expressed in even more canonical terms by John Burgh of Cambridge University, who was writing at the same time that Chaucer was composing the *Troilus* and the *Legend*. Marriage is *ratum* but not *legitimum* when entered into by Christians without solemnity. It is *legitimum* but not *ratum* when performed by the unbaptized according to the laws of their country.[2]

It would be natural, then, to suppose that people not under Church law could enter into clandestine unions free from all guilt. In point of fact, we have not seen a literary case of clandestine marriage even among Christians that was considered sinful. Since, however, ecclesiastical opposition to such contracts was a well-known datum of life in fourteenth-century England, Chaucer might well have wished to make the difference between modern

1. Cf. *Confessio* 8.142–146. Gower, of course, is really speaking of the prohibited degrees of consanguinity. See above, Chap. 5.
2. Burgh 8.1.A and J. For the texts, corrected from the Strassburg 1517 edition, see *Viator* 4 (1973) 446 n. 54.

and ancient law absolutely clear in the *Troilus*, where his aim was
to preserve the lovers from all blame in their affair.

Accordingly, after narrating Pandarus's agreement to help
Troilus in his suit, he begins a new book, in which he discusses
various changes that have taken place over the centuries. Just as
forms of speech differ from age to age,

> Ek for to wynnen love in sundry ages,
> In sundry londes, sondry ben usages.   [2.27–28]

There may be, he says, some lover in his audience who has his
doubts about the way in which Troilus gained his lady's favor,
and who says to himself, "So nold I nat love purchace." But the
truth is, he answers, that there is more than one road and more
than one manner by which to arrive at Rome;

> Ek in som lond were al the game shent,
> If that they ferde in love as men don here,
> As thus: in opyn doyng or in chere,
> In visityng, in forme, or seyde hire sawes.
> Forthi men seyn, "Ecch contree hath his lawes."   [38–42]

He is plainly contrasting public courtship, the practice of openly
requesting the hand of one's beloved, with a furtive approach.[3]
And by means of the concluding proverb he is saying that clandestinity was legal in Troy.

In an earlier chapter we have seen that although Chaucer followed the *Filostrato* as his chief source for the story of Troilus,
he fairly systematically set about to elevate the love of the hero
for Criseyde and hers for him from the dishonorable variety of
Boccaccio's account to one that was as honorable as he could
make it under the circumstances. The result, in C. S. Lewis's view,
is that "the loves of Troilus and Criseyde are so nobly conceived
that they are divided only by the thinnest partition from the lawful loves of Dorigen and her husband. It seems almost an accident
that the third book celebrates adultery instead of marriage. Chau-

---

3. Cf. D. S. Brewer, "Love and Marriage in Chaucer's Poetry," *Modern Language Review* 49 (1954) 463: Chaucer "very obviously has the curious secrecy of Troilus's love-affair chiefly in mind" when he writes these words. But Brewer thinks Chaucer is explaining why Troilus and Criseyde *do not marry*, not why they marry secretly. An independent reading of Chaucer's poem which agrees with mine is given by John B. Maguire, "The Clandes-tine Marriage of Troilus and Criseyde," *Chaucer Review* 8 (1973–1974) 262–278.

cer has brought the old romance of adultery to the very frontiers of the modern . . . romance of marriage" (*Allegory of Love* 197).

We have seen in great detail that there was no frontier between extramarital and marital romance, or if there was, it was easily crossed. Boccaccio passed back and forth over it as the spirit (or the story line) moved him. Lewis is right, however, in saying that Chaucer himself did not cross it; but the reason is that he remained always within the pale of marriage. The partition separating Troilus from Arveragus does not exist. That the third book of the *Troilus* so much resembles a celebration of marriage is no accident, for it is, in Lewis's own words (196), "a long epithalamium," not only "in effect" but in reality.

The model that Chaucer followed for the central event was not the *Filostrato*, but Boccaccio's more juvenile work, the *Filocolo*.[4] In the love story between Florio and Biancifiore in this long prose romance, the frontier between fornication and marriage is to be found in that dim region where all depends upon the direction the lovers intend to take. There are two ways, that of honor and that of dishonor, of righteousness and of unrighteousness. The way of righteousness is straight, but that of unrighteousness is crooked. Neither is difficult to find or to follow, for all depends on one's intention. But to the observer the matter is sometimes obscure. It is not so in the case of Florio and Biancifiore, but the situation is more doubtful with Troilus and Criseyde. There are, however, criteria by which we can judge: when a man talks and thinks of righteousness, purity, chastity, contentment, and of every righteous deed and glorious virtue, we may confidently (at least according to the sixth commandment of Hermas's *Shepherd*) trust him and his works, for they are the deeds of the angel of righteousness.

The Clandestine Marriage of Florio and Biancifiore

The love of Florio and Biancifiore develops and is played out in a completely pagan ambience. Though Biancifiore's parents

4. On the indebtedness of the *Troilus* to the *Filocolo*, see Karl Young's *Origin and Development of the Story of Troilus and Criseyde*, Chaucer Society (London 1908) 139ff., and Robinson's note to *Troilus* 3.512. See also Sanford B. Meech, *Design in Chaucer's "Troilus"* (Syracuse 1959) 60–78.

are Christian, they are both out of the picture after she is born.
As for her maid Glorizia, also a Christian, she does not intrude
her religion into the story until the principals are happily married.
We shall discuss later some of the difficulties this curious arrangement eventually gets Boccaccio into,[5] but in the early part of the
story, as we shall see shortly, the pagan gods are given a free hand.

Florio, the son of the pagan King Felice of Spain (who for
some reason has his headquarters at Verona in Italy), was born
on the same day as Biancifiore, and they grew up together. As
part of their education, they are given Ovid's holy book to study,[6]
in which he shows how Venus's holy fires should be enkindled
within cold hearts (1.45). At the age of fourteen (2.15.5) they fall
in love. Venus has taken note of the invocations they have made
to her with chaste hearts and intercedes for them with Cupid,
who enflames them with love (2.1–2).

They embrace each other and give simple kisses to one another,
but go no further, for they are still too young to know of the
hidden delights of love (2.4.7). Almost immediately, the king and
queen, Florio's parents, find out about their love and take pains
to separate them, since they consider Biancifiore an unsuitable
match for Florio (2.7.9–10). Boccaccio philosophically observes
that this was all arranged by the providence of God, who did not
wish Biancifiore to besmirch her honor by becoming Florio's mistress, but wished to preserve her for marriage:

Ma che is può qui più dire, se non che il benigno aspetto, col quale la
somma benivolenza riguarda la necessità degli abandonati, non volle
che il nobile sanguine, del quale Biancifiore era discesa, sotto nome
d'amica divenisse vile, ma acciò che con matrimoniale nodo il suo
onore si servasse, consentì che le pensate cose sanza indugio si met-
tessero in effetto?   [2.9.8]

We have in this rhetorical question a summary of the plot from
a providential level, that is, a level far above that of the gods who
give immediate supernatural impetus to the actions of the story.
For the sake of the plot Boccaccio is deliberately overlooking, for
the time being, the fact that the young lovers had it in their

5. See below, Chap. 12.
6. See above, Chap. 3.

power from the very beginning to tie the matrimonial knot and thus avoid the dishonor of illicit love.

In explaining his action later, in fact, King Felice says that he was afraid that Florio would become so enamored of the girl that he would marry her ("egli se la facesse sposa"). If he should give her to Florio, or if Florio should marry her in secret ("o che egli da me occultamente la si prendesse"), such a lowborn bride would do great damage to the family honor (2.29.7–9). And Biancifiore tells herself later, after she has been condemned to death through Felice's plots, that she had only to will it, and she could have married Florio, but she did not do so because of her loyalty to the king:

> Io, misera, avrei già potuto con le mie parole tirare Florio in qualunque parte la voluntà più m'avesse giudicato, o congiugnerlo meco per matrimoniale nodo, se io avessi voluto, se non fosse stata la pietà che 'l mio leale cuore ti portava. O vecchio re, per l'onore che io da te ricevea non ti volli mai del tuo unico figliuolo privare, e io del bene operare sono così meritata. [2.53.10–11]

Eventually, of course, the situation is resolved in precisely this way, a consummation which Felice could have foreseen if he could only have interpreted the animal symbolism of the dream Venus sent him, for "il leoncello, occultamente dal cane, si congiugesse con la cerbia amorosamente" (2.3.9). The dog in the dream is not Felice, but the emir or "admiral" to whom Biancifiore has been sold as a slave in Egypt. Florio, now using the name of Filocolo, arrives on the scene and manages to insinuate himself into Biancifiore's quarters, where he finds her maid Glorizia, who hides him until dark (4.104–112).

At nightfall, she brings him into Biancifiore's bedroom and conceals him behind the curtains of the bed. After she has seen Biancifiore to bed, she herself retires to her own room nearby to go to sleep. Florio hears Biancifiore pray that he might now be in her arms, and she would kiss him a hundred thousand times (4.114–117). Florio waits until she goes to sleep, and then undresses and makes his way into her embrace, while she sleeps on. He speaks to her, tells her to wake up, kisses her a hundred times or more at every word. He pulls back the cover and regards her beautiful bosom, he touches and kisses her breasts, and

with his hands explores her most intimate parts, feeling delight that
seems to surpass that of heaven:

Egli la scuopre e con amoroso occhio remira il delicato petto, e con
disiderosa mano tocca le ritonde menne, baciandole molte volte. Egli
distende le mani per le segrete parti, le quali mai amor ne' semplici anni
gli avea fatta conoscere, e toccando perviene infino a qul luogo ove
ogni dolcezza si richiude: e così toccando le dilicate parti, tanto
diletto prende che gli pare trapassare di letizia le regioni degl'iddii.
[118]

Biancifiore finally wakes and is terrified to find someone in bed
with her. She cries out and tries to get up, but Florio identifies
himself and tries to calm her. Her fear is dispelled when she
realizes it is he, and she embraces and kisses him. When she asks
how he got there, he replies that he did so by the will of the
gods ("così ci venni come fu piacere degl'iddii"). They speak
of past and present dangers, and begin to gladden each other with
innumerable kisses. Biancifiore asks to see the ring she gave him,
and he shows it; she takes it as a sign of the truth of King Felice's
ironical augury that she would marry the greatest baron of his
kingdom (119–120).

Taking his cue from these words, Florio proposes marriage. He
tells her that she is not to think that all his travails have been to
acquire her simply as a mistress; rather, he desires her as his inseparable bride. He promises, *per verba de futuro* but before anything else happens between them, to marry her with the very ring
she gave him, and he calls on Hymenaeus, Juno, and Venus to
witness it:

Nè credere che io sì lungamente aggia affanato per acquistare amica,
ma per acquistare inseparabile sposa, le quale tu mi sarai. E fermamente,
avanti che altro fra noi sia, col tuo medesimo anello ti sposerò, alla
qual cosa Imeneo e la santa Giunone e Venere, nostra dea, siano
presenti.

Biancifiore answers that she has always lived with the firm hope
of having the duty of dying as his wife; therefore, she says, let
them get up and perform their marriage before the statue of their
god, Cupid, who can be for them their Hymenaeus, their holy
Juno, and their Venus (120).

She then rises from bed and drapes herself with a rich coverlet, and Florio does the same. They kneel in front of the statue, and Florio prays to Cupid to make their marriage safe and indissoluble:

Questa giovane con indissolubile matrimonio cerco di congiungermi, al quale congiungimento ti priego niuna cosa possa nuocere, niuno vivente dividerlo né romperlo, niuno accidente contaminarlo, ma per la tua pietà in unità il conserva: e come con le tue forze sempre i nostri cuori hai tenuti congiunti, così ora i cuori e' corpi serva in un volere, in un disio, in una vita, e in una essenzia. Tu sii nostro Imeneo; tu in luogo della santa Giunone guarda le nostre facelline, e sii testimonio del nostro maritaggio. [121]

After this remarkable tribute to Cupid's sanctifying power, the statue moves and changes expression, a sign that Florio's prayers have been heard. Then, after Biancifiore makes a similar prayer, she stretches forth her finger and receives the matrimonial ring. Then she rises and like a bashful bride kisses Florio before the holy image, and he returns the kiss. Then she runs into Glorizia's room and tells her the good news. They celebrate together, improvising music as best they can in absence of organ and cither. Finally, after much talk, with most of the night already passed, they all return to bed.

Boccaccio takes this opportunity to address the joyful love that has married the new spouses. He tells those with hard minds to meditate on it, and if they do not soften, no *graziosa vertù* can dwell in them. In the lovers' room, he says, there can be seen torches not lit by human hand; Hymenaeus himself has appeared, and so has Venus and her son. Even Diana is there rejoicing, and she praises the new spouses for having so long preserved themselves chaste for each other under her law.[7] The lovers now delight themselves for a fitting time in loving unions ("amorosi congiugnimenti"); they spend the rest of the night almost until daybreak speaking about various things, and then sleep until the sun is at its full height (122).

The next night too they spend together in pleasant conversation and loving embraces (125), and sleep late again the next

7. Biancifiore had promised Diana that she would be one of her devotees until Hymenaeus arranged her wedding festivities: "infino a quel tempo che l'inghirlandato Imeneo mi penerà a concedere liete nozze" (3.51.7).

morning; but this time the admiral finds them in bed together and consigns them both to the flames. But Florio eventually manages to smooth out his differences with the admiral, who turns out to be his uncle. He tells him that he married Biancifiore: "Davanti la bella imagine del mio signore . . . di lui faccendo Imeneo, per mia sposa con letizia la sposai" (151.5). The admiral asks him if he really means to hold her as his true wife (such clandestine marriages were, as we know, often not sincerely meant): "Ultimamente il demanda se suo intendimento è per vera sposa Biancifiore tenere." Florio answers that he has never desired anything other than Biancifiore as his wife: and since the gods have granted it, while his soul remains united to his body he does not intend to have another spouse apart from her (156.1–2).

At this, the admiral, who hesitated more out of a desire to make him content than to draw him back ("più per contentarlo che per reprenderlo dimorava"), praises his determination. But he adds that it is not fitting that such a great match should have been made furtively: "Non è convenevole cosa che si alta congiunzione furtivamente sia stata fatta." He therefore proposes that they marry in the presence of Florio's subjects ("in cospetto di loro la sposerai") and celebrate the *nozze* with the festivity that such great *sponsalizie* deserve (156.2–3).

On the day set for the wedding, the admiral tells the people the story of the two lovers. He recounts how Florio obtained access to the tower and how he himself found him sleeping with Biancifiore. He makes no mention of their clandestine marriage, strangely enough, perhaps because he did not witness it, but simply says that they desire to join their love with the bond of marriage under his authority: "Desiderano sotto la nostra potenza di congiugnere quell'amore che insieme si portano per matrimoniale legame" (159.4–5). Boccaccio himself alludes to the secret marriage, however, when he says that the priests, after invoking the blessing of Hymenaeus and Juno, make Florio give Biancifiore the ring for the second time (160). The new spouses are content, to say the least, at their changed fortune, and they spend several joyful days in the great festivity that follows their wedding, rendering pious thanks to the gods who brought them to safe haven and put an end to their travails (165).

Such, then, is the love story that Chaucer turned to for inspiration in his effort to purify the love of Troilus and Criseyde. In fact, Chaucer approached his material in the same way that Boccaccio had done in *Filocolo*. For, as we have seen earlier, in the original versions of *Floire et Blancheflor* (and the same holds for the Italian *cantare* and the English version as well), the lovemaking in the tower is a simple matter of premarital intercourse. It was Boccaccio himself who added all of the details of clandestine marriage.

C. S. Lewis has spoken of the *Troilus* in the language of the stable as being "by *Il Filostrato* out of *Roman de la Rose*" (179). It could also justly be described on a human or celestial level as the legitimate offspring of a marriage between *Il Filostrato* and *Il Filocolo* (or perhaps it would be better to speak of Biancifiore and say *La Filocola*).

The Winning of Criseyde

After he has fallen in love with Criseyde, Troilus confides in her uncle Pandarus. When Pandarus offers to help him achieve his desire, Troilus assures him that his intentions are thoroughly honorable. He says:

But herke, Pandare, o word: for I nolde
That thow in me wendest so gret folie
That to my lady I desiren sholde
That toucheth harm or any vilenye.   [1.1030–1033]

We can conclude from this that Pandarus is not acting as Troilus's pandar, at least from Troilus's point of view, but almost as his proctor, empowered to ask for Criseyde's hand in his name. Such negotiations on behalf of prospective bridegrooms were commonplace in Chaucer's day. Even consent *per verba de praesenti* could be conveyed by proxy, or by letter. Pandarus, of course, will be the bearer of Troilus's letters.

When speaking of the matter of proctorial consent, John Burgh gives the example of the marriage between Isaac and Rebecca, referring to the canon *Honorantur* of St. Ambrose in Gratian: it is the parents of Rebecca who are honored with gifts, and Rebecca herself is not consulted about the marriage; she awaits the judgment of her parents in the matter, since it is not becoming to virginal modesty for a woman to choose her own husband.[8] Gratian is illustrating the stipulation of Pope Evaristus in the canon *Aliter,* that a girl must be petitioned and received from her parents or guardians before she can be legitimately married.[9]

By transforming Troilus's best friend from Criseyde's cousin to her uncle, Chaucer at one stroke combined in Pandarus the roles of proctor and protector; Pandarus not only speaks for Troilus, he acts *in loco parentis* for Criseyde. He makes his position clear to Criseyde:

> Think wel that this is no gaude;
> For me were levere thow and I and he
> Were hanged, than I sholde ben his baude,
> As heigh as men myghte on us alle ysee!
> I am thyn em. The shame were to me
> As wel as the, if that I sholde assente,
> Thorugh myn abet, that he thyn honour shente.   [2.351–357]

Just before he brings the lovers together at his house, he again disclaims the office of bawd, this time to Troilus. He admits that he has become a go-between, but the moral nature of his services will depend upon how Troilus deals with Criseyde:

> For the have I my nece, of vices cleene,
> So fully maad thi gentilesse triste,
> That al shal ben right as thiselven liste.   [3.257–259]

As he talks on, he begins to sound too much like Boccaccio's Pandaro, whose speech Chaucer is following at this point. Pandaro freely admits that he has done a bawd's work, but not for the bawd's motive of money. He has cast his honor to the ground out of friendship for Troiolo. Now he only begs him to be discreet, so that his dishonor and that of Criseida may not become common knowledge (*Filostrato* 3.6–10). We have already noticed that Chaucer's Pandarus seems to speak in similar terms of Criseyde,[10] and it could be argued that he, like his Italian original, would be satisfied simply with secrecy and discretion on Troilus's part. But

---

8. Burgh 8.3.B; Gratian 2.32.2.13. Cf. Lyndwood 4.3.1 (*Quia ex*) v. *contractibus matrimonialibus* ("266" [i.e., 273]).
9. Above, Chap. 6.
10. See above, Chap. 2.

Chaucer eventually has him come "to purpos" and clarify his intentions in legal and contractual terms:

> I shal thi proces set in swych a kynde
> And God toforn, that it shal the suffise,
> For it shal be right as thow wolt devyse.

> For well I woot, thow menest wel, parde.
> Therfore I dar this fully undertake.
> Thow woost ek what thi lady graunted the;
> And day is set, the chartres up to make.   [3.334–340]

Troilus responds by vigorously denying that he considers Pandarus's services the work of a bawd. A bawd takes money; Pandarus has acted out of "gentilesse, / Compassioun, and felawship, and trist" (393–403). But so had Pandaro, one might object, in bringing about an admittedly dishonorable affair. In order to distinguish between the two cases, we must take to heart the rule that Troilus cites:

> Departe it so, for wyde-wher is wist
> How that ther is diversite requered
> Bytwixen thynges like, as I have lered.   [404–406]

Pandaro cast his honor to the ground for the sake of Troiolo; but Pandarus has simply put his honor in Troilus's hands to guard along with his own and that of Criseyde, in whichever way he sees fit.

Later, Pandarus sets Criseyde's mind at rest as to the morality of their union:

> Ne, parde, harm may ther be non, ne synne;
> I wol myself be with yow al this nyght.   [913–914]

He will "give her away," in accordance with the formal wedding ritual.[11] She responds by placing herself totally at his and Troilus's discretion:

> For the love of God, syn all my trist
> Is on yow two, and ye ben bothe wise,
> So werketh now in so discret a wise

---

11. Sarum Manual 47: "Deinde detur femina a patre suo vel ab amicis eius."

That I honour may have, and he plesaunce.
For I am here al in youre governaunce.   [941–945]

Pandarus, in fact, had informed Criseyde, in Troilus's presence, what he intended to do. The two of them were to come to his house at his invitation:

"For I ful well shal shape youre comynge,
And eseth there youre hertes right ynough,
And lat se which of yow shal bere the belle,
To speke of love aright!" Therwith he lough.
"For ther have ye a leiser for to tell."   [196–200]

After she is in bed with Troilus, Criseyde admits that if she had not yielded to him already she would not be here:

Ne hadde I er now, my swete herte deere,
Ben yold, ywis, I were now nought heere.   [1210–1211]

Thus, we saw, Pandarus could say to Troilus, "Thow woost ek what thi lady graunted the" (339).

We cannot suppose that either Pandarus or Criseyde is speaking of anything other than what passed between them and Troilus at their original meeting. There, Criseyde asked Troilus to be more specific as to what it was he wanted of her. He answered that he wished only to be allowed

Withouten braunche of vice on any wise,
In trouthe alwey to don yow my servise.   [132–133]

This would include, of course, the vice of lechery, and specifically the branch of fornication.

Before she will allow Troilus to remain in bed with her at Pandarus's house, she calms her fears by making him swear to his honorable intentions (even though, according to Chaucer, such oaths were not strictly necessary in his case):

Soone after this, though it no nede were,
Whan she swiche othes as hire leste devyse
Hadde of hym take, hire thoughte tho no fere,
Ne cause ek non to bidde hym thennes rise.
Yet lasse thyng than othes may suffise
In many a cas. For every wyght, I gesse,
That loveth wel, meneth but gentilesse.   [1142–1148]

Troilus "putte al in Goddes hand, as he that mente / Nothyng but well" (1184–1186); and Criseyde, completely rid now of all dread,

> As she that juste cause hadde hym to triste,
> Made hym swich feste, it joye was to seene,
> Whan she his trouthe and clene entente wiste;

and then she opened her heart and told him her own intent (1226–1239).

Troilus specifies his intent as matrimonial by calling on Hymenaeus, the God of Marriage: "Imeneus, I the grete!" (1258).[12] He also addresses the God of Love in theological terms: "O Love, O Charite!" (1254) and "Thi grace passed oure desertes" (1267), as well as in Boethian philosophical terms: "Benigne Love, thow holy bond of thynges" (1261). Then, after kissing Criseyde, he declares that he is dedicated to her by God and for God: "for the love of God, my lady deere, / Syn God hath wrought me for I shall yow serve" (1289–1290); and he pledges his troth to her forever:

> For certes, fresshe wommanliche wif,
> This dar I seye, that trouth and diligence,
> That shal ye fynden in me al my life.   [1296–1298]

Later, they exchange rings (1368), and still later Criseyde, too, explicitly pledges her troth to Troilus: "I am thyn, by God and by my trouthe" (1512). But the matter is complete and accomplished after Troilus's original protestation, as we know from Criseyde's words:

> For it suffiseth, this that seyd is heere,
> And at o word, withouten repentaunce,
> Welcome, my knyght, my pees, my suffisaunce!   [1307–1309]

And only now is there the least suggestion that they consummate their union physically: "Juggeth ye that han ben at the feste / Of swich gladnesse, if that hem liste pleye" (1312–1313).

12. Cf. *Legend* 2250: "Imeneus, that God of Wedyng is." The same phrase occurs in *Merchant's Tale* 1730.

The Ambages of Clandestinity

Given the honorable and sinless motives of Troilus and Criseyde, these words and actions could hardly have failed to indicate to Chaucer's audience that they had entered upon a true marriage. The matrimonial aura with which Chaucer has surrounded them has been recognized even by modern critics who are totally unaware of the ease with which marriage could be contracted by lovers who were well-intentioned and free to marry. The love of Troilus and Criseyde is admittedly "embodied in an elaborate rite of vows and rings and tender words,"[13] and Troilus at least is said to regard his love as virtuous and legitimate;[14] but further concessions than these have not been thought possible.

The perspective changes radically, however, once we acknowledge that Troilus and Criseyde could be married with nothing more than an "I take you as mine" or its spoken or unspoken equivalent. Criseyde's "Welcome!" would do nicely, as would her response to Troilus's kiss. For, as John Burgh points out, even a toast or a kiss is enough to contract marriage, if the intention of doing so is present (8.3.D).

Nevertheless, we can at the same time hardly fail to conclude that Chaucer took pains to avoid making their marital status explicit. On the one hand, he has given his characters ideals of honor and virtue that would make an extramarital affair unthinkable; he has given them the freedom and opportunity of marrying; and he has surrounded their first union with such compromising details that, if such an account were to be admitted as properly attested evidence, a bishop or archdeacon could hardly do other than order immediate solemnization of the contract that had obviously been made between the lovers. But on the other hand, he deliberately neutralizes the positive statements about marriage in his sources and replaces them with *ambages*, "that is to seyn, with

13. Donald R. Howard, *The Three Temptations* (Princeton 1966) 153.
14. Ernst Käsmann, "'I Wolde Excuse Hir Yit for Routhe': Chaucers Einstellung zu Criseyde," *Chaucer und seine Zeit*, Symposium for Walter F. Schirmer, ed. Arno Esch (Tübingen 1968) 116–119.

double wordes slye, / Swiche as men clepen a word with two visages" (5.897–899).

For instance, when Florio marries Biancifiore, he puts the "matrimonial ring" on her finger, in accord with the standard practice in the West. Chaucer has Troilus give Criseyde a ring, but he also has Criseyde give him one in return, and she gives him a brooch as well. The use of two rings for marriage was customary only in the East.[15] Though this would be very fitting for a marriage that takes place in Troy, the likelihood is that Chaucer knew nothing about the practice.[16] In the West, the ring and other matrimonial *arrhae* were to be given by the man to the woman. In the formal marriage ritual of medieval England, they consisted of a ring, and objects of silver and gold. They were first placed on a plate or book while the priest offered a prayer. Then the groom was to take the *arrhae* and give them to the bride, saying: "With this ring I thee wed, and this silver and gold I thee give, and with my body I thee worship, and with all my worldly cathel I thee endow."[17] The wife of a jealous husband

15. For the Greek rite, see Archbishop Symeon of Thessalonica (d. 1429), *De sacramentis* 276–278 (PG 155.505–508); the medieval Egyptian and Syrian services corresponding to it can be found in Heinrich Denzinger, *Ritus Orientalium* (Würzburg 1863) 2.365, 388–389. See George Frederick Kunz, *Rings for the Finger* (Philadelphia 1917) 202–203. Kunz cites Augustine as speaking of a double ring ceremony (200), but it does not appear in the reference he gives. Two rings were exchanged in the proxy betrothal of Lucrezia Borgia with Giovanni Sforza in 1493 (Kunz 215), but this would be late enough to allow for the likelihood of Byzantine influence. At Luther's wedding in 1525 he was given a ring by his wife, and an unwearable set of "gimmal" (interlocked) rings was made for the same occasion (Kunz 216–217).

16. The same is true of the Eastern use of double crowns, as is pointed out by F. N. Robinson in his note to 2.1735 in connection with the possibility that Pandarus is talking about marriage to Criseyde when he appeals to "the vertu of corones tweyne." One could also object that it would be premature at this point for Pandarus to broach the subject of matrimony. A more promising interpretation has been suggested by Penelope B. R. Doob, "Chaucer's 'Corones Tweyne' and the Lapidaries," *Chaucer Review* 7 (1972–1973) 85–96, who reads the word "corones" as meaning the semiprecious stone ceraunius.

17. Sarum Manual 48.

in the *Confessio amantis* looks back with loathing on this ceremony:[18]

> I wot the time is ofte cursed,
> That evere was the gold unpursed,
> The which was leid upon the bok,
> Whan that alle othre sche forsok
> For love of him.   [5.557–561]

Thus, when descriptions of marriages seem to suggest that the
man receives a wedding ring, as in *The Marriage of Sir Gawaine*
("Thou shalt have gentle Gawaine, my cozen, / And marry him
with a ring")[19] we are normally to assume that it is the bride
who receives the ring. We have seen two ambiguous passages in
Boccaccio that are capable of this kind of resolution.[20]

The matter is not quite so simple, however, and it calls for a
digression on the practice of ring-giving in the Middle Ages.
There was, in fact, some precedent in the West for male wedding
rings. One of the books in Chaucer's library, Vincent of Beauvais's *Estoryal Myrour* (*Legend* G 307), contains a story in which
a man wears a spousal ring.[21] Furthermore, clandestine marriages
are subject to no laws or customs, but can be contracted in any
way the lovers wish. At one such marriage in the diocese of Ely,
for instance, the man gave a kerchief and a little chest to the
woman rather than a ring.[22] It was, moreover, a common practice

18. Macaulay in his notes refers to the much later Anglican Service Book,
where the gold is a stipend for the priest and clerk who officiate at the
wedding.
19. W. F. Bryan and Germaine Dempster, *Sources and Analogues of
Chaucer's Canterbury Tales* (New York 1941, repr. 1958) 238.
20. Above, Chap. 7. In *Decameron* 10.9.111 and *Teseida* 12.62, Boccaccio
indicates that the bride receives more than one ring—he uses the feminine
plural, *anella*. The same is true of Griselda's wedding, but she later returns
only a single marriage *anello* (*Decameron* 10.10.14, 44).
21. *Speculum historiale* 25.29 (Douai 1624) 1012. The story is set in
eleventh-century Rome. Perhaps it should also be mentioned that bishops
were called spouses and wore spousal rings. The imagery gets a bit con-
fused, however, since it is the Church who is the bride and Christ who is
the bridegroom. According to Innocent III the ring is the sacrament of
fidelity or faith in which Christ has given his *arrha* to the Church, and
Christ's guardians are the bishops, who wear a ring in testimony of it. See
Heinrich Kornmann, *De annulo triplici: usitato, sponsalitio, signatorio*
1.15 (Lyons 1654) 15, citing Innocent's *Mysteria missae* 1.61 (in PL 217.796).
22. Sheehan 245, 247.

for women to give men rings and other tokens as pledges of love
and fidelity, and for both men and women to exchange their
rings for the same purpose. In Chaucer's *Book of the Duchess*, the
Lady White gives the Man in Black a ring as the first pledge of
her favor (1269–1274), and Criseyde tells Pandarus to take her
blue ring to the supposedly jealous Troilus,

> For ther is nothyng myghte hym bettre plese
> Save I myself, ne more hys herte apese.   [3.886–887]

In Machaut's *Fontaine amoureuse*, the knight's lady (who happens
to be his wife) speaks to him in a dream, affirms her love "par my
foy," and swears she will never have another beloved, "Car je sui
t'ami et ta drue, / Et ta compaigne." She then exchanges rings
with him and commends him to God, and when he awakes he
finds his own ring replaced by his lady's.[23]

According to Hostiensis, it was common for fiancés to exchange
rings and other jewelry ("Consuerunt enim talia iocalia seu cle-
nodia, munuscula seu munera, inter sponsos fieri"). The point he
is making is that when such exchanges occur after a betrothal,
they cannot be taken without further evidence to mean anything
more than betrothal—that is, marriage cannot be presumed. The
giving of a ring in this case is simply a confirmation of the future
wedding; just as in business, pledges or *arrhae* can be given to
confirm not only past or present sales but future transactions as
well.[24]

From this analysis we can derive the common-sense rule that
ring-giving is simply a sign of what has gone before, whether
the gift is on the part of the man or the woman, or both. The
"turkies" that Shylock had of Leah when he was a bachelor
naturally has a different significance from the ring with which
Portia gives herself and her possessions to Bassanio, or the ring
that Yvain's wife Laudine gives him, which will protect him if he
remembers her, his *amie* (2600–2608). The lady in Machaut's
example who tells her lover always to wear her ring intends it as

---

23. Machaut, *La fonteinne amoureuse* 2327–2524 (*Oeuvres* 3.226–233). See
D. W. Robertson, Jr., *A Preface to Chaucer* (Princeton 1963) 234.
24. Hostiensis, *Summa aurea* 4, *De matrimoniis* § *Qualiter contrahatur*
(Lyons 1568) 289.

a sign of his fidelity, just as her husband (who asks to see it again) could well have considered it a pledge of her fidelity to him.[25] When Olivia sends a ring after "Cesario" (the disguised Viola), the latter naturally concludes, "She loves me, sure, the cunning of her passion / Invites me" (*Twelfth Night* 2.2). When, under the influence of another *error personae,* Olivia secretly marries Sebastiano, the bestowal of her ring confirms her more serious intention. The solitary witness of their agreement, a priest, describes it thus:

> A contract of eternal bond of love,
> Confirmed by mutual joinder of your hands,
> Attested by the holy close of lips,
> Strengthened by interchangement of your rings,
> And all the ceremony of this compact
> Sealed in my function, by my testimony. [5.1]

Some earlier examples can be found in which the "interchangement of rings" in clandestine circumstances accompanies matrimonial intent. In a story told by Aimoin of Fleury, a monk who died early in the eleventh century, Justinian fell in love with the Amazon Antonia in the days before he became emperor. She asked that when he came into his reign he would not consider her unworthy of the embraces of a spouse. Justinian agreed, thinking it impossible that he should ever rule the empire, and exchanged rings with her ("factaque commutatione annulorum"). Later, after he has become emperor, she comes to him seeking justice, almost like a plaintiff before the bishop's court in later times. Justinian does not recognize her, and she puts her case as if it concerned a third person: "Est denique in hac civitate iuvenis qui mecum permutatis annulis fidem pepigit alterni amoris, professus quod me sibi iungeret sub nomine legitimae coniugis." Justinian declares that if faith was pledged, it should not be broken. She shows him his ring; he recognizes it, and thereupon has her brought into his chamber, dressed with royal ornaments, and thenceforth recognized as his consort.[26]

25. Machaut, *Le jugement dou roy de Navarre* 2851–2868 (*Oeuvres* 1.235).

26. Aimoinus, *De gestis Francorum* 2.5 (Paris 1602) 40–41.

In the fifteenth-century romance *Generides*[27] there are more exchanges of rings in an Eastern setting, but this time all of the characters are non-Christian. Generides and Clarionas fall in love:

> And shortly for to say you as it was,
> A full acorde was made betwix them twayn:
> He gave a ryng onto Clarionas,
> And she toke hym another, for certeyn;
> With trew promys eyther for joye or payn,
> In stedefast wise ther hertys to ensure,
> Never to chaunge but alway [to] endure.   [904–910]

The terms of their accord are clearly reminiscent of the formal marriage service, but we are not told explicitly whether their union constitutes a betrothal or a marriage. We are no doubt to assume that it is only a betrothal, for in their subsequent secret meetings we are told that nothing dishonorable was intended; Generides simply served her faithfully (918–924). A similar exchange of rings occurs between Darell and Lucidas (5008–5088), and they eventually are wedded (6722).

Some time after the private contract between Generides and Clarionas, and after Clarionas has been forced to marry King Gwynan (she is rescued before the king can consummate the union), Generides treats publicly of marriage with Clarionas's father, the Sultan. The Sultan agrees to the match and promises half of his heritage as a dowry; but before he will "make an end" of the wedding, Generides wishes to win back the kingdom of India (4642–4647). Later, the ring that Clarionas originally gave to Generides is returned to her, ostensibly by Generides, with the false message that Generides hereby frees her "to wedde where ever ye will in eny lande" (5349–5354), for he himself is now married to Lucidas. When this lie is cleared up, Generides and Clarionas spend the night together:

> That nyght they were to geder, as I rede,
> Nor sownyng to [no] villany ne shame,
> In grete pleasure and in all goodlyhede;
> She made hym chere and he ded hir the same,
> In feithfull wise withoute spotte or blame.   [6338–6342]

27. All references will be to the stanzaic version, ed. W. Aldis Wright, EETS 55, 70 (London 1878). See above, Chap. 7 n. 30.

A similar night is described later (6884–6888),[28] and eventually their "mariage was made in solempne wise" (6911).

The nature of these relationships in *Generides* is complicated by two factors: the possibility of remarriage, and the romantic acceptance of betrothal as the equivalent to marriage. In accordance with pagan practice, which, as we saw, Chaucer took for granted when retelling classical romances, second marriages were accepted as binding. In the same way, it is possible for Generides's father, Auferius, King of India, to marry Queen Sereyne "in honorabill wise" (1281), even though his first wife, the wicked Queen Serenydes, is still alive (she also remarries). In Marie de France's lai *Eliduc*, the themes of the interchange of rings and remarriage are combined in a Western Christian setting. When Eliduc exchanges rings with Guilliadun,[29] she unquestionably has marriage in mind in the end, though Eliduc does not, for he already has a wife. Guilliadun faints dead away when she learns of her; but the situation is resolved in a very uncanonical fashion when Eliduc's wife offers to call it quits, so to speak—"Del tut le

28. Cf. *Sir Eglamour of Artois* (ca. 1350–1400), ed. J. O. Halliwell, *The Thornton Romances*, Camden Society 1.30 (London 1844) 121–176. Eglamour tells Crystabell, "With the grace of God y schalle the wedd," and they plight their troths "thereto" (677–678). They spend the night together and have intercourse, as is evident from Eglamour's words:
> A golde rynge y schalle geve the,
> Kepe hyt wele, my lady free,
>   Yf Cryste sende the a chylde. (715–717)
These lines also show that "schalle" can have present force. There is, however, no indication that the couple consider themselves married. Cf. also *Sir Degrevant* (ca. 1400), *Thornton Romances* 177–256. The heroine, Myldore, tells Degrevant that she will not be touched "Or thou wed me with a ryng / And maryage fulfylle" (1518–1520). To do so, he must get her father's approval. He agrees, and they pledge their troths (1533–1536). Thereupon,
> Thai lay doun in ther bede,
> In ryche clothus was spred.
> Wytte ye wel; or thei were wed,
>   Thei synnyd nat thare. [1541–1544]
They kept this up for the better part of a year. Whether or not Myldore is touched during this preliminary phase we are not told. The same is true in the alternate version, the Lincoln MS. See the new parallel-text edition, ed. L. F. Casson, EETS 221 (London 1949).

29. *Eliduc* 701, ed. Alfred Ewert, *Lais* (Oxford 1944, repr. 1969) 145.

voil quite clamer" (1101)—and allow her husband to marry the
girl. She asks for permission to enter religion, since it would not be
fitting for him to maintain two wives:

> Kar n'est pas vien ne avenant
> De deus espuses mentenir. [1128–1129]

King Horn provides the clearest example of the matrimonial
force of betrothal.[30] Horn's commitment to Rymenhild is clearly
nothing more than a conditional engagement; he must prove his
knighthood first, and then,

> If ihc come to lyve,
> Ihc schal the take to wyve. [559–560]

Rymenhild gives him a ring, which he is to wear for her love
(569). Later, she calls Horn her husband (1039), and he considers
her "his own" (984). Rymenhild is forced to marry elsewhere,
but Horn clears up any possible canonical difficulties by killing
her new husband. In *King Ponthus and the Fair Sidone*, which is
based on *Horn*,[31] Ponthus and Sidone are committed to each other
in the manner of Horn and Rymenhild. Sidone later marries the
King of Burgundy, thinking Ponthus dead. But when Ponthus re-
appears, Sidone considers herself bound to him, and not to the
king; for, as she says, "The laste promys avayles not, bot oonly
the furst" (99).

In the romance *Paris et Vienne*, the original of which must go
back to Chaucer's time,[32] Vienne gives her beloved Paris a ring in
the name of marriage, "en nom de mariage" (506). Whether or

---

30. I use the edition of W. H. French and C. B. Hale, *Middle-English Metrical Romances* (New York 1930) 25–70. This version dates from ca. 1225 and is thought to be based on a lost French version. For the betrothal-marriage, see Gist 27–28.
31. Ed. F. J. Mather, *Publications of the Modern Language Association* 12 (1897) 1–150, translated after 1450 from a French original written some years before 1445.
32. Ed. Robert Kaltenbach, "Der altfranzösische Roman *Paris et Vienne*," *Romanische Forschungen* 15 (1904) 321–621. A later abridged version was translated by William Caxton in 1485, ed. MacEdward Leach, EETS 234 (London 1957).

not this transaction would technically be considered betrothal or marriage, it is enough to make her believe it impossible to marry another (556, 602). The same is true in the shorter version, in which she simply promises Paris that she will have no husband but him and gives the ring so that he may the better remember her, and keep it for love of her (Caxton 39). She later tells her new suitor, "I am married" (55).

A final example of a matrimonial interchange of rings can be found in Thomas Malory's story of Gareth and Lyonesse, which, like *Generides*, is probably based on a lost French original.[33] The story also provides interesting views on clandestine unions. The two lovers "trothplight" each other "to love and never fail while their life lasteth. And so they burnt both in love that they were accorded to abate their lusts secretly." Lyonesse's sister Lyonette, however, is "a little displeased" at their intention, "and she thought her sister Dame Lyonesse was a little overhasty, that she might not abide her time of marriage, and for saving of their worship she thought to abate their hot lusts. And she let ordain by her subtle crafts that they had not their intents neither with other, as in their delights, until they were married." Lyonesse, speaking to her brother, objects against the opinion that such intercourse is dishonorable: "For he is my lord and I am his, and he must be mine husband; therefore, my brother, I will that ye wit I shame me not to be with him, nor to do him all the pleasure that I can" (Caxton 7.22). But Lyonette has her way. Later, Lyonesse gives Gareth a ring "for great love" (7.27 [28]). Eventually, their matrimonial intention is made public, the day of marriage is set, and Lyonesse gives "a goodly and a rich ring" to Gareth, and he gives her another in return; and Arthur too gives her a rich ring of gold (7.34 [35]).

We can only judge the meaning of Troilus and Criseyde's exchange, then, by analyzing the context in which it occurs. The exchange of rings is postponed until after Troilus's initial pledge of fidelity and after they have spoken "of sondry thynges / As

33. Eugène Vinaver, *The Works of Sir Thomas Malory*, ed. 2 corrected (Oxford 1973) 1427. In quoting the text, I use the Caxton variants.

fel to purpos of this aventure," and it is described not as part of
a solemn covenant but as a game: "And pleyinge enterchaungeden
hire rynges" (3.1366–1372). We may ascribe this to Chaucer's
effort to keep the presumption of their marriage from becoming
too obvious. But we can hardly forget Troilus's invocation of the
God of Marriage and his promise of eternal fidelity; nor can we
suppose that they are not in deadly earnest about the love and
loyalty normally signified by such exchanges. Criseyde gave
Troilus a brooch at the same time, and we hear later that Troilus
in his turn gave her a brooch when she left Troy, at which time
she pledged her faith that she would always keep it in remembrance of him (5.1661–1665). The same kind of fidelity was involved here as in the playful interchange on their first night
together.

Another example of Chaucer's efforts to mute the matrimonial
language of his sources has often been noted. When Troilus characterizes his love for Criseyde in terms of Boethius's hymn in
praise of the bond of love that holds all things together, the love
is clearly a holy one. It is not now the pagan God of Love that is
being addressed in charitable terms, but rather "God, that auctour
is of kynde" (3.1765). But at the same time the love that "knytteth
sacrement of mariages of chaste loves"[34] has been transformed to

> Love that knetteth lawe of compaignie
> And couples doth in vertu for to dwelle.   [3.1748–1749]

Still another instance of Chaucer's shying away from the mention of marriage can be observed after the exchange of prisoners
has been arranged, and Criseyde is to be sent to her father in the
Greek camp. Troilus muses over whether he should ask Priam for
her (4.554–560), but he does not speak specifically in terms of
marriage. Boccaccio's hero, however, does, and concludes that
Priam would declare her beneath him, since he intended that his
son should marry a woman of royal blood (4.69). As we have seen

---

34. Chaucer's prose translation of Boethius, *De consolatione Philosophiae*
2 meter 8: "Hic et coniugii sacrum / Castis nectit amoribus." Cf. Stephen A.
Barney, "Troilus Bound," *Speculum* 47 (1972) 445–458, esp. 454–455, for
the context of Troilus's hymn.

from several instances in Boccaccio's own work, in both the *Filocolo* and the *Decameron*, it was not necessary for a determined son in desperate straits to secure his father's permission before he married. But since the plot demanded that Criseida be taken away from Troy, he could not present marriage as a viable alternative.

Chaucer's problem was even more acute, for he rejected Boccaccio's solution of making their love an admittedly illicit affair and bringing up Priam's presumed ill will toward the match as an "impediment" to their marriage. On the contrary, in D. S. Brewer's words, Chaucer "does everything he can to make us understand that their love is ordained by God"; and later, as Brewer sees it, he has the problem of doing "everything he can to make us avoid the question at the turning point of the story of why they did not solve their dilemma by marriage."[35] But if Chaucer's audience would naturally assume that they really were married, then all the more caution would be required.

This, then, is the explanation for the deliberate muting of matrimonial references in the description of the bond between Troilus and Criseyde. There was no incompatibility between love and marriage; lovers usually did get married if they could, and they could do so very easily. It is clear that Troilus and his lady strove to practice the "love that makes couples dwell in virtue," and that this, in Chaucer's book, meant marriage. But since an overt marriage would betray a weakness in the plot, he decided to make it clandestine in a double sense: it was hidden not only from the world of Troy, but also, to a certain degree, from the eyes of his own audience.

To use Gordon Williams's argument again,[36] there was an area of ambiguity about this kind of marriage, and it was precisely this ambiguity that Chaucer wished to exploit. He could reasonably rely on his readers from their own experience to be aware of the uncertainty that existed in all secret alliances. He could treat his characters either as married or as not married, depending on the immediate needs of the story.

35. Brewer, "Love and Marriage" 463.
36. See above, Chap. 8.

Thus, when Criseyde goes to the Greek camp and gradually falls away from her resolve, the ambiguity of her status makes her crime, bad as it is, somewhat less heinous. If it had been explicitly stated that she were married to Troilus, she would have been likened to those bigamists so plentiful in Chaucer's time who simply left one spouse and took another, often in another village.[37] We have seen that almost 90 per cent of the matrimonial cases before the Ely consistory court were concerned with clandestine marriages; but it is another fact that well over 40 per cent involved charges of bigamy.[38]

But since Criseyde was never clearly described as Troilus's wife, she seems less guilty, perhaps, when she denies to Diomede that she is married (5.974–978) and when she enters into a new clandestine union with him and promises to be true to him (1069–1071). If the brooch that Troilus gave her (1040–1041) had been explicitly stated to be part of his matrimonial subarrhation, her action in giving it to Diomede (1660–1666) would have been all the more shocking.

Perhaps we should also remember the medieval acceptance of classical remarriage. After all, Helen is regarded as the wife of Paris in the *Troilus*, not of Menelaus. It is noteworthy that when Robert Henryson read Chaucer's poem in the next century, he considered Criseyde to be married to Diomede, for Diomede divorces her, sending her a "lybell of repudie."[39] He likens the Greek practice of divorce to that of the Hebrews, which, though abrogated by Christ in the Gospel, was previously legal: "Dictum est autem, quicumque dimiserit uxorem suam, det ei libellum repudii" (Matthew 5.31).

Finally, the ambiguity of Troilus's relationship to Criseyde makes Pandarus seem less immoral when he suggests to Troilus that he can find another love (4.400–406). And Troilus seems all the more noble when he remains faithful to Criseyde till the end,

---

37. See above, Chap. 6 and Chap. 7. I am grateful to John Leyerle for suggesting this possible interpretation of Criseyde's conduct.
38. Sheehan 251.
39. *The Testament of Cresseid* 71–75, ed. H. Harvey Wood, *The Poems and Fables of Robert Henryson*, ed. 2 (Edinburgh 1958, repr. 1972) 107.

not because he is bound to her in wedlock, but because he loves her:

> I se that clene out of youre mynde
> Ye han me cast; and I ne kan nor may,
> For al this world, withinne myn herte fynde
> To unloven yow a quarter of a day.
> In corsed tyme I born was, weilaway,
> That yow, that doon me al this wo endure,
> Yet love I best of any creature!   [5.1695–1701]

PART IV

Matrimonial Sin and Virtuous Passion

Arguitur opera nuptiarum quae non sunt causa liberorum mortalia esse, quia luxuria et immunditia nominantur. . . . Sed hoc dicitur non quoad reatum mortalis vitii, sed quoad speciem facti. Speciem enim et similitudinem luxuriae et immunditiae praetendunt et habent designare.

(It is argued that the marriage acts which are not performed for the sake of begetting children are mortal, for they are called lechery and impurity. . . . But this refers not to the guilt of the deadly vice, but to the appearance of the deeds. For they manifest and serve to represent an appearance of, and similarity to, lechery and uncleanness.)

> —Ordinary Gloss to the canon *In eo fornicator*
> of St. Jerome, in Gratian,
> *Decree* 2.32.4.12 v. *immunditiam.*

Departe it so, for wyde-wher is wist
How that ther is diversite required
Bytwixen thynges like, as I have lered.

> —Chaucer, *Troilus and Criseyde* 3.404–406

Chapter 10

The Too Ardent Lover
of His Wife Classified

Motives for Marriage

Now that we have made an honest couple out of Troilus and Criseyde, or at least given them the benefit of the doubt required by our new Code of Courtly Courtship, let us inquire more closely into their moral and religious status. As a noble pagan, Troilus had access not only to the natural, non-Trinitarian theology expounded in Boethius's *Consolation of Philosophy*, but also to the sort of ethical instruction typified by the dictum ascribed to Sextus the Pythagorean: "The too ardent lover of his wife is an adulterer." This saying was brought into prominence by St. Jerome in his polemic *Against Jovinian*, whence it was excerpted by Gratian in the canon *Origo*; and it also found its way into other textbooks of canon law, theology, and pastoral care.[1] A more ardent lover than Troilus is hard to imagine. Have we, then,

---

1. Cited by St. Jerome, *Adversus Iovinianum* 1.49 (*PL* 23.293), and taken up by Gratian, *Decree* 2.32.4.5 (*Origo*); also cited by Peter Lombard, *Sentences* 4.31.6 (*PL* 192.920) or 4.31.5 of the 2d Quaracchi ed. (1916), and St. Raymond of Pennafort, *Summa* 4.2.8 (Verona 1744) 479. Earlier in the passage in which this maxim occurs, Jerome began to quote from a now lost work of Seneca's, and the whole of the chapter *Origo* excerpted in Gratian may simply be a continuation of the words of Seneca. See John T. Noonan, Jr., *Contraception: A History of Its Treatment by the Catholic Theologians and Canonists* (Cambridge, Mass., 1966) 47, 79–80, 196–197. It should be made clear, by the way, that the "discord" in the *Decree* noted by Noonan on p. 196, "Those who copulate not to procreate offspring but to satisfy lust seem to be not so much spouses as fornicators," is not to be taken as Gratian's own belief but simply as a summation of the preceding and following "discordant canons" of Ambrose and Jerome (2.32.2.1–2), which Gratian immediately refutes: "His ita respondetur," etc.

relieved him of the charge of being a "notable fornicator"[2] only
to impale him once again with an accusation of adultery? Let us
review the medieval teaching on marriage before we try to assess
the evidence against him.

Marriage, unlike the other six Christian sacraments, was instituted at the very beginning of the human race, and therefore
all men, even pagans like Troilus, were bound by its laws. The
only difference between pagan and Christian marriage was, as we
have seen, that baptism entailed a special ratification or confirmation of marriage; thus Christian marriage was absolutely indis-
soluable, whereas marriages of nonbelievers could be dissolved by
virtue of the Pauline privilege.[3]

Marriage was first established in the garden of Eden for the

2. The phrase is Donaldson's, "Medieval Poetry and Medieval Sin," *Speaking of Chaucer* 172. Joseph E. Gallagher in his review of Ida L. Gordon,
*The Double Sorrow of Troilus: A Study of Ambiguities in "Troilus and
Criseyde"* (Oxford 1970), in *Medium aevum* 41 (1972) 39–46, esp. 39, sums
up current interpretations of Troilus's love: "Criticism which holds that
there is a consistent Christian vision in the *Troilus* tends to fall into two
groups: the first sees in the poem Chaucer's rejection of false worldly
love in favor of the love of Christ; the second, more recent in origin but
gaining in adherents, claims that Chaucer accepts and praises the love
between Troilus and Criseyde as a limited good which is finally related in
the conclusion to the source of all good"; the first group is hard pressed to
show why Troilus's love is not condemned until the end of the poem; the
second is "often forced to evade assiduously the fact that Troilus does not
love Criseyde in a limited fashion, and that his love by Christian standards
must be deadly sin, if he is truly aware of what he is doing, or a great
error, if he is not." Mrs. Gordon belongs essentially to the first group; for,
though she admits that Troilus is an exemplum "of the heights to which
human love could rise," she adds the rider: "if it were properly directed"
(p. 142). I, of course, have cast my lot with the second group, and will
attempt to show in the remaining chapters that Troilus's love *was* properly
directed, at least according to some medieval "Christian standards."

3. See Burgh, above, Chap. 9, on the difference between *matrimonium
legitimum* and *matrimonium ratum*. His conclusion is: "Unde matrimonium
infidelium separari potest" (*Pupilla oculi* 8.1.A). According to Giles Bellemère, the Avignon curialist writing in the 1390's, it was within the power
of the pope to dissolve nonconsummated Christian marriages. See his *Con-
silia* 89, Vatican MS lat. 2345, f. 236ra. If so, the opinion did not become
common knowledge though the pope exercised the power during the
fifteenth and sixteenth centuries. See John T. Noonan, Jr., *Power to Dissolve* (Cambridge, Mass., 1972) 129–135 and 342–347. It was always recognized, however, that nonconsummated Christian marriages could be automatically dissolved if one of its partners entered religion. See above, Chap. 6.

purpose of multiplying the human race. After the fall, it was reconstituted with the additional purpose of serving as a remedy for the sexual concupiscence that was one of the consequences of the fall. Another way of putting this second purpose was the avoiding of fornication.[4] Other motives were admissible, too, especially the nobler ones of peace-making or the encouragement of love between the prospective inlaws, but also the less noble ones of desire for the intended's beauty or wealth. Though some canonists and theologians admit that anyone who put his mind to it could easily think up other reasons, mutual love between the spouses is notably absent from their lists.[5] "Solace" is sometimes named, even as a quasi-principal cause, but it refers chiefly to the marriage of older people; and when an old man marries a young bride, the expected solace is not even mutual, but the wife is expected to attend on the husband's needs.[6] In fact, even if the old man was impotent and desired the girl chiefly as a bedwarmer, after the fashion of David and Abishag, the marriage was considered good as long as the girl knew and agreed.[7]

4. See Rudolf Weigand, "Die Lehre der Kanonisten des 12. und 13. Jahrhunderts von den Ehezwecken," *Studia gratiana* 12 (1967) 443–478, esp. 447–461.

5. *Ibid.* 462–463. Cf. the commentary on 1 Corinthians sometimes mistakenly attributed to Peter Comestor, Vatican MS Ottob. lat. 445, ff. 94v–123, esp. f. 105ra: "Sunt et aliae minus honestae, ut viri sive mulieris pulchritudo, quaestus quoque et divitiarum ambitio, et alia multa, quae diligentiam adhibenti facile est discernere." (Cf. Friedrich Stegmüller, *Repertorium biblicum medii aevi*, Madrid 1940–1961, no. 6582.1.) Similarly, St. Raymond of Pennafort, *Summa* 4.2.4 (472) calls the motives of beauty and wealth "dishonorable" (*inhonestae*), and love for a beautiful woman (as in the case of Jacob and Rachel) is, in effect, a "perverse intention." Cf. Burgh 8.1.G.

6. Weigand, "Die Lehre" 463 n. 111, 466. On the requirement of "marital affection," which is never listed among the causes for marriage, see John T. Noonan, Jr., "Marital Affection in the Canonists," *Studia gratiana* 12 (1967) 479–509. Such affection seems to have had nothing to do with romantic love or even purely sexual love but, insofar as it referred to love at all, the kind of intellectual esteem for one's wife which we shall see urged by canonists in the name of love (see below, Chap. 12).

7. See X 4.15.4, the decretal *Consultationi* of Pope Lucius III, who, though he finds it incredible that anyone should wish to marry an impotent person, nevertheless allows it: if a man cannot have his wife as a wife, let him have her as a sister. Cf. Nicholas of Lyre, *Postilla* on 3 Kings 1.2 v. *quaeramus*, *Biblia sacra* (Venice 1588) 2.125FG: "Dicunt enim medici quod

What if the man and the woman entered into marriage with no thought of producing children for heaven or, for that matter, for earth, but only because of incontinence, in order to enjoy sexual intercourse? St. Augustine's solution to this question in the canon *Solet* was accepted in the Middle Ages: as long as there is no positive effort made to prevent having children, the union is considered a valid marriage. As Gratian puts it, even if their motive is the fulfilling of lust, *causa explendae libidinis*, they are not therefore considered fornicators but spouses.[8]

The Status of Sexual Pleasure

So far, then, Troilus and Criseyde seem to be in the clear. But does the mere fact of marriage liberate one from sin? Does not Chaucer's Parson, in speaking of the common delusion that a man "may nat synne for no likerousnesse that he dooth with his wyf," warn that one may kill oneself with one's own knife? And does he not say further that almost no act of intercourse, no matter what the motivations behind it, can be performed without sin, because of the corruption and the delight involved in it?[9]

Are we to take this last comment to mean that sexual delight is always sinful in itself? This was the opinion of the twelfth-century rigorists, led by the renowned Huguccio of Pisa, who taught canon law in Bologna until the year 1190, when he be-

---

optimum remedium contra frigiditatem membrorum et paralysin imminentem est amplexus mulieris, maxime iuvenculae et virginis, et ideo talis fuit adducta ipsi David. Nec ex hoc peccavit, quia cum ea contraxit matrimonium, ut magis patebit ex sequentibus. Senes enim quantumcumque possunt contrahere, licet non possint generare. Et sicut dicut doctores, si mulier scienter contrahat cum frigido non potente eam cognoscere, nihilominus tenet contractus, et sic fuit in proposito. Et ideo uti amplexibus huius virginis in statu matrimoniali non videtur fuisse illicitum ipsi David, maxime cum hoc esset ei in remedium tantae frigiditatis." Paul of Burgos (Solomon ben Levi), Lyre's self-appointed corrector, objected to the contention that a beautiful virgin was any more effective in this role than a nonbeautiful nonvirgin, but he did not find anything wrong with the marriage of such a *senex frigidus non potens* (ibid. 127A). Lyre composed his *Postilla litteralis super totam Bibliam* in 1322–1331, and Burgos made his *Additiones* a century later (1429–1431).

8. Gratian 2.32.2.6 (*Solet*), and Gratian's comment before this canon. Cf. Lombard, *Sentences* 4.31.3.

9. *Parson's Tale* 859, 942.

came Bishop of Ferrara. He had the satisfaction of seeing one of his students become pope (Innocent III), and his views carried immense weight. In his *Summa on Gratian's Decree*,[10] he upheld the extreme view that no act of copula could be performed without sinning in some way, because of the delight that invariably accompanied it.

In commenting on Gratian's *Decree*, Part 1, Distinction 13, which deals with choosing the lesser of two evils, Huguccio considers the dilemma of a man whose wife demands payment of the marital debt: if he were to refuse, he would commit a mortal sin; if he should agree, he would, according to Huguccio's doctrine, commit at least a venial sin. Huguccio offers a method whereby both sins may be avoided: the husband should first try to put his wife off by reasoning with her; if he fails, he is to allow her to work her will with him and then depart from her before satisfying any pleasure of his own.[11] However, Laurence of Spain, who taught at Bologna in the generation after Huguccio, found this proposal not so much funny as absurd: "Haec non tam rideo quam derideo."[12]

10. The *Summa* was not yet written in 1188. He died in 1210. See the entry on him in the *DDC*.
11. Huguccio, *Summa* on Gratian 1.13; for the text, see Vatican MS lat. 2280, f. 12rb, given in Weigand, "Die Lehre" 472 n. 141. For a translation, see Noonan, *Contraception* 296–297. Noonan is perhaps overreading when he understands the phrase "saepe in talibus mulier solet praevenire virum" to mean that this sort of interrupted intercourse happened often. When Laurence of Spain comments on Huguccio's suggestion (see next note), he does not give the impression that he thought that such a practice had ever been (or could ever be) used. The phrase could simply mean that the wife often comes to climax before the husband.
12. Laurence of Spain, *Glossa palatina* to Gratian 1.13 *principium*, Vatican MS Pal. lat. 658, f. 3v; cf. Vatican MS Reg. lat. 977, f. 6. Stephan Kuttner informs me that some manuscripts read "Haec non tam video quam rideo." For a similar expression in Bernard of Compostella the Elder, see Alfons M. Stickler, "Der Kaiserbegriff des Bernardus Compostellanus Antiquus," *Studia gratiana* 15: Post scripta (1972) 103–124 n. 33: "Ego propterea scripsi ut derisui habeam, non ut approbem" (referring to another gloss of Huguccio's). It may be worth nothing too that in the two manuscripts just cited Laurence quotes Huguccio as saying *descendere* rather than *discedere*. Cf. January to May, *Merchant's Tale* 1828–1830:
Allas, I moot trespace
To yow, my spouse, and yow greetly offende,
Er tyme come that I wil doun descende.

This was only the beginning of the clash between Huguccio and Laurence. In the second of the two canons of Distinction 13, *Nervi testiculorum* ("The nerves of the testicles of Leviathan are perplexed," etc.), from Gregory the Great's *Morals on Job*, are these words: "Spouses are without blame in having intercourse only when they come together not for the fulfilling of lust but for receiving offspring." Laurence explains the words "without blame" by saying: "That is, the carnal work is not blameworthy only when they come together for the desire of children or for the purpose of yielding the debt." He then brings up Huguccio's view that coitus can never be had without sin, and opposes to it the authority of Peter Comestor, the Master of the Histories. According to Peter, Laurence says, the itching or concupiscence of sexual pleasure is no sin at all, no more than warming one's scabby hand at the fire.[13]

Laurence has thus added to Gregory's single allowable motive, desire for children, a second, that of paying the debt when one's partner demands it. When he comes to the word "receiving," he adds still another, that of incontinence, and he repeats Comestor's alleged view with even greater force: "For though there be

For Laurence's authorship of the Palatine Gloss, see A. M. Stickler, "Il decretista Laurentius Hispanus," *Studia gratiana* 9 (1966) 461–549; see 520–521 for part of the text cited above. Laurence started making his gloss around 1190 and continued working on it until 1214, when he returned to Spain and eventually became Bishop of Orense, which he remained until his death in 1248.

13. Laurence, *Glossa palatina* 1.13.2 (*Nervi*) v. *in admixtione sine culpa.* The last part reads: "P. tamen Comestor dixit quod pruritus ille vel concupiscentia non est peccatum, sicut et cum calefacio manum scabiosam." Since the illustration of warming one's scabby hand is not in the *Historia scholastica* (see n. 15 below), Laurence may have been drawing on Comestor's lost commentary on Lombard's *Sentences*. See A. Landgraf, "Recherches sur les écrits de Pierre le Mangeur," *Recherches de théologie ancienne et médiévale* 3 (1931) 292–306, 341–372, esp. 350–357. On the other hand, Laurence may have contributed the example himself, I am not sure of its force: Does one satisfy the itching of a scab by warming it at the fire, and does this operation even cause a pleasurable sensation? Perhaps fire is used to hasten the healing and removal of the scab by drying it up, but in doing so creates or satisfies an itch. The herb *scabiosa*, which was used against *scabies*, is hot and dry in the second degree; it has the power of dissolving, consuming, and cleansing things. See Vincent of Beauvais, *Speculum naturale* 9.130 (Douai 1624) 648–649.

present an itching and delight, nevertheless it would not be a sin, no more than when I warm my scabby hand at the fire."[14]

In using Peter Comestor in this way to approve of sexual pleasure, Laurence makes him appear much more liberal than he really was. It is true that Comestor stood in opposition to the heretics (no doubt the Cathari) who said that intercourse could not be performed without sin.[15] But he comes close to the side of Chaucer's Parson in holding that it could only rarely be had without sin. Like Gregory in *Nervi*, he believes that there is no sin only when the act is excused by the hope of children. Furthermore, Comestor has nothing to say, at least in his *Histories*, of the delight connected with intercourse. His only thought is for shame involved in the inordinate movements of the genitals. For even when such movement is excused from sin, he says, it still inevitably brings on embarrassment.[16]

It was actually Huguccio himself who first contrasted his doctrine with that of Comestor. According to Huguccio, both Peter

14. Laurence, *Gl. pal.* 1.13.2 v. *suscipienda:* "Et est causa reddendi debiti, 33 q. 5 *Si dicat* [Gratian 2.33.5.1], et cum causa incontinentiae, ut 32 q. 2 § 1 [Gratian 2.32.2.1 *ante:* in setting up his "discord" (see n. 1 above), Gratian seems to identify incontinence and the fulfilling of lust; the Ordinary Gloss later distinguishes between them, as we shall see]. Licet enim ibi sit pruritus et delectatio, non tamen peccatum, sicut et cum calefacio manum scabiosam ad ignem." The Ordinary Gloss omits both of these uses of the example of the scabby hand. But later, at 2.32.2.2 *post* (§ *His ita*) v. *sine ardore*, where Laurence said that unless man had sinned the union of the genitals would be without ardor and itching, as with the other members, e.g, touching one finger to another, the Ordinary Gloss adds: "Vel si esset pruritus, non tamen esset peccatum, sicut non esset peccatum manum scabiosam mittere ad ignem." This use of Laurence's illustration is hardly very logical, for it follows that since man has sinned, then it is sinful to indulge an itch in one's hand.

15. Peter Comestor, *Historia scholastica in Genesim* 10 (PL 198.1064): "*Crescite et multiplicamini*. Quod quia sine coniunctione eorum fieri non potuit, patet quia Deus coniugium viri et mulieris instituit, in quo confutantur quidam haeretici dicentes concubitum sine peccato fieri non posse." Comestor was writing around the year 1170.

16. *Ibid.* 20 (1071–1072): "Inordinatus enim motus membrorum ipsa facit pudenda. . . . Qui [motus] pudendus est et inordinatus, quia non sine peccato fit, nisi raro, spe prolis excusatus. Cum tamen excusari potest a peccato, rubore carere non potest." He adds that when St. Zachary had knowledge of St. Elizabeth to beget the holy Precursor of the Lord, he was unwilling to be seen.

Lombard and Peter Comestor held as heretical the view that no copula was possible without sin.[17] But they are contradicted, Huguccio says, by the canon *Connubia* of St. Jerome,[18] and by many other canons as well. What the heretics mean is that coitus cannot be had without *mortal* sin, whereas his own view is that it cannot occur without at least a venial sin.[19]

Laurence's own position is made clearer by other remarks he makes on the canon *Nervi*. When Gregory says that St. Paul conceded "lesser things" (that is, sins) to the incontinent so that they might avoid greater ones,[20] Laurence says that it was the *immoderate* demand for intercourse ("immoderata exactio debiti coniugatorum") that was so conceded in matrimony. Such activity was still considered sinful, but less so than fornication: "Quod tunc erat peccatum, sed minus quam fornicatio."[21] He interprets Gregory's qualification cited above, "not for the fulfilling of lust," as referring to the use of aphrodisiacs for more frequent intercourse.[22]

When John Teutonicus revised Laurence's gloss to Gratian shortly after the year 1215, he made Laurence's liberal opinion his own in a solid affirmative: "I do not believe that such delight is any sin."[23] He does not, however, reject Huguccio's contrary

17. See Lombard, *Sentences* 4.31.7 (PL 192.921), for his opposition to the idea that no intercourse can be sinless. Elsewhere, viz. 2.31.8 (725–726), Lombard admits that coitus can never be had without libidinous concupiscence, and therefore can never be without sin, in the sense that it always suffers from the effects of original sin.

18. Gratian 2.32.2.4 (*Connubia*); it is while commenting on this canon that Huguccio makes his remarks.

19. For the text of Huguccio's remarks, see P. M. Abellán, *El fin y la significación sacramental del matrimonio desde S. Anselmo hasta Guillermo de Auxerre*, Biblioteca teológica granadina 1.1 (Granada 1939) 23–24; see also Weigand, "Die Lehre" 472. For Comestor's views on marriage, see Abellán 96–97.

20. Referring to 1 Cor. 7.2: "Because of fornication let each man have his own wife."

21. Laurence, *Glossa palatina* 1.13.2 (*Nervi*) v. *minora*. Friedberg, in his edition of Gratian (col. 32), reads *minima*, with *minora* as an alternate (n. 44).

22. *Ibid.* v. *cum non pro explenda*: "Non tamen concessa causa explendae libidinis, ita accedere ut medicaminis utatur ut frequentius coire possit."

23. John Teutonicus, gloss to Gratian 1.13.1 *ante* (*Item adversus*), Vatican

view, but admits it as tenable: "If you wish to hold that there is a venial sin here, you should say with Huguccio," etc. He gives Huguccio's method of *amplexus reservatus* without adding Laurence's derisory remark. Nor does he include the report of Comestor's opinion in the gloss on *Nervi*, though apparently he meant to. When dealing with *Nervi*, he refers to the canon *Vir cum propria*, part of Gregory the Great's responses to the queries of St. Augustine of Canterbury,[24] but when he comes to that canon and takes up once more Huguccio's view of the sinfulness of all intercourse, he refers back to *Nervi* for Comestor's contrary opinion.[25]

Teutonicus does, however, include Laurence's extended refutation of Huguccio in his commentary on *Vir cum propria;* and in the gloss on the canon *Connubia* of St. Jerome he takes over Laurence's first-person statement : "Nevertheless, Peter Comestor says that marital intercourse can certainly be had without sin; and I concede that this is true at times."[26] All of these comments carried over into the final version of the Ordinary Gloss to Gratian, which was basically the gloss of John Teutonicus as revised by Bartholomew of Brescia in light of the *Decretals of Gregory IX.*[27] Furthermore, in the *Rosarium* of the "Archdeacon," Guido of Baysio (composed in 1296–1302), which was widely used as a supplement to the Ordinary Gloss, Laurence's observations in

---

MS lat. 1367, f. 6v, and the Ordinary Gloss: "Non credo quod talis delectatio sit aliquod peccatum." (He stated the objection in these terms: "quia delectatio carnis non potest esse sine veniali peccato.")

24. Gratian 2.33.4.7 (*Vir cum propria*). In recent times the authenticity of this correspondence of Gregory's, which the Venerable Bede included in his *Ecclesiastical History*, has been rather unconvincingly called into question. See the discussion of Paul Meyvaert, "Les 'Responsiones' de S. Grégoire le Grand à S. Augustin de Cantorbéry," *Revue d'histoire ecclésiastique* 54 (1959) 879–894, and the edition of Bede's work by Bertram Colgrave and R. A. B. Mynors, Oxford Medieval Texts (Oxford 1969) 79.

25. Ordinary Gloss to *Vir cum propria* v. *voluptate:* "P. Manducator dixit contra, ut not. 13 Dist. *Nervi.*"

26. Laurence of Spain, John Teutonicus, and the Ordinary Gloss on Gratian 2.32.2.4 (*Connubia*) v. *praesentiam sancti Spiritus:* "Dicit tamen P. Manducator coitum coniugalem bene exerceri posse sine peccato: quod concedo quandoque."

27. See the *DDC* on Bartholomew of Brescia, 2.216–217.

ridicule of Huguccio and in support of Comestor at Distinction 13 are restored and properly attributed to Laurence.[28]

In spite of the prominence given to Laurence's liberal views in the Ordinary Gloss, however, only Huguccio's opinion was cited by Raymond of Pennafort in his *Summa:* "Whether or not the act of intercourse itself is sinful [because of faulty motives], nevertheless, according to Huguccio, it never occurs without sin, because it is always accompanied by itching and pleasure, which cannot be blameless."[29]

Motives for the Marriage Act

So far, then, we have seen that all authorities agreed that marriage for sexual pleasure alone constituted a valid union, as long as there was no positive intention against having children, but that there was disagreement on the status of sexual pleasure itself. The school of Huguccio believed that it always entailed sin; the school of Laurence of Spain believed that it was sinless in itself, but, like everything else, it could become sinful depending upon the partners' motives.

Normally, the motives for intercourse were grouped under four heads, all of which have been referred to in Laurence's commentary on *Nervi:* (1) procreation of offspring; (2) yielding the debt; (3) alleviating or preventing incontinence; (4) fulfilling one's desire for pleasure. They are taken up in detail in commentaries on the canon *Quidquid,* from St. Augustine's *De bono coniugali.*[30] Even Huguccio admits that the first two motives,

28. Guido a Baysio, *Rosarium* (Venice 1577) 16v § 7, 17 § 10.

29. Raymond of Pennafort, *Summa* 4.2.8 (479): "Dicit etiam quod seu coitus sit peccatum sive non, numquam fit sine peccato, quia semper fit cum pruritu et voluptate, quae sine culpa esse non potest." In its original form, Raymond's *Summa de poenitentia* (ca. 1222–1229) did not treat of marriage. He eventually added Tancred of Bologna's *Summa de matrimonio* to his own *Summa,* and then, after editing the *Decretals of Gregory IX* (therefore, around 1235–1236), he revised and expanded Tancred's work to its present form, i.e., Book 4 of the *Summa de poenitentia.* See A. Teetaert, "*Summa de matrimonio*" *sancti Raymundi de Penyafort,* Monographiae iuridicae ex ephemeride *Ius pontificium* excerptae 2.9 (Rome 1929), esp. 25–27; and *DDC* 7.462–463. The discussion of the sinfulness of coitus occurs only in Raymond's expanded version of Tancred.

30. Gratian 2.32.2.3 (*Quidquid*).

procreation and yielding the debt, are sinless (though with the rider that the act itself cannot be done without sin); in fact, one can even *demand* the debt for the sake of children and still commit no sin.[31] John Teutonicus in the Ordinary Gloss, following Laurence, says that not only is there no sin in these cases, there is merit.[32]

The third motive, alleviating or preventing incontinence, is interpreted by the Ordinary Gloss to refer to the times when one is "anticipated by pleasure," that is, when the urge to have intercourse is not deliberately provoked. Huguccio, of course, would consider a request for the debt in such circumstances to be venially sinful, and Teutonicus assumes that this is likewise Augustine's position in *Quidquid*. But he also admits that there are other authorities (and we saw that Laurence was one) who find no sin at all in such a case, on the basis of St. Paul's statement, "Because of fornication let each man have his own wife."[33]

The fourth motive, *causa explendae voluptatis*, applies when one "anticipates pleasure," that is, stirs oneself up by thought or by the use of "hot things" (namely, aphrodisiacs), in order to have intercourse more often. Teutonicus first cites Huguccio's opinion that this constitutes a mortal sin, but a mortal sin that is less severely punished because of the goods of marriage. This, then, is how Huguccio understands Augustine in *Quidquid*, who says that the *immoderata exactio debiti carnalis* was conceded by St. Paul *secundum veniam*. Huguccio also appeals to the sentiment attributed to Augustine in the canon *Adulterii*,[34] and concludes that such copula is a mortal sin which is punished like a venial sin. But Teutonicus then cites the opinion of others who interpret *Adulterii* in an altogether milder light: when the natural use of sex (as opposed to the unnatural use) exceeds the mean, it is venial in a wife, but damnable in a prostitute. They also say that when a husband is said to sin mortally, one should interpret this to mean

31. Huguccio, *Summa* on Gratian 1.13.2 (*Nervi*) v. *sine culpa* and *pro suscipienda prole.* Vatican MS lat. 2280, f. 13ra.

32. Ordinary Gloss to Gratian 2.32.2.3 (*Quidquid*) *prin.*

33. *Ibid.* See the citation in n. 21 above. Laurence's position is that the moderate exaction of the debt is not sinful, and that even the immoderate exaction is only venially sinful.

34. Gratian 2.32.7.11 (*Adulterii*).

that he is acting like an adulterer (that is, the statement is merely metaphorical) or else to read it as an exhortation to continence (that is, as a rhetorical exaggeration). Or, finally, one should say that mortal sin results only when unnatural intercourse is practiced. On this point, they say, all authorities are agreed; according to *Adulterii*, in fact, unnatural practices with one's wife are worse than with a prostitute.[35]

The nobleman in the seventh dialogue of Andrew's *Ars honeste amandi* probably has the canon *Adulterii* in mind as well as *Quidquid* and *Origo* when he propounds his witty argument on behalf of adultery:

Whatever solaces married people extend to each other beyond what are inspired by the desire for offspring or the payment of the marriage debt cannot be free from sin, and the punishment is always the greater when the use of a holy thing is perverted by misuse than if we practice the ordinary abuses. It is a more serious offense in a wife than in another woman, for the too ardent lover, as we are taught by the apostolic law, is considered an adulterer with his own wife.[36]

In the Ordinary Gloss's discussion of the morality of sexual intercourse, then, prominence is given to the Laurentian view that only the inordinate seeking of sexual pleasure is sinful, and that only venially so. It is not sinful, according to this liberal view, even to require the debt in order to satisfy the natural urges for pleasure that arise in one or both of the spouses. This is not quite the same thing as saying that it is permissible to seek moderate delight in coitus, as we shall see, but it approximates this view, especially when taken in conjunction with the teaching that such delight is not sinful in itself.

35. Ordinary Gloss to Gratian 2.32.2.3 (*Quidquid*) v. *ab adulterio*. Laurence of Spain at this point (*Glossa palatina*, Vat. MS Pal. lat. 658, f. 81v) says that some authorities treat the third and fourth motives (incontinence and pleasure) as identical.

36. Andrew 1.6.7 (103). Cf. Bk. 3 (194) for a rigorous view of sexual delight, "which even in married persons is scarcely to be classed among the venial faults which are not [mortal] sins, according to the words of the prophet, who said, 'For behold I was conceived in iniquities, and in sins did my mother conceive me.'" The original reads: "Delectatio carnis, quae inde multa aviditate suscipitur, non est de genere boni, immo constat esse damnabile crimen quae etiam in coniugatos [sic] ipsis vix cum veniali culpa sine crimine toleratur," etc. (*Andreae Capellani regii Francorum De amore libri tres*, ed. E. Trojel [Copenhagen 1892] 362).

This liberal line of thought is developed further a century later by the influential married canonist John Andreae. He lists the reasons for the pre-eminence of the sacrament of matrimony: (1) because of its author, God alone; (2) because of its status, having been instituted before sin; (3) because of the place of its institution, paradise; (4) because of the time when it was instituted, in the beginning of the world; (5) because of what it signifies, and here he refers to his earlier remarks on Innocent III's decretal, *Debitum;* and finally (6) because of its privilege, whereby it makes that work which would otherwise be sinful not to be a sin, as Cardinal Hostiensis says.[37] His own statement, at *Debitum,* of this effect of marriage, is much more striking: "Marriage is of such power that it transforms water, that is, corporal delight, into wine, that is, a good work, which is sometimes meritorious."[38]

On the conservative side, Raymond of Pennafort is still the most important name. When he discusses the motives for intercourse he takes Huguccio as his basic guide, as he did on the question of sexual pleasure. It was, in fact, Huguccio who drew the distinction used by the Gloss between the third and fourth motives, the preventing of incontinence and the fulfillment of "lust" (that is, in the latter, one uses the stimulus of thought, masturbation, or aphrodisiacs). Raymond's view, put simply, is that in the first two motives there is no sin, in the third there is venial sin, and in the fourth, mortal.[39]

Raymond admits, however, that some say there is no sin in the third motive, that of preventing incontinence. But he cites a canon of St. Augustine against them.[40] Then he deals with the opinion of those who see in incontinence two separate motives: (1) When one is so heated by concupiscence that one cannot con-

---

37. John Andreae, *Novella* on X 4.15.7 (*Litterae*) v. *institutor* (4.51 § 6).

38. *Ibid.* X 1.21.5 (*Debitum*) v. gl. *triplex* (1.186 § 15): "[Nuptiae] sunt tantae virtutis quod aquam, id est delectationem corporalem, mutant in vinum, id est opus bonum et quandoque meritorium." Andreae finds this signification in the Gospel account of the wedding-feast at Cana. For more on *Debitum,* see below, Chap. 12.

39. Raymond, *Summa* 4.2.8 (479): "In primo et secundo casu nullum est peccatum, in tertio veniale, in quarto mortale."

40. Gratian 1.25.3 *post,* § 7 v. *Quotiens aliquis,* from Augustine's *Sermo* 41 (*De sanctis sive de anima defunctorum*), where he says that only the desire for children is sinless.

tain oneself; coitus in that case would be a venial sin. (2) When one acts not for pleasure but as a preventative against extramarital coitus; in this case, perhaps, there would be no sin at all. This, however, would make five motives for intercourse, says Raymond, whereas the Masters are accustomed to find only four. In so saying, he seems to think that he has invalidated the opinion.

As for the fourth motive, Raymond gives Huguccio's reasons for considering the satiating of lust a mortal sin. He admits that some say it is only a venial sin as long as the order of nature is observed. This could be conceded, he says, in the case of couples who had intercourse *ex confidentia matrimonii* and would not so act if they were not married. But he reverts to Huguccio's distinctions: if the pleasure is not deliberately stimulated, it is a venial sin. If it is so stimulated, it is a mortal sin.

Raymond's support gave Huguccio's stern views a new lease on life. However, more moderate ideas were gaining ground, as, for instance, in the immensely popular *Somme le roi*. This work was compiled and largely composed by Raymond's fellow Dominican Lorens of Orléans in 1279, not long therefore after St. Raymond had finally breathed his last in what was perhaps his hundredth year. It was translated at least nine times into English during the fourteenth and fifteenth centuries, from the *Ayenbite of Inwit* of Dan Michel to Caxton's *Royal Book*.[41]

Ostensibly, Lorens maintains the traditional four categories of motives for intercourse. The first three—procreation, paying the debt, and preventing incontinence—involve no sin. But his understanding of the third motive is somewhat bizarre and is no doubt based on the liberal distinction cited and dismissed by Raymond. According to Lorens, one acts from this motive by demanding the debt in order to prevent one's partner from committing the sin of incontinence.[42]

The fourth category is simply "all other cases." The case that concerns us here is the first one he names, when intercourse is

41. See W. Nelson Francis's edition of one of these versions: *The Book of Vices and Virtues: A Fourteenth-Century English Translation of the Somme le roi of Lorens d'Orléans*, EETS 217 (London 1942) ix, xxxii–xl.

42. *Ibid.* 246–247. See Donaldson's amusing observations on this point in "Medieval Poetry" (n. 2 above).

sought "only for delight and liking and lechery," to the exclusion of the first three motives. Such an intent does involve sin, either venial or mortal: (1) The sin is venial when the delight remains subject to right and reason and does not exceed the bounds of marriage, and when one would not wish to do such a thing to anyone but one's spouse. (2) The sin is mortal when reason and right are blinded and one would do as much to one's spouse even though she were not one's spouse. The first seven husbands of Sara in the Book of Tobias are cited as examples of men having such adulterous, or equivalently adulterous, intentions. (3) The sin is mortal when the act is against nature.

By Chaucer's time, a middle-of-the-road position like that of Lorens had become the normal view.[43] It relaxed the rigor of Huguccio on the one hand but fell short of the liberality of Laurence of Spain on the other. Against Huguccio, it was held that some acts of intercourse could be without sin and that even immoderate intercourse, for the satiation of lust, was only a venial sin unless it was extramarital in scope. Against Laurence, it was held that all pursuit of sexual pleasure alone was at least venially sinful.

Huguccio and Raymond interpreted the dictum of Sextus the Pythagorean about the too ardent husband being an adulterer as referring to all acts of immoderate pleasure. Laurence of Spain, followed by the Ordinary Gloss, considered this dictum a mere

43. Of the canonists, William Pagula in his widely used *Oculus sacerdotis* simply follows the Ordinary Gloss to *Quidquid* in listing both the rigorous and liberal views, and then adds the moderate view, without stating his own preference: *Dextera pars, De matrimonio*, Vatican MS Ottob. lat. 401, f. 103rv. See Leonard Boyle, "The *Oculus sacerdotis* and Some Other Works of William of Pagula," *Transactions of the Royal Historical Society* 5.5 (1955) 81–110; and "The *Summa summarum* and Some Other English Works of Canon Law," *Proceedings of the Second International Congress of Medieval Canon Law*, ed. S. Kuttner and J. J. Ryan, Monumenta iuris canonici, series C, subsidia 1 (Vatican City 1965) 415–456. Burgh 8.5.K cites as his authority Thomas Aquinas, *In Sent.* 4.32 (see *In Sent.* 4.31.2.2-3), for distinctions which are similar to those of Lorens. In 10.4.O Burgh adds another Thomistic criterion: a sin is mortal if the delight involved is preferred to God. Lyndwood 5.16.15 (*In confessionibus*) v. *matrimonium* (343) says that the fourth motive constitutes a mortal sin, but then he cites the distinction of Thomas and Peter (probably Peter of La Palu, or Paludanus) that it is mortal only when the intention is extramarital.

metaphor: "Just as an adulterer lusts after another man's wife, so the husband lusts after his own. And that he does not sin mortally is evident from the last part [of the canon *Origo*]: for there he is *dissuaded* from doing something he is not *required* to avoid."⁴⁴ But those who held to the *via media* interpreted the saying to refer to mental adultery, which meant that the husband would exercise his lust on his wife even if she were not his wife, and they considered such a condition mortally sinful.⁴⁵

The venial sins that the moderate authorities found in incontinent sexual acts were often not regarded with much concern. Peter Lombard seems to cite Augustine as saying that they are the sort of thing meant in the Lord's Prayer: "Forgive us our debts." (In such cases, perhaps, the petition should be understood as "Forgive us for demanding the debt.") This is applied to spouses "who, overcome by concupiscence, use each other beyond what is necessary to procreate children."⁴⁶ Lombard is doubtless drawing on the *Summa sententiarum*, which dates from around 1138–1141 and is probably the work of Otto, Bishop of Lucca.⁴⁷ Here the sentiment is definitely attributed to Augustine, and the author himself applies it even to those spouses who have intercourse "only for the fulfilling of pleasure."⁴⁸

44. Ordinary Gloss to Gratian 2.32.4.5 (*Origo*) v. *adulter:* "Hic adulter talis dicitur non reatu criminis illius capitalis, sed similitudine adulterinae libidinis. Sicut enim adulter in adulteram ardet, ita iste in propriam. Et quod non peccet mortaliter patet in finali; nam ibi dissuadetur ad quod evitandum non tenetur." Cf. Laurence, Vat. MS Pal. lat. 658, f. 82v.

45. Laurence and the Ordinary Gloss on *Origo* v. *amator* give this sense without drawing the conclusion of mortal sin: "Vehemens amator dicitur qui tantum uxorem diligit ut apud se disponat quod si ipsa esset forte uxor alterius non minus carnaliter se cum ea commisceret."

46. Lombard, *Sentences* 4.31.5, Quaracchi ed. 2 (1916); cf. 4.31.6 of the Migne edition (*PL* 192.920). Thomas Aquinas reads Lombard as referring the sentiment to Augustine (*In Sent.* 4.31.2.3 ob. 1 *contra*).

47. See the third Quaracchi edition of Lombard's *Sentences*, Spicilegium bonaventurianum 4 (Grottaferrata 1971) 16* and 119*; F. Stegmüller, *Repertorium commentariorum in Sententias Petri Lombardi* (Würzburg 1947) no. 837; Roger Baron, "Hugues de Saint-Victor," *Dictionnaire de spiritualité* 7.1 (1969) 909–910. The *PL* edition of Lombard makes it seem as if Lombard is citing a *Sentences* of Hugh of Saint Victor, but this is merely an intrusion of the editor, who attributed the *Summa sententiarum* to Hugh.

48. *Summa sententiarum* 7.3, edited among the works of Hugh of Saint Victor, *PL* 176.156.

It may also be the case that the postulations of sin within marriage were not given as much publicity as we might think from their presence in the textbooks and manuals. One indication of this can be had from the report of Giles Bellemère, Bishop of Avignon, a contemporary of Chaucer's. When he came to comment on the Ordinary Gloss's statement, "I do not believe that such delight is any sin," he said: "Add that once a certain mendicant friar preached the contrary at Angers, and the whole city was greatly scandalized by it."[49] Bellemère went on to specify that no sin was committed when a husband knew his wife for the purpose of yielding the debt or procreating offspring. He said that, as he understood this doctrine, some other circumstance in the act could cause a mortal or a venial sin; for example, a man could know his wife in such a way that he would sin mortally, or have such inordinate delight that he would sin venially. "But such things," he concluded, "should not be expounded too deeply to lay persons in public, lest scandal should arise therefrom."[50]

49. Aegidius Bellemère, *Commentaria in Gratiani Decreta* 1.13 (Lyons 1550) 1.19v §§ 3–4: "Et ibi, *Non credo quod talis delectatio sit aliquod peccatum*, adde, quidam frater de ordine mendicantium semel Andegavis contrarium praedicavit, de quo civitas multum scandalizata fuit." He continues: "Nec mirum, quia ecclesia ad debitum huiusmodi reddendum compellit; et sic, si peccatum esset, compelleret ad peccandum, et sic erraret tota ecclesia, quod non est dicendum. Nec enim peccat qui auctoritate legis facit." Bellemère became Archdeacon of Angers in 1374, the same year that he became an auditor of the Sacred Rota. He wrote his commentary on Gratian in 1402–1404, while governing the see of Avignon. The incident at Angers must have happened fairly recently, for he made no mention of it when he discussed the subject in 1398, in his *Super Decretales Gregorii IX lecturae*, Vatican MS Ross. 832. See Henri Gilles, *La vie et les oeuvres de Gilles Bellemère* (Paris 1966) 17–19, 129.

50. Bellemère, *loc. cit.* § 5: "Non ergo peccat maritus reddens uxori debitum, si hoc facit ut debitum ei reddat vel si hoc facit causa sobolis procreandae. . . . Quod intelligo dummodo aliam circumstantiam in actu non admisceat quae peccatum mortale vel veniale inducere possit; quia vir tali modo posset uxorem suam cognoscere quod peccaret mortaliter, et tam inordinatam delectationem habere quod peccaret venialiter. Sed talia non sunt laicis in publico nimium profundenda, ne inde scandalum oriatur." In his treatise on marriage at the beginning of his *Lecturae* on the fourth book of the *Decretals*, Bellemère at first seems as severe as Huguccio and Raymond; later he shows that he takes a moderate position by citing Thomas Aquinas's distinction that intercourse for lust is only a venial sin if the intention is kept within the bounds of marriage. Vatican MS Ross. 832, ff. 14rb, 19rb, 19vab.

Chapter 11

Sex and the English Poets

From the Parson to the Ultraliberals

A good example of the moderate view of intercourse appears in a treatise on the virtues beginning with the words *Postquam dictum est de morbis ipsius animae,* which exists in several manuscripts of the thirteenth, fourteenth, and fifteenth centuries. It gives the usual four motives for marital copula:

Quattuor de causis cognoscitur uxor: [1] aut causa prolis procreandae; [2] aut debiti reddendi; [3] aut incontinentiae vitandae; [4] aut libidinis explendae. In primo casu potest esse meritorium; in secundo similiter; et in tertio, licet concomitetur veniale. In quarto, distinguendum est utrum maritali affectu cognoscat suam: [si ita agat,] quamvis libidinose, adhuc est veniale; si vero tanta sit libido quod non decerneret utrum suam an alienam, mortale est.[1]

(A wife is known for four reasons: [1] to procreate offspring; [2] or to yield the debt; [3] or to avoid incontinence; [4] or to fulfill sexual desire. The first can be meritorious, and likewise the second; the same is true of the third, though a venial sin may accompany it. As for the fourth, one must distinguish whether a man knows his wife with marital affection: [if so,] no matter how vehement his desire, the sin is still venial; but if his desire is so great that he would not be able to tell whether it is his wife or some other woman, the sin is mortal.

Siegfried Wenzel has recently shown that *Postquam* is one of the antecedents of *The Parson's Tale.* But somewhere along the line (and, I would judge, before Chaucer came into the picture), the moderate view on intercourse was deliberately modified to correspond to the rigorous position of Huguccio and Raymond:

1. Cambridge University Library MS Ff. 1.17, f. 101v, ed. Siegfried Wenzel, "The Source for the 'Remedia' of the Parson's Tale," *Traditio* 27 (1971) 433–453, esp. 449–450.

instead of saying that the third motive is meritorious, though
venial sin may be involved, *The Parson's Tale* states categorically
that it is venially sinful and adds the remark quoted at the beginning of the last chapter, that scarcely any act of intercourse can
be without venial sin, "for the corrupcion and for the delit." As
for the fourth motive, the Parson makes no distinction about
whether the desire or delight is kept inside the bounds of marriage or not: it is categorically a mortal sin "to assemble oonly for
amorous love and for noon of the foreseyde causes, but for to
accomplice thilke brennynge delit, they rekke nevere how ofte"
(940–943).

The Parson has already established, before coming to the *remedium* against lechery, that such intercourse for delight alone
is a species of adultery even for couples who plainly have their
marriage bond in mind: "By cause that they been maried, al is
good ynough, as thynketh to hem. But in swich folk hath the
devel power, as seyde the aungel Raphael to Thobie, for in hire
assemblynge they putten Jhesu Christ out of hire herte, and yeven
hemself to alle ordure" (904–906).

Even the simple statement of *Postquam* that yielding the debt
is meritorious could not be left alone; the Parson adds a dictum
allegedly from Gratian suggesting that sexual pleasure should be
totally repugnant to the wife: "For, as seith the *Decree*, that she
hath merite of chastitee that yeldeth to hire housbonde the dette
of hir body, ye, though it be agayn hir likynge and the lust of
hire herte" (941).[2]

It would be hardly fair to attribute such old-fashioned notions
as these to Chaucer himself simply because they appear in a
treatise that he translated, or perhaps even partially compiled,

2. Wenzel 449 (cf. 452) is unable to find this idea so stated in Gratian,
but can only refer to the section on rape (2.32.5.1ff.), in which virgins are
said to keep their chastity even when their bodies are violated. The canon
cited by Raymond when discussing the second motive of coitus is the *Si
dicat* of Augustine, Gratian 2.33.5.1, but here it is the husband who would
rather abstain from intercourse and the wife who demands it. The part
cited by Raymond, however, does not specify the sex of the spouses except
at the end: "Pay the debt; even though you do not demand it, pay it; God
will count it towards your perfect sanctification if you do not demand what
is owing to you, but render what you owe to your wife." Similar is the
canon *Secundum* (2.33.5.5), also taken from Augustine.

probably in his youth. One might almost be tempted to set it aside as an early indiscretion brought into prominence only because of his rather ill-advised scheme to rescue all of his *juvenilia* by including them in *The Canterbury Tales*. But at the very least we must admit that Chaucer was aware of the stern positions here set forth, no matter how we choose to judge his own mature views.

In *The Man of Law's Tale*, which also seems to be something of a *juvenile*, Chaucer's attitude toward sexual pleasure appears to be rather negative, at least at first glance. We read that after Constance and Alla enter into their divinely arranged marriage,

> They goon to bedde, as it was skile and right.
> For, thogh that wyves be ful hooly thynges,
> They moste take in pacience at nyght
> Swiche manere necessaries as been plesynges
> To folk that han ywedded hem with rynges,
> And leye a lite hir hoolynesse aside
> As for the tyme; it may not bet betide.   [708–714]

This patient endurance of whatever is necessary to please her husband is certainly not taken as a sin on the part of the wife, but neither does it seem to strike Chaucer as being meritorious, but rather as sort of a coffee break from the business of being holy—except that the wife does not particularly like coffee and only indulges in it to please her companion. The husband does enjoy it, however, and he is not condemned. In Alla's case, especially, the pleasure abed is morally enhanced by its intimate connection with the engendering of a son, even though we are not told that it formed part of his intention.[3]

---

3. Cf. the Beggar in Thomas Hoccleve's *Regiment of Princes*, ed. F. J. Furnivall, *Works*, EETSes 72 (London 1897):

> I wote wel, leefful luste is necessarie;
> With-outen that, may be non engendrure;
> But use luste for luste only, contrarie
> To Goddes hestes is; for I th'ensure,
> Thogh thou take of it litel heede or cure,
> A man may wyth his wyf do lecherie.
> The entente is al; be war ay of folye.   [1590–1596]

He takes the position that there are three lawful motives for intercourse—including the prevention of fornication—and all other reasons are forbidden "on peyne of dedly synne" (1573–1584).

It is hard to avoid seeing Chaucer's humor breaking through the serious context of the tale when he speaks of wives temporarily laying aside their holiness. The passage does indeed conjure up the wife that the Parson found in the *Decree*, who acts "agayn hir likynge and the lust of hire herte," but with a tone of bemusement quite foreign to the inflexible categories of the Parson.

The Merchant's Tale, which definitely represents Chaucer's mature period, has even clearer echoes of *The Parson's Tale* and similar treatises. Here there is no doubt whatever about Chaucer's humorous intent, but he seems clearly to disapprove of January's peculiar approach to marriage.

Somewhat contemptuously January cites the main motives for marriage listed by the theorists:

[1]   By cause of leveful procreacioun
        Of children, to th'onour of God above,
        And nat oonly for paramour or love;
[2]   And for they sholde leccherye eschue,
        And yelde hir dette whan that it is due;
[3]   Or for that ech of hem sholde helpen oother
        In meschief, as a suster shal the brother,
        And lyve in chastitee ful holily.   [1448–1455]

We have seen that a marriage would be considered valid even though none of these motives were present, but only that of "paramour or love," as long as there was no positive intention to exclude children. January has made it very clear that he has the first two motives in mind, though not with the precision listed by the experts. If he wishes to replenish his own lineage rather than that of Holy Church, which is how the Parson defines the effect of marriage (920), at least his intention is positive.[4]

4. Joseph J. Mogan, Jr., "Chaucer and the *Bona matrimonii*," *Chaucer Review* 4 (1969–1970) 123–141, esp. 128–130, is a trifle too hard on January, as he himself partially concedes in n. 15. Even Repertoire de Science in Deschamps's *Miroir de mariage*, a main source for the tale, gives as the object of marriage the begetting of heirs ("pour avoir hoirs"), without qualification. See lines 5400 and 5407 (cited by Mogan on p. 133), ed. Gaston Raynaud, *Oeuvres complètes* 9, SATF (Paris 1894). It should be noted that Mogan analyzes this passage from *The Merchant's Tale* in terms of the goods of marriage (*proles, fides,* and *sacramentum*) whereas the controlling paradigm here is the *causes* or *motives* for marriage. When Repertoire pur-

The third motive listed by January, that of *solatium humanitatis*, is not to be taken as an addendum to the first two motives, as it often is, but rather as an alternative to them; when January repudiates it, then, he is not rejecting an essential element or "good" of marriage. We saw in the last chapter that this quasi-principal reason for marriage was meant chiefly for the *vir senex non potens*,[5] and January hastens to assure his audience that he does not fall into this category. There is, however, considerable evidence in the tale to the contrary: that he is, except perhaps at the best of moments, an example of "thise olde dotardes holours" who will kiss when they may not "do" (*Parson's Tale* 857). We must not be too rash in categorizing him among those who use aphrodisiacs in order to have intercourse more frequently. He would no doubt be hard put to make a single payment of the debt should May ever wish to call it in.[6] Even Huguccio by implication allows the aged to take stimulants in order to perform their marital duty.[7] When January himself demands the debt on his wedding night, he labors away at it until dawn; and though he

---

sues this latter subject himself, he says that nowadays many men do not marry to eschew fornication but to indulge in lechery; and others marry more for wealth than for lineage, as Marcia, daughter of Cato, well knew:

Non pas pour fornicacion
Eschuer prannent pluseurs fame
Au jour d'ui, mais que pour le blame
De luxure, et de leur desir
Traicter et aveuc eulx gesir.
Encores prant aucuns aucune
Plus pour argent et pour pecune
Qu'il ne fait pour lignée avoir;
Ce nous fait Marcia sçavoir. [5426–5434]

5. See above, Chap. 10 n. 7.

6. Burgh 8.5.B sensibly observes that if a man should be rendered impotent by the previous rendering, he would not be bound to render again, should the debt be exacted anew.

7. Huguccio, *Summa* on Gratian 2.27.1.41 (*Nuptiarum*) v. *solatium humanitatis*, Vatican MS lat. 2280, f. 258vb, explaining why the aged can marry while the naturally impotent cannot: "Dico quod nullus est adeo senex quod non possit calere vel natura vel artificio vel medi[cis]; quod non est in frigido vel puero." That is, "I say that there is no man so old that he cannot heat himself up to potency, whether naturally or artificially, or by the use of medicines; but this is not true of a frigid man [i.e., one with no sexual heat at all] or of a boy [before the age of puberty]." The Ordinary Gloss to the same canon, v. *in quibusdam*, is similar.

seems well satisfied with the result, obviously May is not (1807–1854). It may, then, be nearly true in his case that he cannot hurt himself with his own knife.

When January broached his fear that his pleasures in marriage would be so great as to deprive him of heavenly bliss, Justinus responded that there was no happiness in marriage so great as to prevent his being saved, provided that he used its delights in moderation:

> I hope to God, herafter shul ye knowe
> That ther nys no so greet felicitee
> In mariage, ne nevere mo shal bee,
> That you shal lette of your savacion,
> So that ye use, as skile is and reson,
> The lustes of youre wyf attemprely,
> And that ye plese hire nat to amorously,
> And that ye kepe yow eek from oother synne.   [1674–1681]

A case could be made for classifying Justinus in each of the three positions we have analyzed in the last chapter. Like Cardinal Huguccio,[8] Friar Raymond, and the Parson, he seems to consider the too amorous use of one's wife a mortal sin that would prevent one's being saved. If so, then, he would consider moderate indulgence in pleasure a venial sin.

Even the moderates like Bishop Peter Lombard, Friar Thomas Aquinas, and Friar Lorens of Orléans considered even the most temperate quest for sexual pleasure alone to be venially sinful. If we should wish to include Justinus in their ranks, we must not be so rigorous in finding mortal sin in excessive amorousness, unless of course it should exceed the limits of matrimony in intent.

When Justinus says that the temperate use of sex is reasonable, he does not necessarily mean that it is sinless, as we have learned from Friar Lorens. When the work is done solely for delight and liking and lechery, Lorens says, it is venially sinful even if the delight remains subject to right and reason. But possibly Justinus was as liberated as Bishop Laurence of Spain and considered the temperate seeking after sexual pleasure to be no sin at all. When

---

8. In order to present the three views without prejudice, I am giving all of the authorities their proper titles, a courtesy that critics usually reserve for Lorens of Orléans alone.

he tells Sir January not to please his wife too amorously and to keep himself from other sins as well, he may mean thereby to exempt moderate amorousness from all blame whatsoever.

In contrast to this speech of Justinus's, when the motives for intercourse are first discussed in one of Chaucer's main sources, Eustace Deschamps's *Miroir de mariage*, only a rigorist-to-moderate range seems possible:

> Maris puet a sa femme traire,
> Et la femme avec son mari,
> Pour hoirs avoir, lors sont gari,
> Ou pour deu rendre par la loy,
> Du pechié mortel ambedoy
> A cellui qui ce deu requiert.
> L'un ne l'autre en ce cas n'aquiert
> Sanz plus que pechié veniel
> Que l'en appelle originel. [9702–9710]

That is to say, there is no mortal sin on either side when spouses have intercourse in order to have heirs or when one spouse pays the debt to the other who asks for it; in such cases no more than a venial sin is committed, of the sort called original.

The speaker is Folie, who is attempting to show Franc Vouloir that marriage is better than fornication. Fornication is always a mortal sin, she says, even when both partners are unmarried. In marriage, on the contrary, she continues, there are two motives for which one can have intercourse without mortal sin, but not without venial sin. This sounds very much like Huguccio's doctrine; but the last line quoted above, in which the venial sin is assimilated to original sin, may be a reflection of Peter Lombard's more moderate doctrine. Presumably, however, even the exactor of the debt acts only to eschew fornication, and we get the impression that even in Folie's book any indulgence in the act for pleasure alone would be rigorously judged a mortal sin.[9]

There is no question about the rigor of Franc Vouloir's own

9. Later (10181–10205), Servitute speaks in favor of sexual pleasure, using the imagery and concepts of Jean de Meun in the *Roman de la Rose*. It does not matter, she says, that some spouses have intercourse for pleasure; pleasure is a necessary stimulus to the act, for otherwise no one would do it and the race would die out. Therefore, Nature, who cares nothing for spiritual law, made the act pleasurable; and there is nothing unnatural about following one's rules and rights.

position, when he finally gives his decision. The law commands one to marry for two reasons and only two reasons: to remain continent and to have a lineage, and not for delight alone. Accordingly, once married, a man must have intercourse solely to beget offspring and to render the debt. The husband must not approach his wife from behind, like a beast, and their ardor must not be chiefly for the exercise of lechery or carnal delight, whether in or out of bed; nor must their ardor drive them to exchange positions and do the act upside down. For those who do so, though married, sin grievously (10708–10728).[10]

In so saying Franc Vouloir is in general agreement with St. Raymond of Pennafort. Raymond asks, "Does a man sin mortally if he has knowledge of his wife by using some other position than the usual one, provided that he does it in the natural receptacle?" He believes, "without prejudice," that if he does so only to gain more pleasure, he does indeed sin mortally. But if his wife is pregnant and he so acts in order to prevent the suffocation of the fetus, it is permissible. The same is true, he adds, if he acts out of consideration for some illness of his wife or any other (reasonable) cause, "though it would be far safer in such cases to hold her as his sister than to know her thus."[11]

Franc Vouloir goes on to give a very sensible explanation of

10. On the particular heinousness of the upside-down position, see Astesanus, *Summa de casibus* 8.9 (Lyons 1519) 203, who considers it contraceptive.

11. Raymond, *Summa* 4.2.8 (Verona 1744) 480. Raymond's stand is the usual one on the question of intercourse during pregnancy; one can still render the debt (and indeed it would be a grave sin to refuse to do so) as long as there is no danger of injury to the fetus. Jerome's condemnation of the practice in the canon *Origo* was taken simply as a counsel. Raymond cites *Origo* not for this purpose but in support of the view that lustful *copula* with one's wife is mortally sinful. It is obvious, therefore, that Zenobia in Boccaccio's *De claris mulieribus* and Chaucer's *Monk's Tale* is an ultrarigorist: after she enters into an arranged marriage with Prince Odenatus, they come to hold each other "lief and deere" and live in joy and felicity, in spite of the fact that she allows him to "play the game" of intercourse with her only at long intervals, and that only for the purpose of having a child and "multiplying the world." For,

Al were this Odenake wilde or tame,
He gat namoore of hire; for thus she seyde,
It was to wyves lecherie and shame,
In oother cas, if that men with hem pleyde.
[*Monk's Tale* 2291–2294]

how intercourse with one's spouse can be performed with extra-matrimonial intent. Spouses can sin, he says, if the wife loves another man more dearly than her husband, or if the husband covets another woman besides his wife. The mere intention is a serious sin, for they are corrupted in thought, and the love and permanence of their union is broken. They would willingly be with these others if they could be, or dared to be. Thus, he says, it often happens that spouses as they lie naked in bed come together without desiring or taking pleasure in each other but rather make love with the wish that they were doing it with someone else. Those who indulge in such thoughts are disordered; their sole intent is to commit fornication; gone is all thought of the debt and hope of lineage. Those who are drawn to such a sin by that perverse intention do not even have the name of lovers, "d'ami ou d'amie" (10729–10768).

Almost without intending it, Franc Vouloir assumes that some sexual pleasure is permissible, as long as one or both of the acceptable motives is present. But later, when he says that he could not stand to be with one woman all the time and would be tempted to sin with another woman, he seems to define delight as the same thing as sin, by way of apposition. Being used to one delight, or sin, makes it easy to fall into another:

> Qui a delit acoustumé,
> Tantost est en autre tumé [i.e., tombé];
> Et usaige fait la coustume
> Que d'un pechié en autre tume [tombe]
> Souventefoiz l' acoustumant.   [10925–10929]

In *The Merchant's Tale*, Justinus concludes his discourse by ironically recommending the excellent declaration that the Wife of Bath has made on marriage "full well in little space." Indeed, her views on the matter under discussion can be summed up in a sentence: The sexual organs were made for "ease" in engendering, provided that we do not displease God. Her statement of principle is beyond reproach, though there can be no doubt that she sometimes fell short of it in practice, even according to her own liberal standards.[12]

12. *Wife of Bath's Prologue* 127-128; cf. Mogan, "Chaucer and the *Bona matrimonii*" 133 n. 21, 138-139.

The Wife certainly did recognize that there was a point at which sin could be committed: "Allas, allas, that evere love was synne!" (614). But probably she would take what we might define as the ultraliberal, or (dare I say it?) the common-sense position, as defined by the Parson: "Many man weneth that he may nat synne, for no likerousnesse that he dooth with his wyf" (859). Again: "By cause that they been maried, al is good ynough, as thynketh to hem" (905). It is the surprised reaction of Thomas Hoccleve in the *Regiment of Princes* when questioned on the subject: "She is my wyf; who may ther-of me lette?" (1570). And it is, of course, January's point of view:

> It is no fors how longe that we pleye.
> In trewe wedlok coupled be we tweye,
> And blessed be the yok that we been inne,
> For in oure actes we mowe do no synne.
> A man may do no synne with his wyf,
> Ne hurte hymselven with his owene knyf;
> For we han leve to pleye us by the lawe.   [1835–1841]

The line about the knife shows that Chaucer (or the Merchant) is making fun at least of January, if not of the principle he is upholding. But William Langland, writing when he himself was admittedly a *senex non potens*, shows that the sentiment could be held seriously in a less absurd match than that between January and May: "Whil thou art young and yeep, and thy wepne keene, / Awreke thee therwith on wiving, for Goddes werk ich holde it.[13] According to Franc Vouloir, many hold this opinion:

> Or y a pluseurs qui entendent
> Que qui prant femme par la loy
> Il ne peche point avec soy
> En conjunction naturelle.   [10702–10705]

When Béatrice de Lagleize was being questioned by Bishop Fournier, the future Pope Benedict XII, she explained that a certain priest told her that it was just as much a sin to have intercourse with her husband as with another man, or rather that it was a far greater sin to do it with her husband, because in so doing she thought that she committed no sin at all. Béatrice unashamedly

---

13. *Piers Plowman* C 11.287–288, cited by Donaldson 174.

told the bishop how she answered him: It is said in the Church that marriage was instituted by God between Adam and Eve, and therefore there is no sin when husband and wife come together ("propter quod peccatum non erat quando coniuges se mutuo cognoscunt").[14] No doubt most of the citizens of Angers held some such very simple and straightforward view as this, to be scandalized by the friar's message of matrimonial sin. And Bishop Bellemère's instinct was to leave them in their simplicity.[15]

Folie in Deschamps's *Miroir* intimated that there was a still more relaxed viewpoint toward sexual sin, one that we might call the radical position: namely, that *simplex fornicatio soluti cum soluta*, intercourse between an unmarried man and an unmarried woman, was only a venial sin, or not a sin at all. This was an obviously attractive opinion, and one that had to be put down periodically. Its condemnation in 1277 by Bishop Stephen Tempier of Paris is well known.[16] It was also denounced by indirection in a constitution of Archbishop Simon Sudbury of Canterbury, issued from Lambeth in 1378: he provided for the frequent inculcation upon laymen of the principle that all sexual intercourse between man and woman, unless excused by marriage, was mortally sinful.[17] If a priest were found negligent in making this salubrious doctrine

14. *Le registre d'inquisition de Jacques Fournier, évêque de Pamiers (1318–1325)*, ed. Jean Duvernoy, Bibliothèque méridionale 2.41 (Toulouse 1965) 1.224. Cf. Albertano of Brescia's *De amore* (written in 1238), which Chaucer seems to have known: Albertano refutes the heretics who oppose marriage, and carnal intercourse within marriage, and declares that if one wishes to lead such a life one may do so: "Quare dicto quod non debes cessare a nuptu, etiam carnali copula, si tibit placet habere uxorem." *Opus de loquendi et tacendi modo [et de amore]* (Cuneo 1507) 39v–40: *De uxore diligenda*. But later, on a different subject (*De luxuria et luxurioso*) he cites Aristotle as instructing Alexander not to seek coitus with women, for it is a characteristic of pigs: "Noli te inclinare ad coitum mulierum, qui coitus est quaedam proprietas porcorum. . . . Coitus est destructio corporis, abbreviatio vitae, corruptio virtutum, legis transgressio, femineos generans mores" (47).

15. See above, Chap. 10.

16. *Chartularium Universitatis Parisiensis*, ed. Henri Denifle with Émile Chatelain, 1 (Paris 1889) 553, error 183: "Quod simplex fornicatio, utpote soluti cum soluta, non est peccatum."

17. "In confessionibus et praedicationibus saepius et multis laicis inculcetur, et praecipue in maioribus solemnitatibus, quod omnis coniunctio maris et feminae, nisi per matrimonium excusetur, est mortale peccatum." Lyndwood app. 59.

known, he was to be canonically punished as if he himself were a fornicator, or a consenter to fornication.[18]

Though William Lyndwood in his commentary on this constitution takes the opportunity to show how sexual congress within marriage can also be sinful,[19] Archbishop Sudbury does not. We may suppose that his doctrine, thus simply stated, confirmed many of the faithful in their view that marriage gave them a free hand to indulge in sex without sin. This is not to deny, of course, that there may have been others for whom sex was never excused from sin, or who considered their sin excused only in the sense that marriage "chaungeth deedly synne into venial synne bitwixe hem that been ywedded," as the Parson put it (920).[20] Such seems to be the assumption of John the carpenter when he acquiesces to Nicholas's warning that "bitwixe yow shal be no synne, / Namoore in lookyng than ther shal in deed" (*Miller's Tale* 3591–3592).[21] But it would be dangerous to assume that his kind of pastorally formed conscience was to be found in the majority of the faithful. A substantial number, no doubt, instinctively held, with Cardinal Hostiensis, that marriage made the work that would otherwise be a sin not to be a sin, or believed, with John Andreae, that it transformed sexual pleasure into a good and even meritorious work.[22]

The most forceful expression of this point of view was made by the author of the alliterative poem *Purity*, in the course of God's denunciation of the unnatural sins of Sodom and Gomorrah. He instituted a natural way of intercourse, God says, which was singularly dear to him. He joined it to love ("drwry"), the sweetest portion of all; and it was he himself who devised the delight of love-making: "The play of paramorez I portrayed myselven." It was the merriest of all things, "when two true togeder had tyghed hemselven." A man and his mate should experience such mirth that "well nyghe pure Paradys moght preve no better," provided that they used each other honestly (that is, not un-

18. *Ibid.*; cf. 5.16.15 (343).
19. See above, Chap. 10 n. 43.
20. This sentiment also appears in William Pagula's *Oculus sacerdotis*, Vatican MS Ottob. lat. 401, *Sinistra pars* f. 251.
21. Cf. Donaldson 165–174.
22. See above, Chap. 10.

naturally, like the Sodomites). The blaze of love that is kindled between them when they meet together in the still darkness burns so hot that all the troubles of the world cannot slake it.[23]

O Moral Gower

It is noteworthy that John Gower, who was composing his *Mirour de l'omme* at the time of Sudbury's proclamation, deals only with extramarital sex in the section on the five daughters of Lechery (8617–9720). Fornication, the first daughter, maintains that it is not a mortal sin for the unmarried to mingle sexually:

> Ainz du meschine et vallettoun
> Procure leur assembleisoun,

23. *Purity* 697–708, ed. Robert J. Menner, Yale Studies in English 61 (New Haven 1920). The whole passage reads:

> I compast hem a kynde crafte and kende hit hem derne
> And amed hit in myn ordenaunce oddely dere,
> And dyght drwry therinne, doole althetswettest,
> And the play of paramorez I portrayed myselven;
> And made therto a maner myriest of other,
> When two true togeder had tyghed hemselven;
> Bytwene a male and his make such merthe schulde come,
> Wel nyghe pure Paradys moght preve no better,
> Ellez thay moght honestly ayther other welde.
> At a stylle stollen steven, unstered wyth syght,
> Luf-lowe hem bytwene lasched so hote,
> That alle the meschefez on mold moght hit not sleke.

See P. M. Kean, *Chaucer and the Making of English Poetry* (London 1972) vol. 2, *The Art of Narrative* 169–172; A. C. Spearing, *The Gawain-Poet* (Cambridge 1970) 72–73. Like the *Purity*-poet and Chaucer, John Lydgate also uses the term "paramours" to include licit love, in his translation of *Les echecs amoureux* (*Reason and Sensuality*, ed. Ernst Sieper, EETSes 84, 89 [London 1901–1903]) lines 3179–3182 (see below, Chap. 12 n. 6). The *Echecs* went on (in the Dresden MS, destroyed in World War II) to describe marriage: it is "the noblest form of friendship, and comprises within itself every kind of love" (summarized by Sieper 2.63). The gloss on the poem, which like it dates from the fourteenth century, says that "Hymen secretly signifies the delectation that is in marriage, in which the people are by the ordinance of the law legally joined together. And this delectation, as they say, is the greatest of them all and the least dishonored by sorrow, because one can more freely, easily, and legally accomplish all these delectations in marriage." Translated by Joan M. Jones, "The Chess of Love" (diss. Nebraska), cited by Emanuel J. Mickle, "A Reconsideration of the *Lais* of Marie de France," *Speculum* 46 (1971) 39–65, 42. Cf. Langland, *Piers* B 9.116–117: "And thus was wedloke ywrought, and God hymself it made; / In erthe the hevene is, hymselfe was the witnesse."

Et dist bien que pour faire ensi
Ce n'est pecché mortiel, par qui
Homme ert dampnez. [8644–8648]

The daughter Avolterie is concerned only with adultery in the literal sense; and Foldelit (Foolish Delight) by implication only adds to what her other sisters recommend. Later, when discussing marriage as a remedy against adultery, he does take up the question of marital sin, but only very briefly (17413–17442).

In the *Vox clamantis* marriage is treated only from a general point of view: the good wife is briefly praised in terms of the *mulier fortis* of the Book of Proverbs, and the bad wife is castigated in the usual antifeminist terms (5.299–438). But in the *Confessio amantis* Gower enters at length into some of the matrimonial questions we have been considering, especially in the story of Tobias and Sara.

In the last part of the seventh book, Genius has taken up the general subject of chastity; now he demonstrates "how marriage, which is a sacramental state that is, as it were, the equivalent of continence, should also be moderated by the discipline of honest delight."[24] The problem with Sara's first seven husbands was that they were motivated more by concupiscence than by marriage (which is perhaps to say that they had no marital affection), and they married her "voluptuously."[25] Or, as Genius puts it, in

24. *Confessio* 7.5309 sidenote: "Hic inter alia castitatis regimen concernentia loquitur quomodo matrimonium, cuius status [est] sacramentum, quasi continentiam aequiperans, etiam honestae delectationis regimine moderari debet."

25. *Ibid.*: "Illi septem viri, qui Sarrae Raguelis filiae magis propter concupiscentiam quam propter matrimonium voluptuose nupsuerunt, unus post alium omnes prima nocte a daemone Asmodaeo singillatim iugulati interierunt." On marital affection as a prerequisite to marriage, see John T. Noonan, Jr., "Marital Affection in the Canonists," *Studia gratiana* 12 (1967) 479–509. In *Mirour* 17413ff., Gower uses the same story to warn against marrying only for beauty or delight, and he cites Gratian (probably he is referring to the canon *Origo*) against loving one's own wife like one's concubine:

Je truis escrit en le *Decré:*
"Vil est a l'omme marié
Et trop encontre loy divine,
Qu'il du sotie et nyceté
Soit de sa femme enamouré,
Ensi comme de sa concubine." [17425–17430]

speaking of her first husband, it was "more for likinge, / To have his lust, than for weddinge" (7.5325–5326). As soon as he got into bed with her on the first night after their marriage, he tried to take her into his arms immediately,

> As he which nothing God besecheth,
> Bot al only hise lustes secheth.   [5331–5332]

But the demon Asmodaeus[26]

> Was redy there, and thilke emprise,
> Which he hath set upon delit,
> He vengeth thanne in such a plit,
> That he his necke hath writhe atuo.   [5338–5341]

We have seen that the standard doctrine in the Middle Ages, deriving from St. Augustine in the canon *Solet,* was that even marrying for lust alone constituted a valid matrimony. But according to the canon *Aliter* of Pseudo-Evaristus, marriage was not legitimately entered into unless the couple spent the first two or three days in prayer before indulging in intercourse.[27] This provision was obviously based on Raphael's instructions to Tobias, when advising him on how to avoid the fate of Sara's previous husbands:

For those who undertake marriage in such a way that they exclude God from themselves and their minds, and give themselves over to their lust like horses and mules without intellect, the demon has power over them. But you, when you shall have received her and entered into your bedroom, remain continent with her for three days, and do nothing other than pray with her.

26. Asmodaeus bears a frightening resemblance to St. Cecilia's alleged guardian angel; she describes him thus to her husband on their wedding night:
> I have an aungel which that loveth me,
> That with greet love, wher so I wake or sleepe,
> Is redy ay my body for to kepe.
> And if that he may feelen, out of drede,
> That ye me touche, or love in vileynye,
> He right anon wol sle yow with the dede,
> And in youre yowthe thus ye shullen dye.
> *[Second Nun's Tale* 152–158]

27. Above, Chap. 6 n. 5.

On the third night, Tobias would be assured of God's blessing, and children would be safely born from their union. At the end of that night, therefore, he is to take the virgin to himself in the fear of the Lord, "led more by love for children than by lust."[28]

Tobias's circumstances were rather special, of course, since a murderous demon was lurking in the bedroom. Gratian and his commentators obviously included the *biduum* or *triduum* of continence called for in *Aliter* among those "solemnities" of marriage that could be omitted without sin. Gower reduces the obligation to asking God's blessing upon the union.

We have seen that Raphael's words were applied to the motives for marital intercourse, as well as to the motives for marriage. Lorens of Orléans brought up the episode to illustrate the principle of "adulterous overflow"; and in the more severe *Parson's Tale* it serves as an example of the excessive lust that constitutes a species of adultery. In other words, the story is a touchstone for mortal sin in marital intercourse. Is the same true of Gower? The action of the seven husbands is clearly mortal, since it results in their being throttled to death, but is it mortally sinful?

If so, Gower would no doubt have to be classified either as a rigorist or a moderate: the former, if we can find no qualification of adulterous intent in the text; the latter, if his remarks on preferring lust to marriage are to be taken as the equivalent of an adulterous intent. It was a corollary of the rigorist position that no act, or almost no act, of intercourse could be sinless; and it shared with the moderate position the opinion that intercourse even for temperate pleasure was venially sinful.

I am not at all sure, however, that Gower can be so easily placed among the conservatives, whether rigorist or moderate. We must remember that he spoke of marriage as being moderated by *honesta delectatio*. Raphael taught Tobias "hou to ben honeste," unlike the previous husbands, who attempted to have intercourse with Sara,

> Noght for the lawe of mariage,
> Bot for that ilke fyri rage
> In which that thei the lawe excede. [7.5351–5353]

28. Tobias 6.17–18, 21–22 (Vulgate).

As a result, in Tobias's case,

> Asmod wan noght at thilke feste.
> And yit Thobie his wille hadde;
> For he his lust so goodly ladde,
> That bothe lawe and kinde is served.   [5360–5363]

Obviously, Tobias desires to enjoy sexual pleasure, and this desire is compatible with honesty. Because he governs his delight (chiefly, it seems, by subordinating it to God, since no mention is made of children), the delight itself remains honest. It is hard to think, then, that Genius (or Gower) considers him to be committing a venial sin. In an earlier context, Genius seemed to regard the actual pleasure of the act of intercourse to be the object of the *debitum:* he spoke of "the lust of loves duete" being ruined by the husband's jealousy when he comes to bed with his wife (5.484–490). The delight of coitus, furthermore, is a requirement not only of law but of love as well: it is "love's duty."

The lesson that Genius draws from the story of Tobias is a bit cryptic at first. A man can clearly see, he says, that "whan likinge in the degre / Of mariage mai forsueie," that is, go wrong,

> Wel oghte him thanne in other weie
> Of lust to be the betre avised.   [7.5370–5371]

This means, I take it, that we are to direct our pleasure in a different way, that is, moderate it with the rule of honest delight, *honestae delectationis regimen.* He goes on to clarify his meaning in a passage quoted in an earlier chapter: God gave the law of nature to both man and beast, but to man he also gave the law of reason, by which he was to set a limit to nature "upon the causes." Whether he means by this the causes for entering marriage or the causes for sexual intercourse after marriage, the import is the same. The net result of this modification of nature is that man avoids lechery but at the same time is able to enjoy sexual pleasure: "And yit he schal his lustes have." The *nota* in the margin emphasizes the importance of this deduction (5372–5383).[29]

29. I quote the full text of this passage above, Chap. 5, in the section on "Nature, Reason, and Incest." Cf. *Mirour* 17187–17191, where he says that marriage frees us to do the natural deed at our pleasure, which otherwise is a mortal sin:

Apollonius of Tyre is then held up for us as another example of
a man who gave his love an honorable and upright foundation by
marriage, and then continued it on an honorable course:

> For he hath ferst his love founded
> Honesteliche as forto wedde;
> Honesteliche his love he spedde.

He had children by his wife, and led his life "as him liste," that
is, he had his "lustes" (8.1994–1998). The actual event is described
thus:

> This lord, which hath his love wonne,
> Is go to bedde with his wif,
> Wher as thei ladde a lusti life,
> And that was after somdel sene,
> For as they pleiden hem betwene,
> They gete a child betwen hem tuo.   [8.968–973]

The child is simply taken as evidence of their lusty play together,
and is not insisted upon as part of their explicit intention. And
even though we are not told of any prayer offered to God beforehand, Apollonius must have played the game correctly, since
he apparently ran no real risk of demonic strangulation, but instead (after passing over some rather troubled waters) survived
as an example to all lovers of what they should understand by
love (2000–2002).

Apollonius's son-in-law, Athenagoras, is no doubt meant to
exemplify the same sort of exemplary conduct. As with all true
lovers, his passion for Thais was irresistible:

> So fell ther into his corage
> The lusti wo, the glade peine
> Of love, which noman restreigne
> Yit nevere myhte as nou tofore.   [8.1762–1765]

But he succeeds, nevertheless, in keeping it within the proper
boundaries:

> Car mariage fin, loyal,
> Nous enfranchist sanz nous blemir
> Selonc nature a no plesir
> De faire le fait natural,
> Q'est autrement pecché mortal.

He waiteth time, he waiteth place,
Him thoghte his herte wol tobreke,
Til he mai to this maide speke
And to hir fader ek also
For mariage. And it fell so
That al was do riht as he thoghte,
His pourpos to an ende he broghte.
Sche weddeth him as for hire lord;
Thus be thei alle of on acord.   [1768–1776]

Temperate Sexual Delight as a Good in Marriage

Would the English poets have had any authority, besides their native intelligence, for considering the pleasures of marital intercourse to be a morally commendable object of one's intentions? John Teutonicus's statement in the Ordinary Gloss to Gratian's *Decree*, "I do not believe that such delight is any sin," comes close, but is, in the end, rather negative. Only John Andreae seems positive: Marriage transforms bodily delight into a good work that is sometimes meritorious.

We have, however, surveyed mainly the canonists and penitential casuists; let us see now whether the theologians and theological philosophers have any such positive encouragement to offer to sexual pleasure.

The twelfth-century canon regular, Hugh of Saint Victor, could perhaps be interpreted in this way, and Augustine along with him; for when Hugh quotes the African doctor's comparison of sex to food, he plays down the connection between lawful sexual pleasure and procreation:

What food is to the safeguarding of the human being, intercourse is to the safeguarding of the race, and neither of them is without carnal delight. But this delight, when modified and restricted to its natural use by the curb of temperance, cannot be lust. Using unlawful food to support life is like using fornicatory or adulterous intercourse as a means to have children. [. . .] And the immoderate seeking of lawful food is like that venial intercourse for spouses.[30]

Omitted is Augustine's penultimate point: "Food that is unlawful because of the belly's and throat's lechery is like intercourse that

---

30. Hugh of Saint Victor, *De sacramentis* 2.11.10 (PL 176.497).

is unlawful because of the lust that seeks no children."[31] Hugh
thereby gives the impression that it is all right to seek delight
moderately, since moderate delight is not the same thing as lust;
and even the immoderate seeking after delight seems to be merely
a venial sin.[32] Gower too, we saw, left out Raphael's reference to
offspring: "When the third night has passed, you shall receive the
virgin in the fear of the Lord, led more by the love of children
than by lust." Obviously, Gower did not mean to exclude the intention of having children; but the only intention he names is that
of seeking delight.

Peter Lombard had the opportunity of making explicit what
Hugh seemed to be suggesting. Lombard compares sexual delight
with the delight of rest after labor or eating after hunger, which
many a holy man has indulged in and which is not sinful unless it
is immoderate. But he does not draw the same conclusion about
sexual pleasure. Such pleasure, he says, is only sinless when the
goods of marriage (he means specifically the intention of having
children) are present.[33] His reason for failing to rank this pleasure
with other carnal pleasures seems to be the special status that he
gives to *omnis carnis concupiscentia et delectatio quae est in coitu:*
even though such concupiscence is not always a *sin*, it is always
evil because it is filthy, and a punishment for original sin: "quia
foeda est et poena peccati."

Even St. Thomas Aquinas was prepared to go no further,
though one can with some justice say that he made it possible for
others to go further. As John Noonan points out, it was Thomas
who was most influential in establishing the Aristotelian notion of

31. Augustine, *De bono coniugali* 16.18, Corpus scriptorum ecclesiasti-
corum latinorum 41 (Vienna 1900) 211.
32. Just above, Hugh defined marital decency as the chastity of procreating and the fidelity of rendering the carnal debt, which Paul defends from
all crime. But immoderate progression (when one is overcome by weakness
or pleasure) is conceded *secundum veniam* (*De sacramentis* 2.11.9). The
venia is usually taken by authorities to mean that a venial sin is committed.
But elsewhere, in his *Questions on Paul's Epistles* (*PL* 175.524–525) Hugh
interprets St. Paul's *secundum indulgentiam* as the concession of a laxer life:
carnal copula would be a sin without marriage; thus by a concession the
illicit becomes licit, and it is customarily performed to avoid a "graver"
sin. The word *gravius*, of course, still leaves room for a venial sin.
33. *Sentences* 4.31.8 (*PL* 192.921).

pleasure as a positive value.[34] Even in his youthful *Commentary on Lombard's Sentences,* he takes the sensible view that no matter how intense sexual pleasure may be, it is not sinful as long as its motivation is kept within the bounds of reason (4.31.2.1 ad 3). But though he cites Aristotle's *Nicomachean Ethics* in his response to the question of what constitutes matrimonial sin, he does not depart from Lombard's view that the willing of pleasure alone in intercourse is venially sinful (4.31.2.3). He never gets around to considering the question again directly in his later works, but he does skirt close to the issue at times. In the *Summa contra gentiles,* for instance, he speaks of the friendship between man and wife as seemingly the greatest there can be among men: not only are they united in the companionship of domestic life, but they also enjoy, in common with animals, the delightful unity ("suavis societas") that comes from the act of carnal copula (3.123). And in his commentary on the *Nicomachean Ethics,* he explains Aristotle's reasons for saying that there should be a certain natural friendship between man and wife, and one of these reasons is the delight had in the act of generation.[35]

Two Franciscan theologians after Thomas's time, Richard of Meneville, or Richard Middleton, who died sometime during the first decade of the fourteenth century, and Astesanus of Asti, who died around 1330, seem to allow, at least by inference, for a positive value to be placed on sexual pleasure. Middleton speaks of the virtue of virginity as influencing the will to reject all venereal pleasure, even that which is licit. Astesanus repeats this definition and also speaks of chastity as a species of the temperate use of generation; chastity is concerned with the principal delight of coitus itself.[36] But this gets us no further than Lombard or

34. John T. Noonan, Jr., *Contraception* (Cambridge, Mass., 1966) 293.

35. *In Ethic.* 8.12 (Parma edition 21.290). Cf. John F. Benton, "Clio and Venus," in Newman 19–42, esp. 21.

36. Ricardus de Media Villa, *Super quatuor libros Sententiarum Petri Lombardi quaestiones subtilissimae* 4.33.4.1 (Brescia 1591) 4.471; Astesanus, *Summa de casibus* 2.41, 2.45.1 (87v, 88v); see Josef Georg Ziegler, *Die Ehelehre der Pönitential-summen,* Studien zur Geschichte der kath. Moraltheologie 4 (Regensburg 1956) 194. On Middleton, see the bibliography by V. Heynck, *Lexikon für Theologie und Kirche,* ed. 2, 8 (1963) 1292. His commentary on the *Sentences* was composed ca. 1285–1295.

Thomas. And in fact Astesanus followed them in considering pleasure-seeking in intercourse as venially sinful.[37]

Middleton, however, offers a ray of hope. In answer to the question whether intercourse apart from the intention of having children or paying the debt is always sinful, he gives two replies, either of which he allows as tenable. The first is the more common one, he says, which agrees with Augustine and Lombard. This opinion makes no distinction between asking for the debt in order to avoid incontinence and asking for it in order to satiate one's lust. The sin is venial whenever the motive for intercourse is not procreation or payment of the debt.[38]

The second opinion is given at greater length, and Richard seems to favor it, especially in allowing it the last word, without contradiction.[39] This opinion is basically the alternative set forth by Laurence of Spain at the beginning of the century and incorporated into the Ordinary Gloss to Gratian. Though Richard does not cite the Gloss explicitly, he does use the one justification for the opinion there contained, namely, the words of St. Paul in 1 Corinthians 7.2.[40] But his first argument in support of this opinion draws on the Aristotelian notion of delight: "To desire a moderate delight in an honest deed is fundamentally no sin, for corporal delight is not *per se* evil. If it were, it would not be a virtue to set limits to it. The virtue of temperance has as its object

37. Astesanus, *Summa* 8.9 (202v); cf. Noonan, *Contraception* 250 for some of the others who took this popular line.

38. Middleton, *Super Sent.* 4.31.3.2 (4.452).

39. John Burgh cites this very section of Middleton to obtain an opinion on whether a spouse may have intercourse in order to cure an ailment. Burgh first brings up the negative judgment of Aquinas, and then adds Middleton's report of what others say, that there seems to be no sin in such a case: "Dicit etiam Ricardus recitando alios . . . quod . . . in casu illo peccare non videtur, quamvis concubitus ille nec sit causa prolis nec causa debiti reddendi" (*Pupilla oculi* 8.5.L). Like Middleton, then, he favors the liberal opinion without overcommitting himself.

40. For Laurence of Spain and the Ordinary Gloss, see above, Chap. 10. Middleton shows himself familiar with Gratian by citing the canon *Nicaena* (1.31.12) for the principle that intercourse with one's own wife is chastity. Astesanus 8.9 admits that there are some who say that there is no sin as long as the intention is kept within the bounds of marriage, but he does not develop the notion.

the delight that comes from touching and tasting."[41] Middleton's word for "set limits to" is *modificare*, the same term used by Augustine and Hugh, to which John Gower's "modifie" corresponds.[42]

Those who hold this liberal opinion, says Richard, point out, in answer to an objection, that "satiating concupiscence and desiring moderate delight are not the same thing." Another objection states that, just as it is sinful to eat beyond what is necessary to maintain the individual, so too it is a sin to use sex for anything else than the conservation of the race. The answer to this is that the example given is false: "A man does not sin every time he eats food for the delight of its taste."

Richard also cites in support of this argument a passage from Augustine's *Good of Marriage*, which Hugh also used:[43] "Marriage does not *require* that kind of intercourse [i.e., for pleasure] to be performed, but causes it to be excused, as long as it is not too excessive, so that it would interfere with the times that should be given over to prayer." Augustine, Richard says, does not seem to mean "excused by penance," for even fornication is excused in this way. Therefore, he seems to mean "excused in the sense of having no guilt attached to it."

To sum up our survey of learned opinions on the morality of sexual pleasure: a great deal of support could be mustered for the view that such pleasure was completely sinless for both husband and wife when children were intended. The writers did not really consider whether the same conclusion would hold if one intended pleasure as well as procreation, or whether one was simply meant to enjoy the pleasure as it came, without intending it. But when the desire for pleasure was isolated from that of having children, the overwhelming weight of authority favored the view that such a desire was venially sinful, even those authors who considered the pleasure itself to be sinless or even good. For all practical purposes, the only dissenters, to my knowledge, were the *quidam* (meaning Laurence of Spain and his followers) mentioned in the Ordinary Gloss to Gratian; Aristotle and the *aliqui* cited by

41. Cf. Noonan, *Contraception* 293–295.
42. *Confessio* 7.5379, discussed above.
43. Cf. Hugh, *De sacramentis* 2.11.9 (PL 176.496).

Richard Middleton; and John Andreae. The last-named was one
of the few recognized authorities on marriage in the Middle Ages
who had experience of the sacrament from the inside. Unfortunately he did not gloss Gratian's *Decree,* and so made no systematic assessment of the problems we have been dealing with.

But in spite of the paucity of liberal authorities, we must not
underestimate the ability of Chaucer and his friends, like moral
Gower and philosophical Strode (the dedicatees of the *Troilus*)
to come to such enlightened conclusions on their own. We have
seen the similarity of Gower's language to that of Hugh of Saint
Victor and Richard Middleton when he allows for the honest enjoyment of sexual pleasure. And Chaucer appeals, directly or indirectly, to the Aristotelian ethic of the golden mean in a nearly
similar context. When describing the courtship of the birds he
sees on May Day in *The Legend of Good Women,* he says that
eventually Pity makes Mercy overcome Right

> Thurgh innocence and ruled Curtesye.
> But I ne clepe nat innocence folye,
> Ne fals pitee, for vertu is the mene,
> As Etik seith.[44] In swich maner I mene.
> And thus thise foweles, voide of al malice,
> Acordeden to love, and laften vice
> Of hate, and songen alle of oon acord.   [F 163–169]

He has already made it clear that Mercy's victory in this context
entails joyful sexual fulfillment: the birds do all the observance

> That longeth onto love and to nature:
> Construeth that as yow lyst, I do no cure.   [F 151–152]

There can hardly be a doubt that they are acting, like Chaunte-
cleer, "moore for delit than world to multiplye" (*Nun's Priest's
Tale* 3345).

44. It is supposed that Chaucer is drawing on John of Salisbury's reference to Horace when he criticizes those who flee a vice by going to the
opposite extreme: "Ut enim ait Ethicus, 'Dum vitant stulti vitia, in con-
traria currunt, recedentes a medio vitiorum, quae regio virtutis est.'" *Poli-
craticus* 8.13, ed. C. C. I. Webb (Oxford 1909, repr. Frankfurt 1965) 2.317,
drawing on Horace, *Satires* 1.2.24, and *Epistles* 1.18.9.

Chapter 12

The Mystical Code
of Married Love

Alla and Troilus

Even by stretching the most liberal moralists to their extreme limits, the most fervent kind of sexual love we can find them sanctioning, it appears, is "honest delectation" or "temperately enjoyed pleasure." This sort of moderation seems a far cry from the fervent passion that exists between Troilus and Criseyde. According to Hugh of Saint Victor, when sexual delight is modified and restricted to its natural use by the curb of temperance, it cannot be lust. But do not these lovers exceed the bounds of reason and fall into lechery?

Let me respond by pointing out that, just as there were different concepts or ideals of womanhood in the Middle Ages, so too there were different attitudes toward love and marriage. The ideal of marriage we have discussed in the last two chapters could be termed the legalistic or moralistic code; it emphasizes carnal copula, lust, and procreation. Even by this standard Troilus does not do too badly, especially in comparison with Gower's Tobias. In neither case is procreation mentioned or excluded, and Troilus spends a good deal of his time in bed with Criseyde in prayer. He does quite enough praying, one would think, in view of the fact that the unusual circumstances of the Tobias-Sara match did not apply. That is to say, there was no demon waiting in the shadows, but only Pandarus, and the fictitious "wikked spirit" of jealousy invented by Pandarus. Gower's other ideal of an honest lover, Apollonius of Tyre, did not bother to pray at all before he commenced his "playing," nor did his bride, who all along had been burning and growing ill with an extravagant ardor for him: "in amorem Appolini exardescens infirmabatur." Pandarus himself corresponds rather to Raphael, who taught Tobias how to defeat Asmodaeus and yet accomplish his desires. Tobias controlled his "lust" so well that both the law and nature were served. Just so, as we have seen, Pandarus tells Criseyde as he is about to bring Troilus to her bed:

> Ne, parde, harm may ther be non, ne synne;
> I wol myself be with yow al this nyght.   [3.913–914]

But another medieval ideal of marriage is more pertinent to Troilus and Criseyde, and this can be termed the mystical code. It is found especially in writings on spirituality, where the relationship between spouses is taken as an analogy for the union between God and the soul. Whereas the legalistic analysis of matrimony centers on engendering and incontinence, the mystical descriptions focus on love. Canonists and casuists are generally obsessed with coitus, while the mystics linger over kisses and embraces. The moralists consider these actions as mere foreplay to intercourse and for the most part ignore them. Writers who concentrate on the love between husband and wife, however, often treat these expressions of love as ends in themselves and rarely refer to orgasmic pleasure. Intense ardor in the former context is vicious; in the latter, virtuous.

Constance and Alla in *The Man of Law's Tale* can be taken as an example of the first tradition. If there is any love lost between them, we are not told of it. We are only told of the kind of pleasure that is connected with getting children, which is incompatible with the active practice of holiness and in which a saintly wife takes no delight. Troilus and Criseyde, on the other hand, can be seen as exemplifying the second approach to courtship and marriage. In their case we have the emotions of lovers, and not the lusts of the sexually excited. Incredible as it may seem, during all the time, and the many times, that Troilus and Criseyde are in bed together, there is only the slightest hint of carnal intercourse between them. Chaucer consistently plays down Boccaccio's more forthright descriptions.

For instance, though it is true that when he first embraces

Criseyde in her bed, Troilus imitates Florio's loving exploration of his lady's body and strokes her arms, back, and sides, her throat and her breasts, he does not proceed to *quel luogo ove ogni dolcezza si richiude.* But he attains to Florio's celestial pleasure nonetheless: "Thus in this hevene he gan hym to delite" (3.1251). As God says in *Purity,* "Well nigh pure Paradise might prove no better" when "two true together had tied themselves." After Troilus's prayer to Love, Venus, and Hymenaeus, and the exchange of words between him and Criseyde that corresponds to Florio's marriage to Biancifiore, Chaucer does not say that they took delight for a fitting length of time in *amorosi congiugnimenti;* much less does he speak of the *ultimo valore d'amor* experienced by Troiolo and Criseida, or offer a basis upon which we could compare their performance with the *sette volte* of Palemone and Emilia.[1] He simply says that he cannot describe their delight and leaves it to the imagination of his experienced listeners:

> But juggeth ye that han ben at the feste
> Of swich gladnesse, if that hem liste pleye.   [3.1312–1313]

"Play," as we have often seen, is a word that Chaucer frequently uses to refer to sexual intercourse. The term connotes lightheartedness rather than ardent erotic passion, and his further use of it in this episode accentuates this impression even more. We have seen one of the instances before, but let us put it in context:

> Therwith he gan hire faste in armes take,
> And wel an hondred tymes gan he syke,
> Naught swiche sorwfull sikes as men make
> For wo, or elles when that folk ben sike,
> But esy sykes, swiche as ben to like,
> That shewed his affeccioun withinne;
> Of swiche sikes koude he nought bilynne.
>
> Soone after this they spake of sondry thynges,
> As fel to purpos of this aventure,
> And *pleyinge* entrechaungeden hire rynges,
> Of whiche I kan nought tellen no scripture;

1. *Filocolo* 4.118, 122 (above, Chap. 9); *Filostrato* 3.32; *Teseida* 12.77 (above, Chap. 7).

> But wel I woot, a broche, gold and asure,
> In which a ruby set was lik an herte,
> Criseyde hym yaf, and stak it on his sherte.   [1359–1372]

The other instance is similar in tone:

> Thise ilke two, of whom that I yow seye,
> Whan that hire hertes wel assured were,
> Tho gonne they to speken and to *pleye*,
> And ek rehercen how, and whan, and where
> Thei knewe hem first, and every wo and feere
> That passed was; but al swich hevynesse,
> I thank it God, was torned to gladnesse.   [1394–1400]

In contrast, after Troiolo shows by his sighs *l'affezion che giaceva nel petto*, he renews *il diletto* (3.37). Chaucer's couple took no sleep that night: the whole of it "was byset in joie and bisynesse / Of al that souneth into gentilesse" (1413–1414). But Boccaccio's lovers desired to stay awake because they could not be satiated with each other, no matter how much they did and spoke what they believed to be appropriate to the act of intercourse; and they did not let the time pass in vain, for all nights were contained in that one:

> Ragion non vi si fece di dormire,
> Ma che la notte non venisse meno
> Per bene assai vegghiar avien disire:
> Saziarsi l'un dell'altro non potieno,
> Quantunque molto fosse il fare e 'l dire
> Ciò ch'a quell'atto appartener credieno,
> E sanza invan lasciar correr le dotte,
> Tutte s'adoperaron quella notte.   [3.41]

We have here a good example of the "expletion of libido" and the "satiation of concupiscence" in carnal copula that the moralists were so fond of denouncing. But it is difficult to see how Chaucer's restrained and elevated account could have provided them with any such evidence of lecherous excesses. One of the reasons that won Criseyde over to Troilus in the first place, she tells him later, was that "youre resoun bridlede youre delit" (4.1678). This seems an eminently fair assessment of his love-making.[2]

---

2. Robert P. apRoberts, "Love in the *Filostrato*," *Chaucer Review* 7 (1972–1973) 1–26, is right to point out the emphasis on sensuality in the

Communion over Coitus

In his *Testament of Love,* Thomas Usk describes a seemingly clandestine marriage of the sort that Chaucer must have intended for Troilus and Criseyde. He makes much of the point that mutual consent is the essential ingredient, not physical consummation. Love defines marriage as "the wedding . . . of two hearts that through one assent in my presence together accord to endure till death them depart." Some "idiots," she says, believe "that such accord may not be but the rose of maidenhead be plucked. Do way, do way! They know nothing of this. For consent of two hearts alone maketh the fastening of the knot. Neither law of kind nor man's law determineth; neither the age nor the quality of persons, but only accord between those two." This mutual consent by itself, she says, without fleshly intercourse, makes marriage, as we see in the case of Mary and Joseph. Therefore, the words of troth (or Truth) agree "that my servants should forsake both father and mother and be adhering to his spouse; and they two in the unity of one flesh should accord."[3] It is not fanciful to suppose

---

Filostrato—though, as we have seen, Boccaccio often gives the same emphasis when dealing with married love. ApRoberts is also right in his conclusion: "Certainly, if Chaucer's changes all set in one direction, no interpretation can be acceptable which moves in an opposed direction."

3. Thomas Usk, *The Testament of Love* 1.9, ed. W. W. Skeat, *Chaucerian and Other Pieces,* supplement to *The Complete Works of Geoffrey Chaucer* (Oxford 1897). The complete passage reads, in Skeat's partially reconstructed spelling: "And if thee liste to loke upon the lawe of kynde, and [that] order whiche to me was ordayned, sothely, non age, non overtourninge tyme but hiderto had no tyme ne power to chaunge the wedding ne the knotte to unbynde of two hertes [that] thorow oon assent in my presence togider accorden to enduren til deth hem departe. What? trowest thou, every ideot wot the meninge and the privy entent of these thinges? They wene, forsothe, that such accord may not be but the rose of maydenhede be plucked. Do way, do way; they knowe nothing of this. For consent of two hertes alone maketh the fasteninge of the knotte; neither lawe of kynde ne mannes lawe determineth, neither the age ne the qualitè of persones, but only accord bitwene thilke twaye. And trewly, after tyme that suche accorde, by their consent in hert, is enseled, and put in my tresorye amonges my privy thinges, than ginneth the name of spousayle; and although they breken forward bothe, yet such mater enseled is kept in remembrance for ever. And see now that spouses have the name anon after accord, though the rose be not take. The aungel bad Joseph take Marye his spouse, and to Egypte wende. Lo! she was cleped 'spouse,' and yet, toforn

that Usk had Chaucer's Troilus in mind as an example of Love's servants who marry in this way; for later Love refers to "my own true servant, the noble philosophical poet in English," and the "treatise that he made of my servant Troilus."[4]

Chaucer himself, in fact, described another such marriage in *The Complaint of Fair Anelida and False Arcite:*

> Her herte was to him wedded with a ring;
> So ferforth upon trouthe is her entent,
> That wher he gooth, hir herte with him went.   [131–133]

Anelida's good intentions are not returned, unfortunately, and, like Ovid's heroines, she sends a letter of reproach to the man who has forsaken her.

John Lydgate's beautiful *Temple of Glass*[5] presents another clandestine marriage which may be modeled upon that of Troilus and Criseyde. Venus instructs the lover:

> But undirstondeth that al hir cherisshing
> Shal ben grounded opon honeste.   [869–870]

His actions are to correspond to Troilus's: "Lete reson bridel lust bi buxumnes" (878). He tells his lady that he will be true to her and secret "whiles that I lyve, bi God and be my trouthe" (1005–1011). The lady is to take him to be hers, Venus says, "for ever-

---

ne after, neither of hem bothe mente no flesshly lust knowe. Wherfore the wordes of trouthe acorden that my servauntes shulden forsake both fader and moder, and be adherand to his spouse; and they two in unitè of one flesshe shulden accorde" (citing Genesis 2.24 or Matthew 19.5: the words of Truth). Love then concludes that such spouses are equal, no matter what the difference between them in status. See above, Chap. 2.

4. *Ibid.* 3.4 (123): "Myne owne trewe servaunt, the noble philosophical poete in Englissh, which evermore him besieth and travayleth right sore my name to encrese (wherfore al that willen my good owe to do him worship and reverence bothe; trewly, his better ne his pere in scole of my rules coude I never fynde)—he (quod she), in a tretis that he made of my servant Troilus, hath this mater touched, and at the ful this question assoyled." The passage quoted in the previous note is reminiscent of *Troilus* 2.890–893:

> But wene ye that every wrecche woot
> The parfite blisse of love? Why, nay, iwys!
> They wenen all be love, if oon be hoot.
> Do wey, do wey, they woot no thyng of this!

5. John Lydgate, *Poems,* ed. John Norton-Smith, Clarendon Medieval and Tudor Series (Oxford 1966, corr. repr. 1968) 67–112.

more, anon here in my syght" and to kiss him "in my presence anon" (1217–1221). Their hearts are to be closed with one lock (1224–1225), and their consent will tie the bond that cannot be undone, as witnessed by the gods:

> Eternalli, be bonde of assurance,
> The cnott [is] knytt which mai not ben unbound:
> That al the goddis of this alliaunce,
> Saturne and Jove and Mars (as it is found)
> And eke Cupide, that first you dide wounde,
> Shal bere record, and evermore be wreke
> On which of you his trouthe first dothe breke.   [1229–1235]

They are to join their desires together forever:

> Therfore atones setteth your plesauns
> Fulli to ben, while ye have life and mynde,
> Of oon accord unto youre lyves ende,

so that they will be steadfast against the "spirit of nufangilnes" (1240–1247).

The instruction over, Venus proceeds to officiate at the ceremony,

> That al atones I shal nou do my cure
> For nou and ever your hertis so to bynd
> That nought but deth shal the knot unbynd.   [1268–1270]

As they stand there in the goddess's presence, the lady takes by the hand her humble servant, who kneels before her, and then kisses him, fulfilling all that Venus set forth (1278–1284).[6]

6. A similar marriage occurs in Lydgate's translation of Guillaume de Deguileville, *The Pilgrimage of the Life of Man* 1905–1979, ed. F. J. Furnivall and Katharine B. Locock, EETSes 77, 83, 92 (London 1899–1904), in which an official or sergeant of Grace Dieu provides the instruction. In Lydgate's translation of *Les echecs amoureux, Reason and Sensuality*, ed. Ernst Sieper, EETSes 84, 89 (London 1901–1903), Venus is the goddess of unlawful love, and Diana the goddess, not of virginity or celibacy, but of chaste and faithful love, whereby warriors loved "paramours" gentlewomen of high degree "nat but for trouthe and honeste" (3179–3182), and wherever the ladies set their lot,

> The knot never was unknet.
> Their choys was nat for lustynesse,
> But for trouth and worthynesse,
> Nor for no transitorie chaunce,
> Nor, shortly, for no fals plesaunce.   [3202–3206]

Venus is then praised with great solemnity by all who are in the temple, to the delight of Cupid, in celebration of this accord and "the affinite / Betwix these twoo not likli to dissevere" (1299–1314). A ballade is sung "in name of tho that trouth in love ment" giving praise to Venus, who has "withoute synne / This man fortuned his lade forto wynne" (1337–1347).

Lydgate stage-managed this sinless union by resorting to ambiguities like those Chaucer used in the *Troilus*. In the original version of the poem the lady seemed clearly to be caught in a bad marriage, a May united to a jealous January (335*–362*). In his revision, Lydgate softened her complaint and made her state more doubtful:

> For I am bounde to thing that I nold:
> Freli to chese there lak I liberte,
> And so I want of that myn herte would,
> The bodi knyt, althoughe my thought be fre.   [335–338]

Even though we might think at this point that her troubles come from the sort of marital plights in which other petitioners of Venus stood (179–195, 209–214), it is later made clear that she is able to enter into honorable wedlock with a man of her own choice.

The wedding service of the Use of Sarum provides another example of the subordination of the coital ends of marriage to considerations of love and spiritual union. When the priest meets the couple at the door of the church, he addresses the congregation in English. He says that they have come here to join together the bodies of the bride and bridegroom, "so that henceforward they may be one flesh and two souls in the faith and law of God, to merit eternal life together, no matter what they have done heretofore."[7]

In interrogating the couple, he asks if they wish to love, honor, and care for each other as spouses ought to do. The bride must also be willing to obey and serve her husband and be meek and obedi-

---

7. Sarum Manual 45: "Ecce convenimus hic, fratres, coram Deo et angelis suis ad coniungendum duo corpora, scilicet huius viri et huius mulieris (*hic respiciat sacerdos personas suas*), ut amodo sint una caro et duae animae in fide et in lege Dei, ad promerendum simul vitam aeternam, quicquid ante hoc fecerunt."

ent in bed and at board; and the husband on his part promises to worship her with his body (47–48). This is as close as the service comes to the subject of carnal copula. It is a far different world from the legal niceties of the procreative intention and of the rights and obligations connected with the marital debt.

The newly married couple then enter the church for the nuptial mass. First they prostrate themselves before the step leading to the altar. In one of the blessings that follow, the celebrant beseeches God to send his benediction upon this young couple as he once sent his holy angel Raphael to Tobias and Sara. In another, he prays that God will sanctify and bless their hearts and bodies and join them in the society and love of true affection (49–50).

During the first part of the mass they stand in the sanctuary. Then, after the Sanctus, they prostrate themselves again at the altarstep, and four clerics hold a veil over them, unless one of them has been previously married. After the Pater Noster, the nuptial prayers are said while the spouses kneel under the veil. It is chiefly the woman who is prayed for: May she be as lovable as Rachel to her husband, as wise as Rebecca, as long-lived and faithful as Sarah (that is, Abraham's wife); may the author of prevarication find nothing to abuse in her actions (a subtle reference to Satan's manipulation of Eve); may she remain faithful to one bed, and flee illicit contacts, and fortify her weakness with the strength of discipline; let her be modest and shamefast, and instructed in heavenly doctrine; let her be fruitful in offspring, and upright and innocent; let her come to desired old age and see the children of her children in the third and fourth generation, and finally attain the rest of the blessed in heaven (53–54). If it is a first marriage for both bride and bridegroom, these prayers are prefaced by the sacramental blessing proper, which consists simply of an address to the God who consecrated conjugal copula by such an excellent mystery that he presignified the sacrament of Christ and the Church in the nuptial covenant.

The rite makes no provision for instructing the spouses in Raymond of Pennafort's inference that Jacob's love for Rachel constituted a perverse intention,[8] or his doctrine that even faithful

8. See above, Chap. 10 n. 5.

brides could sin with their husbands in bed. Children are not to be desired for the glory of God, according to this liturgy, but for the happiness of the parents in their old age.

After the Pax Domini and the Agnus Dei, the veil is removed from the couple, and the groom receives the *pax* or greeting from the priest and gives it to his bride by kissing her. After the mass, bread and wine or some other drink are blessed, and fast is broken. That night, the priest comes to the home of the newlyweds and blesses the bridal chamber, after the couple have come to the bed: May all who reside therein, he prays, live and grow old in the peace and will and love of the Lord. Then he blesses the bed itself: May those who rest in it be kept from all demonic illusions; while awake may they meditate on the Lord's precepts, and may they perceive him even when asleep. Finally, after the spouses are in bed together, he invokes upon them the blessing given to Abraham, Isaac, and Jacob, and calls for the Lord's angel to protect them all the days of their lives (58–59).

Not only is the whole service blessedly free from the casuistry of the confessional, it also largely bypasses the negative instructions of St. Paul by being firmly situated in the pre-Mosaic era of the Old Testament.

We can well imagine that a moral schizophrenia or compartmentalization could easily result from the convergence of the two basic attitudes toward marriage that we have been describing: theoretical and moralistic concepts on the one hand, and practical, liturgical, and instinctive viewpoints on the other. A striking example can be seen in John Gower's *Traitié pour essampler les amantz marietz*, which he composed in his old age, shortly before his marriage to Agnes Groundolf. According to the Latin rubric, the fourth ballade shows how the honesty of marriage is based, not upon the motive of lust or avarice, but only on the motive of procreating children for the worship of God.[9] The ballade itself,

9. *Traitié* 4.1 sidenote: "Qualiter honestas coniugii non ex libidinis aut avaritiae causa, sed tantummodo quod sub lege generatio ad cultum Dei fiat, primordia sua suscepit." In *Mirour* 17197ff., Gower sets out three good motives for marriage: companionship, children, and the avoidance of lechery. But he goes on to speak of marrying for love: "par bon amour loyal et fin" (17248). See Eugene Edward Slaughter, *Virtue according to Love—in Chaucer* (New York 1957, repr. 1972) 193–194.

however, has nothing whatsoever to say about the cause of procreation; it speaks only about the motives of love and loyalty:

> Ovesque amour qant loialté s'aqueinte,
> Lors sont les noeces bones et joiouses.   [1–2]

As he continues, in fact, it is evident that Gower is not speaking
of the motives for marriage but rather of the motives for the love
that leads to marriage:

> Celle espousaile est assetz forte et seinte,
> D'amour u sont les causes vertuouses.   [8–9]

He rejects avarice and other treacherous motives and reiterates
the ideal of loyal and honest love:

> Honest amour, q'ove loialté s'aqueinte,
> Fait qe les noeces serront gloriouses.   [15–16]

Gower's ballade makes me think of nothing so much as Criseyde
when she tells Troilus that it was not for reasons *minus honestae*
that she first loved him, but for his virtue and fidelity:

> For trusteth wel, that youre estat roial,
> Ne veyn delit, nor only worthinesse
> Of yow in werre or torney marcial,
> Ne pompe, array, nobleye, or ek richesse
> Ne made me to rewe on youre destresse;
> But moral vertu, grounded upon trouthe,
> That was the cause I first hadde on you routhe.   [4.1667–1673]

We can also think of the discussion of the motives for love in the
Confessio amantis. There are men, Genius says, who

> Riht only for the covoitise
> Of that thei sen a womman riche,
> Ther wol thei al here love affiche;
> Noght for the beaute of hire face,
> Ne yit for vertue ne for grace.   [5.2518–2522]

Genius is obviously speaking of the motives for marriage as well
as for love, and he considers beauty, virtue, and graciousness to be
worthy reasons for marrying.[10] John maintains that his lady has

---

10. On marrying for love, see also William Langland, *Piers Plowman* B
9.172–176, C 11.279–283, ed. Walter W. Skeat, parallel text ed. (Oxford
1886, repr. 1924) 280–281, and Thomas Hoccleve, *Regiment of Princes*

all of these qualities, and that is why he loves her: she is the mirror and example of good.[11] Not for any worldly good was his heart inclined toward her,

> Bot only riht for pure love.
> That wot the hihe God above. [2623–2624]

Genius responds,

> What man that wole himself relieve
> To love in eny other wise,
> He schal wel finde his coveitise
> Schal sore grieve him ate laste,
> For such a love mai noght laste. [2628–2632]

Which is almost like saying, "Tak love where it mai noght faile" (8.2086). But here he is describing an ideal love between man and woman that will last "until death them depart." At the end of the work he is speaking of a spiritual love that will last for all eternity.

A Full Great Sacrament

We saw that in the sacramental blessing given to first marriages, the act of marital intercourse was said to signify the union of Christ and the Church. This symbolism was based on the interpretation of the Genesis description of marriage (a man shall leave his parents and adhere to his wife, and they shall be two in one flesh) found in the Epistle to the Ephesians: "Sacramentum hoc magnum est; ego autem dico, in Christo et ecclesia." According to the Ordinary Gloss to the Pauline epistles, compiled by Anselm of Laon (d. 1117), the final phrase means that the sacrament is not to be taken as literally referring to carnal copula.[12] But according to

---

1618–1666, ed. F. J. Furnivall, *Works*, EETSes 72 (London 1897) (cf. Gist 20). These passages no doubt go back ultimately to Isidore, *Etymologies* 9.7.29, who joins the motives for marriage with the motives for love: "Item *in eligenda uxore* quattuor res impellunt hominem *ad amorem:* pulchritudo, genus, divitiae, mores. Melius tamen si in ea mores quam pulchritudo quaeratur." Cited by Robert A. Pratt, "Chaucer and Isidore on Why Men Marry," *Modern Language Notes* 74 (1959) 293–294.

11. Cf. the Man in Black's encomium of the Lady White in Chaucer's *Book of the Duchess* 817–1087.

12. Ordinary Gloss to Ephesians 5.32 v. *sacramentum, Biblia sacra* (Venice 1588) 6.96EF. See Beryl Smalley, *The Study of the Bible in the Middle Ages* (Oxford 1952) 60.

Peter Lombard's *Magna glossatura,* the passage could be taken literally as well.[13]

Between the time of Anselm and Lombard, Hugh of Saint Victor had given his great authority to the literal interpretation. A consummated marriage is a "magnum sacramentum in Christo et Ecclesia." But a virginal marriage is even truer and holier because it contains nothing to make chastity blush; it is an even greater sacrament, which signifies the union between God and the soul: "maius in Deo et anima." He bases the symbolism of the unconsummated marriage on the Canticle of Solomon, or Song of Songs, where the bridegroom represents God, and the bride the rational soul. The essence of the sacrament is the mutual love of minds which is guarded by the bond of the conjugal society and covenant.[14]

Hugh's understanding of marriage was brought into great prominence when Innocent III used it in his decretal *Debitum pastoralis officii,* which deals with the problem of widowers who wish to take holy orders. Marriage, says the pope, has two aspects, the consent of minds and the mingling of bodies. The first signifies the charity that exists between God and the just soul,[15] and the second is indicative of the conformity that exists in the flesh between Christ and the Church. A nonconsummated marriage therefore does not symbolize the marriage that was contracted between Christ and the Church through the mystery of his Incarnation. When a man has been twice married or has married a widow, he is forbidden to become a priest, unless one of the marriages was unconsummated. In that case, neither he nor his wife has divided the flesh with a second person.[16]

Bernard of Parma in the Ordinary Gloss on this decretal finds a threefold sacrament in a consummated marriage: in addition to the union of the soul with God and of the Church with Christ, there is the union of human nature with God in the Incarnation.

---

13. Lombard, *Collectanea* on Eph. 5.32 (PL 192.216); see Smalley 64.

14. Hugh of Saint Victor. *De sacramentis* 2.11.3 (PL 176.481–482).

15. The pope takes his text from St. Paul, 1 Cor. 6.17: "Qui adhaeret Deo, unus spiritus est cum eo." The Ordinary Gloss to the *Decretals,* compiled by Bernard of Parma, understands *caritas* as love and union: *dilectio et coniunctio.*

16. Innocent III, X 1.21.5 *(Debitum).*

This third sacrament is not designated by the act of intercourse, but by the marriage itself once it has been consummated.[17] It was in his gloss upon this gloss that John Andreae took occasion to say that marriage between man and woman changes corporeal delight into a good work.

It is noteworthy that *The Parson's Tale* does not refer to the symbolism of the love and union of minds, but only to that of the union of bodies: "This sacrament bitokneth the knyttynge togidre of Crist and of hooly Chirche." "This, as seith the Book, is a ful greet sacrament." "Mariage is figured bitwixe Crist and holy Chirche." The love of husband for wife is taken from the same model, following St. Paul: "A man sholde loven his wyf as Crist loved hooly Chirche, that loved it so wel that he deyde for it." This no doubt is the kind of love meant when the Parson says that husband and wife should love each other with their whole heart, for otherwise their marriage is not perfect.[18] There seems to be no notion that the emotions or passions should play a part in this love. Obviously no romance enters into such a concept of *maritalis affectio* (to use the technical canonical term).[19]

Similarly, when William Pagula says there are eight reasons whereby a husband may be induced to love his wife, he too starts off with the example of Christ and the Church; he then cites the Book of Hosea; he compares the spouses to a single tree; he recalls the husband's promise when he placed the ring on his wife's finger; he points out that such love is pleasing to God, and that God meant wives to be helpmeets, and so on.[20]

Pagula is not addressing himself to husbands who happen to be "in love" with their wives, or who find them personally desirable. John Burgh, on the contrary, does envision such a possibility, but he simply recommends a sincere love and warns against a love that is excessive or inordinate, citing an antifeminist admonition of Seneca's: "The love of a beautiful woman obliterates the reason," etc. (8.18.L).

17. Ordinary Gloss to X 1.21.5 (*Debitum*) v. *sacramentum*.
18. *Parson's Tale* 843, 918, 922, 929, 938; cf. *Merchant's Tale* 1319, 1384–1388.
19. See above, Chap. 10, n. 6.
20. *Oculus sacerdotis, pars sinistra oculi*, Vatican MS Ottob. lat. 401, f. 250rv.

The homilists, too, tended to encourage only the abstract aspects of marital love in those who were so unfortunate as to be already married, and to discourage both love and marriage in those who were not yet so trapped. "Where healthy human nature seems to demand some positive doctrine of sexual happiness, they speak only, as in the realm of public affairs, of sin and temptation, of forbidden pleasures and lusts, of needful fears and repressions, haunted by the same old shadow of Original Sin, the same primitive ascetical ideals as their ancestors." So says G. R. Owst in his study of pulpit literature in the English Middle Ages.[21] Homilies on marriage fit most naturally under the general topic of "The Preaching of Satire and Complaint." As he sees it, "the tragedy remains that, over against the follies of the Venusberg, there was set no other fair castle of Earthly Love to which men and women might be bidden to repair" (383).

We are told, however, that besides the negative ascetic tradition, "there was another tradition, which we might call a *prelatical* one, which concerned itself with canon law and with administrative problems touching marriage ceremonies, remarriage, bearing and raising children, and so on; this tradition was practical and dealt more with applications than with ideals."[22] But where did this more positive tradition reside, apart from the liturgy of marriage? Was it only to be found in an unconscious preference of the people for the ideal of married love over that of contempt for the world?[23] It is my feeling that such a preference was not unconscious at all, but was on the contrary so conscious and common as to be taken for granted. Perhaps for this reason the preachers felt no need to enlarge upon it, but rather saw the need to warn against complaisance in accepting what they considered to be a far lower ideal than the one that they themselves had chosen. To them January's scruple would not have seemed silly:

21. *Literature and Pulpit in Medieval England* (Cambridge 1933; ed. 2, Oxford 1961, repr. 1966) 377.
22. Donald R. Howard, *The Three Temptations* (Princeton 1966) 89–90. This idea, here attributed to Charles W. Jones, unfortunately receives no follow-up in Howard's study.
23. See Howard 157–158.

Yet is ther so parfit felicitee
And so greet ese and lust in mariage,
That evere I am agast now in myn age
That I shal lede now so myrie a lyf,
So delicat, withouten wo and stryf,
That I shal have myn hevene in erthe heere.
For sith that verray hevene is boght so deere
With tribulacion and gret penaunce,
How sholde I thanne, that lyve in swich plesaunce,
As alle wedden men doon with hire wyvys,
Come to the blisse ther Crist eterne on lyve ys?
                                   [*Merchant's Tale* 1642–1652]

No doubt many men and women in Chaucer's time, though perhaps not so foolish as to think that all married people were happy, were optimistic enough to believe that they personally could find happiness in marriage if there was love on both sides and if they and their spouses were suited to each other (conditions not met in January's case). There must have been many preachers who, like Justinus, felt that what was most needed was a warning against possible pitfalls and against the dangers of excess. There may even have been those who, perhaps with a touch of envy, observed that some obviously or apparently happy married couples were without a trace of January's worry and who accordingly felt it incumbent upon themselves to recall to them the Lord's words, "Whosoever does not take up his cross and follow me, cannot be my disciple."

There was at least one context, however, in which the office of preachers might well be called upon, though more likely in a private than a public capacity, to sing the praises of marriage in both realistic and idealistic terms. I am thinking of cases in which heirs or heiresses wished to stay single or live a life of virginity, making it necessary for parents or others to convince them of the nobility and attractiveness of the married state. Such a situation occurs in *Paris et Vienne*, when Vienne's ambiguous answers make her father and prospective fiancé think that she has vowed herself to God (she is in fact vowed to Paris). Her suitor tells her that according to Scripture God instituted marriage, and that therefore one ought to call it holy. He believes, in fact, that marriage is the thing most pleasing to God: "Vrayement, je tiens que la chose que l'om peult fayre en ce monde de quoy Dieu prent plus grant plesir si est l'ordre de mariage." For by marriage the human race is increased and Paradise filled, which was emptied by Lucifer's great sin. Vienne answers that she well agrees that marriage is a good thing, "que c'est ung grant ordre et tres saint, et [je] pense que Dieu l'a bien agreable." But since marriage consists in the union of two hearts accorded together ("mariage n'est seullement que une conjunction de deux courages, faicte par acort"), such a union must not be forced, and it can be made with one person alone; and she has already given her body and heart elsewhere.[24]

Literal Fallout from the Song of Songs

At the beginning of this chapter I suggested that there was a written tradition apart from poetry where descriptions and acknowledgments of passionate but nonlecherous love are to be found: namely, in the exhortations and commentaries of spiritual advisors and mystics. Such passages were chiefly inspired by a book of the Bible, the Canticle of Solomon. The erotic imagery of the nuptial lyrics here contained was, of course, also applied to adulterous love and to excessively lustful marital intercourse, as we know from the use of its "olde lewed wordes" by January (*Merchant's Tale* 2138–2148). But it was also the favorite hunting ground for mystical and allegorical characterizations of divine love.[25] Usually the authors who expounded such meanings were as stern as the general run of moralists when they spoke directly

24. *Paris et Vienne,* ed. Robert Kaltenbach, *Romanische Forschungen* 15 (1904) 554–556.

25. On the probable precedence of sacred love poetry over secular love poetry in medieval England, see Owst, *Literature and Pulpit* 16–17. For a discussion of medieval Continental traditions of mystical and philosophical love unions, see Peter Dronke, *Medieval Latin and the Rise of European Love-Lyric.* 2 vols. (Oxford 1965) 1.57–97 (see above, Introduction n. 20). For Chaucer's use of Canticle imagery in an adulterous context, see R. E. Kaske, "The *Canticum canticorum* in *The Miller's Tale,*" *Studies in Philology* 59 (1962) 479–500; and cf. James I. Wimsatt, "Chaucer and the Canticle of Canticles," in *Chaucer the Love Poet,* ed. Jerome Mitchell and William Provost (Athens, Ga., 1973) 66–90. I do not, obviously, agree with Wimsatt's conclusion that "Troilus is clearly idolatrous" (82).

of love between man and woman. Sometimes, however, often in unguarded moments, their common humanity allowed them to give honest and even extremely sympathetic accounts of such love in real life.

Nicholas of Lyre, for example, who was the most widely used and respected modern exegete of the Bible in Chaucer's day, has the usual sort of canonical and theological account of marriage in his commentary on the First Epistle to the Corinthians. But he takes on a much different tone when he deals with the Canticle. He does not believe that the book is a literal account of the love between Solomon and his first wife, the daughter of the Pharaoh, though he defends this marriage of Solomon's as possibly legitimate;[26] and therefore, he says, if the Canticle were to be taken literally, the love described in it could be licit, that is, contained within the bounds of matrimony. His own reason for not accepting the book on the literal level is that the love is carnal, "and such love frequently has something indecorous and illicit attached to it." (He is not saying, one should notice, that this is true of the love described in the Canticle itself.) Nicholas accordingly thinks that "the description of such love does not seem to pertain to the canonical books of Holy Scripture, especially since these books were written at the dictation of the Holy Spirit, whereas Solomon had knowledge of his love for his wife, and her love for him, and the delights (*delectamenta*) that followed upon it, from experience, and not through the revelation of the Holy Spirit." He prefers instead to read it as an allegory of salvation-history, encompassing both the Old and the New Testaments.[27] But in the course of explicating this allegory, he describes literal love-making with understanding and without condemnation.

Sometimes the Ordinary Gloss to the Canticle also betrays this kind of sentiment. For instance, in explanation of the first verse, "Let him kiss me with the kiss of his mouth," it says: "Here she speaks like a lover who because of the fervor of her love is not able to observe the normal order of speech. For as two diverse

26. Nicholas refers to his gloss on 3 Kings 3.1 v. *attamen* (or *et tamen*), *Biblia sacra* 2.128FGH–129A.
27. Nicholas of Lyre, *Postilla* on Cant. 1.1 v. *osculetur*, *Biblia sacra* 3.355CD.

bodies are joined together in a kiss, so too in the Incarnation of the Son two substances . . . are united."[28]

There is no reference to intercourse or procreation in the Canticle, and very seldom is there such in the commentators. The fact that the man and woman are called *sponsi* rather than *coniuges*, and the wife *sponsa* rather than *uxor*, might have suggested that the marriage was not yet consummated, since this was the technical import of these words.[29]

On one occasion, however, Nicholas may be using the term "cohabitation" in the sexual sense. He is commenting on the dialogue between the lovers:

He: Behold, thou art beautiful, my love, behold, thou art beautiful. Thine eyes are the eyes of doves.
She: Behold, thou art beautiful, my beloved, and fair. Our bed is filled with flowers.

At the words *Ecce tu pulchra*, Nicholas says: "After the cohabitation of the groom and bride, there occurs here a gracious mutual colloquy of the spouses, which customarily arises from cohabitation in the corporal sphere" (that is, on the literal level).[30] But *post cohabitationem* could simply mean "after they are in bed together"; or it could even have the more usual meaning: "after they have come to live together."[31]

Commenting on the bride's desires for flowers and apples, "quia amore langueo" (2.4), Nicholas says that "the woman, whose body is languid, delights in the odor of flowers and fruits, and the embraces of her husband." On the same passage, the Ordinary Gloss remains entirely on the supernatural level: languor of the flesh is brought on by the ardor of one's love for God, because of its excess, or the pains that accompany it.

When he comes to the familiar praises of the bride's physical charms (4.5), Lyre dutifully expounds the meaning. For instance,

---

28. Ordinary Gloss on Cant 1.1, *Biblia sacra* 3.355B.
29. See Peter Lombard, *Sentences* 4.27.9 (PL 192.913).
30. Lyre on Cant. 1.14 (357D): "Post cohabitationem sponsi et sponsae, ponitur hic colloquium gratiosum sponsi et sponsae, quod solet esse in corporalibus ex cohabitatione."
31. In the next section we shall see Richard Rolle using this word nonsexually.

when her breasts are said to be like twin fawns, he says, "that is, swelling out at the same height; not too much, however, but decently, enough to show her female sex." When he explains the same expression later (7.3), he makes a rare reference to offspring, and in doing so somewhat contradicts the small-breasted ideal just formulated: "that is, swelling out equally, and abounding in milk to nourish offspring."

Some of the verses of the Canticle are very suggestive of descriptions of love in the secular romances. For example: "Thou hast wounded my heart, my sister, my spouse, thou hast wounded my heart with one of thine eyes, and with a single hair of thy neck" (4.9). Nicholas's comment is a very obvious one: "This is a way lovers have of expressing their love." But later he has a more perceptive observation to make on lovers' talk. Nicholas says that the husband's words, "Turn thine eyes away from me, for they have put me to flight" (6.4), are to be understood as meaning the opposite of what they say. Lovers speak in this way to express mutual love, as when a husband says to a beloved wife, "Go on, I don't care for you," by this expression insinuating that he loves her dearly.

At one point Nicholas perceives a quarrel between the spouses and says that when the husband desired to be reconciled, his "bad spouse" refused from within her locked bedroom, excusing herself by saying that she had taken off her tunic and did not wish to put it back on, and she had washed her feet and did not wish to soil them. Then she recounts what her husband did next: "My beloved put his hand through an opening, and my belly trembled at his touch" (5.4). Nicholas concludes that the irate husband reached in through the window with his staff to strike her. The Ordinary Gloss, however, ascribes the bride's actions to timidity and says that her beloved touched her with his hand and set her trembling, and by his touch she was vehemently inflamed and hastened to open the door to him. That is to say, she opened up the door to her heart in order to enjoy not just the touch of his hand but his most blissful embrace—which, of course, is interpreted as the sweetness of divine illumination.

The most celebrated medieval exponent of the Song of Songs was St. Bernard of Clairvaux. He was one of the founders of "romantic spirituality," in which sacred love between God or the Virgin Mary and the soul was described and expressed in terms of passionate love between man and woman.[32]

The affection of love, according to Bernard, is the highest gift of nature, especially when it is directed to God. And no sweeter words can be found to express the sweet emotions of the Word and the soul than "bridegroom" and "bride." For all things are common to spouses: heredity and home, board and bed—even their flesh is one. On the wife's account the husband leaves his parents and clings to her; and the wife is commanded to forget her people so that he may desire her beauty: "ut concupiscat ille decorem eius."[33]

If, then, love is especially and principally fitting for spouses, there is good reason for calling a loving soul a spouse. She does not seek liberty, reward, heredity, or instruction, but only a kiss, like a chaste bride breathing out sacred love, who is totally unable to hide the flames that consume her. She does not use the usual blandishments and circumlocutions, but suddenly breaks forth from the abundance of her heart, nakedly and boldly saying what she wants: "Let him kiss me with the kiss of his mouth" (7.2).

She loves chastely who seeks him whom she loves only for himself, and not for something he possesses (7.3). It follows that one who loves perfectly in this way has married: "Ergo si perfecte diligit, nupsit." Again: "Sic amare nupsisse est." For when such love is returned, there is a mutual consent that constitutes an integral and perfect marriage (83.3, 6).

Nothing can be more pleasing than this conformity, Bernard says. It is truly a contract of spiritual and holy marriage. In fact, "contract" (literally, a "dragging together") is too weak a word

32. See Christine Mohrmann on Bernard's metaphorics of love: "En harmonie avec les tendences de l'époque et s'inspirant d'une interprétation traditionnelle du Cantique des cantiques, Bernard applique, sans aucune restriction, à l'expérience mystique, la terminologie de l'amour terrestre." Introduction to Bernard's *Sermones super Cantica canticorum*, ed. J. Leclercq, C. H. Talbot, and H. M. Rochais, Editiones cistercienses, *Opera* 1–2 (Rome 1957–1958) 2.xx. The eighty-six sermons were composed between 1135 and 1151.
33. Bernard, *Serm. Cant.* 7.2 (referring to Psalm 44.11). I use the Cistercian edition mentioned in the previous note and cite only the arabic-numbered subdivisions, which correspond to those of *PL* 183.

—it is a mutual embrace: "Parum dixi, 'contractus'; complexus est." There is clearly such an embrace where two persons are of one will in their likes and dislikes. The two of them become one spirit. No disparity between them can matter. Love recognizes no reverence or respect for degree. It betrays and captures all other affections. One who is in love can only love, and knows nothing else. It is enough to be man and wife; beyond the give-and-take of love no other bond is necessary: "Sponsus et sponsa sunt; quam quaeris aliam inter sponsos necessitudinem vel connexionem praeter amari et amare?" (83.3).

The union of husband and wife conquers even nature's strong bond between parents and children. The affection of spouses is greater not only than all other affections, it is even greater than itself—it is not self-seeking, but is self-sufficient; it seeks no reward and requires no other cause than itself (83.3–4).

Love is a great thing; but there are degrees of love, and the love of a bride stands highest: "Magna res amor; sed sunt in eo gradus: sponsa in summo stat." Children also love, but they think of their inheritance as well. They revere their parent more than they love him. That love is suspect which seems to be sought for some gain. It is weak if it fails or lessens when hope fails; it is impure if it seeks something *other*. Pure love is not mercenary, does not draw its strength from hope, nor does it suffer injury from lack of hope. Such is the love proper to a bride; this is what a bride is, whosoever she is; the possessions and hope of a bride are a single love: "Sponsae hic est, quia haec sponsa est, quaecumque est; sponsae res et spes unus est amor." She abounds in this, and her husband is content with it. He seeks nothing else, and she has nothing else. He is thereby her husband and she his wife. This is the love proper to spouses, and no one else can attain it, not even a son: "Is sponsis proprius, quem alter nemo attingat, ne filius quidem" (83.5).

Honor is demanded of children, love of a wife. The love of a husband seeks only the return of love, and fidelity. Should not love be loved, "Quidni ametur amor?" Therefore, renouncing all other affections, she gives herself whole and entire to love, by which she responds to love itself. She gives her all, so that nothing can be said to be lacking in her love (83.5–6).

In a spiritual context, "excess" is not a negative word for Bernard. *Excessus* in fact is his word for *ekstasis*, mystical ecstasy.[34] The love of the bride for her husband, as detailed in the Canticle of Solomon, is not only as full and intense as she can make it, it is also irrational, consuming, inflamed, incoherent, intemperate, unashamed; and all of these are praiseworthy attributes.

We saw that Bernard defined the bride's love as chaste because she loves her beloved for himself, and not for something he possesses. He goes on to say that her love is holy, because it is centered not in the concupiscence of the flesh but in the purity of the spirit. At the same time, however, she loves ardently, because she is so inebriated with her love that she forgets her lover's majesty. "O quanta vis amoris!" Bernard exclaims (7.3). In speaking of the husband's majesty, Bernard makes it clear that he means God, but his analogy remains firmly rooted in the human relationship between the bride and her royal lover.

The bride is inebriated but not satiated. She demands a kiss, which is a sign of love (8.6) and can be of such efficacy that it would cause her to conceive and her breasts to swell with milk in evidence of it (9.7). She justifies her greed not by reason but by love and desire:

I am not ungrateful, but I love. I confess that I have received more than I deserve, but not more than I asked for. I am carried along by desire, not reason. Do not, I pray, call it presumption where affection is brought to bear. It is true that shame holds me back, but love overcomes it. Well I know that "the honor of the king loves judgment"— but headlong love does not wait for judgment, nor is it tempered by counsel, or held back by shame, or subordinated to reason. I ask, I beg, I beseech!   [9.2, citing Ps. 98.4]

At the words, "Heap flowers about me, surround me with apples, for I languish with love" (Cant. 2.5), Bernard observes that love increases because the incentives of love are more abundant than usual. For after their passionate exchange the husband goes off in his accustomed way, and his bride is left to languish in her love. The more pleasing his presence, the more grievous his absence. "Separation from a thing you love increases desire, and the

34. See Mohrmann, Introd. to *Sermones* 2.xxi.

more ardently you desire something the more painful it is to be without it. . . . When the loved object is near, love flourishes, but languishes when it is absent. This languishing is nothing more than a certain weariness of impatient desire, which necessarily affects the mind of one who loves strongly when the beloved is gone." When one is entirely taken up in waiting, even the other's haste seems slow. Therefore, the bride gathers good works around her to rest in the sweet scent of fidelity while her husband delays (51.1, 3).

Even when her husband has only started to leave, she wants him to come running back. She shows no shame (*verecundia*), which doubtless would ordinarily be part of her character, but is overridden by her intemperate love: "Amor intemperans facit hoc." Such love it is that triumphs over and leads captive all sense of shame (*pudor*) and moderation in what is fitting, all hesitation and considerations of modesty and timeliness (73.1). Her sudden summons to her husband to return argues not only her great love for him but also his great loveableness. They are such untiring practitioners of their love affair, *tam indefessi sectatores amatorii negotii*, that an unquiet love pursues the one and urges on the other (74.1).

When he is gone for too great a time, her desire and ardor are so intense that she goes out at night to seek him in the streets. She can be held back by no reason, impeded by no difficulty, and restrained not by her love of quiet, her sense of shame, or her fear of the night (75.1). Such a burning and violent love, especially divine love, cannot restrain itself but speaks out incoherently, in any order of words or lack of words. Sometimes it speaks no words at all, but only breathes out sighs. Thus it is that the bride, burning with a holy love to express however little she can of the ardor she suffers, bursts forth with whatever comes into her mouth (67.3).

A girl may dare to think of marriage the more marriageable she finds herself, that is, the more similar she is to her beloved. No matter that he is more eminent than she; for insofar as they are alike they are brought together, made equal by love, married by their profession of fidelity: "Quidni audeat, eo se nubilem quo similem cernens? Nec terret celsitudo, quam sociat similitudo, amor conciliat, professio maritat" (85.12).[35]

But she must also be physically mature, with her breasts developed: "Alioquin parvula est, et nondum nubilis, sed nondum ubera misit" (10.1). Though Bernard has much to say about the function of the wife's breasts in nourishing her infants, he also acknowledges that they are important in her love-making. They are redolent with perfumes, and their fragrance is greatly commended. But the bride attributes her fragrance not to herself but to the oils and perfumes given her by her husband (13.8), and she desires to have her beloved rest between her breasts (43.1).

Bernard makes the marriage bed look both delightful and chaste, when for instance he says that "the bride and groom are inside together alone, enjoying mutual and secret embraces." He immediately elevates it to a spiritual level by saying that they are away from the noise of carnal desires (14.5), but the damage is already done. When he contrasts his spiritual birth with his physical generation, he disparages the latter by saying that it was done with the goad of carnal cupidity (16.4); but in another context he admits that not all carnal love is bad: there is a carnal love for Jesus whereby the heart is moved by his human words and deeds; it leads to spiritual love and becomes spiritual love (20.6, 9).

Sometimes, Bernard says, God appears to the soul like a modest husband seeking secret embraces and taking delight in kisses: "Nunc quidem instar verecundi sponsi sanctae animae secretos petat amplexus et osculis delectetur" (31.7). There is no suggestion that such delight in a real husband would be at all improper or sinful, no more than when he speaks of a wife who finds more pleasure in making love to her husband than another woman rejoices in her children: "Et quidem laeta in prole mater, sed in amplexibus sponsa laetior. Cara pignora filorum, sed oscula plus delectant" (85.13).

When the bride sings her epithalamium, she shows her spouse how the bed and bower have been adorned and invites her beloved to rest in it and sleep the night with her (46.1, 5). The

35. Cf. Thomas Usk, *The Testament of Love* 1.9 (41): "Two that wern firste in a litel maner discordaunt, hygher that oon and lower that other, ben mad evenliche in gree to stonde."

husband, like an ambitious lover, *ambitiosus amator*,[36] gracefully shows his beloved that all the splendor she glories in and the sweetness (*suaveolentia*) of the bed is his doing (47.1). He lifts up her head, as she lies there, with one of his arms, and cherishes her to his bosom with the other: "Denique uno brachiorum suorum sustentat caput iacentis, alterum ad amplexandum parans, ut sinu foveat" (51.5).

Such love as this gives rise to "naked demands" and incoherent outbursts at times, but there is room also for blandishments and loving terms of endearment. He calls her his very own dove; and he asks of her what she so often asks of him with such fervor: to see her and speak with her and enjoy her delicious company like a modest husband, not in the open, but in a quiet and secluded place:

Amat et pergit amatoria loqui: columbam denuo blandiendo vocat, suam dicit, et sibi asserit propriam; quodque ipse rogari obnixius ab illa solebat, ipsius nunc versa vice et conspectum postulat et collo- quium. Agit ut sponsus, sed ut verecundus, publicum erubescit, de- cernitque frui deliciis suis in loco sequestri.

He assures his dear one (*amica*) that if they go to work in the vineyard it will not interfere with the business of love, "negotium amoris impedire seu interrumpere." There will be opportunity for that which they both seek, for the vineyards have retreats and byways pleasing to the modest (61.2).

This is the literal play, "Hic litteralis lusus," Bernard says, catching himself up a bit, perhaps out of a fear that he has gone on too long and too far. Let us not remain on the literal level, he says, nor repeat, God forbid, the bawdry of sordid loves, *lenocinia turpium amorum.* "When you think of lovers, it is necessary that you imagine not a man and a woman, but the Word and the soul."

Bernard expresses a similar caution when he tells of the hus- band's overlong absence from his wife. He stays away to increase her desire, to try her affection, to "exercise" the business of love. But, Bernard asks, does he not carry his dissimulation too far? Such pretense on the part of lovers can serve a good and useful

36. Cf. Ovid, *Amores* 2.4.48: "Noster in has omnis ambitiosus amor."

purpose when it is a simple matter of going away and being called back ("esto quod pie utiliterque interim fuerit dissimulatum donec in sola adhuc vocatione seu revocatione res erat"); but what good can it do when one must be sought with such great effort? If the question is about carnal spouses and shameful lovers, as it seems to be on the literal level, it is of no interest to him—let them see to it: "Si de carnalibus sponsis et pudendis amoribus quaestio est, sicut litteralis superficies praelusisse videtur, et si inter illos talia contingere queant, mea non interest: ipsi viderint" (75.1–2).

Again, he says that the marriage that he speaks of as an embrace of great sweetness, *tantae suavitatis complexus*, is nothing other than an "amor sanctus et castus, amor suavis et dulcis, amor tantae serenitatis quantae et sinceritatis, amor mutuus, intimus, validusque." It does not join two in one flesh but in one spirit: "Qui non in carne una, sed uno plane in spiritu duos iugat, duos faciat iam non duos, sed unum, Paulo ita dicente, 'Qui adhaeret Deo unus spiritus est'" (83.6, citing 1 Cor. 6.17).

But in spite of these reminders that he is speaking of spiritual and mystical union, it is clear that Bernard presupposes and reflects an ideal of married love that is both passionate and chaste, both physical and spiritual, both delightful and uplifting. Though he seems at one point to imply that the *amores* of *carnales sponsi* are *pudendi* ("shameful") by definition (75.2),[37] he has admitted

---

37. Cf. his remarks on remarriage because of incontinence: Such a remarriage is only a venial fault, but the incontinence that prompts it is filthy, *turpis*, and it is shameful that reason cannot achieve the decency in men that nature produces in birds (59.7). In heaven men will be much happier, for there will be no more marriage (59.8). In his sermons against the heretics of Cologne, Bernard maintains that to be always alone with a woman and not know her carnally is a greater work than resurrecting the dead (*Serm. Cant.* 65.4). He asserts that the Church does not allow men who vow continence to cohabit with women (65.6). Apparently Bernard is conveniently forgetting the tradition of virginal marriage. See John T. Noonan, Jr., *Power to Dissolve* (Cambridge, Mass., 1972) 84–85, and the canons of St. Augustine on husbands and wives vowing continence, Gratian 2.27.2.3 (*Beata Maria*); 2.33.5.4 (*Quod Deo*), 5 (*Secundum*), and 6 (*Una sola causa*). When the heretics retort that the Gospel does not forbid such a practice, Bernard replies that the Church does, because the Church forbids scandal (65.7). The heretics think that wives are filthy, whereas it is only with a wife that the filth of coitus can be excused (66.1). Some of the heretics allow marriage, but only for those who are still virgins; Bernard objects against thus restricting the generous blessing, *larga benedictio*, of marriage (66.4–5).

more than once that they can also be *verecundi* ("shamefast"). Though he distinguishes spiritual marriage from the marriage that unites two persons in one flesh, the union of two spirits into one was considered to be an essential aspect of marriage on the literal level: it was the union that came before the union of bodies; and Innocent III would cite the same verse from St. Paul to show that this *consensus animorum* signified the *caritas quae consistit in spiritu inter Deum et iustam animam*.[38]

When, therefore, we encounter sexuality in medieval literature, and see that "it must be kept secret, it must not be given too freely (or withheld completely), it must be regarded with a devout awe,"[39] we should hesitate before we conclude that "it is a reversal of the sexuality which orthodox medieval social institutions approved."

The Age of Richard Rolle

Bernard's sermons on the Canticle were very popular in England from the very beginning, to judge from the large number of twelfth- and early thirteenth-century manuscripts still extant. And though there are fewer manuscripts of a later date, on the Continent as well as in England, undoubtedly his influence lingered on, especially in contemplative circles. But England, or at any rate the pulpit in England, "had to wait for its school of literary mystics until the age of Richard Rolle in the [fourteenth century], to tell of love-longings for Jesus, of mystic unions with the Queen of Heaven, or of the wooing of our Lord."[40]

Rolle himself belongs to the first half of the fourteenth century; like John Andreae and perhaps John Acton, he was carried off by the Black Death. And though his influence seems to have reached its greatest intensity in the fifteenth century, his message of love must have been in the air by Chaucer's time. His most popular work, the *Incendium amoris*,[41] can serve as an example of

38. Above, n. 15.
39. Howard, *Three Temptations* 101.
40. Owst, *Literature and Pulpit* 17–18.
41. *The Incendium amoris of Richard Rolle of Hampole*, ed. Margaret Deanesly, Publications of the University of Manchester 97 (Manchester 1915). Only three of the surviving MSS of the *Incendium* are definitely of the fourteenth century. Two others are either from the late fourteenth or the early fifteenth century. The work was translated into English in 1435 by

the way in which intense love on the human level was used to illustrate divine love.

Like Bernard, Rolle often speaks of love in general, without specifying its object. For example, he says, "No creature can love too much. In all other things, too much of anything becomes a vice. But the greater the excess of the strength (*virtus*) of love the more glorious it is." "What else is love," he asks,

but the transformation of affection into the thing loved? Or, love is the great desire for what is beautiful, good, and lovable, with thoughts continually set upon what one loves. When one possesses it, then one rejoices, for joy is not caused by anything but love. Everyone becomes like that which he loves. Now neither God nor any creature disdains or refuses to be loved. Rather all admit to joy in being loved, and to delight in love. For they experience no sadness in love unless the object of the love is unresponsive (*ingratum*), or if they despair of attaining that which they seek with their love. [17:194–195]

Again: "There is nothing better than mutual love, nothing sweeter than holy charity. For to be loved and to love is the sweet business of the whole of human life. It is also the delight and prize of angelic and divine beatitude. If therefore you seek to be loved, love. For love receives return in kind" (25:214). And: "Love is the constant thought about and great desire for what is lovable because of its beauty and goodness. For if the thing that I love is beautiful and not good, I prove that I love unworthily. But if it is good, then it is to be loved" (40:268). Love conquers fear and pain and pride (26:217); it makes one virtuous, and eliminates sin (22:207).

Friendship is like love: a true friend loves his friend only for his own sake, and not for profit or pleasure. Friendship can be defined as a union of wills that agree and disagree about the same things.[42] True friendship is the solidifying of lovers, the solace of

the Carmelite friar Richard Misyn, ed. Ralph Harvey, *The Fire of Love*, EETS 106 (London 1896). The Latin text followed by Deanesly consists of a prologue and forty-two chapters. The English version is divided into two books: The first contains the prologue, which is counted as chapter 1, and the first 30 chapters, counted as chapters 2–31. The second book contains chapters 31–42, numbered as 1–12. I will cite the chapters as given by Deanesly, followed by her page numbers.

42. "Amicitia est connexio voluntatum eisdem consentientium et eisdem dissent[ient]ium" (39:261). Cf. Bernard, *Serm. Cant.* 83.3: "Complexus plane, ubi idem velle et nolle idem unum facit spiritum de duobus."

minds, the relief of anguish, the expulsion of worldly sadness, the correction of sins, the increase of holiness, the decrease of evil deeds, the multiplication of merited goods; one friend is in turn drawn by the other from evil by salubrious advice and inflamed to do good, and the one desires (*concupiscit*) for himself the grace that he sees in the other (39:264).

Friendship between men and women can be good, even meritorious, if entered into with a good mind and treasured for God's sake, and not for fleshly sweetness (263). Rolle is speaking, of course, of friendship that does not have marital affection as its goal. He never discusses the kind of physical love that is permitted to married couples. At one point, when speaking of the supremacy of celibacy as a way of life, he admits that marriage in itself is good, but he does not pause to describe how a good marriage works. Instead he rushes on to explain how it is perverted by men who marry only for the purpose of fulfilling their lust ("pro explenda libidine") or for riches (24:211).[43] He uses the erotic language of the Canticle only to describe divine love.[44]

It is possible, however, to deduce something of what he might have said of married love if he had put his mind to it. He says, for instance:

There is a certain natural love of man for woman and woman for man which no one lacks, not even saints. It was established by God in our nature from the beginning, and because of it, when men and women are together and sympathetic to one another, they rejoice in this companionship by a natural instinct. This love also has its delights, such as arise from talking together and touching each other honestly, and from a pleasant life together (*grata cohabitatio*). But nevertheless a man does not gain merit by such love unless it is informed by charity, nor is he given demerits, unless it is blackened by guilt. (For if evil motions arise, whereupon they think about lust and direct themselves to it, without doubt they are mortally culpable, because they sin against God.) Therefore, it is a foul error on the part of those who say that all our deeds, whether interior or exterior, are either meritorious or demeritorious, for they are trying to deprive us, or at least attempting to deny the existence of, delights and actions that are natural, and so they do not hesitate to bring confusion on our noble nature. [39:263–264]

43. For other descriptions of lechery, see 23:210–211; 29:228.
44. E.g., 26:218; 28:223.

This doctrine of love between the sexes is an outgrowth of his teaching on friendship in general earlier in the same chapter:[45]

Such friendship is purely natural, and therefore gains no merit, nor is there demerit unless it involves something against a precept of God. It also has great delight attached to it, which likewise involves neither merit nor demerit. For true friendship cannot be without the mutual delight of the friends, their desirable speech together, and the solaces they speak to each other. And this friendship, if it is informed by the grace of God and takes place wholly in him, and is referred and directed to him, is then called holy friendship, and gains much merit. If, however, this friendship causes the friends to do anything against the divine will, it is a perverse, foul, and impure friendship, and brings great demerit. [262–263]

Therefore, the morality of friendship and love depends entirely upon one's intentions:

If we touch a woman and at the same time think nothing but good in our heart, certainly it should not be called a sin, even though some temptation of the flesh should arise from it. For one does not fall into evil while the mind remains fixed on God. But when the heart of one who so touches is rushed into various desires, or when in other circumstances he is even turned aside into evil pleasures, and is not at once restrained by the love of the Creator and the constancy of his virtues: know beyond a doubt that that man bears in himself the guilt of impurity, even though he should be far removed not only from the company of women but also from that of all human beings.[46] [24:212–213]

Spiritual Counsel for Troilus and His Sympathizers

If we take seriously Troilus and Criseyde's expressions of honesty and good intentions and allow them a moderate amount of sensual pleasure in virtue of their marital affection, is there any

45. The relationship between Troilus and Pandarus can, of course, be analyzed in these terms. See, for example, Robert G. Cook, "Chaucer's Pandarus and the Medieval Ideal of Friendship," *Journal of English and Germanic Philology* 69 (1970) 407–424; Cook, however, is unduly disturbed by the deviousness practiced by Pandarus in bringing Troilus and Criseyde together.

46. These sentiments come in the midst of the discourse on the bad uses of marriage, though it is evident that Rolle is not thinking of a specifically marital relationship here. He goes on, however, to speak of the dangers of marrying an infidel wife.

reason to consider their love evil? In the light of its subordination to God in his holy bond of love, should it not also be considered meritorious?

If so, what went wrong? A simple answer is that Criseyde, through weakness, became unfaithful. For, as Rolle says, "Friendship that is kindled by some thing that is not the beloved object itself fails and is extinguished when the thing that incited the love is no longer to be had. For example, when manners, riches, or beauty keeps the friendship going, it evaporates when the manners go astray, the riches decrease, the beauty disappears; and it must be said of him who had that friendship that 'there is nothing unhappier than to have been happy.' "[47] Rolle, however, is here speaking of imperfect friendship, for "the friendship that nature inspires in friends is overthrown by no poverty, is destroyed by no going astray, is ended by no deformity, as long as the nature remains which exists on account of that friendship" (39:262).

If we grant that Criseyde was sincere and accurate in telling Troilus that she first loved him for his "moral vertu grounded upon trouthe," did not her nature change? Rolle tells us that "nature compels a man to seek a faithful friend; since he himself intends to be faithful and to keep himself responsive, nothing is done in vain. Therefore, that friendship which exists naturally will not be dissolved as long as nature remains, unless the beloved nature becomes repugnant, to the neglect of nature itself; and one's nature could in no way do this, unless it were overcome by corrupted morals."[48]

Troilus might have had cause, even by the canons of true friendship, to repudiate his love of Criseyde, but he did not do so. Despite the sorrow she made him suffer, he continued to love her more than any other creature, and prayed to God, the promoter of fidelity and the punisher of wrong, not to punish

47. Loosely quoting Boethius, *Consolation of Philosophy* 2, prose 4.
48. "Natura enim cogit hominem sibi quaerere fidelem amicum; cum et ipse fidem et gratitudinem servare intendit, nihil frustra agit; ergo ipsa amicitia quae naturalis est, non dissolvetur, natura existente, nisi in iniuriam ipsius naturae natura amata repugnet; quod nullo modo natura facere potest, nisi corruptis moribus fuerit oppressa" (262). In the case mentioned above, the *mores* were only *errantes;* here they are *corrupti.*

Criseyde, but to allow him to wreak vengeance on Diomede, the instigator of the misdeed (5.1695–1708).[49]

For Criseyde's fall was not entirely her own fault. As Rolle points out, women are by nature weaker than men. "For reason is less vigorous in them, and therefore they are easily seduced and quickly vanquished. On this account they need the counsel of good men. But by bad men they are badly treated, for they are much more inclined to the delight of pleasure than to the clarity of sanctity" (263).[50] Though Chaucer in the prologue to *The Legend of Good Women* denies that he held such a doctrine of feminine weakness, it is easy to see how Cupid and Alcestis could conclude from the *Troilus* that he did.[51]

Apart from Criseyde's weakness and infidelity, however, there was another, more fundamental defect in their love. It was earthly, and so had to come to an end in one way or another.

> Swich is this world, whoso it kan byholde.
> In ech estat is litel hertes reste.
> God leve us for to take it for the beste.   [5.1748–1750]

Chaucer's final advice to young people who feel the impulses of love is for them to come "home" from worldly vanity and regard the world as nothing but a fair "that passeth soone as floures faire." They should look to God, who made them in his image, and love Christ, who for love of them died on a cross;

49. See above, Chap. 9. Cf. *Incendium* 39:261–262: "Immo si fuerit vera amicitia, magis sollicita erit revocare errantem, etsi oporteret ut amicitia dicatur amor, quo vult et procurit amico bonum sicut sibi ipsi, et nullo errore potest rumpi dum vivunt"—i.e., "till death them depart."

50. Peter Comestor, in a sermon for the feast of All Saints, contends that women are by nature so handicapped in the struggle for sanctity that they deserve all the more credit when they actually achieve it (*PL* 198.1805). Even before the fall, Eve was weaker than Adam. In Horace's phrase, she was "wax to be twisted into vice," and for this reason the devil chose to tempt her rather than Adam. So Comestor in his *Historia scholastica in Genesim* 21 (*PL* 198.1072). See my essay "The Metamorphoses of the Eden Serpent during the Middle Ages and Renaissance," *Viator* 2 (1971) 301–327, esp. 308, where however I neglected to give my reason for emending the *PL* reading of *certam in vitium flecti*, "certain to be twisted into vice," to *ceream in vitium flecti*: the latter is the reading of Vincent of Beauvais's citation of Peter in the *Speculum naturale* 30.68 (Douai 1624) 2265–2266, and it agrees with Horace, *Ars poetica* 163.

51. See above, Chap. 4.

For he nyl falsen no wight, dar I seye,
That wol his herte al holly on hym leye.
And syn he best to love is, and most meke,
What nedeth feynede loves for to seke?   [1845–1848]

Whereas Boccaccio at the end of the *Filostrato* warned only against false human love and still hoped for true love, Chaucer characterizes all human love as false or fictitious.

Many readers have been distressed by this total rejection of human love at the end of the *Troilus;* others have seen it as proof that Chaucer was condemning the love of Troilus and Criseyde all along. Both reactions are misguided. The unqualified and exaggerated statements at the end of the poem are typical of the rhetoric of spiritual counsel. We have seen an example of this sort of overemphasis in the so-called palinode of Gower's *Confessio amantis;* and the common occurrence of such exaggeration is taken for granted in the Ordinary Gloss to Gratian when overly severe sentiments are to be explained away. For instance, St. Jerome is not really saying that excessive pleasure in marriage is mortally sinful, but only that it resembles such culpable behavior: "Sed hoc dicitur non quoad reatum mortalis vitii, sed quoad speciem facti; speciem enim et similitudinem luxuriae et immunditiae praetendunt et habent designare."[52] Again, the series of canons forbidding intercourse at certain times are to be understood simply as counsels, not commands, or they are to be taken as referring to purely lustful motivations.[53] Chaucer has the Wife

52. Ordinary Gloss to Gratian 2.32.4.12 (*In eo fornicator*) v. *immunditiam.* For the whole text and a literal translation, see above, epigraph to Part IV. See also Chap. 6 and Chap. 10.

53. Ordinary Gloss to Gratian 2.33.4.1 (*Sciatis fratres*) *prin.* See also the Gloss on Gratian's comment *Quod autem* preceding this canon: Some say not to demand the debt in times of prayer is a precept, others say it is a counsel; the Gloss recommends a compromise: "Tu mediam viam teneas." The "middle way" is that sometimes it is a precept, sometimes merely a counsel, depending on one's motives. It should be obvious that the apparent contradictions caused by overstated counsels of perfection have nothing to do either with the two-truth system or the "gradualism" by which Alexander Denomy and Douglas Kelly respectively account for Andrew the Chaplain; see Denomy, "The *De amore* of Andreas Capellanus and the Condemnation of 1277," *Mediaeval Studies* 8 (1946) 107–149, and Kelly, "Courtly Love in Perspective: The Hierarchy of Love in Andreas Capel-

of Bath protest at length against the tendency to oversell the
"higher life." One may counsel a woman to be a virgin, she says,
"but conseillyng is no comandement" (*Wife of Bath's Prologue*
66–67). She grants that

> Virginitee is greet perfeccion,
> And continence eek with devocion,
> But Crist, that of perfeccion is welle,
> Bad nat every wight he sholde go selle
> Al that he hadde, and gyve it to the poore,
> And in swich wise folwe hym and his foore.
> He spak to hem that wolde lyve parfitly;
> And lordynges, by youre leve, that am nat I.
> I wol bistowe the flour of al myn age
> In the actes and in fruyt of mariage.   [105–114]

Rolle's *Incendium amoris* offers some examples of the kind of
contradictions that result from transforming counsels—that is,
recommendations as to what is the safer course or the more perfect way of life—into absolute declarations or precepts. For instance, he is often severe in his attitude toward women and sometimes almost sounds like Boccaccio at the end of the *Filostrato*.[54]
Rolle says, "I think it is better to do without their inimate friendship (*specialitas*) than to fall into their hands, for they do not
know how to be moderate either in love or in contempt" (12:
179).[55] It is almost impossible for a young man to achieve sanctity

---

lanus," *Traditio* 24 (1964) 119–147. According to both of these explanations,
there was a real contradiction or incompatibility between a human love
approved of by "philosophy" but condemned by God.

54. *Filostrato* 8.30–31: "Giovane donna e mobile e vogliosa / È negli
amanti molti," etc. See above, Chap. 2.

55. He came to this conclusion after having been rebuked by a woman
who said he was all words and no deeds; she spoke not in reproof (to help
him reform), but out of contempt. Just before this he recounted three other
recent reproofs from women which he took (so he says) in good part. He
had reproached one for wearing a horned headdress, and she retorted that
he should not be looking at her to see what she was wearing. A second
reproved him for speaking of her large breasts as if they gave him pleasure
("quasi me delectarent"). She wanted to know what concern it was of his
whether they were large or small. The third playfully touched him and said,
"Quiet, brother," because he had boisterously threatened to touch her or
had actually done so. It was as if she had said, and rightly so, that it was
out of keeping for him, a hermit, to play with women (178–179). Later he
returns, almost out of the blue, to speak with more bitterness of the thank-
less task of reproaching women for their vanity in dress (39:266).

in the midst of feminine charms (8:166). If women love men, they go insane, for, as he said before, they know no moderation in loving.

But when they are loved themselves, then they inflict the most bitter pain. They have one eye full of snares, and the other full of sorrow. Love of them distracts the senses, perverts the reason, changes all the mind's wisdom to foolishness, alienates the heart from God, and subjugates the captive soul to demons. And if one looks at a woman with carnal love, even though without a desire to fulfill lust, one does not keep oneself immune either from illicit motions or impure thoughts.

He continues in this way, and the upshot once again is a command to be wise and flee women, and keep one's thoughts far from them. For though they be good, nevertheless, because of the devil's instigation and suggestion, and the allurement of their beauty and the weakness of the flesh, one's will could delight in them beyond measure (29:228).[56]

But later, in the context of true and even meritorious friendship between men and women, he expresses concern for the effects of antifeminism on women: "For if women should perceive that they were despised by men, they would complain against God, who created them in such a way that they should be disdained by men; and perhaps they would despair of their salvation. For they feel themselves forsaken if they do not receive counsel and help from men." We have seen his conclusion to this line of thought earlier: since their reason is weak, they stand in great need of good men's counsel (39:263). God does not want women to be either despised by men or seduced by them, but in all sanctity they should be instructed faithfully and charitably for the health of soul and body (264).

Similarly, in spite of his statements on the natural goodness and even supernatural meritoriousness of the delights of human love, Rolle categorically renounces such love elsewhere, in precisely the same terms that Chaucer uses at the end of the *Troilus*. "Every object of delight that men have seen in this exile is like grass, which now flowers and waxes green, but soon it has vanished as

56. Cf. 24:213, where he speaks of the danger of marrying an infidel and being tempted by her to her infidelity, which happened even with so wise a man as Solomon.

though it never existed. . . . But this is the nature of love that is faithful and not feigned (*fictus*), that is remains in perpetual stability, and does not change for any newcomer whatsoever" (41:273).[57]

But truly, carnal love shall grow and perish like a flower of the field in summer, and shall no more exult and exist than if it were of only one day's duration, so surely does it last only for a little while, and then at the end it shall decline into sorrow, and so without doubt it shall become bitter in foolish lovers. Their pride and their playing in false beauty shall be thrust down into rottenness and filth, for they are already hurled into torment, which will remain with them forever. [275]

When Rolle is in this mood, no quarter is to be given to the delights of human love. "For God gives beauty to men and women not so that they might become inflamed over one another, to the contempt of their Creator, as now happens in almost everyone, but in order that they might recognize the benefits of the Lord their God and glorify him with their whole heart and love him incessantly, and constantly aspire to that everlasting beauty, compared to which all worldly attractiveness and glory is nothing." If the servants of this world have a lovable form, what will the beauty of the sons of God in heaven be like? Therefore our ardent love should be directed toward Christ, whose love conquers all—"amor omnia vincit" (275). "For Christ hastened to the cross with such great ardor in order to gain possession of us" (42:276).

On this note, then, the treatise on "the fire of love" is brought to an end. But it is a note that was often sounded throughout the course of the work. In the very first chapter, Rolle comes perilously close to the "foul error" he denounces later of leaving no room for natural goods but dividing everything up into what is supernaturally meritorious or injurious.[58] He warns us that "all

57. The opposite of *exilium* or *via* is "home" or "homeland" (*patria*), as in 7.163. For his analysis of *amicitia ficta*, see 39:262. The word *fictus* does not mean deliberately feigned; rather it means "not true" because centered wrongly (on profit or pleasure, not on the beloved himself) and not enduring.

58. See 39:264, cited above: those persons err *turpiter* who say that "omnia facta nostra, sive interiora sive exteriora, sunt meritoria vel demeritoria;

love not directed to God is iniquity, and renders iniquitous all
its possessors," a sentiment only grudgingly qualified: of all the
objects of love, worldly things are the least deserving and should
never be loved beyond strict necessity (1:148). If one does not
love the Creator with his whole love, one thereby loves a creature
of God more than is licit or honest. While the rational soul is "on
the way," it cannot exist without love. Therefore love is the foot
by which it is brought after this pilgrimage either to God or to
the devil (23:210).[59]

When speaking of the bad uses of marriage, Rolle suddenly
moves from a condemnation of lust and immoderate *ardor* for
one's wife to a denunciation of excessive *love* for women in general:

There is nothing more dangerous and nothing fouler, nothing
filthier for a man than to pour out his mind in love for woman, and
to pant after her as if she were a blessed repose. After doing so, it is
no wonder that that object soon becomes vile which beforehand he
had desired with great distress as his ultimate beatitude. For he knows
afterward, while meditating on the brief delight and long anxiety, that
he had foolishly and most foully gone astray by falling into such a
love.

A man like this comes to see the light only after it is too late, that
is, only after he is dead, because in this life "he seeks only external
and visible solaces, and is blinded to those that are internal and
invisible, and goes to the fire as if with eyes closed. But when the
unhappy soul is freed from the body it shall know immediately
and without a doubt, in the manifestation that is given to it, how
miserable an existence it led while in the flesh, where it thought
itself not only unharmed but also happy" (24:211–212).

Inevitably, this passage reminds us of Troilus's postmortal re-
flections, which Chaucer inserted as something of an afterthought,

---

quia auferre nituntur, vel saltem in nobis non esse contendunt, delectationes
et actiones naturales, et sic confusionem nobili naturae inducere non verentur."

59. He goes on to describe how one fixes one's eye on a woman because of
lechery. The sight inflames the soul, and soon thought about what is seen
enters and generates concupiscence in the heart and deforms the interior
nature. Then at once one is caught up in the burning of the noxious fire,
and is blinded lest he see the Judge's sentence.

in which he condemned all human activity as inspired by blind desire and destined to come to an end.[60] But there is an important difference. Rolle is speaking of a man who "cares nothing about the words of God and his precepts," who is not enlightened about earthly love until after his death, when he is about to be cast into hell-fire. Troilus, on the contrary, has always followed God's precepts and is disillusioned about Criseyde, and therefore presumably about all human love, before he dies. Furthermore, his soul leaves his body "full blissfully" and rises on the way to heaven, rather than descending to hell. He is, moreover, not referring specifically to the love of women when he condemns the operation of "blind lust," but is speaking generally. The observation is immediately inspired by the sight of his friends weeping over his death. He laughs at this kind of preoccupation, when we should instead "cast all our heart on heaven." For, in comparison to the perfect felicity of heaven, he considers everything else vanity, and completely despises this wretched world (5.1816–1825).

Troilus's final words, therefore, and Chaucer's subsequent observations, should be taken in conjunction with some of Rolle's more measured judgments upon worldly love, not as leading one to hell, but as interfering with one's spiritual perfection here on earth and limiting the quality of one's happiness in heaven.[61] When Rolle, speaking of the nature of love in general, said that no one is saddened by loving unless the object of love prove *ingratum* or unattainable, he added that this never happens with the love of God, but it often—note that he does not now say always—it often occurs with the love of the world and of women. "I do not dare," he continues, "to say that all love is good. For

60. *Troilus* 5.1823–1824: "And dampned al oure werk that foloweth so / The blynde lust, the which that may nat last."

61. A later example of the need to balance extreme statements in religious writing can be seen in Calvin's *Institutes*. Calvin has often been considered a "voluntarist" in his theism, in placing primary stress on God's will rather than on his reason: God's actions are right because he wills them, not because they are reasonable. It is true that he sometimes speaks in this way, but he usually does so in order to stress the unknowability of God's mind and the puniness of man's intellect. Elsewhere he makes it abundantly clear that he assumes that God always acts for the justest of reasons, even though these reasons are incomprehensible to us.

that love which delights more in a creature than in the Creator, and prefers the delectability of visible beauty to intellectual clarity, is bad and hateful, because it turns away from eternal love and turns toward temporal love, which cannot last. But perhaps it shall be less punished, because it rather seeks and rejoices to love and be loved than to defile and be defiled." (17:195).

In this chapter, Rolle distinguishes between the love of the beautiful and the love of the good: the former, which he suddenly limits to carnal beauty, is evanescent, like grass, whereas the latter is enduring (196). But toward the end of the book, as we saw earlier, he defines love in such a way that the beautiful and the good are put on more equal terms. Though he admits that one can have a worthy love for beautiful creatures that are also good, he says, speaking for himself and all who share his aspirations:

The love of a creature, though it be good and beautiful, is forbidden to me, in order that I might offer and reserve all my love to the font of goodness and beauty, so that he may be my love who is my God and my Jesus. For he alone has beauty and goodness from himself, nay, he is Beauty and Goodness itself. Everything else is neither beautiful nor good except from him, and the greater the extent to which it approaches him, the greater is its beauty and goodness.[62] [40:268–269]

Lesser loves, of course, are not wrong, though they can be called bad in the sense that they bring with them all sorts of grief:

For if I love anything else [other than God], my conscience nags at me for not loving correctly, I am fearful lest that which I love does not love me in return. And even if I did not have this fear, I am still crushed by death, which separates those who love in this bad way, so that it devastates all their vanity. Besides, there often occur other adversities that disturb the serenity and sweetness of the lovers. But he who loves God truly and with his whole heart remains all the more pure in his conscience the more ardent he knows himself to be in divine love.[63] [269]

62. See also the prayer of one who is languishing of divine love (35:246).
63. Cf. the stronger statement two chapters earlier (258): "Those who languish with impure love and for the beauty of rotten flesh, which is nothing but a veil over rottenness and corruption, are led without sweetness to death."

Neither Rolle nor Chaucer speaks of the hope earthly lovers have of being reunited in heaven after death. When, in *The Knight's Tale*, Theseus discusses the fate of Arcite, Troilus's alter ego, he reconciles his bereaved wife Emily and his cousin Palamon to death by linking it to the will of Jupiter—that is, Providence—and connecting it to the Boethian doctrine of the chain of love (2987–3066). But there is no talk of reunion in the hereafter, perhaps because Emily is to marry again in the present life. Similarly, it would be out of place to speak of Troilus's reunion with Criseyde, given her present pledge of fidelity to Diomede.

Earlier, Troilus and Criseyde did look forward to being together in Elysium, or wherever Minos placed them.[64] But when Troilus dies, he does not take a downward journey to the netherworld, but an upward flight, for Chaucer has transformed Boccaccio's description of Arcita's ascent in the *Teseida* to Troilus. He is noncommittal about the final destination of both Troilus and Arcite. Perhaps he did not want to enter into the contemporary discussions of the fate of virtuous non-Christians.[65] But we are given the clear impression that wherever it is their respective psychopomps take them, they are better off than they were in the "foul prison of this life."[66]

If Chaucer had in mind, not the pagan notions of sidereal immortality,[67] but the dispositions of Christian theology, as Dante

64. *Troilus* 4.785–791, 1187–1188. In lines 470–476, however, Troilus expected to die and sorrow over his separation from Criseyde forevermore in the netherworld. John M. Steadman, *Disembodied Laughter: "Troilus" and the Apotheosis Tradition—A Reexamination of Narrative and Thematic Contexts* (Berkeley 1972) 41 n. 48, would like to allow for the possibility that Chaucer was thinking of a superterrestrial location for Pluto's kingdom. But the phrase "down with Proserpyne" (4.476) shows clearly that he had the ordinary Ovidian arrangement in mind. Cf. also 3.592: Pluto is deep in hell.

65. On the wide extent of this concern, see Thomas G. Hahn, "God's Friends: Virtuous Heathen in Later Medieval Thought and English Literature" (diss. U.C.L.A. 1974).

66. *Knight's Tale* 2809–2815, 3057–3061; *Troilus* 5.1807–1827. Arcita's psychopomp Mercury does service for Troilus; but Arcite is apparently to be guided by Mars, the deity he chiefly served.

67. See Morton W. Bloomfield, "The Eighth Sphere: A Note on Chaucer's *Troilus and Criseyde*," *Modern Language Review* 53 (1958) 408–410;

did, Troilus's upward flight would serve only to give him his outer-space view of the earth and vision of heavenly felicity, and perhaps also to bring him before his Judge, before being returned to earth and placed in Limbo to await the harrowing of hell after Christ's passion and death. Only then would he be placed in one of the spheres of heaven. One pagan that Dante describes as achieving salvation in this way is the Trojan hero Rifeo, who, because of his love of justice, was assigned to the sphere of Jupiter (*Paradiso* 20.118–129).

Swich Fyn Hath Troilus for Love

Rifeo appears in the *Filostrato* as one of the companions-in-arms of Troiolo. He is captured by the Greeks along with Antenore and others (4.3). Chaucer takes him over as Rupheo in the same context (4.53) but makes no other use of him. Probably, then, Chaucer was not thinking of Dante's hero or Virgil's "iustissimus unus" (*Aeneid* 2.426), but it is clear that he wished to elevate Troilus's character at the end of the poem just as he had done during the course of it.

Troiolo in effect calls for Criseida's death and damnation when he finally has irrefutable proof of her infidelity (8.18). Troilus instead continues to love her:

> Thorugh which I se that clene out of youre mynde
> Ye han me cast; and I ne kan nor may,
> For al this world, withinne myn herte fynde
> To unloven yow a quarter of a day!
> In corsed tyme I born was, weilaway,
> That yow, that doon me al this wo endure,
> Yet love I best of any creature! [5.1695–1701]

According to the testimony of Love in *The Testament of Love*, when two hearts in her presence enter into a marriage "till death them depart," this agreement, sealed by their consent, is placed in her secret treasury; "and although they break forward both, yet such matter ensealed is kept in remembrance forever."[68]

Steadman, *Disembodied Laughter;* and John W. Conlee, "The Meaning of Troilus's Accension to the Eighth Sphere," *Chaucer Review* 7 (1972–1973) 27–36.

68. Usk, *Testament of Love* 1.9 (the entire text is given above, n. 3).

But Troilus did not break his forward, even though Criseyde
broke hers. The intensity of the love he felt for her was not a
vice but a virtue: "Virtus amoris quanto plus excedit tanto
gloriosior est" (Rolle 17:194). He did not love her more than
God, which would have been a vicious excess, but "best of any
creature." His love was not feigned or fictitious except in the
sense that its object was transitory, like everything else on earth.

In his original ending of the *Troilus*, Chaucer simply followed
Boccaccio in speaking of the end that the hero came to for love,
immediately after describing his miserable death at the hands of
Achilles. But he does not call it an ill-conceived love, *mal concetto
amore*, or a vain hope, *speranza vana*, as Boccaccio does (8.27–28),
nor does he call Criseyde base, *villana:*

> But weilawey, save only Goddes wille!
> Despitously hym slough the fierse Achille.
>
> Swich fyn hath, lo, this Troilus for love!
> Swich fyn hath al his grete worthynesse!
> Swich fyn hath his estat real above,
> Swich fyn his lust, swich fyn hath his noblesse!
> Swich fyn hath false worldes brotelnesse!
> And thus bigan his lovyng of Criseyde,
> As I have told, and in this wise he deyde.
> [5.1805–1806, 1828–1834]

Boccaccio's only reference to Troiolo's possible fate after death
comes in his request that his readers pray for Troiolo so that Love
might bring him to where Love dwells (8.33). Chaucer omitted
this mythological conceit but must have considered it necessary
to give Troilus a more sublime finish than a simple death in the
field. He therefore inserted the three stanzas modeled on Arcita's
ascent in the *Teseida*. He left the following stanza unchanged,
however, producing this transition:

> And forth he wente, shortly for to telle,
> Ther as Mercurye sorted hym to dwelle.
>
> Swich fyn hath, lo, this Troilus for love!

and so on, thus giving the distinct impression that the "fyn" for
his love, great worthiness, and royal estate is the reward of
heavenly bliss "above." Such too is the end of his desire or "lust."

This ambiguous word is given a noble connotation by being placed next to his "noblesse." But the last three lines of the stanza bring us back to his final disappointment and death: such is the end brought about by the false world's brittleness, such is the story of the way Troilus fell in love with Criseyde, and such is the way he died. Then, instead of following Boccaccio in advising young men to be more careful than Troiolo was in choosing the women they love, Chaucer contrasts the feigned loves of the false world with the love of Christ:

> And syn he best to love is, and most meke,
> What nedeth feynede loves for to seke?   [1847–1848]

Some readers have supposed that Chaucer in these lines is allowing or even encouraging well-ordered love on the human level. But there is no hint of such measured optimism here; he is saying categorically that all human loves are feigned. He does not say that it is morally wrong to seek them, only that it is unnecessary and unwise to do so, for they will ultimately prove transitory and disappointing.

This statement demands qualification but does not receive it, for the time for such qualifications is past. The same is true of the concluding stanza before the dedication to Gower and Strode and the final benediction; the pagan religion, in contrast to the Christian, is dismissed as absolutely hopeless and debased:

> Lo here, of payens corsed olde rites,
> Lo here, what alle hire goddes may availle;
> Lo here, thise wrecched worldes appetites;
> Lo here the fyn and guerdoun for travaille
> Of Jove, Appollo, of Mars, of swich rascaille!
> Lo here, the forme of olde clerkis speche
> In poetrie, if ye hire bokes seche.   [1849–1855]

As a summary of the main action and sentiments of the poem it is almost as inaccurate as the *Beowulf*-poet's initial characterization of the diabolical nature of the religion practiced by the pre-Christian peoples he portrays in his work. Pagan worship figures more importantly in *The Knight's Tale* than in the *Troilus*, but how does the tale end? After Palamon is married to Emily, we encounter this prayer:

> And God, that al this wyde world hath wroght,
> Sende hym his love that hath it deere aboght.   [3099–3100]

The *Troilus*, however, had an unhappy ending, and Chaucer must have felt that a sterner statement was called for. It was, in fact, the familiar medieval mood of *contemptus mundi* that was called for; and Chaucer was determined to be held in contempt not just of the world in general but of the ancient pagan world in particular.

The stanza may strike us as intellectually and emotionally inept, in spite of any claims that can be made for its rhetorical and dramatic fittingness. Perhaps Chaucer was led astray by the example of the *Filocolo*, which concludes with even greater ineptness.

Boccaccio's work is set in time at the transition point between paganism and Christianity, and his treatment of the two forms of religions gives rise to a startling inconsistency, which could have been corrected only by massive revision. At the beginning of the *Filocolo*, the concepts of Christianity are freely expressed in pagan terms: God is Jove, the devil is Pluto, and mankind was saved from Pluto by Jove's only son. In the same breath we hear of such gods as Hymenaeus, Pallas, and Saint James of Compostella. Juno appears to the pope and tells him to get moving against his enemies; and in Boccaccio's own prayer to Jove he describes his current studies in canon law at Naples thus: "Ora nelle sante leggi de' tuoi successori spendo il tempo mio" (1.1.30). Though he takes a passing swipe at the false gods, "i bugiardi iddii" (1.3.15), once the main story gets going these gods initiate most of the action, good as well as bad, and only vague references to divine providence give any hint of the Christian order of reality. Then, at the end, all the principals are converted to Christianity; the gods who have served the protagonists so beneficially and so actively are dismissed without more ado, and there is no more clothing of Christian concepts in pagan terms—except that the old deities retain their job of running the heavens (5.95.1).

In his address to his work at the end, "O piccolo mio libretto," Boccaccio says that the long instruction on the Christian faith given by Ilario in the last book is to bear witness against those who object to the more pleasant things contained therein: "A' contradicenti le tue piacevoli cose, dà la lunga fatica di Ilario per veridico testimonio" (5.97.10). Probably the complaints of such contradictors, then, prevented Boccaccio from reassuming his original method of integrating paganism with Christianity. Chaucer may have felt it incumbent upon him to end his work with a similar religious flourish. He did, after all, rely on the *Filocolo* earlier to purify the morals of his lovers, and he was almost certainly drawing on the apostrophe to the work at the end when he addressed his own "little book."

At any rate, the fact is that the main body of the *Troilus* reflects an atmosphere of pagan morality like that of the body of the *Filocolo*, and the end of the *Troilus* is like the end of the *Filocolo* in its rejection of the pagan gods. But in neither case are the gods of love and marriage singled out for repudiation. In the *Filocolo* Jove is given special mention at one point (5.52.7), but for the most part all the gods are lumped together as *vani iddii e fallaci* (5.60.2). No taint, however, is attached to the love and marriage of Florio and Biancifiore, which was brought about by these very gods.

Chaucer mentions only Jove, Apollo, and Mars by name. And while there can be no doubt that the love affair of Troilus and Criseyde is implicated in the general indictment of paganism, this is mainly because they shared in the universal ignorance of the truths spoken and enacted by Christ. Insofar, then, as the stanza can be read as referring specifically to the story of the *Troilus* and not to the whole heathen world, it encompasses all the events of the Trojan War, which was the result of travail on behalf of rascally gods like Jove, Apollo, and Mars.

In light of this great handicap of ignorance, Criseyde's fall becomes all the more excusable, and Troilus's constancy all the more stunning. Even after his death, Troilus was vouchsafed nothing more than the Boethian revelation that all is vanity on earth compared to the plenary felicity of heaven. Lady Philosophy's implied objection against too much trust in marital love was borne out in his case. As Chaucer awkwardly puts it in his translation of Boethius, book 3, prose 7: "The gladnesse of wyf and children were an honest thyng, but it hath ben seyd that it is

overmochel ayens kynde that children han ben fownden tor-
mentours to here faders [*subintellege:* and wyves to here hous-
bondes], I not how manye." Yet perhaps he could hardly be
blamed for taking this unwise course, since in so acting he was
following another Boethian doctrine: that the holy bond of love
makes couples dwell in virtue (3.1748–1749). It was, in fact, by
virtue of this love that he fled from pride, envy, wrath, avarice,
and every other vice (1804–1806). If it left him a sadder man at
the end of his life, he had also become thereby a better man.

Envoy

I have given Chaucer's *Troilus and Criseyde* a lion's share of the attention in this study, not only because it is one of the best of the medieval romances, but especially because it has been singularly subject to misunderstanding and mistreatment at the hands of modern critics. I hope that I have removed some of the bases of faulty interpretations of the poem by explaining and clarifying several of the traditions upon which Chaucer and his contemporaries were dependent.

Marriage was considered the most desirable conclusion to serious love. There was no tradition of incompatibility between love and marriage, except in the literature of satire and complaint; and in such literature neither love nor marriage was taken seriously or sympathetically. The practical founder and main preceptor of the romance of marriage was Ovid, and his lessons were inescapable in the Middle Ages.

For authors like Chaucer, to whom the ideals of marital fidelity were important, most of Ovid's heroines were easily assimilable to medieval notions, though in some cases it was necessary to resort to the simple device of a clandestine marriage in order to satisfy the requirements of honesty. The same was true when Chaucer came to deal with Boccaccio's hero Troiolo; and Troiolo resembled the Ovidian heroines further in being reduced to writing hopeless letters in an effort to recall a love already vanished and betrayed.

Evidence of the widespread practice and prosecution of clandestine marriage reveals how importantly the canon law on marriage figured in the lives of the medieval faithful. Furthermore, the alacrity with which the Church's solemn ban against such

[333]

marriage was violated lends support, I think, to the suggestion that stern views on marital sexuality were also widely ignored, even granted that they were widely known. The pronouncements of moralists on the ease with which husband and wife could sin while making love must surely have invited a good deal of disbelief among those whom human nature had inspired with a more positive attitude toward love and marriage. We saw evidence of such optimistic views not only in the literary romances (and we might have added further testimony from love lyrics), but also in the liturgy of marriage and in writings on spiritual marriage. Especially in the latter, though it is often half hidden beneath the mystical allegory, there can be seen an ideal of marriage at once passionate and virtuous, in which both the sexual and the spiritual delights of love are unashamedly sought and enjoyed. That such an ideal could coexist with moralistic inhibitions is evident from the writings of both Chaucer and Gower.

The aspirations of asceticism and the demands of humanity can never hope to live together at all times in perfect peace. Or, to admit the human qualities of both ideals, eschatological humanism has always, from the beginning of Christianity, challenged the extreme assumptions of incarnational humanism, and vice versa.[1] There is a natural tendency to exaggerate on both sides. In particular, we saw that it was common in medieval literature for supererogatory counsels to go about disguised as absolute precepts, and for perfectionist hypotheses and probabilities to solidify into categorical terms. The incidence of such metamorphoses was especially high in moments of stress, as, for instance, when one approached the end of one's life or the peroration of one's sermon. At such junctures it became easy to condemn as "sowning into sin" works which in other circumstances could be seen to ride quite comfortably along the middle way between excess and defect.

1. See John Courtney Murray, *We Hold These Truths* (London 1960) 185–193.

Index

In listing medieval authors, Latin epithets and patronymics and all foreign place-name designations are arbitrarily treated as surnames: for example, Peter Comestor, John Andreae, Thomas Aquinas, and John de Meun are indexed under Comestor, Andreae, Aquinas, and Meun respectively. But when the epithets or designations of place are translated into English (for example, Andrew the Chaplain, Laurence of Spain, Nicholas of Lyre), the Christian names are indexed.

*Love and Marriage in
the Age of Chaucer*

Designed by R. E. Rosenbaum.
Composed by York Composition Co., Inc.,
in 10 point linotype Janson, 2 points leaded,
with display lines in Weiss and Goudy Text.
Printed letterpress from type by York Composition Co.
on Warren's No. 66 Text, 50 lb. basis
with the Cornell University Press watermark.
Bound by Colonial Press, Inc.